AF608270

MINDING ANIMALS IN THE OLD AND NEW WORLDS

A Cognitive Historical Analysis

STEVEN WAGSCHAL

Minding Animals in the Old and New Worlds

A Cognitive Historical Analysis

UNIVERSITY OF TORONTO PRESS
Toronto Buffalo London

Toronto Buffalo London
utorontopress.com

ISBN978-1-4875-0332-1

Library and Archives Canada Cataloguing in Publication

Wagschal, Steven, 1967–, author
Minding animals in the old and new worlds : a cognitive historical analysis / Steven Wagschal.

Includes bibliographical references and index.
ISBN 978-1-4875-0332-1 (hardcover)

1. Literature, Modern – History and criticism. 2. Literature, Medieval – History and criticism. 3. Animals in literature. 4. Anthropomorphism in literature. 5. Animals – Symbolic aspects. 6. Animal psychology. I. Title.

PN56.A64W34 2018 809′.93362 C2018-901786-4

This book has been published with the help of a grant from the Federation for the Humanities and Social Sciences, through the Awards to Scholarly Publications Program, using funds provided by the Social Sciences and Humanities Research Council of Canada.

University of Toronto Press acknowledges the financial assistance to its publishing program of the Canada Council for the Arts and the Ontario Arts Council, an agency of the Government of Ontario.

Canada Council for the Arts Conseil des Arts du Canada

Funded by the Government of Canada Financé par le gouvernement du Canada

To Sandy, Molly, and Marlena

Contents

Acknowledgments

I would like to thank the members of Indiana University's SPACKLED group (Studygroup for the Philosophy/Psychology of Animal Cognition, Knowledge, Learning, Evolution, and Development), and especially the convener, Colin Allen, who welcomed me to biweekly discussions about a host of animal cognition issues; Berta Ares at the CSIC Escuela de Estudios Hispano-Americanos in Seville for offering support and for introducing me to the work of Tomás López Medel; and Juan Montero Delgado at the Universidad de Sevilla for his support of my research exchange in Seville. I would also like to thank Maria Medina and the staff at the International Office of the Universidad de Sevilla for financial and logistical support; Indiana University's Office of the Vice Provost for International Affairs (OVPIA) for financial support of research travel to Seville; the College Arts and Humanities Institute (CAHI) for a teaching release during which time I began the research on this book; Executive Dean Larry Singell's support of my sabbatical leave; and the Social Sciences and Humanities Research Council of Canada for the award of a generous publication grant.

Several colleagues and friends at Indiana University and other institutions read chapter drafts and offered truly invaluable suggestions: Abel Alves, Kate Myers, Ryan Giles, Carolyn Nadeau, Colin Allen, and Sandy Shapshay. The people with whom I discussed the project in brief or at length is too long to list but I will try: Stephen Hutchinson, Mercedes Alcalá, Frederick De Armas, Cathy Larson, Adrienne Martín, Howard Mancing, Barbara Simerka, Chloe Ireton, Stan Shapshay, and Ivan Kreilkamp. I've been extremely fortunate to work in the Department of Spanish and Portuguese at Indiana University Bloomington, where wonderful colleagues have been supportive of my research; in particular, I owe a debt of tremendous gratitude to Kim Geeslin and Deb Cohn, who made it possible for me to write while I was department chair by taking on additional responsibilities themselves. I'd also like to thank my immensely supportive friends Alain Barker, Liz Rosdeitcher, and Yael Ksander, who took care of many important things in Bloomington while I was abroad researching and writing.

It has been a pleasure to work with my editors at the University of Toronto Press, Suzanne Rancourt, Barbara Porter, and Charles Stuart, at all stages of publication. I'd also like to thank the anonymous readers who offered valuable suggestions for improving the manuscript. Any remaining errors are entirely my own.

To my research assistants at Indiana University, Dan Qaurooni and Beth Boyd, I owe a debt of gratitude. In particular, I would like to thank Christie Cole for her help in preparing the final manuscript and obtaining images and permissions for publication, and Robert Fritz for his help on many aspects including identifying original sources, offering invaluable criticisms, and translating passages for publication in chapter 3.

I would like to offer thanks to several non-human family members now and in the past – canines Cheddar, Pretzel, Kelly, and Missy, and felines Frisky, Lucan and Pussy-Nous-Nous – for their affection and indirect help in my gaining a first-hand appreciation of the perils of and insights owed to anthropomorphizing. Finally, I deeply appreciate all of the support of my human family members Sandy, Molly, and Marlena, who not only tolerated moving to Southern Spain, where I wrote a large portion of this book, but who are always ready, willing, and eager to talk about the minds of animals and help individual animals whenever they can.

MINDING ANIMALS IN THE OLD AND NEW WORLDS

A Cognitive Historical Analysis

Minding Animals with Anthropomorphism

In an October 2015 landmark legal decision in Buenos Aires, Argentina, Judge Elena Liberatori ruled that an orang-utan named Sandra held certain rights usually reserved for humanity, defining Sandra as a "non-human person" (Liberatori n.p.) (see fig. 1).[1] Determining that Sandra did not want to remain captive in a zoo, Judge Liberatori ordered the City of Buenos Aires to provide Sandra with what was "necessary to preserve her cognitive needs" (Liberatori n.p.). Since Sandra doesn't speak a human language, how did the ethologists, psychologists, lawyers, and ethicists who provided *amicus* testimony know what she did or did not want? The evidence presented in the case in a human court, on behalf of this non-human animal, included information about the similarity between orang-utan and human DNA,[2] species-typical behaviour,[3] and reports of her activities and appearance at the zoo. According to the plaintiff's lawyer on behalf of her case of *habeas corpus*, "her physical and mental state had profoundly deteriorated, with an evident risk of death" (Baggis 5). Her suffering was due to "the illegitimate and arbitrary denial of freedom, as well as unjustified confinement of an animal with proven cognitive capacities"; the remedy sought was to "request that she be allowed to live among her conspecifics in an adequate place, soliciting her liberation and transfer to a primate sanctuary" (Baggis 3). Judgments on Sandra's unhappiness were achieved through interpreting her behaviour with regard to her "psychological wellness" (Liberatori n.p.) and relied on knowledge of her cognitive abilities alongside the use of anthropomorphism. The biologist who argued on behalf of the zoo to keep Sandra confined made the point that using anthropomorphism in judging her "depressed" was a categorical error: "To say that an animal is depressed is to speak of a human behavior transferred

Figure 1 Sandra the orang-utan. Juan Mabromata / AFP / Getty Images.

to a wild species" (qtd. in Brumec, n.p.). Yet the suit prevailed, a win not just for one orang-utan but for anthropomorphism.[4]

My study explores the anthropomorphic understanding of non-human animals in the Iberian world, from the Middle Ages through the early modern period in different contexts and through various modes of discursive writing. The overarching thesis of this book is simple: People tend to conceptualize the minds of animals in ways that reflect their own uses for the animal, the manner in which they interact with the animal, and the place in which the animal lives. Often this has little if anything to do with the cognitive abilities of the animal as understood scientifically. These conceptualizations employ anthropomorphism in varying degrees, from extreme, gratuitous anthropomorphism to its opposite, anthropectomy, which relies on the complete denial of anthropomorphic traits. The four chapters utilize historical evidence from the Iberian world in order to substantiate this thesis, analysing the ways in which animals were conceived of implicitly and explicitly. I start with the symbolic use of animals in medieval Christian and didactic texts; I then examine attempts at understanding actual animals' minds in Spain in early modern farming and hunting books; later, I study animals that were conceptualized under the aspect of novelty in what the Europeans considered the "New World"; and finally, I analyse the complex ways in which Cervantes navigated the forms of anthropomorphism that preceded him before moving beyond these and creating the first embodied animal minds in literature, whereby he incorporated meaningfully and realistically an animal's sensory modalities and cognitive abilities into that animal's characterization.

The fields of cognitive science and philosophy of animal cognition inform this study in order to ascertain which are realistic or plausible representations of animal minds and which are not. I find that animals' minds are represented in accordance with their actual abilities infrequently; more often abilities are downplayed or ignored. Relying on current research in cognitive science and the philosophy of animal cognition, I demonstrate that specific modes of interaction between human animal and non-human animal (interactions that favour an appreciation of the animal's sensory modalities and emotions, along with specific habitational parameters that allow for individualized, close contact between human and animal) contribute to the most insightful and accurate discursive conceptualizations of non-human animal higher cognition. Conversely, representations that ignore higher cognition and tend towards treating animals as automata tend to involve modes of interaction that favour greater anthropocentric utility (e.g., considering the animal as an object harvested for food or for a useful by-product) and/or habitational parameters that severely limit human-animal interactions. Providing evidence mostly from European sources but also offering complementary evidence from indigenous-informed texts, my study points to the importance of culture alongside human cognitive embodiment as determinative factors in how humans conceive of the minds of non-human animals. By combining these areas, my work contributes to the interdisciplinary field of Animal Studies while also developing a novel line of inquiry into Cognitive Literary Historicism, which has been theorized amply by Lisa Zunshine, Ellen Spolsky, and others, and practised in recent work on early modern Spanish literature by Howard Mancing, Barbara Simerka, Isabel Jaén, Julien Simon, and others.[5]

In broad strokes, anthropomorphism has been mischaracterized pejoratively because the extensive and diverse phenomena to which it refers are erroneously conflated. Some forms of anthropomorphism amount to fanciful personification in the ascription of fantastical faculties; this includes human speech to non-human, and even inanimate, objects (such as in fables). But it also ranges to subtle, informed, and careful inferences about cognition in non-human animals whom humans have good reason to believe are feeling, thinking creatures (such as the arguments in favour of Sandra's unhappiness). Yet many critics of anthropomorphism dismissively lump these strands together. In the twentieth and twenty-first centuries, cognitive ethologists have employed varying degrees of anthropomorphism and have developed different ways of talking about it. As will be detailed, Kristin Andrews, Frans De Waal, and others argue that anthropomorphism is more appropriate than what used to be the dominant mode of animal psychology, namely, denying that animals have consciousness, thoughts, and emotions. Such denials often occur under the influence of psychological behaviourism, which is guided by a restrictive reading of Morgan's Canon that states the following: "in no case is an animal activity to be interpreted in terms of higher psychological processes, if it can be fairly interpreted in terms of processes which stand lower in the scale of psychological evolution and development" (292; qtd. in Andrews 32).[6] In contrast, what I call "constructive anthropomorphism" relies on the interpretation of appropriate cues, knowing about species-specific behaviour, and making appropriate inferences as to what the animal is feeling, so as to generate a model of the animal's mind. Being open to constructive anthropomorphism begins with the underlying assumption that there is something in the mind of an animal to be known. Throughout history, many thinkers have held such an assumption including Michel de Montaigne (1533–92), who famously wondered whether he was playing with his cat, or his cat was playing with him (2.12:156).[7] As cognitively embodied and highly social creatures, humans have an innate[8] tendency to inquire about the intentionality of other beings and inanimate things, especially if they have motion, which Matthew Hutson defines as "Magical Thinking," that is, "overattributing mental states to physical objects" including animals (170). While we can never know what is going on even in another person's mind with absolute certainty, this does not stop us from meaningfully communicating our interiority to others reasonably well. We regularly use similar abilities and techniques when dealing with animals that we care about because this kind of inference comes to us naturally, even though these beings have different sensory modalities and, arguably, different kinds of phenomenal consciousness. We may never know exactly what it is like to be another animal, but that certainly does not mean that there is nothing to know.

Modern thinking on the cognition of animals begins with one of the greatest scientific minds of the nineteenth century, Charles Darwin, who argued that humans must share with animals many cognitive abilities. He emphasized the continuity of abilities across species, as this made the most sense in his evolutionary view. In light of more recent knowledge about the link between genetics and evolution, the animals most closely related to humans share the most genetic information, which forms the basis of the plaintiffs' arguments on Sandra's behalf, in which they stressed the percentage of DNA that humans have in common with orang-utans. Holding a line opposed to the influential Aristotelian distinction between reasoning humans and non-reasoning beasts, Darwin argued that "[t]here is no fundamental difference between man and the higher animals in their mental faculties" (448). Like the cases of many early moderns and others before him who will be examined in this study, "Darwin attributed cognitive states to many animals on the basis of observations of particular cases rather than controlled experiments ... [and] the clear attribution of feelings and emotions to nonhumans" (Allen and Bekoff 24). Furthermore, "Darwin used behavioral evidence, such as the animal pausing before solving problems, to support his contention that even animals without language are able to reason" (24).

Today, cognitive ethologists and comparative psychologists construct experiments to test hypotheses about animal thinking, problem-solving, consciousness, and emotion – whether in the lab or in the wild – rather than relying only on anecdotes as in Darwin's case. Mark Bekoff and Colin Allen, Jane Goodall, Donald Griffin, Irene Pepperberg, De Waal, and others have used forms of anthropomorphism to guide their investigations into animal cognition while striving for scientifically sound results and interpretations. For philosopher of animal cognition Kristin Andrews, the opposite of anthropomorphism – which she calls "anthropectomy," and is sometimes referred to as "anthropodenial" – may be a kind of error that predisposes the thinker or researcher to bias (42). The ethologist, De Waal, distinguishes between kinds of anthropomorphism, labelling the scientifically inappropriate type "gratuitous anthropomorphism," while favouring the type that assists scientists in understanding an animal's cognition. As De Waal puts it, "[t]he closer another species is to us, the more anthropomorphism assists our understanding of this species and the greater will be the danger of anthropodenial" (n.p.). Gratuitous anthropomorphism is, for De Waal, "distinctly unhelpful" from a scientific point of view. Yet it is important as a category, for instance, to identify the ways in which typical fables personify animals and have them behave and speak as if they were human beings.

The historical analyses of my book provide evidence from historical sources (often lacking from the work of cognitive scientists and philosophers) regarding the unchanging nature of human cognitive processes, which are often assumed to be constant insofar as *Homo sapiens* has not significantly evolved in tens or hundreds of thousands of years.[9] Some thinkers in cognitive science, including Allen, Bekoff, Luciano Floridi, Stephen J. Crowley, and Andrew Aberdein, have indeed made forays into historical texts, especially philosophical ones, for their explicit ideas about cognitive ethology.[10] In contrast, my work analyses fictional and non-fictional texts in various genres of writing for both their explicit and also implicit ways of considering non-human animals, as teased out through literary analysis. I demonstrate the importance of what historian Marcy Norton has called the "mode of interaction" between humans and animals (for instance, hunter-hunted, farmer-farmed, etc.), as well as what historian Arturo Morgado refers to with the term "habitational parameters."[11] These two factors often explain a culture's conceptual understanding of animals' minds, overriding counter-evidence about an animal's cognitive faculties. I find that contingent human interests (such as whether or not the taste of an animal's flesh appeals to societal members) tend to guide appraisals of animal cognition, including whether animals feel pain and suffering, demonstrate self-awareness and consciousness, have emotions, thoughts, and intentional agency.

Since ideas about suffering are inextricably tied up with human morality, a lack of appreciation for animal suffering tends to lessen the sense of moral responsibility humans have towards specific individuals or groups of animals. I argue that factors that lead to species-specific bias, in favour of or against certain species (i.e., speciesism),[12] include whether the animal has "affordances" within embodied human culture for the animal's cognition to be appreciated by humans. An example of an affordance would be a human lap on which house cats and lapdogs find opportunities for seating and warmth as well as the giving and receiving of grooming/affection. This is only possible because of their diminutive size (unlike, for instance, an elephant), and because of the biological fact that they require similar habitational needs as humans, including a certain ideal room temperature, pressure, and humidity (unlike, for instance, an octopus). This affordance, then, allows a particular mode of interaction (e.g., human caretaker to pet), through which humans are able to gain greater appreciation of the animal in question and of his or her cognitive faculties. This occurs through what I call "constructive anthropomorphism," which means relying on appropriate cues, knowing about species-specific behaviour, making appropriate inferences as to what the animal is feeling, so as to generate a model of the animal's mind.[13] Constructive anthropomorphism is how we mind animals appropriately. While animals have minds independent of human's beliefs about them, my title, *Minding Animals*, refers to this construction of the animal's cognitive faculties, while including that animals are often dependent on humans who should act responsibly and ethically in caring for them.[14]

In the historical texts of my study, the habitational parameter and the mode of interaction often prove determinative of the human constructions of non-human animal minds. In exceptional cases, constructive anthropomorphism demonstrates that closer interaction with an animal or species leads to greater understanding of the animal's cognitive faculties. While such non-scientific appraisals are just that, they generate an understanding that can be called "folk animal psychology," which has explanatory value and is often in line with current ethological appraisals or studies. In other words, later scientific study has often borne out the folk psychology of those with expertise. Through constructive anthropomorphism and animal-centric perspective-taking, early modern authors created the first realistic, scientifically plausible representations of non-human animal phenomenal consciousness.

An analysis of Hispanic texts from before, during, and after the encounter with and conquest of America, along with the radical cultural changes and shifts that ensued, show a pervasive continuity among ways in which the human mind conceptualizes animals and interprets (or ignores) facets of animals' cognitive abilities, thoughts, and emotions. Cultural constructions are important to these ideas, which are often naturalized and considered scientific. Yet there is a generalized lack of awareness among humanities scholars of the impositions that human cognition places (across cultures) on the conceptualization of animal cognition. Indeed, as psychologist John S. Kennedy has argued, "anthropomorphic thinking about animal behavior is built into us. We could not abandon it even if we wished to" (qtd. in Andrews 41).[15] While his case is overstated and necessarily so, since some people, including Kennedy himself, refuse to engage in anthropomorphic thinking, I would argue that it remains an innate tendency, and while we can overcome said tendency, humans transculturally and over time have always approached animate beings in this way. In some sense, anthropomorphism is similar to the way in which we engage trying to understand other people through Theory of Mind and empathic understanding. Ultimately, trying to understand what it is like to be another person is easier than, but not altogether different from, trying to understand what it is like to be, say, a bat.[16]

The refusal to engage in any kind of anthropomorphism, which still has adherents in animal behaviourism[17] as well as in the thinking of some philosophers, has its own history that can be traced to sixteenth-century Spain. The Spanish medical doctor Gómez Pereira was the first philosopher to call animals "automata" in his *Antoniana Margarita* (1554). By *automata* he meant that they were like machines, and he denied them sentience, knowledge, emotions, and suffering.[18] Everything animals did could be explained by instinct, rather than emotion, intention, or choice. For instance, the feelings that a mother sheep and her baby have for each other can be explained with a simile relating the emotion to the physical property of attraction, a literary device which Pereira takes literally: "like iron and magnet" (Pereira 6).[19] As historian Abel Alves has pointed out, this view attempted to counter the Scholastic one, prominent in Spain, which held that animals were not rational but could feel pleasure and pain (Alves, *The Animals of Spain* 6). Better-known versions of the automaton claim were made by René Descartes, who saw animals as "reflex-driven machines, with no intellectual capacities" (Allen and Trestman 12).[20] His follower in mechanistic philosophy, Nicolas Malebranche, went further and insisted that animals had no emotion. For Malebranche, since they had no reason or soul, animals could not suffer (Allen and Trestman 12–13). These views projected a philosophical and medical view of non-human animals that conveniently made the abhorrent cultural practice of vivisection palatable, upholding the status quo deemed important by certain elites; in this case, anatomists who wished to continue dissecting live animals for what they considered its benefits to research and teaching.[21]

I believe that most people would agree that the cries, heavier breathing, increased heart rate, and attempts to flee that a restrained mammal displays when cut open with a scalpel indicate the animal's suffering. And they would arrive at this conclusion on suffering precisely because of anthropomorphic projection: As Shakespeare's Shylock noted with another context in mind, when we are pricked, we also do bleed.[22] While Pereira had many followers in Spain, his book was the object of a scathing reply in Francisco de Sosa's *Endecalogue against the Antoniana Margarita* (1556). Here his ideas are ridiculed and sentenced "to hell" by a series of eleven anthropomorphized animals who speak and defend the notion that animals have appetites, know things, and have memory and feelings (Barreiro Barreiro, in Pereira 18). Even Alonso Martínez de Espinar, who encouraged the practice of hunting towards all manner of animals in his treatise on hunting, *Art of Archery and Hunting*, recognized that people must steel themselves in order to inflict suffering on the creatures that they are killing. For Martínez de Espinar, humans must learn to avoid feeling empathy, and this is precisely why hunting made such good practice for killing people in war.[23] As Alves has pointed out, Thomas Aquinas had made a similar point from the opposite point of view in writing that a "'pitiful affection for animals increases the disposition to pity humans" (*The Animals of Spain* 6). To deny the feeling and suffering of animals is not in the interest of knowledge or science, but in the self-interest of those who wish to continue exploiting animals in the cruel practice of vivisection or some other means of exploitation.[24] The idea that the animals were suffering and would have preferred not to be there is a form of anthropomorphism, in which these human desires, feelings, and emotions are projected onto the subjects of the vivisection. But does that make the sentience and the suffering of the animals any less true?

Undoubtedly, it is not merely a twenty-first-century view that regards animals as potential sufferers, as feeling and thinking beings. Many early modern writers in philosophy, literature, medicine, hunting, and husbandry made these inferences too, in limited cases, for certain animals. As Andrews explains, modern psychology is based on folk psychology, and modern comparative psychology is based on "folk animal psychology," a practice by which human beings with expertise, including "farmers, zookeepers, and pet owners who pay close attention to the animals in their care," can develop such expertise and use it quite well for prediction of future animal behaviour (41).

Beyond paying close attention to an animal's behaviour and noting anecdotes to appreciate an animal's phenomenal consciousness, we need to have some idea of what it would be like to be that animal. This requires understanding the species' sensory modalities as they operate in what biologist Jakob von Uexküll called the animal's "Umwelt" (the organism's relevant environment) as well as knowing the species-typical behaviour (Andrews 29). Thus knowing through observation that dogs, for instance, have a superior sense of smell to humans is correct, even though it is based on anecdote; this particular notion was held around twenty-five hundred years ago by Aristotle and by many posterior thinkers, and to this day it helps us to understand what is going on in the dog's mind, where olfaction is often more important than what the dog sees.[25] Subsequent modern scientific research on dogs and on other animals (revealing, for instance, that dogs have significantly more olfactory receptors, and have bi-chromatic rather than human-like tri-chromatic vision) often draw on such pre-scientific folk observations and will be brought into this study to assess the accuracy of folk animal psychology.

In early modern texts we see that, using anecdotal cognitivism and folk psychology, writers gained a significantly reliable understanding of non-human animal sensory modalities for certain modes of interaction, for select habitats, and for several animals with which humans, by necessity or choice, spent significant amounts of time during which they were able to carefully study and make anthropomorphic projections about individual animal's minds. Horses and dogs are the best examples, as they were used in warring, hunting, farm work, and other ways. Not unremarkably, horses and dogs were often considered the most intelligent non-human animals, treated with greater respect and care in many cultures (less likely to be eaten, for one), given individual names, and sometimes treated to special rites because of their acknowledged cognitive capacities (such as their own burials).

At the other end of the spectrum of human knowledge of an animal's mind were "fish," animals that most Westerners still discount from folk psychology, indicating a significant limitation to anthropomorphic projection. In the end, this projection is strongest for animals that seem most like humans and may bias us from recognizing the cognitive life of animals that are very distinct or arbitrarily not of interest (for instance, animals that are less cute than another animal). In Sebastián de Covarrubias's dictionary of Spanish entitled the *Treasure of the Castilian or Spanish Language* (*Tesoro de la lengua castellana o española*, 1613) he offers this revealing definition: "Fish: Latin *piscis*, the fish that is raised in the water" (Pez: Latine piscis, el pez que se cría en el agua; 1360). This ten-word entry is surely one of the shortest in Covarrubias's often verbose tome in which the lexicographer defines this grouping of animals by its habitat alone.[26] In contrast, Covarrubias writes hundreds of words on dogs, including significant tidbits on their intelligence, morality, and emotions, confirming in his entry that "on the topic [of dogs], entire books have been written, with very special cases" (desta materia ay libros enteros escritos, con casos muy particulares; 1357).

With an implicit recognition that the length of an entry relates proportionally to the animal's worth, Covarrubias therefore implies a lack of importance for "fish." The attitude of Americans towards fish vis-à-vis other animals today suggests that people still view them as less interesting than mammals, and in general much less sentient than so-called warm-blooded animals.[27] Just as Covarrubias's definition from 1613 implied, the term "fish" reflects a habitat – water – more than a useful taxonomical designation. Fish were, and are, commonly treated as "cold-blooded" objects without feeling or conscious awareness. In an illuminating article in the *Journal of Agricultural and Environmental Ethics*, philosopher of science Colin Allen recently called into question the usefulness of the category of "fish" for making scientific generalizations (25–6). Importantly, as Allen points out, they live in the depths of the sea, where their ordinary natural behaviour is far from the gaze of humans.

Yet current research on "fish" suggests that these human intuitions, which are not helpfully informed by folk animal psychology, are full of biases. Until the eighteenth century, even sea mammals, like whales, were usually classified as fish. It was during the early modern period, and especially in light of New World encounters with certain aquatic mammals and reptiles, that this taxonomic categorization was at times challenged by early natural historical writers in the Indies. This led to an impetus for a renewed classification system, one which would eventually eject mammalian animals and some reptiles; however, the category "fish" remains massive and disparate nonetheless. For instance, as will be explored in chapter 3, sixteenth-century naturalists such as José de Acosta were confronted with the problematic status of the American manatee, which seemed to spend its life in the water but also tasted like veal. This provided a need to challenge the category of "fish" well before whales and dolphins were excluded. While the category is improved, lumping everything that moves in the water (with the exclusion of mammals and reptiles) is still not a taxonomical category, but what Allen calls "a folk category." Allen notes the tremendous number of species (more than thirty thousand) included in today's concept of "fish" as well as the extreme disparities among its exemplars that betray their co-categorization:[28]

> [T]hese species account for around 60% of all vertebrate species ... These include the jawless fish (lampreys and hagfish), and the Gnathostomata, or jawed fish (the latter a paraphyletic group). The jawed fish include

> cartilaginous fish (sharks, rays, and ghost sharks), the ray-finned fish (comprising the nearly 95% of all known species, including the Teleosts, or "bony" fish that make up the majority of the forms most familiar at fishmongers, pet shops, and touristic snorkeling spots), and the "lobe-finned" or "fleshy-finned" fish. This latter group includes the "living fossil" Coelacanth, the lung fishes, and is the lineage that gave rise to all the land vertebrates. This makes the latter group paraphyletic, since some of its descendants (including ourselves) are not classified as lobe-finned fish. The lobe-finned fish separated from the ray-finned over 400 million years ago, whereas the Teleosts do not appear in the fossil record until the Triassic period, between 250 and 200 million years ago. It is perhaps edifying to remind ourselves that tuna are more closely related to us than they are to sharks, and that coelacanths are more closely related to us than they are to tuna. (32; see also fig. 2)[29]

At stake in the classification of "fish" is the undervaluation of their cognitive abilities, a form of bias. Allen argues that because fish live under the water people assume (unscientifically and incorrectly) that these animals have no relevant cognitive life. To this effect, a perusal of recent research on fish bears out the following. For example, studies have revealed that manta rays recognize their reflections in mirrors, indicating self-awareness (Ari and D'Agostino); surgeonfishes "repeatedly sidled up to a realistic mechanical model of a clear fish that was rigged to deliver gentle strokes," in which decreased cortisol levels in their blood showed that fish feel both pain and pleasure or relief from pain (Balcombe).[30] According to Andrews, the philosopher of animal cognition, feeling pain and pleasure are an indication of phenomenal consciousness. This bolsters the suggestion by Allen and others that many of the species subsumed under the unscientific category of "fish" have consciousness.

Recent groundbreaking research has borne out the value of anthropomorphism in assessing animal cognition in other types of animals that are often held to be cognitively uninteresting, including dismissing the commonly held bias of a "bird brain," i.e., the pre-conceived notion that birds are not intelligent (which often implies that they are less worthy of moral regard). The work of comparative psychologist Irene Pepperberg stands out in this regard. In her book *Alex & Me* (2007), she recounts the experiences and knowledge of her thirty-year research relationship with Alex, an African grey parrot, who learned to use English to communicate complex ideas. Pepperberg has documented in scientific studies how Alex could count, label colours, perform arithmetic functions,

Figure 2 A coelacanth. Photo courtesy of Laurent Ballesta, Andromède Océanologie. Blancpain Ocean Commitment.

and even developed his own concept of "zero." One of the ideas behind the notion that birds were not intelligent has been the comparative size of the bird versus the mammalian brain. Yet, in 2016, it was shown that bird neurons are denser than mammalian neurons, such that the estimates, by weight, of how many neurons comprised a typical species brain were highly faulty and lopsided to the benefit of mammals, especially primates. According to Seweryn Olkowicz, Suzana Herculano-Houzel, and their colleagues:

> [B]rains of songbirds and parrots contain very large numbers of neurons, at neuronal densities considerably exceeding those found in mammals. Because these "extra" neurons are predominantly located in the forebrain, large parrots and corvids have the same or greater forebrain neuron counts as monkeys with much larger brains. Avian brains thus have the potential to provide much higher "cognitive power" per unit mass than do mammalian brains. (1)

Increasingly, the findings of cognitive science journals are making their way into mainstream media like *National Geographic* and the *New York Times* such that an increasing number of people are coming to accept that many species of animals are highly cognitive. Meanwhile, viral YouTube videos have provided a significant body of anecdotal evidence of emotional relationships among animals, including creatures of differing species, such as between a goat and a donkey, indicating that these can be rich and emotionally charged.[31]

Human exceptionalism is becoming less pervasive and less defensible in many regards. Even what once seemed like the biggest difference between humans and non-human animals – based on the Aristotelian distinction of voice (φουη) versus articulate discourse (λογοσ),[32] that humans are the only species with meaningful language – has been challenged by twenty-first-century research in cognitive ethology. Discoveries have shown that certain species of parrots not only mimic sounds but also create utterances that are meaningful to other parrots. Still unable to understand the exact meaning of whale utterances, by analysing patterns of clicks and pauses in varying social settings in the ocean, some scientists are now confident that sperm whales not only have a common language, but also use distinct dialects depending on social context, something that would be indicative of culture (Cantor et al.).

With emphasis on close reading and a long tradition of discourse analysis that teases out how words and sentences create explicit and implicit meanings, literary critical analysis is a particularly apt discipline for analysing the different tropes and mechanisms of anthropomorphism that take place in writing. While many researchers in the humanities eschew relying on current science, I hold that scientific cognitive models of animals, informed by folk animal psychology and constructive anthropomorphism, ultimately make the best case for animal studies and animal rights and protections. This is in line with pioneering animal welfare philosopher Peter Singer, who often focuses on animals' pain and suffering as a locus of moral concern. Thus, in analysing texts about animal minds, I examine their reliance on folk psychology and compare this with findings from current cognitive ethology and knowledge of species-typical behaviour when possible. Surprisingly, historical folk psychological accounts often predicted current scientific findings from cognitive ethology. And importantly, many of the biases and speciesism that permeated the medieval and early modern world continue to have a hold on people today because human-animal interactions remain limited by habitat and mode of interaction, despite the massive cultural differences and world views between then and now, and despite scientific evidence and philosophical argument to the contrary.[33]

My book is divided into four chapters that track changes and developments in anthropomorphic understanding of non-human animals, from the Middle Ages through the early modern period in different contexts and through different modes of discursive writing.

Starting with chapter 1, "Deploying the Animal in Medieval Miracles, Bestiaries, and Fables," I analyse ways in which animals were conceived of implicitly and explicitly in Iberia before the encounter with what historians Miguel de Asúa and Roger French have called the "unexpected menagerie of the New World" (1). The parts of the chapter lay out three main symbolic vehicles in which these conceptions were realized. I delve into the complexity of these symbolic readings that relied on implicit or explicit assessments of animal cognition using various anthropomorphic approaches that correspond mostly to human cognitive capacities. I also play close attention to other valences as the symbolic and the realistic, factual and literal were intertwined in important ways. First, I analyse Marian and hagiographic narratives involving animals, with particular emphasis on the rich Iberian repository of animal lore in Alfonso X's *Cantigas de Santa María* (thirteenth century) and other sources of animal miracles associated with the Virgin or with certain saints. In many miracles, the Virgin takes possession of the animal's mind in order to cause it to act in certain ways that will serve divine and human purposes symbolizing devotional practices; the implicit view of the animal mind in these *cantigas* relegates the animal to a position of cognitive and ontological inferiority, for the animals portrayed seem to lack intentional agency as compared to humans, who behave differently in those miracles involving human actors. Nonetheless, a few animal miracle stories demonstrate the strong affection of humans towards animals – both humble and prized – and this offers a positive evaluation of human-animal emotional relationships.

Continuing with this chapter, I then turn my attention to the portrayal of animal minds in the sole Castilian example of the European bestiary tradition. This thirteenth-century translation and adaptation of Brunetto Latini's *Tesoro*[34] has much in common with the classical *Physiologus* tradition and the seventh-century *Etymologies* of Isidore of Seville, and is based on fanciful anecdotes borne of invention and passed on through literary tradition for symbolic uses. The portrayal of the animal mind reveals much about anthropocentric biases of human cognitive development. Such portrayals frequently correspond with the appropriateness of the animal's habitational parameters for human contact as well as with certain modes of interaction that are privileged over others, similar to the Marian miracles. The insights into actual animal minds that may be gleaned demonstrate how our human cognitive embodiment, which anthropomorphizes and tends to view the world anthropocentrically, often determines these conceptualizations.

Finally, in the last part of this chapter, I analyse animal fables and *exempla* that treat sentient animals. Filled with didactic potential, the fable was a popular genre in the Middle Ages and was included in literary texts such as the *Book of Good Love* (*Libro de buen amor*, c. 1330) and *Tales of Count Lucanor* (*El conde Lucanor*, c. 1335). The fable's popularity achieved its apogee at the dawn of the Spanish Renaissance from whence are preserved three incunabula editions of *Aesop's Fables* printed in the Castilian vernacular, the earliest of which is attributed to Aesop (Esopo) and known as the *Esopete ystoriado* (Toulouse, 1488). Although many scholars have viewed the genre as obvious and straightforward, the animals in the fables are not always highly anthropomorphized. Sometimes they reflect an attempt to represent actual animals as they were thought to be minded. Through the process of storytelling, fables can reveal human emotional capacities and cultural norms – such as under which conditions animals become objects of human empathy – as well as cognitively embodied aspects of human cognition. This genre can reveal intercultural elements of human cognitive evolution that are too easily overlooked when assuming the dominant mode of cultural and literary criticism, that is, an assumption of difference among cultures based on an unchallenged ideological belief in the non-biological constructedness of cultures.

In chapter 2, "Exploiting the Animal through Hunting and Husbandry," I focus on the minding of real living animals in Spain in the sixteenth and seventeenth centuries, analysing tomes devoted to the practice of hunting and animal husbandry, and studying the differences in sentience that can be attributed to differences in mode of interaction. The earliest animal husbandry text of this type is Gabriel Alonso de Herrera's *General Agriculture* (*Agricultural general*, 1513), which was published and widely disseminated only some two decades after the conquest of Granada, in response to the mass expulsion of Muslims and Jews, which contributed to a sharp decline in Spain's agricultural production. Like other books about caring for farm animals, Herrera responds to a practical need and is often informed by valid folk psychology and a clear knowledge of certain animals' behaviour, such as a sow's resistance to leaving her young alone; at other times, however, the information it purports seems hard to believe, such as when the author claims that female goats are are so stupid that they will allow a bird to suckle without recognizing that the bird is not a baby goat.[35] In Herrera's book, the animals that have the least favoured positions on the farm and have the greatest burden placed on them are generally equated as the least intelligent based on spurious anecdotes. Their emotions and suffering tend not to matter to the author, although he is against inflicting suffering unnecessarily. I also examine the minding of animals in hunting manuals of the sixteenth and seventeenth centuries, for instance Martínez Espinar's, in which vivid accounts of a dog's cognitive capabilities demonstrate the authors' folk psychology and knowledge of canine behaviour and sensory modalities, as well as noting the importance of the mode of interaction – hunter to hunting companion – to appraisals of cognition. The hunted animals in these tomes tend to have limited emotional range, often noted as "furious." However, some surprising exceptions appear as well, including an appreciation in Miquel Agustí's *Secrets of the Country Estate* (*Secretos de la casa de campo*, 1617 in Catalan, 1625 in Castillian) for the higher cognitive functioning of deer, who are alleged to use Theory of Mind to outsmart canine hunters.

With the the status quo for the state of affairs of European animals established, chapter 3, "Describing the Animal in New World Habitats," examines the theorization of the animal mind under the aspect of novelty in major natural historical works of the sixteenth century in what came to be known in Europe as the New World. It is divided into sections that demonstrate the importance of habitational parameters to views of cognition, that is, demonstrating that the factors associated with the environmental context in which an animal lives determines to a great extent the way in which authors conceive of the animal's mind, which works in conjunction with the mode of interaction of the animal. Rather than be subsumed entirely under cultural factors, I demonstrate that these conceptions of the animal are interculturally anthropocentric. Indeed, speciesist biases based entirely on habitational parameters continue to permeate contemporary US and other global cultures, especially as pertain to fish, farm animals, and grazing animals. Focusing on cognitive abilities, I compare the accounts of newly encountered animals and imported European animals in the works of Spain's royal chronicler Gonzalo Fernández de Oviedo (*Sumario* [1526] and *La historia general de las Indias* [Part I, 1535]). I also draw on histories by Jesuit missionary

José de Acosta (1539–1600), by legal functionary Tomás López Medel (1520–82), and other sources for comparison. While the information found throughout these tomes is varied, interesting intercultural values come through, such as the unquestioned speciesist notion, in Oviedo, that people should not eat dog meat; a pre-Enlightenment and pre-Romantic fascination with the exotic (through the collecting of animals from other lands), both among Spanish royalty including Alfonso X and Charles V, and independently, by Moctezuma II of Tenochtitlan; and how certain features of newly discovered animals can spur on what today we call scientific investigation. Finally, I turn to the the natural historical manuscript that has come to be known as the *Florentine Codex* (1545–90), written and edited by Franciscan friar Bernardino de Sahagún (1500–90) with the participation of multiple indigenous informants to compare the European world view of Oviedo, Acosta, and others with the partially indigenous world view in Sahagún's manuscript, for similarities and differences in the minding of animals.

Chapter 4, "Embodying Animals: Cervantes and Animal Cognition," explores animals, both sentient and not, in Cervantes' fiction. I focus on *Don Quixote,* where the creator of the first modern novel utilizes all of the means of anthropomorphism and anthropectomy previously studied in the earlier parts of the book in the creation of hundreds of animals. In his fiction, Cervantes navigates human experiences of real animals with the history of writing on animals from the Middle Ages onwards. Thus, some of his animal creations have symbolic value, like the hare who Don Quixote interprets as an omen related to his beloved Dulcinea; others, like Cipión and Berganza from the "Colloquy of the Dogs," are gratuitously anthropomorphized and speak as in an Aesopian fable; still other non-human animals are anthropectomized, as mere objects of exploitation, as they are killed or ingested as food without reflection on their former live selves; and a few of the creatures, like the cat, the lion, and the goat, are complex beings with an interiority that cannot be fully fathomed because of the lack of a common language between humans and animals. Ultimately, through what I have called "constructive anthropomorphism," Cervantes carefully crafts two equids who are full-fledged characters, reflecting a realistic appraisal of their *Umwelt*, sensory modalities and cognitive abilities. Like his human characters, Cervantes's horse Rocinante and his unnamed donkey friend, El rucio, are textually embodied beings. His endeavour ultimately yields a new way of representing human-animal relationships unlike any before it across Europe, ushering in the novelistic model of the vital human-animal relationship, one that requires a deeper understanding of the animals' species-typical behaviour and is achieved through constructive anthropomorphism that textually represents embodied animal cognition.

Chapter One

Deploying the Animal in Medieval Miracles, Bestiaries, and Fables

"If animals could still talk the way they did in the days of Guisopete."
– Cervantes, *Don Quixote*

As knight and squire return to their village in the penultimate chapter of *Don Quixote* Part II, they become embroiled in a hare hunt, when the terrified prey seeks refuge from the hounds underneath Sancho's donkey: "[Sancho] saw a hare racing across the field, followed by a good number of greyhounds and hunters, and the terrified animal took refuge and shelter between the feet of the gray (...) '*Malum signum*! *Malum signum*! A hare flees, with greyhounds in pursuit: Dulcinea will not appear!'" (929) ([P]or aquella campaña venía huyendo una liebre, seguida de muchos galgos y cazadores, la cual, temerosa, se vino a recoger y a agazapar debajo de los pies del rucio (...) "*Malum signum! Malum signum*! Liebre huye; galgo s la siguen: ¡Dulcinea no parece!"; 2.71:581). The people and animals involved in the hunt live on one plane, in which the hare is portrayed naturalistically, empathetically described as feeling fear (*temerosa*). On another plane, the scene is a symbolic one, a *signum* in Don Quixote's conceptual framework at a moment in which he is reflecting on the end of his long journey and interpreting the scene subjectively. Although the hare utters no words, its actions explode with meaning. For the eponymous character, the animal expresses a dark foreboding that symbolizes his sense of loss for Dulcinea.[1] His rare use of Latin here combined with his unusually choppy syntax of two- and three-word phrases strung together sound oracular, harking back to a time when interpreting the symbolic meanings of animals was customary.[2] In this older sense, according to Jacques Voisenet, the medieval animal was always a means to an end.[3] For Augustine, as Voisenet explains, the *signum* was "a thing that, in addition to the impression that it causes the senses, allows us to know something more" (qtd. in Voisenet 194).[4] As Umberto Eco put it, Nature – in particular fauna – is converted into an abundance of interpretable and signifying material (qtd. in Voisenet 195).[5] Thus, this scene in *Don Quixote* signals a reversion to an archaic or medieval manner of interpreting the world, what in another chapter of Cervantes's novel is referred to as "the time of Aesops,"[6] that is, when animals "talked" (1.25:300). As Duoda, the ninth-century duchess of Septimania and countess of Barcelona wrote in the *Liber manualis*, "What to say of the lions, of the bees and of other intelligent animals? (...) What do they teach us? Many things are shown to men as examples and their utility is discovered (...) There is a useful meaning in everything" (qtd. in Voisenet 187).[7] While the practice of interpreting natural omens in the world was recognized, it was not universally approved. For instance, Saint Isidore warns of using anthropocentric anthropomorphism to know the future: "It is a great sin to believe that God would entrust his counsels to crows" (*Etymologies* 267).

This chapter lays out the ways in which animal minds were conceived of implicity and explicitly in Medieval Iberia, examining three main symbolic vehicles in which these conceptions were realized: 1. Marian and hagiographic stories involving animals, 2. the bestiary tradition, and 3. animal fables and exempla. Often the role of the animal and its mind in these stories is symbolic, whereby the animals serve a purposive authorial intention.[8] To give just one preliminary example, the symbolic uses of animals figure prominently in European medieval bestiaries, for instance, in the section dedicated to animals of Thomas de Cantimpré's encyclopedic *Liber de naturis rerum* (c. 1244), in which the five human senses are symbolized by a lynx (vision), a boar (hearing), a monkey (taste), a vulture (smell), and a spider (touch) (qtd. in Nordenfalk, 1).[9] George Pencz's engraving "Taste," based on de Cantimpré, illustrates this association (see fig. 3). Animals could symbolize abstract notions as well, such as the seven deadly sins (Voisenet 192).

However, as I will argue, this symbolic manner of interpreting was never quite so simple. For one, it often relied on implicit or explicit assessments of animal cognition – intelligence or emotions – using various anthropomorphic approaches that correspond to human cognitive capacities. To reduce the writing on animals of this vast swathe of textual and artistic practices from many places over ten centuries to the merely "symbolic" overlooks important ways in which symbolism

Figure 3 Georg Pencz's *Gustus, The Sense of Taste.*

reveals significant aspects of human cognitive functioning and in which the various kinds of symbolic representation reveal a plethora of ideas about animal cognition.

In addition, since the court of Alfonso X (1221–84) was the site where Aristotle's writings and other works from Arabic and Greek were being (re-)integrated into Western thought, we can in fact see hints of scientific tendencies entering into European discourse at this time through the use of animal representations, tendencies that we risk overlooking by subsuming them under a sweeping generalization of "symbolic." Thus, while analysing symbolism for how it operates and what it says about human cognition, this chapter pays close attention to other valences of represented animal minds, beyond the merely "symbolic." The symbolic and the realistic, factual and literal were intertwined in important ways.

Richard P. Kinkade and John E. Keller write of a "proto scientific" medieval "renaissance" (no oxymoron intended), in which animals played an important role. As an example, they point to the way in which the animal illustrations of Alfonso X's *cantigas* – strictly speaking, a non-scientific work, focused on devotion to the Virgin – are drawn from life and often attempt to be as naturalistic as possible, resulting in at least one case of exotic animals being rendered in what Keller and Kinkade call "near-photographic realism" (see fig. 4).[10]

At the same time that such exotic non-human animals had currency in the symbolic imaginary, animals were also commonplace beings of everyday importance to most people, playing an important part in the daily fabric of life. As Francisco Ruiz Gómez has noted, daily contact between humans and a variety of real animals was far greater in the European Middle Ages than it is today, and not divorced from the symbolic but interwoven, as for instance in the way that domestic animal and human interdependency was reinforced by the story of Noah's ark, which demonstrated that the success of humans and animals depended in some respect on the other, or as Ruiz Gómez paraphrases it, "we are all in the same boat" (todos vamos en un barco; 267–8). Indeed, unlike today's cartographic property boundaries for individual homes or estates, in Alfonso X's *Partidas*, the legal definition of an inhabited household even included, under certain circumstances, the *minima* of certain, specific animals, to wit, "at least a dog, and a cat, and a rooster" (a lo menos can, e gato, e gallo; qtd. in Ruiz Gómez 268).[11] As Dolores Carmen Morales Muñiz puts it, "no realm in the universe had as much importance in the life, culture, society, religion, politics, and naturally, in the imaginary of medieval man, than the animal world" (207). Thus, it is not surprising that animals play a significant role in the main literary genres of the era. As Susan Crane has written on medieval Britain, which is just as true for medieval Iberia, "[l]iving with animals in the Middle Ages, [was] so intensive and pervasive in contrast to our century's curtailed living contacts" (12).

Figure 4 "Cantiga 29" of *Cantigas de Santa María*. Photo credit: Album / Art Resource, NY.

In these narratives, the role of the animal is often symbolic. But this chapter also examines examples of human-animal interaction that, while assumed to be fictional, demonstrate an attitude of respect and caring for animals, as well as an implicit and emergent notion of "pet," a concept often conceived of as the cultural invention of the modern urban bourgeoisie, paradigmatically in Britain and the United States. Theorists of modernity have asserted that, in earlier times, only the leisured ruling classes conceived of a personal relationship with a domesticated animal, and extended this only to lapdogs and exotic menagerie animals. But medieval texts also provide examples of respect and caring for humble animals who live among humble people, with one-to-one bonds and anthropomorphic concerns for the animals' well-being.[12] Thus the chapter will investigate divergences from these symbolic ways that anticipate other strands of thinking about animal minds, including empathically imagined anthropomorphic embodiment. Indeed, while symbolic relations are the most obvious and important ones in medieval literature, we can mine these writings for their observations on animal cognition, as well as for what those say about human cognition.

While the cultural conditions associated with these medieval Iberian images of animals are unique and fascinating unto themselves, equally compelling for this study is the fact that – despite hundreds of years and largely disparate world views, social organizations, and political structures – some of the same processes for animal conceptualization are at work in the twenty-first-century Western imaginary of animals. Indeed, this is owed partly to the fact that the most basic circumstances of life on the planet (gravity and other laws of physics, the experience of temperature change and other sensations, living as social beings) as well as the human body, along with the concomitant use of complex symbolic languages and subsequent dominion over the non-human animal world, remain largely unchanged. Thus, brain processes such as cognitive metaphorizing, embodied metaphor, Theory of Mind, anthropomorphizing, and empathy are as important today as they were five hundred years ago (as well as hundreds of thousands of years ago). Furthermore, animals are frequently categorized into descriptive cognitive categories based not so much on their actual cognitive functioning, emotions and abilities, but rather on assumptions having to do with their habitational parameters and their mode of interaction with humans, as conceptualized through our own human cognitive faculties and our own habitational parameters and conditions (which to a large extent determine the possibilities for our most basic and tenacious ideas about animal minds).[13] For instance, as will be exemplified in the very few examples in which fish come up in these stories (as well as in certain others such as the fable of the ass and the lapdog), the human ability to interact with an animal in certain ways determines in large respect the unexamined view of that animal's cogition.[14] Furthermore, in this period, we see the stirrings of a more naturalistic description of animals in the Iberian bestiary.[15] Alfonso X "The Wise," and others in his circle such as his nephew, the "Infante" Juan Manuel, are at once towering writers of the Middle Ages and central figures in thinking about animals. To wit, not only did Alfonso author and edit the miracles of the Virgin (many of which involve animals) and a hunting treatise (now lost),[16] but he also collected a renowned menagerie in thirteenth-century Iberia.[17]

Divine Intentions and Animal Agency in Miracle Stories

In this section, I seek to disentangle the imaginative human (cognitive) processes through which animal miracles are produced. It would be facile to lump all of these animal stories together as mere "miracles," for not only do these tales shed light on ways in which animals were conceptualized by humans (at times in ways that are continuous with current conceptualizations) but also on the human mind itself. To this end, I analyse the rich Iberian repository of animal miracle lore in Alfonso X's *Cantigas de Santa María*, while similarities to other animal miracles, associated with the Virgin or with certain saints, will be mentioned for comparison.

Several of the Marian miracle stories in the *Cantigas* share a common cognitive animal model in which animals appear in the stories as passive recipients of Mary's commands. In such stories, the Virgin intercedes to save a worthy person or people from a ferocious animal, whose habitational parameter is either *the wild* or *the cage*, and in which the typical mode of interaction for the animal is that of *hunter to hunted* or *hunted to hunter*. This is the paradigm *par excellence* for what happens in Cantiga 144, in which the Virgin "saved a good man of Pracença from death by a bull" (guardou de morte un home bo de Pracença d'un toro).[18] As explained in the poem and through the excellent miniatures, the captured bull in question is being stabbed and baited by cruel townspeople at a celebration and, in this enraged emotional state, is about to charge a good cleric (see fig. 5). Not only is the "good man" (home bo) innocent of any involvement in the bull-baiting, but he is purposively attempting

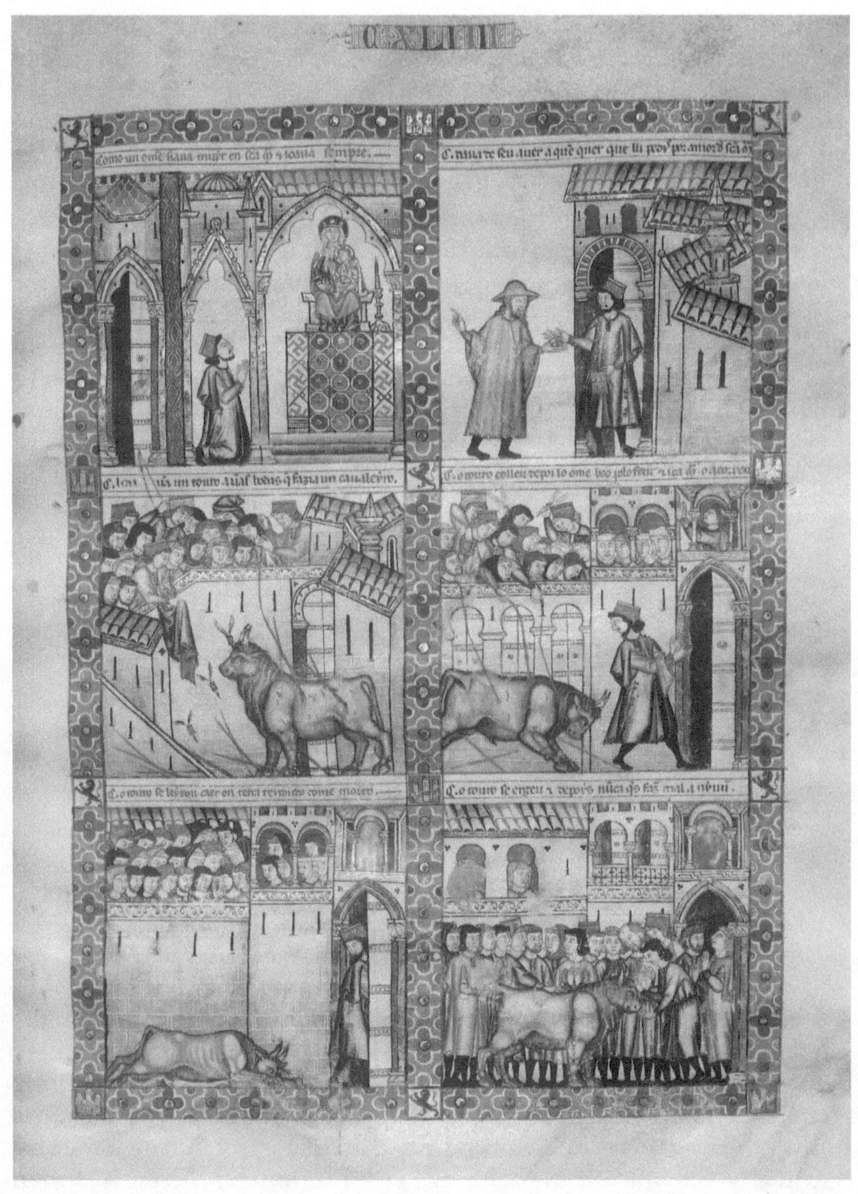

Figure 5 "Cantiga 144" of *Cantigas de Santa María.* Photo credit: Scala / Art Resource, NY.

to avert his gaze, in accordance with the proscription against watching such bloody spectacles in the Alfonsine *Partidas*.[19] As the bull is about to hurt the good man, Mary intercedes and makes the bull drop to the ground and "stretch out as though dead" (assi como sse quisesse morrer; 144.54), thus causing no harm to the man.

This same paradigm for (1) kind of animal, (2) habitational parameter, and (3) mode of interaction is the operant one in Cantiga 9, in which a monk who is supposed to bring an image of the Virgin to an innkeeper is about to be attacked by a fierce lion approaching him. Once again, the violence is averted by Mary, who takes over the mind of the lion. With a slight twist, in Cantiga 398, the violence averted by Mary's involvement was not aimed at a good person but metonymically, at a good person's animals:

> Don Domingo had lost thirty lambs ... and he wandered over valleys and hills all that day looking for them anxiously ... his wife worried that they would be eaten by wolves ... after the third day, he saw the sheep gathered together, surrounded on all sides by wolves. He then was relieved of the great grief he had suffered and went to gather his flock ... [Mary] *caused* the lambs to have the wolves as guards.
>
> (e Don Domingo avia – nom', e triinta cordeyros/ que y tiin(n)a perdera; – e per vales e outeyros / os andou tod' aquel dia – bsca[n]do-os mui coitado [...] Enquanto os el buscava – con mui gran coita sobeja, / a ssa moller, Dona Sancha, – foi chorand' aa ygreja / e diss': "Ay, Santa Maria, pela ta merçee seja / que aquel gãado aja – de lobos per ti guardado." [...] mais depois a tercer dia – viu o gãad' u estava / de consũu, e de lobos – tod' en derredor çercado [...] E do pesar que ouvera – grand[e] ouv' enton conorto, / e foi fillar seu gãado – e levóo ao Porto [...] porque *fez* que os cordeiros – ouvessen por guardadores / os lobs. [398.24–46, emphasis added])

Again, as she did with the bull in Cantiga 144, Mary controls both the emotions and the intentional agency of the wolves here, making them behave not just in some strange way, but in a manner that is entirely counter to their nature;[20] instead of hunting the sheep, the wild wolves protect them.[21] This is a case of complete mind control in which the animal involved in the miracle behaves like an automaton. As the historian Alves puts it, in reference to similar Marian cults in Catalonia, "nonhuman animals were meant to be guides to natural sites and artifacts that were imbued with spiritual significance and supernatual power.

In turn, they themselves were used as ciphers, often (though not always) leaving the real animal behind" ("Sanctification" 165).

This model is the same one at work in some miracles outside of the *Cantigas*, for instance, in the miracle of the disciples of Saint Yago (Santiago).[22] The disciples are making the prilgrimage with his body to Compostela, initiating what will one day become the Camino de Santiago. As they are very tired, they ask the pagan Queen Lupa about borrowing some oxen to help ease the burden of carrying Yago's body; angered by this, instead, Lupa has the disciples thrown into a dungeon with raging bulls, ferocious animals that she keeps in order to kill people. Yet Mary's power overcomes the bulls, and instead of rage they themselves are filled with fear: "she ordered that the disciples be thrown to the bulls, which nobody dared approach; but as soon as they saw the disciples they were filled with fear" (mandó que arrojasen los discípulos á los toros, á que nadie osaba acercarse; pero en cuanto los vieron se llenaron de terror; 96) In light of this, Queen Lupa converts to Christianity, making the miracle even grander: "the Queen, moved and terrified by these miracles, converted to the faith of Christ with all of her people" (la reina [...] conmovida y aterrada con tales milagros, se convirtió á la fé de Cristo con todos los suyos; 97). Later, she provides these once terrifying bulls as the animals for the pilgrimage that the disciples had initially requested; miraculously, the beasts carrying the saint then come to a complete stop at the same time that a star in the heavens becomes immobile. For a second time, Mary overpowered the minds of beasts and controlled their actions, thus indicating the exact site at which Yago should be buried.

And in the *Poema de Fernán González*, a similar if less explicit model of animal mind control can be found in the story of the wild boar. This miracle seems very similar to the paradigm involving Mary with the bulls. However, in this case, the action of her miracle is not made explicit. In addition, the *Poema*'s boar miracle takes the best interest of the boar in mind as well, as not only does it not charge at the human hero, but it is saved from him by entering the sanctuary.[23] There is not much detail here about the boar's actions and nothing explicit about the animal's thoughts, but it does seek refuge away from the man who is hunting it in the small hermitage that one day Fernán González will turn into a major monastery. The animal is spared because it enters holy ground, where the man is too ashamed to kill it.[24]

According to the *wild animal made miraculously peaceful* paradigm, animals first feel a basic emotion (rage, fear) and have some *intentional agency* insofar as the animal seeks to express the emotion in action. While humans, endowed with free will, should be judged by their actions, these wild creatures, in contrast, seem to have no will. Instead, their nature is ferocious, and the Virgin, or in other cases, the saint in question, controls an awesome and miraculous power to enchant and subdue, transforming their nature, in a way that would not be theologically sound if it were done to a human. Thus through what Kinkade and Keller have seen as an Orphic process, the animals' minds are taken over by the power of a more intelligent being.[25] This effect on the animal mind seems possible because of the widely held Aristotelian belief, echoed in Scholastic thought, and specifically reiterated in Alfonso X's *Partidas*, that only humans have a rational mind that makes decisions: "Only men have reason, and no animal whatsover" (la razon han los onbres tan solamente, et no otra animalia alguna; [P II, T XII] 260). This is one of the common justifications that "the intellectual capacity of man" is what allows humankind "to take advantage of the fruits of Nature and of the animals" (Ruiz Gómez 260), a corollary of what came to be known as the Great Chain of Being or *Scala Naturae*, explicated by A.O. Lovejoy in the first half of the twentieth century.

While the change is especially striking in miracles involving furious, dangerous animals such as bulls, a similar Orphic process is at root in miracles involving harmless animals as well. When the Virgin cures a mule of gout in Cantiga 228, the cured animal is made to circle the church not once but thrice, a numerologically significant event. She thus overcomes whatever elements of intentional agency that the animal may have had and provides the animal with a cognitive faculty that is symbolic of Mary's agency. After circling, and as if to leave no doubt as to the divine cause of the circling, the cured mule was made to "kneel humbly in front of the altar" (mostrando grand' omildade [...] E ben ant' o altar logo – ouv' os gēollos ficados; 228.45–7). The actions of the animal then are clearly a *signum* of heavenly power over the mule and by extension and synecdoche, over the Earth. In the case of the mule, there is significant compassion expressed towards the dying animal. To begin, a boy is ordered to kill the sickly animal out of what is called compassion;[26] he only then discovers that it has been cured, in what is also a compassionate act by Mary, who causes its cure and then causes the mule to symbolize devotion. The use of the term "cause" indicates explicitly that Mary's control is key, that she is the one with agency, not the mule. Such loss of will or conscious intentional agency is not what happens in *cantigas* in which she controls humans. For instance, in the story of the man who while eating chokes on a bone and is about to die, Mary indeed causes something to save him, but it is much less mentalistic – she causes him to have a coughing fit, an action that is typically not regulated by human intentional agency.[27]

In Cantiga 354, about King Alfonso's ferret, his beloved hunting companion animal is stepped on by a horse. The King fears for its life, expressing his deeply felt ties, and wants its body returned to him even if it is dead: "Give it back to me however you find it, be it dead or alive, and I shall console myself with it as one who is inconsolable" (Dademia qual quer que seja, – sequer viva, sequer morta, / e conortar-m-ei con ela – come quen se mal conorta; 354.35–6). But it does not perish for Mary has it come out from under the horse's hoof alive and well.[28] Animating both horse and ferret, Mary rescues the animal in a miraculous way. She *causes* the horse to put its hoof down in a certain way so as not to kill the ferret and causes the ferret to come out from under the hoof.[29] Ultimately this kindness seems more directed at the King than to the ferret, but it validates the strong emotions that the King feels towards this "clever" ferret who delights him.

Cantiga 366 provides a paradigm of animal control that adds further cognitive complexity and again involves recognizing the great affection of a noble for a hunting companion animal. In this case, the nobleman is King Alfonso X's brother, Don Manuel, who loses his greatest falcon on a hunting trip. After looking for the falcon for weeks, it comes back miraculously, delivering to him a small bird it had caught. In addition to the miracle of the falcon being led back by Mary (overcoming any intentional agency it may have had), there is some further naturalistic complexity that attempts to provide an explanation as to why the falcon was lost in the first place. Indeed, the falcon demonstrates some Theory of Mind, and the narrator demonstrates cultural awareness of falconry and an understanding of folk animal psychology about raising falcons that informs the miracle story, and which makes sense considering Alfonso X wrote a treatise on hunting, which would have included a section on falconry:[30] "Although they called it very loudly, it would not come to them, try to coax it as they might, for a falcon, until its hunger is satisfied with the prey it has seized, is fearful that its master will trick it to take it away from it and tries to eat its fill, as quickly as it can" (446) (chamaron quanto podian / o falcon que lles vẽesse. – Mais macar braadadores [...] Eran muito en chama-lo, – nen per siso nen per arte / sol vĩir non lles queria; – ca falcon, tra u se farte / da caça que á fil[l]ada, – con medo que o enarte / o que o trage en toller-lla, – punna d'aver seus sabores [...] En comer quanto mais pode; 294.57–65). Indeed, current research demonstrates some mind-reading abilities of many species of animals, including some birds. The human-animal mode of interaction of hunting companion is common to both the story of the ferret and this one; and the fact that such different species with different natural habitats and capabilities are treated so similarly demonstrates the overarching importance of this human-animal mode of interaction. In the case of the falcon, it also lends this *cantiga* a richer naturalistic and mentalistic view of animal cognition than others in which humans interact with creatures they would have less occasion to understand well. Despite this, Mary's agency involves miraculous mind control of the falcon, just as it might for other animals.

Animals are at times animated by another consciousness that, in dire oppostion to Mary's or the Saints', is malevolent. For instance, in Cantiga 82, a group of pigs that are controlled by the Devil approach and harass a monk. Cantiga 47 is similar, and like its precursor in Gonzalo de Berceo's *Milagro* 20 about the "drunken monk" (monje embriagado; 461–99), the various animals who approach the monk and threaten him have been sent by the Devil. In Berceo's version, the main character is a very good man and avoids almost all sins, but heads to a tavern one night and gets drunk. On his walk home, he is threatened by three animals – a bull, a dog, and a lion – all of whom are enraged and furious, and who seem possessed by or at least placed there by the Devil. In the case of the bull who is about to gore the monk, Mary intercedes by putting herself and her cape in between the man and the bull, instantly taming the ferocious animal, who becomes "tamed" (amansado; 468.4). The dog scenario is similar, although the details of her intercession are not mentioned. Regarding both the bull and the dog, the animals are first possessed by the Devil and then unpossessed and tamed by Mary, who does not touch them. But when the lion approaches, Mary varies her involvement: here she uses a stick to deliver a serious beating to the king of beasts, who then retreats; the poem does not clarify why she does not just tame the lion by overpowering his mind and instead resorts to significant force against him.[31] Despite the supernatural elements of this story, the way in which Berceo depicts the furiosity of the animals is in line with anthropomorphic understandings of their emotions and reflections of these in their outward behaviour: thus the bull digs in with his feet and the dog bears his teeth and stares with wide open eyes (466–73).

While the boar's action in *Poema de Fernán González* was not explicitly caused by a supernatural force, here the animals are overpowered by the devil in precisely the same way that they were controlled by Mary in Cantiga 144. But of course, this is not the miracle, but the problem. In Cantiga 47, Mary intercedes in a different way – indeed, she behaves more like an animal tamer, using methods of the era to control the animals, to wit, a cape for blocking and dissuading the bull and dog, and a stick for beating the lion, all three of which seem to alter their intentional agency and leave the monk alone. As Kinkade and Keller explain, this control over animals, whether through invisible mind control, or with animal taming skills, is linked to the Orphic tradition, as it became Christianized. This Orphic quality of peaceful animals is explored further in Cantiga 29. From Hesiod's description of Orpheus to the New Testament Christ, and then to Mary and other saints, a recurring fantastic depiction imagines animals, including wolves and sheep, living in harmony around a central human figure (64). As Kinkade and Keller point out, this is precisely what is represented in the panel 5 miniature of Cantiga 29, in which "God caused the animals to venerate Mary in the Garden of Gethsemane" (68) (see fig. 6).[32] It is in this tradition that Saint Francis serves as lover of animals, and he is reported to have delivered real sermons to birds (67). For Saint Francis, all animals praise God: "Praised be you, My Lord, for the sister our mother Earth, and receive the praise of all creatures that are in the sky and on the earth, and those that are found below the ground and the sea" (translation mine) (Alabado seas, mi Señor, por la hermana nuestra madre tierra, y recibe la alabanza de toda criatura que hay en el cielo y sobre la tierra, y las que hay debajo de la tierra y del mar; Ruiz Gómez 268).[33] Keller and Kinkade observe, in reference to a miniature accompanying Cantiga 29, that "the miracle as verbalized declares that even savage brutes ought to adore Our Lady, and there in proof are painted a giraffe, a zebra, a dromedary, an elephant, what resembles a hippopotamus, and many rare species of birds and fish" (10), some of which surely belonged to Alfonso X's famous menagerie of exotic animals.

A different kind of animation occurs in Cantiga 147, in which an animal behaves entirely anthropomorphically. While speech is one of the most significant abilities that many thinkers posited as a fundamental difference between human and non-human animals, in Cantiga 147, one of the sheep suddenly bleats in meaningful language, disobeying the distinction set up by Aristotle that animals have "voice" but lack "discourse," a difference that leaves the

Figure 6 "Cantiga 29" detail of animals, of *Cantigas de Santa María.* Photo credit: Album / Art Resource, NY.

transmission of reasoned ideas to *Homo sapiens* alone (Ruiz Gómez 264).[34] A poor old woman has been lied to by a shepherd with a large herd to whom she had entrusted her lone sheep for safekeeping. When he claims out of greed that her animal is dead, the Virgin causes the stolen sheep to cry out and be rescued. In an attempt to represent human speech, the sheep bleats, "Here I am, here I am" (ei-me acá, ei-m' acá; 147 [proem] 516P). From this, the woman is able to get her sheep back.[35] The miracle here, thus, reflects the belief that animals do not communicate in meaningful utterances – it is miraculous for them to "speak," for this is an ability reserved for humans (and gods or spirits apparently).[36] If the sheep's utterance were an intellectual act, it would entail a host of other intellectual abilities, including knowing that the woman was looking for the sheep, as well as desiring to be returned to the woman, knowledge and desire that are, not surprisingly, completely in line with the woman's wishes. As such the sheep's desires are anthropocentrically imaged.[37] Speech in this case does not entail the sheep's reason, belief, or emotion, but instead symbolizes Mary's care for the woman who needs the sheep for her own subsistence. Apart from the novel ability with which the sheep is empowered, the animal seems to behave just like a sheep – i.e., its emotions are not contrary to that of a typical sheep and it does not seem to engage in unsheeply intentional agency; this miracle is concentrated on the granting of one exceptional ability.

In other *cantigas*, the miracle is that of resuscitation (or resurrection), similar to the miracle performed on Lazarus by Jesus in the New Testament. Cantiga 178 begins with a hypothetical, evoking an explicit comparison between humans and non-human animals: if the Virgin can bring a man back to life, then clearly she can do the same for an animal.[38] This tale involves a little mule that a farmer gives to his beloved son: "Caressing the boy tenderly, he said: 'Let this mule be a gift to you, and I shall give you barley and straw for it'" (que log' a seu fillo deu, / e faagando-o muito, – dizendo: "Este don teu / seja daquesta muleta, – e dar-te-ll-ei org' e palla"; 178.12–14). Although the boy takes good care of the mule, she dies. The boy's endearing emotional bond with the animal leads his father to try to hide the animal's death from him, implying that the father does not see anything wrong with his son caring so deeply for a non-human animal.

The boy presents a large candle to the Virgin, and even though the mother has had the animal skinned, she hops back to life and good health. Such is the power of the Virgin. Early notions akin to the modern notion of "pet" are generally associated with aristocrats, and applied only to a few select animals, like lapdogs or royal menagerie animals; yet clearly in this case, the humble mule is loved by the boy, and the loving father condones and even encourages this emotional bond.

Finally, a drastically different view of animal control is seen in two miracles that have to do with fish. Unlike the ferocious animals who experience altered emotional states and intentional agency, or the lamb who begins to talk, fish do not have any mind to begin with. It becomes clear that habitational parameter and mode of interaction are not independent variables, and both play an important role. Fish live beneath the surface of the water, and seldom interact actively in their habitat with humans; the mode of interaction is a simple one: fishing. The naive appraisal of fish cognitive functioning that results from these relations is one of "no cognition." For instance, in Cantiga 183, the reader is told that Moors threw a statue of the Virgin in the water, so the Virgin makes it so that they could not catch any fish. Unlike the wolves' minds in Cantiga 398, when she explicitly caused them to be sheep protectors instead of hunters, here the change is not cognitive but from "catching" to "no catching" in which the fish are objects rather than subjects. The text explains that "She caused them not to be able to catch any fish while they left that statue lying in the water" (Ca fez que niun pescado – nunca poderon prender / enquant' aquela omagen – no mar leixaron jazer; 183.25–6), but nothing of the fish minds. The reader is not privy to what she caused exactly and whether fish have had any cognitive abilities, but it implies that fish do not.[39] Miraculously, when the Moors remove the statue, they catch more fish than ever. Again, how she caused the fish to change is not made plain, an inexplicitness that is rare in the *Cantigas*.

A second miracle story that deals with fish and that portrays their cognition similarly is Cantiga 339, in which, en route from Cartagena to Alicante, a group of sailors in a sinking ship pray to the Virgin, who intercedes. She saves them by having fish miraculously plug the leak in such a way that it looks as if it were done by an engineer: "She inserted three fish so that no water could get in nor out through it nor cause any damage" (412) (tres peixes enton exerir, / assi que non pod' entrar nen sayr / agua per y pois nen enpeecer; 339.45–8). Two of the fish that Mary puts in the hole die, and they are eaten, while the third is later placed in front of the church altar as a sign of devotion. Like Cantiga 183, it does not seem that the fish in this tale have any consciousness, awareness, intentional agency, or emotion. Were they explicitly ordered to swim into the hole? It is unclear what "fish agency" would mean in this story. Do they experience any pain on dying? The experience of fish pain and/or any awareness or consciousness is not found in the *Cantigas*. In the end, there is no empathy or care for the fish who die, a treatment that is radically different from the mammalian and ornithological bonds of the King and the Prince towards the ferret and the falcon, respectively, and of the humble boy who loves his mule. All three of these animals survive because of heavenly intercession, which validates the human-animal relationship and the emotions that humans feel towards these animals in the relationship of hunter-hunting animal, and boy-pet.[40] These medieval stories demonstrate a long-standing speciesist bias against fish that is largely habitat-related. Viewed anthropocentrically, their fish lives matter less, as they live in an aquatic environment far from our own. Below the surface of the water, their experiences are out of sight, which is not coincidentally the dominant sense of *Homo sapiens*. The idea that fish are like automata – an unreasoned notion based on the conditions of our own cognitive embodiment about which we are not generally aware – has only recently been challenged by cognitive scientists who have conducted studies on fish pain revealing that indeed, fish do feel it; this aspect of fish consciousness, as well as fish learning, will be explored in greater depth in later chapters.

The Centrality of Humans in the Castilian Bestiary

Like Aristotle's *On Animals* and Pliny's *History* (Books 8–11), medieval texts in the line of the *Physiologus* and the bestiary tradition classify and discuss animals, with greater or lesser scientific accuracy, anecdote, and oftentimes symbolic associations. In Castilian, there is only one extant bestiary, a translation and adaptation of Latini's *Tesoro*.[41] This version was popular in thirteenth-century Iberia and based on a translation of Latini's French version; it is considered among the least symbolic of the medieval bestiaries, more in line with its precursor text, the *Physiologus*, which hundreds of years earlier, Isidore of Seville (seventh century) would imitate in the section on animals of his own *Etymologies*.

In the thirteenth-century bestiary, based on fanciful anecdotes borne of invention and passed on through literary tradition for symbolic uses, the portrayal of the animal mind reveals much about anthropocentric (speciesist) biases of human cognitive development as the portrayals correspond frequently with the appropriateness of the animal's habitational parameters for human contact as well as with certain modes of interaction being privileged over others, similar to how these are conveyed in the Marian miracles. The insights into actual animal minds that may be gleaned demonstrate how conceptualizations are largely determined by our human cognitive embodiment, which anthropomorphizes and tends to view the world anthropocentrically.

There is little about non-human animals that could be said to be "cognitive" in the Castilian version of Latini's *Bestiary*.[42] Starting with fish (*pescado*), the author discusses mostly their habits in the water, for instance, that some lay eggs, others have live births. Cognitive aspects are, at best, fantastic or spurious: fishermen are able to outsmart and catch the eel (*morena*) by whistling like a snake, a sensory stimulus to which it cannot help but come: "the fishermen call it by whistling with the voice of a snake, and it comes to the sound, and they take it" (la llaman los pescadores [quando las quieren tomar] silvando en boz de serpiente; & viene a aquel silvo, & toma[n]la; 4). In what starts to sound like an appraisal of intellectual ability, the echinus fish is called "wise" (sabia), but then the reader learns that this is only for superstitious reasons: the echinus allegedly knows when there will be a storm and prepares for it: "Echinus is a small fish of the sea which is so wise that it can perceive a storm on the sea before it comes, and it quickly picks up and carries a stone to use as an anchor to defend against the force of the storm and for this reason (Saint Peter is an anchor like this) very often the fishermen will observe them" (Echinos es un pescado pequeño de mar que es tan sabia que aperçibe la tenpestat de la mar ante que venga, & toma luego una piedra que lieva con sigo ansy como un ancora por se defender contra la fuerça de la tenpestad & por ess [es Sant Pedro asi commo ancora] muchas vezes los marineros los guardan; 4). The echinus is, thus, symbolic in the sense that it is a sign for humans that helps them anticipate a real threat about the awesome deadliness of nature, allowing them some measure of control (however fictitious or self-deceptive).[43] Quite typically for the *Bestiary* in general, and of many of the animals that will follow, the echinus is treated extremely and entirely anthropocentrically, as if the cares of humankind were the only ones in the universe. This tendency to treat some animals as if their own concerns are irrelevant while those of humans are important without solid reasons is a symptom of human speciesism that is still prevalent today.

It is in this vein that the author mentions the crocodile, a vicious predator but one who it is believed will cry if it kills a man: "if it overcomes the man, it cries while eating him" (si vençe el ome, comelo llorando; 5). In a similar manner, of all the creatures in the world, "the dolphin is a big fish of the sea and goes in search of men's voices"

(Delffin es un grant pescado de mar, & va en pos de la boz de los omes; 8). Furthermore, the dolphin's voice is described anthropomorphically, as it is compared to that of a man crying. The lore recounted includes the tale of one dolphin in Jaca [in Babilonia] who loved a boy so much that it followed him and beached itself only to be captured. Snakes, too, are scared not of men, but of "naked men" (10). While all anthropomorphism is to some extent anthropocentric, these spurious accounts of animal cognition are what I call "anthropocentric anthropomorphism" for they belie an obvious self-interested fantasy about an animal's emotions or thinking centred on humanity, which shares a similarity with the Weltanschauung espoused in the Marian miracles about animals, for instance, of a mule circling a church; in these cases, too, the animal's behaviour was symbolic of the role of divine choice and commitment to humans through animals, and of humans' preferred status in the Great Chain of Being. Nevertheless, it is important to point out that the habitational parameter of "under the water" does not play out here as decisively as it does in the Marian miracles, where fish seemed, *tout court*, treated as non-cognitive automata.

Despite the spurious accounts and unapologetically anthropocentric view, there is the occasional stirring of scientific ideas here. While not directly involved with accounts of animal cognition, they are worth mentioning. In the section devoted to the dolphin, the author says that some live up to thirty years.[44] He explains that we know this because dolphins mark their tails each year. While the detail is spurious, it does demonstrate an attempt, like much of modern science, to rely on quantitative factors for accuracy. Also, while dolphins and whales (both mammals according to modern taxonomy) are called "fish," the fact that these animals are fundamentally different than most other water creatures is not lost on the author, who juxtaposes them against common fish in mentioning that these special ones give birth to just one live offspring.[45] Also, it is noteworthy that the emotional bond described in the anecdotes of human-dolphin interaction are only found in these and not in stories with regular "fish," which suggests that the author appreciated some important taxonomical distinctions (without mentioning it explicitly) between fish that lay many eggs and "fish" that are more like humans and other land mammals that expend more energy caring for individual young. This mode of interaction with humans is *possible* because sea mammals rise to the surface much more commonly than do "fish" and hence have the possibility of interacting with humans in a human zone, above water.[46]

At times, the anthropocentric human-animal interactions in these stories are described in loving terms, such as the dolphin who followed the boy he loved to the beach (even though the emotion was not reciprocated), or another dolphin story in which a boy trained a dolphin with bread to allow him to ride on top of the animal (8); later when the dolphin learned that the boy had died, the animal "let himself die" (8). While some anthropomorphic cognitive abilities stand out in these stories, they tend to be subservient to the value of the symbolism, that is, the anthropomorphism has a moral valence about human morality. This is the case of the serpent who is evil and cruel,[47] expressed through lore about how the female is lustful, enjoys coupling, and then decapitates the male who sticks his head in her mouth; the offspring who are born of this union break out of her belly and kill her, continuing the cycle of evil.[48] An example of the snake's wickedness involves complex anthropomorphic cognition, featuring Machiavellian Intelligence, in this instance, knowing what the eel (*morena*) will think and acting accordingly to trick her: "And know that this snake, when she goes off to the water with the taste of lust or when the eel moves and she calls the eel with her voice, whistling as a whistle and the eel quickly comes to her" (Et sabet que esta serpiente quando a sabor de luxuria vase a las aguas o anda la morena & llamala en su boz, silvando en manera de silvo; & la morena vienese luego para ella; 14). The animal is at once anthropocentrically anthropomorphic and symbolic, in a re-enactment symbolizing how the snake tricked Adam and Eve in the the story of the Fall.

The habitational parameters and the related category of mode of interaction play a significant role in the conceptualization of these animals, which can be seen by contrasting the type of information and beliefs about fish with those of other types of animals. In contrast to the richly creative but spurious entries on "fish," much of the section on birds, especially hunting birds, is accurate, demonstrating the familiarity of the author with bird-training practices or the influence of medieval falconry treatises. Birds are defined initially in an entirely anthropocentric manner, as objects created for human delight: "possessed by men for their enjoyment, with which they take other birds" (que tienen los omes por su deleyte, con que toman otras aves; 16); yet the anthropomorphism involved in adducing their intelligence and emotions is not gratuitously anthropomorphic. Given the closer mode of interaction and the fact that success in arduous and costly falcon training depends on correct instrumental knowledge of how falcons act and learn, the attributes are not spurious, but based perhaps on observation and constructive anthropomorphic projection: So the goshawk (*azor*) is "daring, such that it is not cowardly before any bird, not even does it fear the eagle" (atrevido, en guisa que por ninguna ave no es covarde; nin aun del aguila non a miedo; 17); "they are so proud that they will not take anything except in flight" (son atan orgullosos que non quieren ninguna cosa tomar si non en bolando), elements that depict a worthy colleague partaking in the hunt. However, of all species, the gyrfalcon (*girafalte*) is best,[49] not only because it is endowed with superior physical characteristics, but also for its cognitive attributes including Machiavellian Intelligence ("it is courageous and full of guile" [es de grant coraçon, & engañoso; 21]).

Where Latini deals with birds that are not used in hunting, their value is more centrally symbolic. As it was for the echinos fish, naturalistic symbolism is attributed to birds too. The heron (*garza*) warns humans of an approaching storm, by flying very high in the sky (23). Note that while symbolic, this is a different kind of symbolism than the archaic or medieval omen associated with interpreting birds' flights and positions more broadly.[50] Other examples of what I call "naturalistic symbolism" include that of the common raven (*cuervo*) – the author draws on the biblical story of Noah's ark, and explains naturalistically a couple of reasons for which the crow did not return: "because it found much dead flesh, or died in the water's depths" (por que fallo muchas carnes muertas, o que morio en las aguas fondas; 27).

Like the dolphin mentioned earlier, the carrion crow (*corneja*) also demonstrates naturalistic symbols and anthropocentric anthropomorphism, as it knows what will happen to men revealing the future to those who know how to read the signs: "they guess the things that will befall men, and they show those to him who masters the signs such that he can perceive them" (adevinan las cosas que an de acaesçer en los omes, & las muestran aquel que sabe la maestria por muchas señales, en guisa que los puede aperçebir; 27). Yet these are sometimes naturalistic things, such as increased squawking when it is going to rain: "we can perceive the rain that is to come when they make loud cries and voices" (podemos aperçebir la luvia que a de venir quando ellas meten grandes gritos & grandes bozes; 27). These birds also demonstrate human-like emotions – they "love" their offspring immensely and show it: "they love their children so much that after these have left the nest they follow them for a long time and feed them regularly" (aman tanto a sus fijos que despues que son salidos del nido van muy grant tienpo en pos ellos, & çevanlos mucho a menudo; 27).[51]

Turtle doves (*totora*) provide a symbol of Christian marriage for humans: "there is in this way great love for her beloved; if she happens to lose one, she never takes another spouse and keeps the faith that she had with him and this is due to the virtue of chastity, or because she hopes that her beloved returns to her" (a asi grant amor con su conpañero que sil pierde por alguna ventura, nunca toma otro marido, & guarda bien la fe que tenia con el; et esto es por vertud de castidat, o por que cuyda que torna su amigo a ella; 34). Doves can also teach of negative behaviour, as they engage in licentiousness: "they are moved to lust by kissing, and they unite instead of singing" (muevensse a luxuria besando, & lañen en logar de canto; 26). In the discussion of doves (26), there is an implicit assumption of cross-modal perception,[52] as the symbolic and literal value of looking at a painting is supposed to have an effect in the same way that it would on a human female, that is, according to the widely held (but, of course, erroneous) belief that a woman's visual field at the time of conception would affect her offspring, which led to a series of medieval and Renaissance prescriptions for what types of images women should look at while conceiving lest they ultimately give birth to demons or monsters. Indeed, this same type of prescription is implicitly supported here for doves: those who want good-looking doves (*palomas*) should have a visual representation of a handsome one kept near the place where they mate: "they create a painting of a dove, so that they engender offspring in the likeness of that painted dove that they see in front of them" (fazen una pintura de paloma, porque engendran fijos a semejança de aquella paloma pintada que veen ante sy; 26). Similarly, the stork (*cigueña*) is also an example (according to the science of the day), because it demonstrates how to give itself an enema, which is useful to humans (anthropocentrism); concomitantly it also symbolizes dirtiness (29). The pelican is another highly symbolic bird: according to the text, the mother kills the offspring, cries, and then observes a three-day mourning period, after which she injures herself with her beak and drips her blood on them, which resuscitates them: "the blood brings them back to life" (la sangre los torna bivos a vida; 32), which Latini compares to sacred scripture: "The Sacred Church gives testimony of it, where Our Lord says: I am made a pelican by likeness" (Santa Yglesia da testimonio dello, do Nuestro Señor dize: yo so fecho pelicano por semejanza; 32).

While much anthropomorphism is implicit, cranes are portrayed anthropomorphically through simile, in a direct comparison with humans: "they are birds that go in armies like knights who go to battle and one always go ahead like the lieutenant and leader of the others, who guides them and yells with her voice, and all the others follow that one and they obey her" (son aves que van en azes asi como cavalleros que van a batallas & sienpre va una delantre asi commo alferze & guiador de las otras, que las lieva & las castiga de su voz, & todas las otras siguen aquella & la obedesçen; 30). This commonplace anthropomorphism can be distinguished from the gratuitous anthropomorphism treated earlier.

While there is anthropocentric interest in many of these animals, the instrumental value of taste (i.e., flavour, from the point of view of human eating) is rarely on the surface, but it comes up a couple of times. In contrast with most species about which Latini is silent, partridge (*perdiz*) meat is very tasty.[53] This bird is also believed to be highly intelligent and to engage in Theory of Mind as explained by the anecdote of the mother partridge who hides the offspring in the nest and moves the young around, in order to "trick the male" (33).

Another intelligent bird is the parrot (*papagayo*), an exotic animal from India.[54] It was known at the time that these birds can learn to say words, as the author puts it, "words formed in the manner of men" (dize palabras formadas en manera de ome; 33). There is some folk developmental psychology proposed by the author, who comments that the parrot learns best before its second year, when it is very young. Current cognitive science does not bear out this observation entirely, as certain parrots will continue to learn words and concepts; and in the case of an African grey parrot named Alex, comparative psychologist Irene Pepperberg showed that he not only learned to "parrot" sounds of human words, but also their meanings; in addition, Alex learned various numerical operations when he was more advanced in age.[55] However, some research does hold that, like humans who need to learn a language while young or end up without the ability to learn a language at all, parrots need to develop their language faculty early on if they are going to be able to continue to learn words.

After fish and birds, the author moves on to "beasts," starting with the lion, considered in traditional anthropomorphic manner as the "King of Beasts" (36), metaphorically equating the wild animal world with that of humans. Interesting anthropocentric details on the lion's alleged cognition emerge in the description, as the reader is told that the animal is merciful to humans who beg on their hands or knees,[56] that a lion will only attack women or children if he is very hungry, and that, demonstrating Theory of Mind, the lion literally covers his tracks with his tail, thus he has no reason to fear hunters (37).

The ass (*asno*) is regarded with gratuitous anthropomorphism as "jealous" (*celoso*); he is so jealous, in fact, that he tries to castrate his male offspring; mother asses, however, endowed with Theory of Mind, hide their offspring to avoid this. Like the fanciful claims made about many other animals, the ass has a (spurious) anthropocentric utility to humans, in that he gives a call every hour of the day and the night exactly on the hour, thus making himself useful as a clock (39). While it is not made explicit, one reason that the author/translator may include this claim about the ass's castration of his offspring may be the belief or fear that many animals will engage in "incest." This fear is brought up explicitly in the discussion of the camel, alleged to be the exception to the rule (i.e., the male camel will *not* mate with his own mother). The camel, thus, is more like proper humans in this regard, while other animals have an essential difference, which can be considered a moral failure.

Anthropomorphic anthropocentrism abounds: the beaver (*castor*) is brought up with reference to castration as well, but it is not the father beaver who castrates, but human hunters seeking musk oil. To avoid this fate, the beaver castrates himself with his own sharp teeth. This spurious idea – which projects an understanding of anthropocentric desires through Theory of Mind to the beaver – can also be found in Pliny and Isidore (the reality is that male beavers have internal testicles, which is the reason why these authors cannot see them). This is another case of anthropocentric anthropomorphism, for the animal's behaviour seems guided with man at the centre (in this case, fear of castration from men is guiding the animal's actions). The hyena also allegedly uses Theory of Mind anthropocentrically to trick dogs and humans, by imitating the voices of men and then hunt what is man's (52). Likewise, the monkey (*ximio*) is defined anthropocentrically as a beast that can imitate the things that he sees a man do ("The monkey is a beast that copies very well all of the things that he sees men do") (Ximio es bestia que contrafaze muy de buena mente todas las cosas que vee fazer a los omes; 55–6).

Yet some animals are treated less anthropocentrically, demonstrating the utility of appraisals of cognition using constructive anthropomorphism.[57] In these cases in particular, symbolism plays little role. The ox is said to "love" his companions, and this is inferred through comparison to humans – when an ox companion is lost, the ox cries out (40);

while the text does not say this explicitly, the inference of love, then, is based on the apparent suffering from loss, noted from the cries that seem like something a loving human would emit upon losing a loved one. In his book on the emotions of farm animals, animal-rights author Jeffery Moussaieff Masson states that cows mourn the loss of their young (when taken away to be sold for instance) by calling out, with cries, and with searching behaviour, demonstrating what he also calls "love." While little if any research has yet been done on ox cognition to confirm the claim that they feel strong bonds towards "friends," it is certainly conceivable that such mother-child emotional bonds could be more widely experienced by other members of the species in non-familial relationships.

Other animals in Latini's *Bestiary* have incredible cognitive abilities that nonetheless are not highly anthropomorphic: For instance, deer are said to use teamwork to cross wide rivers, "And when they cross big rivers, the one behind always holds its head above the haunches of the one in front, and in such a way that they support one another" (Et quando pasan rios grandes, el de tras syenpre lleva la cabeça sobre las ancas del delante, & en tal manera se tienen los unos a los otros; 44). Some of these cognitive abilities are ascribed to nature and specifically not consciousness, that is, it is instinct: when avoiding dogs, deer use smell to their advantage, but the text says it is "by nature" (por natura; 44), not learned.[58] However, if they are followed, they don't keep running away, but face death, "to die in front of them more quickly" (por morir delante dellos mas ayna; 45). In this sense, we have come full circle to the symbolic, for this manner of dying seems like one that could be used to instruct men in battle how to die bravely.

The sections on dogs and horses are the longest in the *Medieval Castilian Bestiary*, and contain many obviously spurious anecdotes purported as true. Interestingly, both species enjoy significant treatment of their cognition, much of which is surprisingly accurate. As with the falcons, habitational parameters and mode of interaction breed familiarity and first-hand knowledge replacing some of the kinds of spurious information handed down for other species, especially those who live in the wild far from civilization (e.g., beavers' self-castration). For canines, the author deals with how dogs "love" humans more than any other species, how they respond to their names when called, how they recognize the voice of their master, and how they are loyal (45). Regarding the ability of hounds to track through scent, the author recognizes that this superior sensory adaptation is an ability achieved through breeding, and alleges that learning only plays a small role (thus he advises the reader to be careful to breed one's dog not with just any dog). Like the dog, the horse is also anthropocentrically described and explained, and, similar again to the dog, this is realistic anthropocentrism, because breeding of the two animals over millennia has led to the characteristics most desired by humans. That is, domesticated dogs and horses are by their breeding anthropocentric to some extent. For instance, a large body of recent research has shown that dogs are attentive to human eye contact and will follow the gaze of preferred humans.[59] The author of the *Medieval Castilian Bestiary* says that the horse (*cavallo*) is a very smart animal, and one that has understanding (*entendimiento*), because it lives among humans. There is some wishful anthropocentric projection of emotion, when the author says that the horse gets "happy" in battle; attacks and bites the enemy; the horse will also become "sad" and will "shed tears" (echar lagrimas) when his master dies.

The treatment of both the horse and the dog is different than that of other animals except the falcon, and the subtlety and complexity of their descriptions seem to benefit from the author having had relationships with these common domesticated animals. On the other hand, the cognition of the elephant – an exotic animal for Europeans – is explained only insofar as it is symbolic, and rests on spurious lore about elephants mating for life; as such, they serve an important symbolic role for they are "chaste," and if their mate dies, male or female, the other will wander off in solitude into the desert (51). Such distinctions in treatment are not warranted by any unbiased treatment of animal sentience, for elephants are known to be among the most intelligent and emotional large mammals.

Most of the animals treated in the *Medieval Castilian Bestiary* are real ones, both common and exotic. Yet a couple of fantastic, symbolic animals emerge, one of which has cognitive properties: the unicorn. Here, the treatment of the unicorn and the effects of a virgin on him are the same as those repeated elsewhere in medieval unicorn myths. The process through which the unicorn is made docile is reminiscent of how wild animals are tamed by the Virgin Mary in the *Cantigas*, as the unicorn puts up no struggle and just settles down into the lap of a virgin, going to sleep.[60]

This examination of bestiary animals with explicit cognitive faculties demonstrates that the two relations of habitational parameter and mode of interaction are fruitful in categorizing kinds of representations, and that speciesism abounds due to preferential modes of interaction and habitational parameters that allow for closer contact, scrutiny, and ultimately compassion or empathy towards the animal in question.

Speaking Animals and Voiceless Beasts in Fables and Animal Exempla

The fable can be traced back millennia to Greece and India. It is commonly considered to be a fictional tale in which highly sentient animals speak, often serving a didactic purpose. At the dawn of the Middle Ages, Isidore of Seville (c. 560–636) set down the three main generic conventions of fables in his *Etymologiae* (c. 620–5):

> 1. Poets named "fables" (*fabula*) from "speaking" (*fari*), because they are not actual events that took place, but were only invented in words. These are presented with the intention that the conversation of imaginary dumb animals among themselves may be recognized as a certain image of the life of humans. Alcmeon of Croton is said to have been the first to invent these, and they are called Aesopian, because among the Phrygians, Aesop was accomplished in this area. 2. And there are both Aesopian fables and Libystican fables. They are Aesopian fables when dumb animals, or inanimate things such as cities, trees, mountains, rocks, and rivers, are imagined to converse among themselves. But they are Libystican [Libyan] fables when humans are imagined as conversing with animals, or animals with humans. 3. Poets have made up some fables for the sake of entertainment, and expounded others as having to do with the nature of things, and still others as about human morals.[61] (66)

In many fables, the animal characters display, to a greater or lesser extent, the speech, reasoning abilities, and anthropocentric concerns of people, such that they may seem human in almost every way except for their animal shape. The animal body may amount to little more than a mask or disguise leading to what Isidore calls "an image of the life of humans."

Filled with symbolic and didactic potential, the fable was a popular genre in the Middle Ages, and included in literary texts of the period, such as *Libro de buen amor* (LBA) and *El conde Lucanor* (CL). Its popularity culminated at the dawn of the Spanish Renaissance, from whence are preserved three incunabula editions of *Aesop's Fables* printed in the Castilian vernacular. The earliest of these collections in Castilian

(Toulouse, 1488) is attributed to Aesop (Esopo) and known as the *Esopete ystoriado* (EY]).

Typically, these allegorical stories depict an animal exemplar who interacts with another animal, or on occasion, with an object.[62] Looking to create a strong contrast between types in most cases, the other animal is most frequently of a different taxonomic species, genus, family, or even order. In such situations, the animals are depicted in what is generally an unnatural situation (unusual to obtain in natural settings), rather than in real animal social groupings (where animals of the same species gather together in pairs, families, flocks, packs, or herds). There is a considerable variety of animals depicted in medieval and Renaissance fables, and they are often found in pairs of unlike animals: for instance, the dog and the sheep, the wolf and the crane, the lion and the donkey. Land animals abound – mostly those that today we call mammals – while birds are next in number. Most of the fables in the LBA, the CL, and the EY depict short narratives in fictional worlds with few or no humans, in which animals speak a mutually intelligible language. In Isidore's terms, they are, for the most part, "Aesopian fables"; much fewer in number are those of the type Isidore calls "Lybistican," in which humans converse with animals. Still fewer are those in which animals do not speak at all.

As might be expected, most of the individual fables as well as fable collections as a whole would, at first glance, seem to provide little insight into how the medieval or early Renaissance mind conceived of actual non-human animal thinking or feeling, nor what human attitudes towards relations with non-human animals were like. Rather, it might seem that fables are fantastic stories that mostly reveal how humans abstracted elements of human morality for entertainment or didactic purposes. Indeed, such literature could be used to educate the unlearned, and the *Esopete ystoriado*'s anonymous prologuist makes clear that "the common and unlearned" (los vulgares et non doctos) are the volume's intended audience (133v, qtd. in Burrus xiii).[63]

What can we learn about animal minds or about how humans felt towards or interacted with animals by reading medieval and Renaissance fables? Although many scholars have viewed the genre as obvious and straightforward, the animals in the fables are not always highly anthropomorphized. Sometimes they just reflect an attempt to represent actual animals as they were thought to be. Through the process of storytelling, fables can reveal human emotional capacities and cultural norms (such as when animals become objects of human empathy) as well as cognitively embodied aspects of human cognition that reveal intercultural elements of human cognitive evolution that are too easily overlooked when assuming the dominant mode of cultural and literary criticism, that is, an assumption of difference among cultures based on an ideological belief in the non-biological constructedness of cultures.[64]

An analysis of fables sheds light on contemporaneous views of animal cognition and helps to re-centre the animal in the Middle Ages and early Renaissance. Obscured or below-the-surface elements can be fruitfully extracted from fables. Moreover, the implicit thinking about animal minds generally mirrors the kind of thinking that humans do about other human minds, providing historical evidence that our Theory of Mind abilities have been used on non-human entities as well as on members of our own social groups. As will be explored, there are also traces of human-to-animal empathy in some of these fables. With close attention to how minds are portrayed, often implicitly, I will point out, for instance, that "fables" sometimes involve animals in which no animal actually speaks. Accordingly, I have categorized the fables or exempla in the *Libro de buen amor* (c. 1330–45), *El conde Lucanor* (c. 1330–5), and *Esopete ystoriado* (1488) dealing with animals into three categories,[65] based on one principal element of the human/animal cognitive divide: whether or not they speak,[66] along with the concomitant but graded issue of thinking, feeling, and reasoning. This division lays bare the fact that many fables do not meet Isidore's basic criterion of animals possessing human speech, and it is indeed these generically unexemplary fables that are most instructive of cultural views and insights about animal minds, human-animal relations, and human cognitive embodiment.

Type 1: Speaking Animals: Zoophonic Fables

In what I call Zoophonic Fables, which make up the largest group of the ones I have analysed, the fable meets the traditional criterion, spelled out by Isidore of Seville, for a fable to be a fable, that is, "dumb animals" speak, whether it be (a) with other animals or things (Aesopian, type 1.a), or (b) with humans (Lybistican, type 1.b). Since animals in the actual world do not speak in words, sentences, and paragraphs,[67] representing them as such is clearly fantastical, not indicative of a writer's belief or inexplicitly held view that animals truly possess this kind of intelligence. Rather, the imagined words that are spoken tend to make obvious that the non-human animals are indeed stand-ins for humans, the ones who, under different guise, might actually engage in such conversations and discourse. In other words, having animals speak out loud in human-sounding discourse is a performative counterfactual that relies on the notion that animals not only do not speak, but also, given the historical philosophical tendency to link speaking with reason, reinforces the unargued supposition that they do not think rationally either, and/or that they lack self-awareness, thereby implicitly strengthening the human-animal dichotomy in which human uniqueness is celebrated along with "man's" rightful dominion over the animal world.

As an example, in "The fable of the mouse from Monferrado and the mouse from Guadalaxara" (LBA 1.370–9), the first mouse is rural and displays manners and possessions more consistent with those of a peasant, while the other one hails from the city, serves lavish foods, and shows himself to be sophisticated in his manners. Indeed, these mice are "gratuitously anthropomorphized," a term I borrow from primatologist Frans De Waal, as they speak to each other in a comprehensible language replete with opinions, beliefs, and arguments. Other significant elements of gratuitous anthropomorphization include their human-like emotions and societal customs: the mice enjoy eating fancy food; engage in guest-host reciprocity, each taking turns to invite the other to dine in his home; by making plans to visit each other again in the future, they demonstrate "mental time travel," which Kristin Andrews explains as "[t]he ability to project oneself mentally either backward or forward in time, which allows one to remember past events or envision future events" (188); and they display human-like sociocultural class distinctions in the thematized disparity between their taste, wealth, and customs: performing his higher-brow class, the city mouse even sets the table using expensive table linens ("buen lienç"), a detail that for some twenty-first-century readers may evoke the animated film *Ratatouille*, about a rodent who becomes an important Parisian chef.[68]

Another example that exemplifies well the gratuitous anthropomorphic nature of many fable "animals" is that of the lion and the mouse in LBA 1.425–32. The mouse disturbs a lion, is caught, and pleads for his life, using sophisticated reasoning skills and appealing to the lion's anthropocentric sense of "honour." Indeed, the lion is moved by these reasons and "pardons" the mouse. When the lion is later caught in a net by hunters, the loyal mouse comes to the rescue, using his teeth, which he anthropomorphically recognizes in human technological terms as a knife (buen cochillo), to cut a hole in the net, thereby returning the favour to the lion, by saving his life. Drawing out the human connection further, it is worth pointing out that this fable is similar to a vignette told by Pliny in the *History* about the woman from Getulia who is pardoned by the lion after pleading for her life; it is also reminiscent of the hagiographic tradition of Saint Jerome, who removes a thorn from a lion's paw and is then loved by the lion forever after.

The type of anthropocentric concerns that the mouse-lion story bring to the fore are even more pronounced in the fable of the dog, the wolf, and the sheep (EY 1.4:35). The gratuitous anthropomorphic elements there include a verbal accusation of larceny, a trial before a judge, a perjured statement (which itself implies a type of Theory of Mind known as Machiavellian Intelligence), and a criminal sentence. In this fable, the animals are far removed from the normal habitational parameters of, respectively, the house, the forest, and the farm, and placed in a most gratuitously anthropomorphic setting.

Yet despite the generic conventions and similarity in all of these fables in which animals speak, there are important differences in the treatment of the animal world and animal minds that stand out when we analyse for types of animals portrayed, habitational parameters, modes of interaction, and degrees of anthropocentrism, which vary accordingly. For instance, in the Lybistican version of the thief and the mastiff fable included in EY (2.3:50),[69] the dog reveals, implicitly, that he is but a human "in disguise" when he worries aloud about the Christian afterlife! Indeed, since animals are not considered to have souls by Catholic doctrine, they sadly have no place in Heaven. Indeed, Lybistican fables tend to be the least verisimilar and most outrageous of set-ups. In contrast, while the Aesopian fable about the country mouse and the city mouse is largely a paean to the humble but preferable life of the country – based on the Horatian topos of the *Beatus ille* – despite all of the gratuitous anthropomorphism, we see some cognitive imagining or animal perspective-taking, involving empathy towards animals, on the part of the author, who has given some thought to what living like a tiny creature would entail. To wit, while many of the desires of the mice are highly anthropomorphic, not all of them are: indeed, some are constructively anthropomorphic, reflecting a wild animal's desire to be left alone, to nourish itself, and to flee from predation by humans.

The mice are reflected in a social-cognitive world that is somewhat *separate* from the human world, that is, the mice speak to each other (personification) in an Aesopian fable way. The alternative type of arrangement, what Isidore calls a "Lybistican fable," would be *even more* gratuitously anthropomorphic. Elements of the narrator's "animal-perspective-taking"[70] include focusing on the animals' diminutive size, as well as the corresponding verisimilar plot features that arise because of these conditions: they eat small things, like a bean (*fava*); the mice literally live in holes (*forados*) in the wall; they remain in fear of much larger and more powerful predators (e.g., they scurry away when a person spots them).

Animal perspective-taking also comes into play in the fable about the wolf and the dog, in which the wild wolf and domesticated dog discuss their situations. While they are stand-ins for humans, the particular attention to the mode of being and way of life of each animal is striking as they discuss the benefits of domesticity and of being wild; while at first the wolf is envious of his interlocutor's plumpness and apparently comfortable life, when he sees the restrictive collar worn by the dog, he extols the virtues of freedom (libertad), which he chooses (2.15:65–6). Again the issue of freedom, or lack thereof, comes up, one that is central still today to considerations of animal rights and justice.[71]

In sum, in these Zoophonic Fables (Type 1), the treatment of animals can be more or less anthropomorphizing, and this element corresponds in large respect to how anthropocentric or zoocentric a particular story is. Indeed, in some cases and respects, the animals may be accurately and verisimilarly represented, for instance, being the right size for their species, living in an appropriate animal habitus (such as a domesticated rooster on a farm). On the spectrum of verisimilitude, the stories that are the most jarring to its realization seem to be the Lybstican (Lybian) fables (Type 1.b) in which animals and humans speak to each other. With a diminution of the gratuitous aspects of anthropomorphizing, the treatment of animals becomes even more nuanced in Types 2 and 3 fables, in which animals do not speak, which will be explored in the sections to follow.

Type 2: Fables of Limited Anthropomorphism / Zoo-Aphonic Fables: *Bestia sapiens*

In Zoo-Aphonic Fables, animals seem to express their thoughts and emotions in discourse, but do not voice them aloud; that is, their silent thoughts or intentions are represented to the reader, but when the creatures communicate to other beings, they do so in a species-appropriate way, rather than in spoken language; if they do make an utterance, it is a growl, chirp, bark, or other sound, respecting the distinction proposed by Aristotle that animals have a voice (φουη) but lack the capacity to emit a reasoned and articulate discourse (λογοσ) (qtd. in Ruiz Gómez 264). Strictly speaking, then, these are not "fables" according to Isidore's strictures on the genre, which include the necessary condition that animals (or inanimate objects) speak; yet they are considered fables by readers, critics and the writers themselves.

Although clearly fabulous, these types of fables on the whole seem more verisimilar than those of Type 1, since there is not such an extreme difference in what animals can and cannot do (speak Latin or Spanish or English). For instance, the LBA's "The Fable of the Envious Donkey and the Lapdog" ("La fábula del asno envidioso del perro faldero," LBA 1.401–40) represents the thoughts of the donkey, who is envious that the Lady of the house allows the lapdog to "kiss her hands with his tongue and mouth" (con su lengua y boca las manos le besaba) and feels and expresses love ("grand amor que la amava"). The reader is taken through the donkey's reasoning: he ponders that he is more useful to the household than the useless dog, and then decides to act on his desires by leaving his stable and jumping up on the Lady in his own way. Given his size, he cannot sit on her lap, but instead puts his arms (braços) on top of her shoulders (onbros). In his musings, the donkey uses human-like Theory of Mind; but the conclusions he draws (that she will like his getting on top of her) are incorrect; instead, she is appalled, and he is badly beaten by her servants for his actions. While highly anthropomorphized in his thinking and reasoning, the donkey does not speak (if he did, he might have explained his intentions). The story also demonstrates striking details that help the reader glean important elements of human conceptualizations of animals: while the lapdog is given the opportunity to demonstrate "love," it is because of his small size relative to humans, something related to what today we might call a "cuteness factor," one that is based not on proven information about the animal's mind, but on anthropocentric criteria that have to do with human contingent preferences; the donkey, oblivious to the dog's cuteness, lacks the affordances offered to a much smaller animal, but as a non-human, is unaware of this: from the human and lapdog points of view, the human lap is an affordance on which the lapdog may sit; for the donkey, there is no lap to sit on, and his head and tongue are much too big for him to gently lick or kiss the dainty lady. Yet none of these issues associated with body size and shape have much to do, necessarily, with the cognitive potential and emotions of the animal; it is only with respect to the human's perspective (anthropocentrism) of the animal's abilities and uses that the ass becomes an animal fit for a barn rather than a pet fit for kisses and caring, based mostly on the relative size and humanly determined concept of cuteness. Interestingly in the story, the reader receives no direct portrayal of the dog's thoughts or emotions, only dog actions from which the lady, the donkey, and the reader can infer his thinking. There is significant donkey perspective-taking in the fable: the donkey is housed in a stable (where he doesn't enjoy living), he makes the sounds of a donkey (rrebuznando), which is considered indecorous noise (cazorría) by humans and is not speech; the perspective-taking includes the detail that the poor animal suffers the pain of the heavy beating of "sticks and stones" (palos y piedras), a detail which, by contemporary cognitive standards, would be an ascription of consciousness to the donkey.

Indeed, Type 2 stories generally demonstrate significant animal perspective-taking as well as significant anthropomorphism, without actual speaking or other impossible scenarios (like mice using table linens); they usually involve situations depicting animals alongside humans rather than animals interacting only among other animals. For instance, in an alternate version of the fable of the mastiff and the thief (LBA 174), the guard dog chases away the human thief, refusing to be enticed by a deceptively delivered gift of (deadly) food. While he does not utter a word to the thief in this version, gratuitous anthropomorphic details include the dog's second- and third-order reasoning about abstract concepts, as he reflects on loyalty and how much he owes his generous master. The dog is highly intelligent and somehow susses out that the bread has been tampered with (deadly objects are hidden inside of the food, placed there with the intention of killing the guard dog). The mastiff, therefore, demonstrates that he has Theory of Mind, and uses it correctly to outwit the thief's Machiavellian Intelligence; the mastiff's explicit reasoning concerns mostly his moral concerns,[72] and exemplifies what, prima facie, is not borne out from experience with or research on dogs. Canines are known to be highly food-motivated, seeking food rewards continuously, which is a main form of training. They are not the mental time travellers that the story makes this one out to be, as the dog concludes epigrammatically, projecting himself into the future: "better to have bread and other things every day than just a little bit of extra bread today." Yet he acts like a dog in other ways. The perspective-taking shows him as canine when he threatens the thief: "He began to bark a lot; the mastiff was a carnivore" (Començó de ladrar mucho; el mastín era mazillero); he is socioculturally a guard dog in the employ of a master; he barks loudly and chases the thief away ferociously.

Type 3: Voiceless Animal Fables

In the final and smallest grouping of stories, the animals remain important actors yet do not speak out loud nor are their thoughts conveyed directly to the reader. Nor do they engage in other exceptionally human activities the way non-human animal characters often do in Type 1 or Type 2 fables (e.g., a dog worrying about the eternal afterlife, etc.). These stories do not meet Isidore's criteria for fables, yet they have important animal characters and were considered fables by their authors and translators, or included in collections as fables. The LBA, the CL and the EY (1488) each have a few.

In voiceless fables, humans are involved, but rather than engage in the Lybistican fantasy, the author resists having the animal speak to the human and instead makes the story considerably more verisimilar, with constructive anthropomorphism relying on folk animal psychology. Indeed, in "The Fable of the Peasant and the Young Bull" ("La fábula del rrustico & del nouillo") (EY 21:126–7), given that the young bull does not speak, the reader cannot know exactly what he is thinking for lack of access to any discourse, yet, along with the story's human farmer protagonist, the reader can infer the bull's thoughts and emotions through its behaviour and bull-body language. The young bull is described as "fierce and wild" ("bravo e indomado"), and the way the farmer treats him initially reflects contemporaneous farming practices: wanting to make use of the animal as a beast of burden – as an ox – he attempts to train the animal by yoking him together with a tamed, probably castrated, older ox: "the other tame ox and put the yoke on his neck" (otro buey manso & echar le el yogo sobre el pescueço; 126).[73] The young bull protests this by moving his body around and threatening everyone with his horns: "he began to threaten by throwing off the yoke and the straps and also with his horns he wanted to injure and tear apart anyone who was around" (començo de bravear echando de sobre si el yugo & las correas et allende queria ferir & despedaçar conlos cuernos a todos los que estavan al derredor; 126). The farmer intends to win this war and thus goes to greater lengths to tame the animal, sawing off his horns and tying up his "hands and feet" (pies y manos). Yet the bull continues to demonstrate to the farmer that he has a mind of his own, that is, intentional agency, by protesting these constraints, through the actions of stomping his feet and raising dirt, in lieu of working. Unfortunately for the poor animal, the explicit human moral of the story is that, in certain cases, enough is enough, and an extreme sentence is necessary. In this case, the bull is brought to the butcher for punishment and to provide anthropocentric utility; if the bull cannot be broken and made useful to humans, then *it* will be slaughtered and made useful to humans; if the animal will not provide labour, then the man will profit through *its* dead flesh. This fable of failed domestication and death is hardly fantastic, and indeed, if we fail to use anthropomorphism here to understand the bull's resistance to the yoke as intentional agency – his continued desire to be free of chains – we would be misunderstanding the animal's behaviour and cognition, as well as misreading the story. Despite the dénouement being less than animal-friendly, the animal's concerns in this story, unlike those of so many fables, are fully zoocentric, even if the story line is easily adaptable to provide an anthropocentric moral for humans. Thus the story is a good one to illustrate and defend the importance of constructive anthropomorphism based on folk psychology versus accounts that engage in radical anthropectomy.

Another voiceless animal fable featuring human-animal interaction is that of the snake and the gardener. In the "Exemplum of the Farmer and the Serpent" ("Enxiemplo del ortolano e de la culebra," LBA 1.348–53),[74] a farmer comes across a snake in winter and is concerned about her well-being since it seems very cold. The farmer is kind and uses constructive anthropomorphism in imagining how it would feel to live outside without clothes or fur – in some sense, he is imagining how *he* would feel if he were a snake and outside in the cold, and he feels empathy for the wild animal. It likely does not take modern scientific knowledge to realize that snakes and other lizards sun themselves and therein must derive warmth that they lack. He is a "pious man" (omne piadoso) who feels pained that an animal suffers: "he felt very badly for her" (dolió se mucho della), leading to his rescue of her. Like the gardener, the reader also lacks direct access to the mind of the snake. However, like the bull's actions in the previous example, we can also make inferences from the snake's behaviour. After the gardener saves the snake, she thrives in his home as he takes excellent care of her, treating her almost like a pet or even a child, feeding her "bread and milk" from his own table: "from whatever he ate" (de quanto él comía). We can deduce from this that the farmer's original assessment that the snake was suffering (judging anthropomorphically) was spot on. Later on, the animal is specifically not understood by the narrator in a gratuitously anthropomorphic manner: not grateful or ungrateful, she acts like a wild animal, and seems driven by her instincts to attack and poison people. How different from the moralizing tales of animals who are grateful to another who has helped them in the past, such as the "mouse and the lion," in which the mouse, after being pardoned by the lion and not devoured, returns the favour by gnawing the lion out of a net (LBA 1.425–32). Regarding the snake, the story warns allegorically of hidden danger and of mistaking a foe for a friend, and also, on a more literal plane, of a certain kind of misguided anthropomorphism, a lack of respect for the wildness of wild animals.[75] The distinction here is between different kinds of anthropomorphism, and the limits on this activity; while his original ideas and empathy – based on one kind of anthropomorphism – prove to be correct, the animal is then misguidedly (gratuitiously) anthropomorphised by the farmer who mistakes the snake for a friend and puts his life at risk. Yet the snake is barely anthropomorphised by the narrator – rather, the textual representation involves perspective-taking of the snake, who acts as a snake in a zoocentric manner.

Another fable of this type also involves misguided (gratuitous) anthropomorphism, but offers a twist on this motif. In "What Happened to a Young Man who Married a Young Woman of Very Bad Character" ("Lo que sucedió a un mozo que casó con una muchacha de muy mal carácter," CL 150:35), the main character uses Machiavellian Intelligence to beguile his new bride in a misogynistic tale about terrorizing a woman into subservient behaviour. Our main character thus feigns holding the belief that animals have the ability to understand and comply with his verbal command to bring him water to wash his hands. Apparently unwilling (and actually unable), one by one, each of the animals is punished by the man with a gory death when they do not carry out his wish. "Bring me water for my hands" (Agua a las manos), he cries out, first to his dog, then to his cat, and finally to his horse, only to act as if he were enraged at each of them when they fail to comply. In the final instance, he addresses the personified steed as "Sir Horse" (Don Caballo), and uses abstract reasoning and hypotheticals to explain that, if his wishes are not followed, he will be undeterred from killing the horse too, just as he killed the dog and the cat. As the narrator says, without granting access to the horse's mind, "The horse stayed still" (El caballo se quedó quieto), after which the young man cuts off Don Caballo's head and chops him into pieces for the benefit of his astonished bride.[76] The man explicitly makes the point to his horse, that he is willing to kill him despite his being his *only* horse, a detail intended to be appreciated by his *only* wife. The story presents the animals in a somewhat pseudo-counterfactual: the character acts *as if* they understood human speech and had the intentional agency to comply with the task if they wanted to, but he knows full well that they cannot. In the purpose of training his bride to acquiesce to his future whims, the animals are symbolic here, but not in the same way that animals are symbolic in the Marian stories, in the bestiary, or in some of the other fables. Here they are metonymies for the woman herself, as she is forced to learn through the animals' exemplary punishment. Thus she becomes animalized with the threat that she too will be beheaded by her terrorizing husband.[77]

Most of these voiceless animal fables have human actors, but not all: for instance, in "The Fable of the Dog and the Piece of Meat" ("La fábula del perro y el pedaço dela carne," EY 1.5:34), a dog carrying a piece of meat across a river drops it because, seeing the morsel's larger shadow cast in the water, he becomes greedy for what he believes is a larger piece than the one in his mouth, winding up with nothing (see fig. 7). The story blends anthropocentric anthropomorphism (exhibiting greed, being foolish) with animal-perspective taking (carrying food in mouth, walking on all fours). Perhaps unwittingly, the author has failed to sufficiently take into consideration a dog's sensory modalities; a visual image would not likely become dominant over the dog's other senses the way this would typically occur in humans (through cross-modal perception relying on humans' large and developed visual cortex and excellent colour vision); rather, a real dog would likely not have been tricked by a shadow, reflection, or mirage because the animal would be so much more reliant on the sense of olfaction and gustation to locate food. This sensorial anthropocentrism makes the story more human and accessible, and gets its intended message across – about being content with what one has rather than covet that which one does not – more readily.

The medieval literature of animals is rich, varied, and often symbolic. Ruiz Gómez writes that "The medieval mentality thought that the symbol and the represented thing were the same" (274).[78] While symbolism had its heyday in the Middle Ages, the symbolic deployment of animals would continue well beyond the period, in Renaissance emblem books, and in Renaissance and Baroque painting, such as, for instance, in Jacob Jordaens' *A Maidservant with a Basket of Fruit and Two Lovers* (1630, Glasgow Museum), in which a live parrot in the outer frame serves to symbolize lust and luxury (see fig. 8). I have focused largely on one aspect of this duality, on the non-symbolic role, in an attempt to glean elements of what medieval Iberians *thought* and *felt* about real animals. Animals played a vital role in these texts that point to important aspects of human cognition, as they demonstrate, cross-temporally and cross-culturally, certain realities about our understanding and empathy

Figure 7 The Dog and His Shadow, an Aesop Fable. Granger, NYC –

towards other living beings and how their described or imagined cognition is part of that. In some instances, the stories demonstrate, implicitly, the usefulness and hazards of different varieties of anthropomorphism. The kinds of animals in the various genres differ significantly. While in the most symbolic genre, the bestiary, the vast majority of the animals are exotic ones, and readers would surely enjoy reading about them but would not have had much, if any, contact with them. In the miracle stories and in the fables, in contrast, most of the animals mentioned are common and typically found in Iberia. The only exception is the lion, which appears in many fables. But even lions, while imported from Africa, were commonly found in Iberian palaces. Most of the animals are of the land and sky, and very few of the animals are "fish," which seem never to have sentience except in the cases of cetaceans in the bestiary. Also, the habitats from which animals come differ depending on whether humans are involved in the fable. Typically, when only animals are involved, the habitats are the wild and the farm; but when humans

Figure 8 Jacob Jordaens's *A Maidservant with a Basket of Fruit and Two Lovers.*

are involved, the mode of human-animal interaction generally restricts the species to farm animals with only occasional wild animals.

This survey of Iberian textual animals has analysed the major ways in which animals were conceived in the Middle Ages. It provides the backdrop and corresponds to the ways in which animals were deployed in literary works against which I shall analyse how actual animal minds were understood implicity and explicitly starting in the early Renaissance in hunting and husbandry books.[79]

Chapter Two

Exploiting the Animal through Hunting and Husbandry

The primary column that the Monarchy sustains, defends, and augments is that of arms. Given the knowledge of their usefulness in making men capable, much has been written about this profession. Yet because in peace and at leisure, only theoretical texts serve, it is recognized that for the sake of practice, the most useful exercise is that of hunting, the perfect school of militias, the lively imitation of the harshness of arms and of war; for, in its practice, the senses become vigilant, strengths become more agile, limbs are hardened, spirits find encouragement, hearts are enlargened, the horror of blood and the scandal of death are lost.

(La principal columna, que sustenta, defiende y aumenta la Monarquía, es las armas; conocido este útil, para que los hombres se hagan capaces, hay mucho escrito en esta profesión; mas porque en el ocio y la paz sólo pueden servir los documentos para la teórica, habiendo reconocido que para la práctica es el más útil ejercicio el de la caza, Escuela perfecta de milicia, viva imitación de la dureza de las armas y de la guerra; pues en su uso se hacen vigilantes los sentidos, se agilitan las fuerzas, se endurecen los miembros, se alientan los espíritus, se engrandecen los corazones, se pierde el horror de la sangre y escándalo de la muerte.)

– Alonso Martínez de Espinar, *Arte de ballestería y montería*

When Don Quixote and Sancho meet the Duke and Duchess for the first time, the aristocrats are leading a sizeable hunting party.[1] Mounted on a beautiful white horse, the huntress carries a goshawk (*azor*) on her left hand, performing an aristocratic hunting practice of the type explained in medieval hunting manuals and alluded to in a plethora of medieval literary works. Interrupted by the arrival of the novel's protagonists, the hunt ends abruptly and the reader learns nothing as to the thoughts and emotions of the bird, the equid, or the creature that they were hunting. Yet closure will be brought to this episode of hunting, since several chapters later, the knight and squire will be invited on another hunt. This time, instead of a goshawk, the hunters will use dogs and spears (venablos), as the intended prey is a wild boar: "finally they reached a forest that lay between two high mountains, where, having set up their posts, their blinds, and their traps, and assigning people to different positions, the hunt began with so great a clamor, so much shouting and calling and barking of dogs and sounding of horns, that they could not hear one another speak" (684) (llegaron a un bosque que entre dos altísimas montañas estaba, donde tomados los puestos, paranzas y veredas, y repartida la gente por diferentes puestos, se comenzó la caza con grande estruendo, grita y vocería, de manera que unos a otros no podían oírse, así por el ladrido de los perros como por el son de las bocinas; 2.34:305). While the furious boar is an animal of myth and legend – retold in numerous literary versions including Lope de Vega's *Adonis y Venus* and in paintings such as Rubens's *Calydonian Boar Hunt* (c. 1611) (see fig. 9) – the way in which to hunt boar was also the subject of practical books. In fact, the manner in which the hunters in *Don Quixote* use barking dogs and loud horns to create noise that will stir up the forest animals is similar to the way in which these activities are described in tomes such as Gonzalo Argote de Molina's *Book of Hunting* (*Libro de la montería*, 1582).[2] Led by the Duchess, the hunters move to a location where they know the boars roam, a detail also prescribed by Argote de Molina. The hunters in *Don Quixote*, however, do not use the recommended method for killing the boar, which would have been that of using a spear from a perch in a tree and was considered the best and safest way. Instead, the Cervantine characters stand on foot, and as a group they stab the boar with their spears.[3] The only one to be found in any kind of perch is Sancho, comically dangling from a tree while screaming. Other than the description of the boar as "excessive" (desmesurado) and depicted as foaming at the mouth while charging at them – from which we can infer the beast's ferocity – no other cognitive process of the animal (such as intention, consciousness, thought) is described. Like other animals and people, the wild boar, who is implicitly anthropectomized, is one more plaything for the aristocrats who constantly seek their own amusement. As Alonso de Herrera mused darkly in his *Agricultura general*, it is best to let aristocrats keep themselves busy with their hunting lest they otherwise inflict greater harm on the populace with their leisure. When the boar is killed abruptly, no further thought is given to the animal's life or

Figure 9 Peter Paul Rubens's *The Calydonian Boar Hunt*. Digital image courtesy of the Getty's Open Content Program.

death. Rather, in the course of the same sentence, the narrator's attention turns away from the boar, and lights on Sancho's comic dangling, which leads him to muse on the friendship between Sancho and his donkey:

> Finally, the tusked boar was run through by the sharp points of the many javelins it encountered; Don Quixote, turning his head in the direction of Sancho's shouting, for he had realized that the shouts were his, saw him hanging upside down from the oak, his donkey beside him, for the gray did not abandon him in his calamity, and Cide Hamete says he rarely saw Sancho Panza without his donkey, or the donkey without Sancho: such was the friendship and good faith that existed between the two of them. (684–5)

> (Finalmente, el colmilludo jabalí quedó atravesado de las cuchillas de muchos venablos, que se le pusieron delante; y volviendo la cabeza don Quijote a los gritos de Sancho, que ya por ellos le había conocido, vióle pendiente de la encina y la cabeza abajo, y al rucio junto a él, que no le

> desamparó en su calamidad; y dice Cide Hamete que pocas veces vio a Sancho Panza sin ver al rucio, ni al rucio sin ver a Sancho: tal era la amistad y buena fe que entre los dos se guardaban. [DQ 2.34:306])

While the relationship between Sancho and his mount is put into focus along with significant emotions of "friendship and trust" [amistad y buena fe], the other animal in the sentence is mentioned only to be killed off.[4] This variation in the way that animals' cognition is treated, and the considerable reflection that was granted to some versus the lack of attention given to others, is one of the threads of this chapter, which examines sixteenth- and seventeenth-century Spanish books on hunting and animal husbandry.[5] Like Cervantes's boar and donkey, the animals in these tomes receive different treatments, which I have analysed by the varying "mode of interaction" of their species with humans, using Norton's category, and in conjunction with their distinct "habitational parameters," relying on Morgado's concept.

In the early modern period, the genres of writing that developed to shed light on the contemporaneous understanding of animal minds often revealed functional folk animal psychology in heterogeneous treatises that included chapters on one or more of the following: agriculture, ranching, animal husbandry, proto-veterinary care (known as *albeytería*), and hunting. With varying degrees of anthropomorphism, emotions and thoughts were frequently attributed to animals' minds in real-life situations that were meant to represent the actual world and prescribe ways of dealing with animals on the hunt and on the farm. While these nonfictional genres are concerned primarily and most explicitly with the practicalities of farming, raising, and/or hunting animals, an implicit early modern understanding of how certain animals think and feel emerges, in expressions of intuitive folk animal psychology based on close and frequent contact with the animals, anticipating the "anecdotal cognitivism" of Charles Darwin and other nineteenth-century animal researchers.

In the sixteenth and seventeenth centuries, amid significant interest in cataloguing and describing all kinds of animals,[6] there is special emphasis in Spain on dogs or horses – and sometimes on both, as in Luis Pérez's *On the Dog and the Horse* (*Del can y del caballo*, 1568) – as well as on animals that are the object of the hunt, like deer, bears, and boars. In addition, other works, like Herrera's *Agricultura general*, treat animals that are raised on the farm and used for labour and/or food. These texts differ in orientation from the natural histories treated in chapter 3, which were largely descriptive in purpose. In contrast, the hunting and husbandry tomes aim primarily towards the exploitation of the animals they treat. While some of these works are largely compilations of statements by authorities, they also rely on recent, local anecdotes, as well as on careful observations and intuitions of their authors. Such works have the practical purpose of explaining how to breed, raise, care for, and train certain species of animals, and there is often an increasing empiricism indicative of a modern scientific tendency in such writings.[7]

Authors mind animals in order to explain complex behaviours, often directly involving the animals' sensory modalities, imagined as different from human modalities. In works that are specifically about the hunt and related activities, Argote de Molina and others describe the emotions and thoughts of animals whose mode of interaction is to help with hunting – mostly dogs – with far greater depth and specificity than those for whom the mode of interaction is to be hunted, whether these be boars or bears.[8] These imaginative understandings utilize varying degrees of anthropomorphism, including gratuitous and constructive anthropomorphism, for anthropocentric ends, almost always incorporating elements of a somewhat accurate description of non-human animal sensory capacity into the cognitive make-up. That is, they frequently take into account the importance of the animal's senses – in most cases, smell, but also hearing, sight, and touch – to the animal's emotion, thinking, and implicit consciousness. Often they delve into processes including memory and learning. But as might be expected, these mindings are not always accurate when compared to current cognitive research findings. While sometimes the animals' thought processes are gratuitously anthropomorphic, at other times the descriptions fail for making certain kinds of animals sound like *automata* through implicit anthropectomy.[9]

The following three sections analyse the minding of animals by their mode of interaction. In the first, I begin with the minding of hunted animals; I next turn to animals raised for food and other animal products, as well as for labour on the farm; and finally, I discuss dogs who, among other tasks, played a prominent role in hunting and shepherding, as well as horses, involved in hunting. The analysis will show that the mode of interaction and the habitational parameters are highly significant as to whether and how emotions, thoughts, intentional agency, self-awareness, and consciousness are portrayed.

The Hunter to Hunted Mode of Interaction

Historically, human attempts to understand animals' minds well are almost always reserved for the most beloved animals, which in Europe have often been dogs and horses. Both animal species offered humans anthropocentric instrumental benefits, shared similar habitats, and were fairly easily dominated or trained by humans. They responded to human commands (verbal and/or haptic) and lived among humans, if not always sleeping in the same spaces, then sharing at least their days in a cooperative task or occupation. Thus, just as today, individuals of these species could be fairly well known. In contrast, as pointed out by contemporary ethologists, there are serious limitations to what can be studied and learned about wild animals, precisely because they are free, often skittish, and tend to avoid people.[10] Furthermore, wild predatory animals may attack a human and can present a serious danger. While today's ethologists are interested in knowing more about wild animals for the sake of scientific knowledge, the authors of hunting tomes had little need to understand a wild animal's mind beyond what was needed to be known for the sake of killing it safely and effectively, in order to exploit its flesh and/or its head for a trophy. While an increasing number of ethological studies are done today in the wild, many more are performed on animals in the laboratory, which – like the hunting tomes – similarly privileges the study of certain kinds of species (e.g., mice), which can be kept and bred in captivity with ease, and thus studied in controlled locations.[11]

That animals' cognitive capacities are to a large degree imagined to be a certain way because of humans' mode of interaction with the animals is the organizing principle of this chapter. The approach will facilitate the illustration of how unexamined notions of animal minds arise and are constructed through cognitive embodiment and cultural particularity in early modern Spain as well as elsewhere today. Despite their similar outward appearance in broad strokes (morphology), their closer evolutionary ties, and genetic proximity (more similar even than that of, say, an eel and a tuna), there are stark contrasts between the way that authors treat boars, bulls, and other ferocious animals, on the one hand, and dogs and horses that assist in the hunt, on the other (see fig. 10). Indeed, in addition to the animals' mode of interaction, I will argue that the place, context, and manner in which an animal lives – what Arturo Morgado García has called an animal's "habitational parameter" (26) – are *directly* related to the way in which its cognitive faculties are conceived by humans.

Figure 10 Diego Rodríguez Velázquez's *Cardinal-Infante Ferdinand of Austria*. Photo credit: Erich Lessing / Art Resource, NY.

Just as Cervantes's brief allusion to the boar's mind focused on the emotion of fury (implied through the animal's typically foaming mouth),[12] likewise, in his "Discurso," Gonzalo Argote de Molina describes mostly the fury of the animal. Akin to bulls in the ring who were (and still are) deliberately enraged by specific people tasked with this assignment, boars were provoked with noise and pain. Yet, sometimes the human-inflicted injury was too harsh, it would seem, since it might lead to the animal reacting with significant violence against the horseman and his horse: "a fierce wild boar, and having injured it from his horse with the sword, the boar became more fierce with the pain of the injury, it reared up against him and injured his horse in the flank" (vn Brauiſsimo Iauali, y auiẽdole herido, deſde el Cauallo cõ en el Eſtoque, el Iauali embraue-cido con el dolor de la herida, ſe empino contra el y le hirio el Cauallo por la Ijada).[13] Boars indeed foam at the mouth, and this is a sign of their rage and of when they will charge. In his chapter on the boar hunt, in *Secretos de la agricultura*, Miquel Agustí pays a little more attention to the cognitive depth of the boar, to say that (in his view) the animal is not scared of dogs (no tiene temor a los perros; 432), such that he does not recommend chasing them but only tracking them with bloodhounds. Agustí also recommends not putting collars that make sounds on the dogs, because in such cases the boar is forewarned and runs far ahead of the dogs, thus implying that the animal's sense of hearing is quite acute (434). Using anthropomorphizing language, Agustí comments on how boars "delight" (deleyta) in eating the fruit of hazelnut (*avellano*) and elm (*olmo*) trees, thus indicating where a hunter may hope to find one (434). While the cognitive description is clearly richer than Argote de Molina, it is clear that the rationale for the details is entirely instrumental, answering the implicit question, how best can the hunter track and kill the boar? If an animal has a known preference for certain foods, then it is helpful to know what it "likes," and in this case, then, it seems that to say that the animal "delights" in these fruits is a case of gratuitous anthropomorphism. Agustí also makes one comment about a non-emotional cognitive process, about the memory of their birthplace, because, apparently, while running in a chase, if they happen upon their birth area, boars will take refuge (refugio) and "feel safe" (estar a salvo) there (434).

As these specific details presented by Agustí and Argote de Molina demonstrate, the point of mentioning what we can broadly call the "cognition" of the animal is all about more effectively hunting it. To wit, the hunter needs to know where to locate it (kinds of places it will choose to roam, which may rely on knowing what it tends to or "likes" to eat), what will or will not make it angry, feel pain, and therefore run, whether the animal feels fear under certain conditions, under what circumstances the hunter should be wary of being attacked by the animal, and also which of its senses are most acute. Right or wrong in their particulars, it is the cultural understanding, and importantly, the purpose of the writer's understanding, that leads to the selection of elements to represent in the conception of the animal's mental life.

As in Cervantes's story (and more generally in the literary and artistic traditions), the boars in these tomes are always huge and ferocious, and although they might inflict serious damage beforehand, they are always ultimately killed, either by humans or by their dogs, in vignettes of particular hunting parties. For instance, Argote de Molina concludes one boar hunt narrative with the words, "in the end it was killed by the hounds" (al fin fue muerto por los Lebreles; fol. 6r). Their ferociousness was legendary and perhaps stoked by classical myths of the Calydonian boar, or of Venus and Adonis, the latter of whom was killed by a wild boar (see fig. 11). One boar was so ferocious that it killed or injured dozens of dogs before being put to death by the emperor: "so ferocious that it killed fifteen hounds and injured seventeen, and one huntsman named Diosdado; His Majesty, the Emperor [Charles V] killed it" (tan feroz que mato quize Sabueſſos y hirio diez y ſiete, y aun montero que ſe dezia Dios dado, y matolo ſu Mageſtad del Emperador; fol. 6r). Obliterating such a fierce opponent seems to reflect well on the man who eventually slays the animal, as Abel Alves points out: "respected as an opponent, brave nobles ... were praiseworthy for their predatory skill" (*The Animals of Spain* 64). Unlike the way that Cervantes's Duke and Duchess participate in the hunt from start to finish, in Argote de Molina's description, the royal leaders of the hunt are called in only at the end, notified by the call of a horn (bozina) that signified that the animal in question had been cornered, netted, or otherwise prepared to be killed, limiting the interaction between prey and slayer in a manner similar to the way a modern bullfight leaves the matador's involvement for the end.[14]

Akin to the way in which the boar was conceived, the bull was another animal treated in hunting tomes and considered primarily as "ferocious" (furioso) and little else. Bulls receive little, if any, empathic treatment from treatise writers or from Cervantes.[15] In Part II of *Don Quixote*, the knight and squire are trampled by a group of "fierce bulls" (toros bravos) along with the "tame lead oxen" (cabestros mansos) who are being brought to a ring where they will fight: "the crowd of fierce bulls and tame lead oxen, and the multitude of herders and other people who were taking them to a town where they would fight the next day" (841) (el tropel de los toros bravos y el de los mansos cabestros, con la multitud de los vaqueros y otras gentes que a encerrar los llevaban a un lugar donde otro día habían de correrse; 2.58:481). The reader does not learn the precise fate of these Cervantine bulls, what precisely will be

Figure 11 Titian's *Venus and Adonis.* Digital image courtesy of the Getty's Open Content Program.

involved when they fight (habían de correrse), since there were and still are a plethora of bullfighting practices in different parts of Spain, from the codified *corrida* in official rings, to the famous Running of the Bulls (the eight-day Festival of San Fermín through the streets of the Navarrese city of Pamplona), to less well known local practices such as the town of Tordesillas's "Toro de la Vega" in the Castille and León Autonomous Community, where some two hundred youths annually chase, attack, and spear one bull that is let loose on their streets.[16] We may also get some idea about what was in store for Cervantes's bulls from Argote de Molina's "Discurso," where he describes and celebrates several ways of slaying bulls. The lack of empathy and attention to cognitive features through implicit anthropectomy is noteworthy, as Argote de Molina describes the killing of bulls in any form as "the most enjoyable celebration in all of Spain" (la más apacible fiesta que en España se usa).[17] Here, the *fiesta*'s sacrificial victim is not treated with any reverence, and apart from fury, the animal's cognitive elements remain almost entirely unexplored.

It is useful to see how poorly the bull is treated in a couple of these practices in order to appreciate how implicit anthropectomy is operating, that is, how no attention is paid to the other emotions, or pain and awareness of the animal. In one of these practices, mentioned by Argote de Molina, after separating the bulls from the cows who are freed, a group of citizens lets loose on the bulls and cuts their legs at the knee joint so that they cannot move:[18] "They bring the bulls together with the cows from the country to the city, with people on horseback ... they trap them in a closed-off place in the square where they will fight, leaving the bulls inside and then returning the cows to the countryside" (Traen los Toros del campo juntamēte con las Vacas a la Ciudad, cō gente de a Cauallo ... encierrā los en vn ſitio apartado en la plaça, dōde ſe an de correr y dexando dentro del los Toros, bueluen las Vacas al Cāpo; fol. 16r–v). Ultimately, the townspeople let the dogs do the killing as the bulls are left to bleed to death.[19] In a different regional variation of bull-slaughter from Baeza, Argote de Molina narrates how the youth of the town descend on the bull and stab it with pikes (*picas*), then as a group lift the massive animal up in the air on these same implements.

While for Argote de Molina these activities are all good sport, his favoured way to "hunt" (cazar) a bull contains elements of the modern bullfight in prioritizing the killing of the animal by one man and emphasizes the ideal of his delivering a single, lethal blow: With "great Spanish gallantry" (gran gentileza española), one mounted *caballero* should kill the bull with a single thrust of the lance (*lançada*): "and killed it dead with one thrust of the lance, so well and with such grace, as did Don Peroponce of Leon in Andalusia, the son of the Marquis of Zahara, and as did Don Diego Ramirez, an important knight of Madrid in Castille" (y derribarlo muerto de una lançada, con tanta desemboltura y ayre, como lo usaron en el Andaluzia Don Peroponce de Leon, hijo del Marques de Zahara, y en Castilla Don Diego Ramirez, Caballero principal de Madrid; fol. 16v). In this explanation, while leaving the bull's cognition out of the picture, Argote de Molina pays some implicit attention to that of the gentleman's horse.[20] Argote de Molina points out that the horse should have a "phlegmatic" temperament and be (mentally) prepared in ways that have cognitive implications: "The way in which the knight should thrust the lance is as follows: enter on a large horse with a strong back, raised in front, phlegmatic, one that does not go too fast on his feet; his ears should be covered with cotton, and his eyes covered with taffetta then covered with blinders, *so that he cannot sea or hear*" (La forma quel Cauallero a de tener para dar lançada a de ſer, ſalir en Cauallo crecido, fuerte de lomos, leuantado por delante, *Flegmatico*, que no acuda a prieſſa a los pies, a le de traer cubiertos los oydos con Algodon, y pueſto por los ojos vn tafetan, cubierto con vnos Antojos, *por que no vea ni oyga*; fol. 17r, emphasis added). That the horse be "phlegmatic" is a directive referring to the humoral theory of psychology. Applied to a non-human animal, the term corresponds to trying to select a horse with a well-behaved and obedient temperament. Argote de Molina also makes explicit reference to the reasons for covering up the horse's eyes and ears, which imply the active cognition of the animal and the relation between cognition and the sensorium: indeed, the taffetta (*tafetán*) and blinders (*antojos*) and cotton (*algodón*) are to prevent the animal from seeing sights and hearing sounds and thus to prevent the animal from feeling certain emotions that might inhibit his obedience and responsiveness. Indeed, the minds of horses and dogs – animals that were *de rigueur* for aristocrats for large prey hunting (as well as in the related practices of warring for which hunting had long been considered the dress rehearsal) – are understood largely for practical reasons, for the efficacy of getting the animal to help the man kill effectively while remaining safe. However, as will be seen in the sections on dogs and horses, additional elements come up that seem to go beyond the practical, which may be attributed to the hunters' spending so much time with them that they get to *know* these non-human animals the way they might know their human companions, since familiarity and shared exploits breed friendship, something that is also seen in the colonial texts that mentioned the relationships between the conquistadors and their dogs (see chapter 3).

Writing on the history of the bullfight in the ring, María del Valle Ojeda Calvo explains that most early modern volumes that discuss horseback riding (including hunting books like Argote de Molina's *Libro de la montería*) contained a chapter on what would later become known as bullfighting (el arte de torear; 84).[21] While today the bullfight is no longer considered a form of hunting, in the early modern period, practitioners and theoreticians noticed a significant similarity between hunting and the various bull running, baiting, and fighting practices, given the use of multiple men on horseback, strategies, lances, spears, and other weapons. That the bull is kept trapped in a man-made ring (coso) may at first glance seem disanalogous to hunting. However, in fact, one of the intermediary goals in the hunting of certain wild and often "furious" animals was to isolate and contain them in an area from which they could not escape, sometimes with artificial barriers such as nets that are spread from tree to tree. Thus, stags (*gamos*) as well as wild boars are often confined in a limited area by nets and then killed by dogs[22] (see figs. 12 and 13); alternatively,

Figure 12 (top) A Stag Hunt with Nets and Dogs and Figure 13 (bottom) Hunting Boar with Nets and Dogs. Both images from Gonzalo Argote de Molina's *Discurso sobre el libro de la montería*. Courtesy of the Biblioteca de la Universidad de Sevilla's Fondo Antiguo.

but similar in terms of confinement strategy, stags are sometimes purposefully chased into a river and then killed in the water or as they are getting out of it;[23] in Galician pit hunting, deer, wolves, boars, and other animals are forced into a covered pit that is filled with pointed stakes that stab and kill the animal as it falls;[24] and similarly, Peruvian jaguars are chased by barking dogs into a tree, whence comes the hunter with his quiver to shoot the trapped feline, a detail also mentioned by Argote de Molina that he had learned second-hand. All of these diverse hunting techniques employ the strategy of containing the animal before killing it, making bullfighting a kind of ritual hunting that re-enacts the last stage of one of these hunts of wild animals.

While the foremost emotion of large prey animals, like bulls and boars, in these texts is their ferociousness, there are exceptions. For instance, leading to a gruesome description of what a wolf will do to itself if trapped in a tree by a lasso, the animal is first tricked into feeding on bait where he gets part of his body caught in the noose or lasso; there is something a little anthropomorphizing about the mental life of the wolf in Argote's use of the term "descuidado," literally, caught with no cares: "arriving unsuspectingly to the bitter taste, they are caught in the lasso by the foot, hand, or body" (llegando deſcuydados alguſto amargo, ſon aſidos del Lazo por el pie, mano, o cuerpo; Argote fol. 12r). In this "amusing" technique, the snare lifts and hangs the animal up in the air, in what Argote describes as "amusingly hanging in the air" [colgado en el ayre gracioſamente; 12r). He provides a disturbing anecdote, which surprisingly depicts the significant, if grim, problem-solving cognition of one trapped wolf: "not finding another solution to free himself, he took apart and cut off his own hand with his teeth and escaped" (no hallando otro remedio para librarſe, deshizo, y corto con los diẽtes ſu propia mano, y eſcapo reparando; 12r). While this helped the wolf save his life temporarily, the hunters win in the end: "when the huntsmen found the severed hand, they followed the wolf the next morning by scent and found him in the hills, and they let loose the dogs to chase him, and they quickly reached and killed him" (como los Monteros hallaſſen la mano depedaçada, ſiguieron otro dia el Lobo, por el raſtro y hallaronle en el Monte, y corrieronlo los Lebreles, y luego le alcançaron y mataron; 12r).

Less ferocious hunted animals are sometimes treated as cognitively more complex.[25] Deer (*venado*)[26] in particular were treated by Miquel Agustí (1560–1630), prior of the Order of Knights of Saint

John of Jerusalem in Perpignan, with an eye to significant cognition, in what appears to be the influence in Catalonia of the French medieval hunting tradition on Agustí's *Book of the Secrets of Agriculture, Rustic and Pastoral House* (*Llibre del secrets d'agricultura, casa rústica y pastoril*, originally published in Catalan in 1617, with translation into Castilian in 1625). While the vast majority of his references to higher animal cognition are reserved for dogs, Agustí minds deer in a way that he and other Iberian authors typically do not for the fiercest game animals such as wild boars and bears. In this peculiar case for Iberian hunted animals, the ideal of representing a challenging adversary – typical of the portrayal of the enemy in epic – helps explain the robust mindedness of deer, which is more typical in the French hunting tradition.

For Agustí, deer are self-aware and demonstrate intentional agency by actively trying to evade hunting dogs: "It is also important to pay attention to the deceitfulness of deer" (conviene tambien tener advertencia del engaño del ciervo; 427). Is this a case of gratuitous or rather constructive anthropomorphism? Attributing "engaño" to the deer may seem similar to the fable's manner of analogy, in which one animal is pitted in trickery against another, such as the tale of the fox and the crow.[27] But at the same time it suggests the cognitive abilities associated with Theory of Mind, and in particular "Machiavellian Intelligence," used by the deer to save its own skin. The deer is deliberate in its evasion, engaging in a range of activities in this vein. The deer *knows* things about dogs – how they use their senses of sight and olfaction – employing this knowledge to his own material advantage:

> [W]hen he sees the dogs hunting him close by, *he strives to move out of their [line of] sight*, and free himself and pursue the most diverse methods, such that at times he looks for other domesticated animals and places himself among them in order to get the dogs to run back; they cannot find the scent nor the smell of him, because he puts all four feet under his belly and exhales into the cold, humid ground; and it is natural malice that *he knows that dogs smell his breath and the [scent] of his feet* more so than any other part of his body.

> ([Q]uando se ve cazado cercano de los perros, *se esfuerza de salir de su vista*, y librar, y dar los mas diversos modos, porque va algunas vezes a buscar los otros animales domesticos, y se pone entre ellos, para dexar discorrer

los perros, los quales no pueden hallar el viento, ni el olor dél, porque se pone todos los quatro pies de baxo el vientre, y respira su aliento al fresco, y humedad de la tierra, y es malicia natural en *conocer que los perros sienten mas su aliento, y el de sus pies*, que de otra parte de su cuerpo. [428, emphasis mine])

While at times the anthropomorphism may be gratuitous, I would characterize the passage as mixed. Agustí pays attention to elements of deer sensory perception that are often overlooked. His folk animal psychological assertions are constructive in that Agustí pays attention not only to dog cognition but also to deer sensory processing and behaviour. The deer tricks the dog, he asserts, by "hiding" his feet under his body and by breathing into the ground. In particular, this explanation that the deer "knows" which parts of the body are most easily sensed by dogs may seem a human-inspired exaggeration. In general, the "escape behaviors" performed by deer and other prey animals have been scantily explored in cognitive ethology (Stankowich and Coss 358). But DeYoung and Miller find that deer demonstrate advanced cognition: "[w]hitetails appear able to *assess* predation risks in their environment and *weigh* the costs and benefits of various behavioral options (Ozaga, 1995)" (319). In the small body of scientific literature on deer (which belong to the family of even-toed ungulates) in the wild or near-wild settings, it is clear that "hiding is an anti-predator strategy that evolved in ungulates, which live in habitats providing cover" (qtd. in Vannoni et al. 558). It has been documented that deer fawns hide in vegetation, in plain sight, in a location chosen by the fawn, where they lay with their body and feet to the ground, just as Agustí describes. After foraging, the doe returns to the site where she last left her fawn, communicates by uttering sounds that are recognized by the fawn, who then gets up and approaches her; then, the mother uses olfaction to ensure that this fawn is indeed her own before nursing (Vannoni et al. 558). This complex behaviour, especially on the part of the mother, would seem to indicate that she "knows" something. What about Agustí's other claim, that the deer mixes with other animals *in an attempt* to evade the dog by relying on Theory of Mind? As I mentioned, little research has been done on prey animals in general. Of mammals that come into close contact with humans regularly, deer are one of the most understudied, and to my knowledge, no studies on their potential Theory of Mind have been undertaken, which is not to say either way that they lack or that they have Theory of Mind, just that it is far from clear that they do not. But studies have been conducted on comparable species and strongly suggest that two other members of the even-toed ungulates family (*Artiodactyla*), pigs and goats, possess Theory of Mind to some degree, which makes it at least plausible that cervids might also possess it. Agustí's claim that the deer posits the dogs' line of sight and knows from which vantage point it will *not* be seen (se esfuerza de salir de su vista) is precisely the kind of test that has been done on pigs to determine whether they can use knowledge of another pig's line of sight for their own benefit, and research suggests that pigs can do this (this may be understood as a rudimentary Theory of Mind; see Held et al. 2000). Ethologist Valerius Geist has observed the phenomenon anecdotally (285–90). It is also in line with ethological research already done on other species as well – especially gorillas – that demonstrates that apes will engage in certain actions more readily, including mating without permission from the group's dominant male, when they are out of the latter's line of sight, thus avoiding potential punishment. A number of cognitive researchers have thus posited Theory of Mind for gorillas, bonobos, dogs, certain kinds of birds, and as I mentioned, pigs and goats. Admittedly there is no consensus among scientists that these experiments definitively prove that these non-human animals hold Theory of Mind. So while Agustí's assertions are certainly not facts, his claims are at the very least something that today might be able to attract scientific research and verification or disproving (none of which has yet happened), and given the findings for pigs, the assertions seem to be within the realm of plausibility, although they are not yet warranted by current scientific knowledge.

Among other tactics, Agustí's deer runs against the wind, in order to "trick" (engañar) the olfaction of dogs as well as to better hear the sounds of those chasing him: "Sometimes the deer runs against the wind, *in order to trick the dogs' sense of smell, and in order to better hear the pursuing dogs' howls and sounds*" (Algunas vezes el ciervo corre al contra viento, *por engañar el olfato de los perros, y para mejor oir los alaridos, y vozes de los perros* que le persiguen; 429, emphasis added). Deer will also run through areas of the countryside that have been burnt, because, according to Agustí, they somehow know that the smell left in the wake of fire is greater than their own odour, and thus, that the dogs will lose the scent they seek: "Sometimes it happens that the deer will travel over fields by way of certain burnt areas, where the dogs cannot track a scent, because the smell of fire is greater than that of the deer, and the dogs cease running, having taken in this terrible smell in their noses" (Algunas vezes acontece, que los ciervos passan el campo al traves de ciertos lugares quemados, de donde los perros no pueden hallar ningun sentido, por lo que el sentido del fuego es mayor que aquel del ciervo, y los perros desisten de correr, aviendo tomado esta ruin olor por la nariz; 429). Similarly, deer will run into water and head with the current, to hide their scent from the dogs:

> In addition to a lot of running, a deer has many tricks in order to flee when he is injured or mistreated, and can no longer offer any resistance, fearing a total loss of hope, he leaves the low and thick woods, takes the path to the fields, and will get in a river or pond, because it happens frequently that he gets away from the dogs, because in the country, the sensation of deer's scent is tiny, and when he gets in the water he procedes in this way, that he travels more quickly with the water, rather than against the water, in order to remove his odour from the dogs.
>
> (además de mucho correr, tiene muchos engaños el ciervo para huir quando es herido, o mal tratado, y que no puede hazer mas resistencia, temiendo perdida toda la esperanza, dexa los bosques baxos, y espesos, y toma el camino de los campos, o se pone en algun rio, o estanque, porque muchas vezes sucede, que se libra de los perros, porque en campestre el sentimiento del rastro del ciervo es muy pequeño, y quando se pone a la agua procede de esta manera, que va mas presto segun va la agua, que no contra la agua, por quitar el olor de si a los perros. [430])

According to Agustí, the evasion tactics often work (430). In fact, with such incredible cognitive and sensorial abilities, it seems a wonder that a deer would ever be caught by dogs! While the elaborate description of these cognitive strengths may seem to stretch credulity, hiding in water behaviour is actually described by biologists Randy DeYoung and Karl Miller: they include an anecdote about one particular deer who "successfully elude[d] trained hunting dogs by entering a ditch and remaining submerged with the exception of her nostrils, forehead and eyes" (319). Moreover, Agustí describes the stag's vulnerabilities in even more human terms. Indeed, the stag is so fixated on mating during the rut, he becomes "careless" about other things. Here the gratuitous anthropomorphism rises to the level of unbelievable, whereby Agustí calls the stag's desire for the female by the name of sin:

> In September and October, the deer leave the dense forests and go in love, and then they have no food, nor any secure location, because due to the scent and vestiges of the doe, they put their noses to the ground, *in order to smell without breathing*, and regardless if they go by night or day, *moved by lust*, thinking that there is nothing that can do them harm, and they live off of little, because they do not eat except for what presents itself right before them, purely following the scent of the doe.
>
> (En Setiembre, y Octubre dexan los bosques espesos, y van en amor, y entonces no tienen comida, ni lugar cierto, porque segun el rastro, y vestigio de la cierva, ponen la nariz en la tierra, *para sentir el olfato sin respirar*, y a si van de noche, como de dia, *llevados de la luxuria*, que piensan no ay cosa que les pueda hazer daño, y viven de poco, porque no comen sino solo de lo que se les representa delante, siguiendo puramente el rastro de la cierva. [426, emphasis added])

The use of olfactory and visual signs that the deer uses rises to the status of a secret code that is transmitted beneath human perception and requires inference and philosophy; in deciphering the code, the dog has his own part to play in interpreting the signs, which will be studied later in this chapter. In this gratuitously anthropomorphic cognitive model, one that is socially inflected by Catholic mores and gendered norms for males and females, the deer are not just distracted from their self-preservation by the sin of lust, but rather seem also to hold the additional belief that nothing can harm them (piensan que no ay cosa que les pueda hazer daño), and this then is when they are most vulnerable, not unlike the way humans are often warned by Christian authors to remember that they are not eternal and that judgment and the afterlife will come.

Yet these gratuitously anthropomorphic descriptions of animal thinking are not mere replications of human thinking, despite their indebtedness to a human model.[28] Furthermore, they are not meant symbolically, as were the Aesopian "irrational animals from which the image and customs of men were known" (animalias irracionales de vnas a otras la ymagen and costumbres delos ombres fuessen conoscidas), but rather to teach the reader about animals in their own right, for specific, practical purposes, including the safety of the hunter and the success of the hunting expedition. While they are often gratuitously anthropomorphic, the introspective intuitive details are not always far off in practical terms. I would suggest that the exceptional treatment of deer owes much to the medieval French tradition in which the deer was considered a great adversary, propped up in order to make the hunters who killed them more noble.

While Agustí's attention to deer cognition is general and applies for him to all deer, some writers provide anecdotes of special instances of one animal displaying certain behaviours that were not necessarily typical of the species. For instance, in his chapter on bear hunting (montería de osos) in the "Discurso," Argote de Molina generally explains the ways to hunt bears unproblematically. But he provides an anecdote about one bear who fought back: When he was cornered by the royal hunting party, and arrows (dardos) and spears were coming at him, the bear took those in his "hands" (manos) and threw them back against his attackers. The human emotional reaction to this event focalizes its uniqueness, for the event left the King and Queen in awe (admirados): "He defended himself against them all, and he became free and safe in the countryside, without being harmed at all, instead he caught the arrows and spears that they threw at him in his hands and threw them back with great force at the backs of those who where throwing them, leaving the monarchs astonished by his fierceness" (ſe defendio de todos ellos, y ſe boluio libre y ſeguro al Mõte, ſin reſcibir daño alguno, antes los dardos y lanças que le tirauan, las recogia con las manos, y las tornaua a tirar con grande fuerça contra las eſpaldas a los que ſe las tirauan, dexan do a los reyes admirados de ſu braueza; fol. 8r). While this bear's thoughts are not made explicit, his behaviour seems to indicate that he understands that the weapons are harmful, and that they can be aimed against the humans who shoot them. Of course, it could also be the case that the bear is merely "aping" the behaviour that he has seen, without any awareness or understanding. Comparative psychologist Michael Tomasello studied this type of behaviour not in bears but in chimpanzees:[29] the animals were divided into two groups, one that saw humans twisting bolts off of rings in order to access food, and another group that saw the humans pushing the bolts through the rings; the ones who saw the twisting were more successful at twisting the bolts when left alone. But the jury is still out on whether this type of behaviour represents Theory of Mind. For Gordon Gallup (1982) and Daniel Povinelli (1997), such capacity for imitation means that the imitator is representing the demonstrator's mental state, but C.M. Heyes disagrees, calling this "emulation learning" which does not prove the representation of any thoughts (Heyes 104). Returning to Argote de Molina's bear, we can say, however, that the author does not gratuitously anthropomorphize the animal, since his narration merely involves repeating the actions that the bear takes without mentalistic language, unlike, for instance, Agustí's deer, who were involved in trickery. That discrete exemplars of a species – brute or otherwise – can be conceived of as an individual in itself signals at least the possibility that the species as a whole might be capable of such cognitive capacities, which is similar to the attention given to animals in experiments today in which these abilities are being tested.

Alonso Martínez de Espinar's *Arte de ballestería y montería*, an important tome published some twenty years after Agustí's *Secretos*, continues in the trend towards the empirical, the practical, and the profitable, paying ever greater attention to the prey's mind, for the sake of better killing it. The text is noticeably almost devoid of appeals to authority, save for the occasional reference to Pliny. Instead, Martínez de Espinar replaces such appeals with a significant number of references to the authorial voice's many years of experience (e.g., "having followed the countryside for so many years" [haber seguido el campo tantos años; 55]). The practical exigencies of agriculture, animal husbandry, and, in this case, hunting require hands-on knowledge and as little spurious science and incorrect anecdote from received authority as possible. Indeed, the subtitle of Martínez Espinar's book indicates what he finds to be the irksomeness of repeated incorrect information that leads to ignorance: *The Art of Hunting and the Hunt, Written as Method to Avoid the Annoyance that Ignorance Provokes* (*Arte de ballestería y montería, escrita con método, para excusar la fatiga que ocasiona la ignorancia*).

Espinar expands upon one of the commonplaces of the practice of hunting, the idea that it is a preparation for war, with a complex elaboration that, I will argue, bears upon the representation of animal minds in his book. As many medieval manuals explained, and as many fictional texts reiterated,[30] hunting was not merely a relaxing leisure pastime, but also great practice for war, in which one has opportunity to practice, while at peace. Common rationales for hunting include gaining strength, staying fit and prepared, and practising weaponry. For Martínez Espinar, it is also good for developing strategy, in an explicit simile between soldier and hunter: "The good *soldier*, in order to defeat his *enemies*, among other tasks that he performs, has to ambush them in order to catch them off-guard. The *archer* must do the same thing with *game*, occasionally using tricks to his advantage in order to defeat it" (El buen *soldado*, para vencer a sus *enemigos*, entre otras diligencias que hace, es ponerles emboscadas para cogerlos descuidados. Lo mismo pretende *el ballestero* hacer con *la caza*, aprovechándose en algunas ocasiones de ardides para vencerla; 113, emphasis added). He then describes war as a mode of interaction, with the hunter and the animal adversary continually referred to in the language of "friend and foe" (amigo y enemigo) while animals are also gratuitously anthropomorphized as "enemigos" to other species. For instance, he writes on deer: "their greatest understanding is with their olfaction; with it, they distinguish friend and foe" (el mayor conocimiento tienen en el olfato; con él, diferencian y conocen el amigo y enemigo; 135); on other animals he comments that "man is not their sole enemy" (no es sólo el hombre su enemigo; 189).

Furthermore, Martínez de Espinar gets graphic and gory about why hunting is such great practice: indeed, those who hunt get used to "the horror of blood and the scandal of death" (el horror de la sangre y escándolo de la muerte; xvii). That is, the benefits are not just tactics, strategies, physical exercise, or technique with weapons, but about getting used to killing one's adversary, about becoming accustomed to copious amounts of blood and guts. This analogy is not merely linguistic, and it relies on the obvious similitudes between humans and non-human animals, especially mammals, some of which require cognitive anthropomorphism: that they have similar bodily systems and organs, that they can bleed to death, and that they feel pain and suffering. That when they are pricked, they also do bleed. Getting used to "the horror of blood and the scandal of death" means overcoming one's inherent, natural aversion to causing suffering and death, and it is tantamount to becoming a great warrior. Martínez de Espinar repeats the idea that hunting is good practice for war many times in his book.[31] In a nation almost continually at war in all four cardinal directions, as well as within its own borders (e.g., uprising of the Alpujarras, the wars of succession of both Catalonia and Portugal), this is indeed an excellent rationalization for hunting at a time when it was receiving ever greater criticism from various sectors in society as a wasteful pastime (and, if only rarely, as cruel and unnecessary).[32]

Other rationalizations for hunting include Martínez de Espinar's etiological tale in which animals hunted other animals before humans ever hunted anything; he claims that humans learned from animals by imitation, as he uses the gratuitously anthromorphic term "murderers" (homicidas) to refer to non-human animals who kill other non-human animals: "humans learned this from animals, because they practiced it first for their sustenance ... the animals that she [the land] raises are murderers of one another" (esto aprendieron los hombres de los animales, porque ellos lo usraon primero para sustentarse ... los animales que ella [la tierra] cría son homicidas unos de otros; 80). He also provides anecdotal examples that he has witnessed of animals killing their own kind, such as the case where two stags locked horns so hard that they killed each other (123).

The rationalizing digressions in Martínez de Espinar are a good context in which he develops the psychology of the hunted animals. In his book, the animals of the forest seem systematically to have emotions and especially higher thinking. For instance, with their senses of smell and sight hindered on very windy days, deer become "anxious," in a description that highlights their awareness (*conocen*): "they know the harm that will befall them by not being able to use their vision and their hearing as they do when the weather is calm; because the noise that the wind in the countryside makes is so great that it leaves no opportunity for him to hear or to see, and because of this, on such days he is very anxious and gets upset about anything" (*conocen* el daño que les viene de no poderse valer de la vista y los oídos como cuando está el tiempo sosegado; porque el ruido que hace el viento en el monte es tan grande, que no le da lugar que vea ni oiga, y por esta causa, en tales días está con gran inquietud y de cualquier cosa se alborota; 112). Whether this anthropomorphism is gratuitous or not is open to debate since so few studies have been conducted on deer – the description may or may not be apt. Rhetorically, however, the effect is to portray a better adversary in the animal, one that is more worthy of the hunt, and thus retaining the hunt's privileged status as an increasingly important practice for war, as well as a more worthy topic to which to dedicate a book. In addition, the more cognitively advanced the animals are, the more praise should be granted to hunter's tricks or "ardides" which he describes repeatedly. This leads to a palpable tension in his work between calling animals "beasts" (bestias) – assuming that they do not have reason – and depicting these "foes" (enemigos) as complex cognitive beings, the kind of tension that is found in epic, as the poet strives to demonstrate at once the might and right of the heroes, while depicting a noble adversary who is (almost) worthy of them, such as Hector who dies by the hand of Achiles.

Among these stratagems, Martínez de Espinar explains a stealth method for killing deer and other grazing animals that contains a trace of the mythological Trojan Horse and Daedalus's wooden cow. He calls it "buey de cabestrillo," referring to the use of a live ox as an olfactory and visual blind behind which the hunter can stealthily approach the prey animal (see fig. 14).[33] Not paying any attention to the mind of

Figure 14 Hunting with Ox in Alonso Martínez de Espinar's *Arte de ballestería y montería*. Courtesy of Hathitrust.

the ox – an animal that is instrumentalized and automatized through implicit anthropectomy – Martínez de Espinar attends explicitly to the associative learning of the deer, insisting that the hunter should never reveal himself even after the kill, so that the survivors do not associate the humans with the ox. Indeed, the deer will not forget the association quickly, he admonishes, explaining that the deer would associate the experience of the ox with the killing by the hunter. He employs the verb "escarmentar" to describe such learning: "One should never uncover oneself to the hunted animal nor abandon the ox, even after shooting at the animal, because the one that was not killed will *learn the lesson* having seen the man alongside the ox, and they will not forget this apprehension so quickly" (Jamás se ha de descubrir a la caza ni desamparar el buey, aunque sea después de haberla tirado, porque la que no mató, *quedará escarmentada* con haber visto al hombre junto al buey, y este recelo no se les olvida tan presto" (my emphasis, 233). The term "escarmentar" (to learn a lesson) is an interesting vocabulary choice to use for these animals, since its definition and asserted etymology involve self-awareness, learning, and the avoidance of future deception, all things not generally associated with mindless "beasts": according to the *Diccionario de Autoridades*, the verb means,

> Take heed and learn from what one has himself or in others seen and experienced, so as not to fall or err in the future, and avoid risks and dangers. The etymology of this verb is troublesome, and the most versimilar [explanation] is that it is a compound form of the nouns "responsibility" [cargo] and "mind" [mente] and that *escarmentar* signifies the same as "making the mind take responsibility," such that it can recognize and forwarn about harms and errors before they happen, in order to flee and avoid them.
>
> (Tomar advertencia y enseñanza de lo que en sí mismo o en otros ha visto y experimentado, para no caer ni errar en adelante, y evitar los riesgos y peligros. La etymología deste verbo es dificultosa, y la más verisimil es que es compuesto de los nombres Cargo y Mente, y que Escarmentar vale lo mismo que hacer cargo a la mente, para que advierta y reconozca los daños y yerros antecedentes, y los huya y evíte. [*Autoridades* 1732])

By keeping his presence unknown to the surviving deer, the advised hunter will, in effect, prevent the deer from linking cause and effect, an ability that he has, and one which here seems to belie an element of instrumental and logical rationality (as evinced by his use of the word "escarmentar").[34] Because of this, the prey animals are deprived of sensory information (sight of or smell of the hunter), and will not be able to ascertain the actual cause of their conspecific's killing. All of this implies anthropomorphically that deer have concepts like "cause" and "effect," and that they have a "mind" that can "take charge" (hacer cargo), ultimately implying that they reason like humans.

In a separate passage, however, using a counterfactual, Martínez de Espinar more carefully suggests that deer act only "as if" (literally, "just as") they had reason. He offers the example of how they "know" enough to avoid "thick vegetation" (espesuras) on windy days, which they do "to take advantage of both their sight and their olfaction ... with this they defend themselves, just as one who has reason could avoid it" (por aprovecharse de la vista como del olfato ... con esto se defienden, como lo pudiera prevenir quien tuviera uso de razón; 119). The implication of this hypothetical is that they don't have reason. Why not? It would seem that non-human animals lack reason *merely* by virtue of being non-human. The author's unstated Aristotelian theoretical foundation is at odds with his practical folk animal psychology, which is informed by decades of contact with animals. In sum, the tension remains that these animals are highly intelligent, have excellent sensory perception, use something like reason, and have the capacity to link causes and effects, which would allow them to alter their behaviour for self-preservation. In fact, by Martínez-Espinar's admission, these creatures are better than humans in this last regard: "in regards to their self-preservation, animals have known advantages over humans" (que los animales, en lo que toca a su conservación, nos hacen conocidas ventajas; 119).

While he generally does not think as highly of the intelligence of boars, Martínez de Espinar brings up the anthropomorphic scenario of the "squire boar," in which a mature animal ("Sir") brings along a smaller and younger boar "that we call a squire" (que llamamos escudero). Still playing on the martial metaphor introduced earlier, the older boar is likened to a knight who, in the author's explanation, is not virtuous and yet is "astute" (130), who brings the younger, less astute boar along with him so that when they find themselves in dangerous situations (such as being hunted by humans), the old boar remains quiet and still, allowing the squire to take the fall, in a way that seems rational, in a calculated, instrumental way, with a nod towards Machiavellian Intelligence. While to a lay person this pairing may seem unlikely, hunters and ethologists have documented the existence of the squire boar phenomenon. And while the thought processes of wild boars are not well understood and would be difficult to test, these animal actions do have their basis in fact rather than fable.

While the mode of interaction in earlier texts – paradigmatically, Argote de Molina's "Discurso" and his publication of Alfonso XI's manuscript on hunting – relinquishes the cognitive status of hunted animals to the most basic, unitary affective states (such as the emotion of "fury"), in the seventeenth century more attention was paid to non-human prey as complex, thinking beings, anthropomorphically portrayed as worthy adversaries. Both Agustí's and Martínez de Espinar's wild animals have emotions well beyond fury; they have memory and are capable of associative learning, understood not in a purely behaviouristic manner, but with self-awareness and metacognition. The intelligence and abilities of these animals thus require excellently trained hunters who will make great warriors when called upon, warriors who are adept at stealth methods, like the ancient Greeks, who overcame the Trojans with the wooden horse trick. These modes of hunting are required in order to avoid clever animals sensing the human hunter who wishes to make his kill, just as a warrior will be successful in certain cases if he can ambush the enemy without first being detected. Portraying the quarry as actual enemies engaged in war, anthropomorphically, with emotions, intelligence, and metacognition, Martínez de Espinar develops the idea that hunting is necessary, and not just a cruel and wasteful pastime for the leisured class, writing against a critique of hunting that was becoming more common at the time. At war with France, England, Holland, and all of Islam, and having finished campaigns in Catalonia and Portugal, a solid preparation for war would seem ideal for early modern Spaniards, and to some extent, rational.

The Farmer to Barnyard Animal Mode of Interaction

Animals kept on the farm were considered altogether different from the wild animals that humans hunted in large respect because of their mode of interaction. Given this mode, the animals' cognitive abilities are generally portrayed as extremely limited. They did not need to be outsmarted in the hunt. There was no need to portray them as worthy adversaries, since they were already captive and for the most part obedient. Nor were they generally befriended (as were dogs and horses) given that they were a constant food source and/or provided other products, such as leather, lard, or wool. In tomes about animal husbandry, in contrast to fictions that gratuitously anthropomorphized animals as valiant "foes" of the forest, here, on the contrary, animals are automatized and implicitly anthropectomized, in such a way that they seem less intelligent, less sentient, and less emotional than they actually are. In some sense, the animals are animalized.

In the first work of this kind published in Spain, Gabriel Alonso de Herrera's *Agricultura general*, the author relies on authority and incorporates learning from Greek, Latin, and more recent Arabic sources from reconquered Granada. Herrera's stated purpose was to provide practical, effective advice for raising crops and animals, and indeed it was commissioned by Cardenal Cisneros (Gonzalo Ximénez de Cisneros), who paid for the printing and distribution of thousands of copies of Herrera's work, making it free and available to any farmer who wanted it, which Cisneros saw as a practical way to reverse the decline in agriculture that had been wrought through periods of war and the expulsion of Jews and Muslims following the capture of Granada (Baranda 96).[35] It should not be surprising that animals raised to be consumed as food are not generally considered sentient since this is pretty much the same thinking that permeates contemporary considerations that allow agribusinesses to flourish, in which cows, pigs, chickens, and other animals are kept out of sight of the vast majority of consumers, until they are cut up and packaged at the supermarket.[36] Another way that animals in this mode of interaction are generally conceived and described rhetorically, and with similar repercussions, is as a group, a mass as one and the same of every other member of their species, not as individuals. In fact, in no case does Herrera relate anecdotes about the exceptional qualities of individual members of the species. This stands in stark contrast to the writing of colonial natural historians (e.g., Oviedo's monkey who communicates to his conspecifics the need not to touch the arrow lodged in his head),[37] or hunting treatise authors (e.g., the bear who throws arrows back at the hunting party). Even when, in Herrera's work, there are individuals mentioned, they stand for the whole, not as exceptions, but as synecdoches, as will be explored.

Herrera treats goats, sheep, cows, bulls, and pigs. Most of his advice concerns how to raise them with the greatest benefit to the owner, maximizing profit, in order to become rich, in a budding capitalistic way: "What I will say about them, in brief, it is a kind of possession that makes the owner rich without costs, but not without labor or science" (Lo que brevemente dellas quiero decir, ser una manera de hacienda que hace rico á su dueño sin costa, mas no sin trabajo y esciencia; 265). The animals he describes seem bereft of thought, and Herrera writes mostly about their physical characteristics. He suggests ways of selecting types of animals based on certain characteristics in order to have the animal behave the way the farmer wants. For instance, he claims that bulls with a certain kind of tail will reflect certain traits that we might call psychological: "the thick tail is a sign of little strength, and also of little heart, lazy and stupid" (la cola gorda es señal de poca fuerza, y asimismo de poco corazón, flacos ó lerdos; 530). A seemingly unrelated physical characteristic, therefore – in this case, the girth of a tail – is correlated directly with a cognitive faculty. The positive and direct correlation laid out in the claim would seem to lower the value of any implied cognition that may be perceived in the pejorative descriptors of "lazy" (flaco), "stupid" (lerdo), or "cowardly" (poco corazón). In addition, it implicitly assumes that exemplars of a species are not unique since properties come in physical packages, shared by a multitude of conspecifics with the same defining physical trait and hence psychological characteristic.[38] This treatment of the animal amounts to making it a part of an unindividuated mass.

While Herrera's farm animals are considered for intellect, they seem outright stupid, as the bull example above suggests. For instance, pigs are portrayed implicitly as automata, machines whose sole activity is eating. Farmers should beware that pigs will, quite literally, bite the hand that feeds them and worse: "in trying to take the bread from the hand, eating the hand, and after it, the whole body" (aun por tomarle el pan de la mano comerle la mano, y tras ella todo el cuerpo; 499). Furthermore, they will eat, kill, and ingest their own offspring (499). He repeats this idea later, emphasizing that they will eat their own young out of hunger: "often the very same mothers will eat their own children out of hunger, thus it is good practice to feed young mothers very well, so that they do not eat their children out of hunger" (aun muchas veces las mismas madres de hambre comen sus propios hijos, por ende conviene que á las paridas les den muy bien de comer, porque con la hambre no coman sus hijos; 503). Also, the farmer must take special care to keep an eye on the little ones since the mother may squish her young by accident.[39] As might be expected, these assessments of pig intelligence contradict what cognitive ethologists have found in recent studies. Without going into great detail, a couple of points can easily dispel the notion that pigs are "stupid" and that they don't care about their young. In their recent review of pig cognition studies, Lori Marino and Christina M. Colvin found that pigs are capable of "complex object discrimination ... requiring a robust memory" and have the capacity for "long-term memory" (4). They rely on both colour vision and olfaction not only to locate food when foraging, but are able to follow one or the other sensory modality in order to find the source of the food. Like dolphins and sea lions, pigs have been shown to recognize human gestures and to use sound stimuli "to successfully process semantic and syntactic components of an artificial language," for instance, selecting correctly from among three objects, and responding appropriately with an action to a task such as "fetch the frisbee" (5). They are "highly social animals" (2), who "discriminate among conspecifics and show a preference for familiar individuals over strangers" and can distinguish their own offspring from others using olfaction and by recognizing vocalizations. "Thus, not unlike canids, pigs appear to have strong abilities to flexibly discriminate among conspecifics using various cues and under a variety of circumstances" (9). Whereas of course it is possible that a pig would eat his or her young (just as it is possible, although it is to be hoped, very infrequent, that a human would eat his or her young), natural selection would not have led to this level of sensory discrimination for pigs, if it generally led to their treating their own young like any old food source; rather, it most likely provides for the possibility of a more nurturing relationship.

For their part, female goats are alleged to be so stupid they will let the nightjar (choto cabras) suckle from their bosom, unable to distinguish between a bird and their own kids: "they come to the nannies at dusk at the time when they are going to breastfeed the kids, such that the nanny, *thinking* it a kid, consents to this" (ellos vienen sobretarde á las cabras al tiempo que han de mamar los cabritos, que la cabra *pensando* que es cabrito le consiente; 361, emphasis added). Although Herrera uses the verb "pensar" (to think) implying some conscious awareness, it sounds like goats are simply stupid in his estimation, like pigs. While the claim about the nursing bird is spurious[40] – cervids have a strong sense of olfaction and are known to use olfactory stimuli to verify that the young are indeed their own before allowing suckling – taking this at face value reveals an implicit anthropectomy of intentional agency; indeed, it does not allow for the possibility that the goat may not mind the additional suckling, or may enjoy it; instead, Herrera judges the animal's mind by anthropocentric standards related to maximizing her teat's utility for humans (i.e., preferring that milk to be consumed by humans, or that milk be consumed by goat kids who will become goat meat that can be sold, etc.).

In the various descriptions of what to look for in animals, and how to practise farming, Herrera places considerable emphasis on the taste of the meat, which supersedes discussion of animals' cognition. For instance, he provides specific instructions on when to castrate a baby goat in order to improve the quality of the meat: "Kids are to be castrated before one year of age, because the younger they are the better they tolerate it, and it will make for better meat" (Los cabritos de se han de castrar antes de año, porque mientra que mas tiernos son mejor lo sufren, y hárase mejor carne; 359). For their part, male pigs should be castrated, fattened up, and eaten before the age of three, and not after four because they are not "good" when old (501); the older animal tastes awful apparently, which he emphasizes with a litany of adjectives: "but the meat of such [animals] is bad, hard, disgusting, of bad flavour and smell" (mas la carne de los tales es mala, dura, butionda, de mal sabor y olor; 501). These animals are, for the most part, things to be used and enjoyed, objects that provide not only nourishment but also flavour. Such views are pervasive and can be found much later, in widely read sources like Covarrubias's early seventeenth-century dictionary, *Tesoro de la lengua*, when he compares the qualities of wild and farmed pigs, only by taste: "If the domestic pig is so tasty and of so many flavours, the wild boar is much more so, having been raised in the countryside and having leaner and healthier meat" (Si el puerco casero es tan sabroso y de tan diversos gustos, mucho más lo es el javalí, por ser criado en el monte y tener carne más enjuta y más sana; "jabalí," 1113), an idea that Covarrubias inserts into the classical tradition, citing a poem by Juvenal about the excellence of serving wild boar at banquets. Somewhat contradictorily, on occasion, Herrera suggests some positive anthropomorphizing emotions (despite these emotions, there is never respite from the implicit or explicit understanding of the animals as singularly unintelligent). For instance, the farmer must contend with the possibility that the sow will not leave her pen to eat because she "loves" (con amor) her young so much (504). The farmer should follow Herrera's suggestion and construct an extra way out of the pen for her. Here he is dealing with the practical problem of how to get the sow out of her pen to fatten her up, so understanding and controlling her motivations are key. The emotional bond comes into play for a practical reason. It is a porcine inclination against which the productive farmer must strive.

Regarding other emotions, there is the occasional mention of a bull being either "wild" (bravo) or "meek" (manso; 531). Herrera also recognizes that animals feel pain, as he suggests ways to diminish it for the goat (360). About his recommended method of using a burning-hot, sharp implement to remove the testicles in bull castration, with a rhetorical flourish, he notes that this one action causing one pain will achieve two goals (castration and cauterization): "it is very good that the tool with which they are cut be sharp like a knife and that it be burning, such that in one occurrence it cuts and burns in cautery, and with one brief pain two benefits will take effect" (es muy bien que la herramienta con que los cortan sea aguda como cuchillo, y vaya ardiendo, porque de un trance corte y queme como cauterio, y con un dolor breve obrará dos beneficios; 547). It is worth nothing that he qualifies the pain as "brief," and views this in a positive light, implicitly suggesting that it is preferable to a longer pain. While he gives no explicit reason for caring about the bull's suffering, it might be because he recognizes an analogue to human suffering. After all, this is a commonly held view for Catholics as is the regularized ascetic practice of not eating meat on certain religious days.[41] This may be a remnant of the Catholic proscription against taking pleasure in suffering, in the same way that the cleric in the *Cantigas* (chapter 1) averted his gaze from the bull-baiting and was then saved by the Virgin. Alternatively, it could be because of an unarticulated belief that animal suffering – understood today as the stress-induced release of cortisol – causes the flesh to toughen up, a belief shared by many gourmands today.[42] Furthermore, in a passage on inflicting unnecessary suffering in pigs, it is implicit that Herrera believes that they feel pain and that pain should be avoided. He has no qualms about the idea of fattening up an animal in order to slaughter it, but he criticizes making the pig suffer unnecessarily. In particular, Herrera frowns on the practice of "blinding," that is, gouging out the pig's eyes in the (misguided) belief that this will fatten them up more quickly. Herrera says this practice sometimes leads not to fattened pigs, but to dead ones: "those who blind their pigs by destroying their eyes are very much in error, thinking that they will fatten up more: they do this to those that they raise at home, *and in addition to being cruel*, most pigs who lose one eye will die, and many more if they lose both" (mucho yerran algunos que ciegan los puercos quebrándoles los ojos, pensando que engordan mas: esto hacen á los que ceban en casa, que *allende de ser crueldad*, los mas de los puercos mueren perdiendo un ojo, pues mucho mas si los pierden entrambos; 507, emphasis added). Herrera also recognizes that pigs have appetites and preferences, and suggests varying the diet of pigs, so that they will eat with greater pleasure, offering an alternative to blinding – a strategy that works, according to him – while making explicit the pigs' *feeling towards* their food: "and in order to fatten them up, change their feed sometimes so that they eat more willingly and will fatten up more" (y para bien engordar múdenles algunas veces los cebos, porque los coman de mejor gana, y engordarán mas; 507).

In sum, farm animals are treated by Herrera as pain-feeling creatures with extremely limited cognitive faculties who at times seem downright stupid and who must be helped along by humans who can exploit them for profit. For unstipulated reasons, he frowns on the unnecessary infliction of suffering on the animals. Yet when the animals' emotions are mentioned, it is eminently for practical reasons, like understanding the emotion in order to ensure that the farmer can fatten the animal up according to his plan to get rich and live well. The mode of interaction and habitational parameters are main factors that contribute to these implicitly anthropectomized assessments of cognition.

In *Secretos de la casa de campo*, Agustí – who had posited elsewhere highly complex thinking for certain hunted animals (see above) – is seldom concerned about understanding the cognition of farm animals, who are assessed explicitly for their utility to humans.[43] At times, like Herrera before him, Agustí seems to propagate stories that make animals in this group seem less intelligent. The pigs he describes seem foolish, as they will eat so much during the (farmer-driven) fattening process to the point at which they are so immobile that mice will build nests on their backs (348).[44] They lack in other cognitive capacities too: Some animals have no memory, even for the most important things. Thus, ducks "do not remember the place where they first laid [an egg]" (no se acuerdan del lugar donde han puesto la primera vez para colocar; 379). From the standpoint of our knowledge of ducks today, this is hard to fathom, since migrating animals, like ducks and geese, could more plausibly be assumed to have incredible memories, even without a robust understanding of the cognitive mechanisms of migration. Similarly, he claims that rabbits have "no memory" – a cognitive factor that would make having an individual identity somewhat impossible – and as a corollary, that they will even forget, surprisingly, where they have built their own nest: "the rabbit has no memory, it does not even remember its den" (el conejo no tiene memoria, ni se acuerda de su madriguera; 365). Memory is something that humans prize and rightly value for ourselves. We consider it an important aspect of intelligence, primarily human but with some animal exceptions. The thought or fear of losing one's memory entirely entails the devastating corollary that we lose our identity.[45] Thus, we are surprised and impressed by "Chaser," the Border collie trained by psychologist John Pilley to recognize over one thousand different nouns, as well as several verbs to act on those (see fig. 15).[46] Other animals can learn to have trained memories as well, such as the pigs mentioned earlier. Parrots have been

Figure 15 Chaser learns a new trick. Photo courtesy of Cass Sapir.

shown to recognize words that are spoken or written, and can even learn to distinguish correct from incorrect spellings; rodents, primates, and more recently pigs have all been studied in terms of learning and memory, which "are considered to require higher brain functions and are not merely the acquisition of a series of elicited responses" (Gieling et al. 151); pigs have also been demonstrated to be "self-aware" through the use of mirrors in experiments (Broom et al. 2009, qtd. in Gieling et al. 159).

With anthropocentric rationales in mind, however, and the taste of rabbit meat at stake, in particular, Agustí suggests that these creatures are capable of some learning in spite of himself, when he prescribes taking young rabbits who have been bred in captivity to a "fenced-in park" (dehesa; parque), where they will run as if wild and learn to avoid foxes; if not "they would be domesticated and become like dopey and stupid ... and would not be able to save themselves from the fox's cunning and they would be quickly devoured" (se domesticarían, y quedarían como adormecidos y pesados ... y no se podrían salvar de la astucia de la zorra, y sería luego devorados; 365). Reminding the reader of the anthropocentric utility of this park, he instructs the farmer to plant specific species that the rabbit will feed on; the rabbit will have the "freedom to run" (la libertad de correr), which in turn will improve the quality of the meat, which is the ultimate goal: "better meat, and less melancholic than from those of the pen" (la carne mejor, y menos melancolica que los del corral; 367).The key point in this exercise is that, in his estimation, the wild flesh tastes better, and in his attempts to explain how they can survive in this semi-natural environment, Agustí undoes his claim, at least implicitly, that rabbits are naturally stupid. Indeed their stupidity and inability to flee from the cunning fox is a by-product of their captivity in pens by humans.

In Agustí's account, while he does not explicitly endorse the idea that they are intelligent, he shows that hens are capable of learning. Well before B.F. Skinner developed his behavioural theories and practices that would come to be known as "operant conditioning," something akin to this was already practised according to Agustí's account. While he portrays chickens as irrational, they seem capable of learning. In fact, for Agustí, a hen can be taught not to break her own eggs. The farmer should use hard fake eggs for the lesson: "[for] the enraged hen who breaks her eggs ... you will form an egg out of plaster or out of mortar made from lime, and sand, you will put it in the nest, without leaving another one there; and after having pecked one or two of these eggs, it will be enough for her pacification and improvement" (La gallina arrabiada, que rompe sus huevos, conviene poner yeſſo con yemas de huevos, tanto que venga á endurecerſe, y ponerlo en el nido, ò ponedor, y esto le sirve de yeſca, y cebo; y formareis un huevo de yeſſo ò de mortero hecho de cal, y arena lo pondreis en el nido, ſin dejar alli otro; y con uno, ò dos huevos que avrà picado, ſerà harto para ſu recogimiento, y enmienda; 369).

Oxen provide a particularly interesting case of how determinative for the animal's conceptual mindedness is the conjunction of an animal's mode of interaction with its habitational parameters. Whereas bulls in the ring or running wild had some cognition in the accounts of hunting-tome authors – i.e., the bull should be feared, their emotions contained, they must be outsmarted lest they escape and cause injury, their rage is usually stipulated – the same species of animal, now under different conditions, is barely minded at all. Evolutionarily, oxen are close to horses, as both mammalian species belong to the same clade of large mammals known as ungulates. Yet their mind is imaged quite differently, despite the fact that the ox works for the farmer and in some respects is like horses and dogs; it is important that the ox's labour is of a different kind. The ox is seen through the mode of farming and husbandry rather than as hunted animal or hunting assistant, which explains why Agustí pays so little attention to cognition. First, Agustí explains how to castrate the bull, but he heeds no thought to the animal's pain, even though Herrera had reflected on animals' castration pain over a hundred years earlier. Then he describes how to examine its behaviour before making it the member of an ox team. But Agustí does so with little attention to how the animal's mind works; the problems, rather, are about behaviour, as if cognition and behaviour were completely independent in what amounts to implicit anthropectomy. Regarding behaviour, then, if the ox does something the farmer doesn't like, then he must be punished: "If he is lazy, if he is too fast, raging, quick in getting up, kicking or goring ... it is necessary to punish him for these defects before trying to tame him with the yoke" (Si es perezoso, si es demasiado pronto, furioso, ligero en levantarse, dar de piernas, o cornadas ... los quales defectos es necessario darle castigo primero antes de domarlo al yugo; 313).[47] Most telling about the way in which the ox's cognition is delimited by his status as a simple farm animal, that is, as an object of husbandry who inhabits the barnyard and provides labour, is the heartless advice that Agustí gives on what to do with the animal as he ages: "Once the herdsman knows that the ox who he has tamed to plow can no longer pull, you will fatten him up for some time without work, and then you will kill him and cure him whole, or in pieces, for your family's annual food" (Deſpues que el Vaquero conocera que el buey que habra domado en arar, y que ya no puede mas tirar, lo engordareys por algun tiempo ſin trabajar, y deſpues lo matareys y cecinareys entero, o a pedaços, para comida annual de vueſtra familia; 430). In the course of one single sentence, the nameless ox goes from tired to fattened, killed, and cured, whole or in pieces. There is no mention of feeling or remorse, nor any mention that the animal has served the farmer well over the course of his hard life; Agustí only considers the ox in terms of its antropocentric utility, and thus, when no longer providing labour, he turns to killing the animal and transforming *it* into food. Not only does the animal not receive any of the respect or admiration often given to a dog or horse after years of service, but no attention is paid to any cognitive process the ox might have, nor to any feelings the farmer may have for this work companion, despite the fact that an ox is a close relative of the horse, is able to respond to commands, and would learn a name if one were taught to the animal.

Likewise, another beast of burden, the donkey, is treated with anthropectomy as well. For Agustí, despite its being a "vile and despised animal" (animal vil y despreciado; 345), it is still "necessary" on the farm for the kinds of work it can do. Unlike the horse, who will be pampered with caresses, the donkey is praised merely for being an animal who can suffer hunger and beatings well. It would seem that the mode of interaction of farm animal, along with particular societal biases, strips the donkey of any regard – far from the horse. Some of the humour of Sancho's riding a donkey, as a squire to Don Quixote, arises from his position and his care for this farm animal with lowly status, an animal who, unlike the horse, was not typically used in battle or hunting. Beyond the mode of interaction, certain long-held societal biases lead to the donkey's overall poor treatment, and obliviousness to an appreciation of donkey cognition.[48]

Hunter to Assistant Mode of Interaction

In branches of cognitive science dealing with animals' minds – ethology and comparative psychology – until very recently, little was written about canines. For comparative psychologist Alexandra Horowitz, they were not seen as a species from which anything could be learned: "There is no *data* in dogs. That was the conventional wisdom among scientists" (Horowitz 4). For Horowitz, the reasons for this trend – which in the last several years has been reversed – include their ubiquity in human societies and proximity to humans for many thousands of years, in what is sometimes referred to as co-evolution. While the topic of Horowitz's research is dog cognition, a similar (but not quite as strong) case can be made for horses, which, like dogs, have been bred for characteristics that made them increasingly useful to humans in hunting and warring, as well as for other tasks. Similar to dogs, special horses have regularly been given names by their owners, memorialized in writing, and even buried in sacred locations.[49]

Ironically, it is this same closeness to humans that made dogs and horses the most widely written-about animals in earlier times. Many people had close relations with both dogs and horses. Hunters, farmers, shepherds, warriors, and proto-veterinarians all had a practical, vested anthropocentric interest in the successful training and manipulation of one or both of these animals, from whom they benefitted greatly. Their own success depended to some extent on knowing how the animals' minds worked, at least in a reliable folk psychological way.[50] In contrast, one does not need to know how a sheep's mind works in order to slaughter and eat it.[51] However, it is helpful to know as much as you can about a dog's mind if you plan on successfully training it to, say, receive your commands and herd the sheep that you expect to use for wool or meat.

As noted above, royalty and high nobility organized hunts of large game, relying on numerous dogs and horses, led by a dozen or more men who worked collaboratively to track and kill the selected game. In the fourteenth-century *Libro de Montería*, written for Alfonso XI, the anonymous medieval author often mentions the importance of selecting the best dogs for specific purposes, which mostly tracks the canines' sensorial strengths and cognitive abilities.

On the sheer size of the hunting party and the number of animals involved, Argote de Molina recounts an anecdote of the wild boar hunted by Charles V and his men, who "was so ferocious that it killed fifteen bloodhounds and injured seventeen" (fue tan feroz que mato quinze Sabueſſos, y hirio diez y ſiete; "Discurso," 6r), demonstrating that only counting the dead or injured, there were at least thirty-two hunting dogs working together. Argote de Molina proposes what he thinks should be the ideal number of royal hunting workers in his day, writing for Philip II. While he is revising down a larger party size, whereby, in Argote de Molina's opinion, too many people and animals were employed in the hunt, the magnitude is still huge:[52] "from here on, there should not be more than twenty-four squires on foot, sixty archers, twenty-four hunters on horseback, four accountant hunters, four mastiff boys" (que de aqui a delãte, nõ ſean mas de veynte y quatro Eſcuderos de a pie, ſeſſenta Balleſteros, veynte y quatro Monteros de a Cauallo, quatro Monteros dela ventura, quatro moços de Alanos; "Discurso" 2r).[53] As the mention of "mastiff boys" implies, there were young men dedicated to working with specific breeds of animals, each having a group of dogs in his care, thus having the opportunity to get to know each individual animal. Indeed, naming all the men in the current employ of Phillip II, Argote de Molina points out their respective roles in taking care of dogs, as well as the prestige of having this honourable occupation, in a chapter entirely devoted to this (2v).

There is ample evidence from these tomes that this collaborative work leads to the possibility for humans and animals to have deeper interspecies bonds, described in some cases as "love." For instance, Argote de Molina mentions the anecdote of Don Lorenzo Xuares de Figueroa, the master of the Order of Santiago, who had an alabaster statue of his dog Amadis created for his tomb, along with the tender inscription "beloved Amadis" (amad Amadis; fol. 5r). That humans had such deep feelings towards dogs, and considered the animals in some way noble or heroic (named in this case after the most famous fictional knight of chivalric romance, Amadis of Gaul), most likely reflects their belief that the dogs too were capable of "human" feelings, which is borne out explicitly in some texts on the topic.

While most of Herrera's *Agricultura general* is devoted to crops and harvesting, and the section on animals is mainly devoted to animals and by-products that the farmer will eat or sell, he has a relatively lengthy section on dogs. He begins by repeating what he has read in authorities about canines, mentioning that they "love their masters," are "faithful," that they are great "friends," and also useful to the farmer as great "enemies" of those who mean the farmer harm. For Herrera, class-based considerations mean that he eschews farmers having hunting dogs, and thus the advice offered in his book is very different from that of hunting manuals. Nonetheless, given the anthropocentric resilience of canines, Herrera thinks dogs are necessary on a farm and for shepherds, and his practical advice shows some of his implicit thinking on dog cognition. For instance, he repeatedly mentions that they respond to their name, highlighting a kind of cognitive ability that was entirely absent in his sections on pigs, goats, and oxen. Also, he recommends specifically that dogs should have short names, at most two syllables, for they respond better to this type of word as their name. Pups shouldn't be allowed to fight too roughly when they are little, because if they are hurt badly, it may make them cowardly, what today we might call a psychological scar (345); he considers them not entirely bereft of reason – which is much more than the seemingly irrational goats and pigs – which he adduces from the manner in which they will fight together, especially with a family member, against a fox: "although they are beasts without reason, they do not lack it entirely" (aunque son animalías sin razon, no carescen del todo della; 346).

While Herrera's was a book on agriculture that included chapters on animal husbandry, related genres included books devoted entirely to the care of dogs, horses, or both. One of the most widely read works of this type was *Del can y del caballo* (Valladolid, 1568),[54] in which Luis Pérez describes in two lengthy parts what he knows about the "dog" and the "horse," relying sometimes on observation and more frequently on classical authority. In a humanist vein, it is largely based on the authority of Greek and Roman writers, especially Pliny and Aristotle, which Pérez blends with some recent local anecdotal information.

In the section on dogs, Pérez describes the early conditions of the litter, and ascribes to the newborn puppies excellent sensory abilities of hearing and olfaction, as well as – in stark contrast to the treatment of "ferocious" animals – the very human emotion of "love": "puppies are born blind (...) and although blind, they love their mother so much that the recognize her by her voice, and by her smell, and they search for her teats by touch" (los Cachorros nascen ciegos ... [y] aunque ciegos, aman tanto la madre, que la reconocen en la boz, y en el olor, y a tiento le buscan las tetas; 72).[55] The recognition that their desire for the mother is "love" allows us to infer that he identifies human-like bonds between the offspring and the mother. Note that Pérez does not say that what the animals feel is *as if* or *like* the human emotion of love, but rather, he simply employs the verb "love." Is this use of love merely a reflection that the mother breastfeeds her young? In a society that placed significant emphasis on raising cattle – to produce food, leather, and bulls for running and fighting – it would have been widely known that cows also bore live young and nursed like dogs and humans; yet such anthropomorphizing on emotion is hard to find in the period when discussing cows and bulls.

Beyond this anthropomorphic capacity for love, Pérez also discusses other emotions and the intellect of dogs. He goes on to describe a fascinating theory, based (it seems) on his observations, of how dogs have a special kind of knowledge based on their olfaction, that is also human-like. At bottom of these cognitive abilities are superior sensory adaptations: Pérez and other early modern authors were correct in holding that canines had a sense of smell that far surpassed that of humans. Careful observers in early modern Spain noted, for instance, as did Aristotle, that dogs had a much greater capacity for smell than do members of our species, hence their utility for the hunt in those days, or as border-patrol agents for sniffing out drugs or explosives today.[56] But of course they did not know the empirical details as we now know them, and how a standard clinical neuroanatomical text divides mammals into macrosmatic and microsmatic, based on the level of development of the olfactory system (ten Donkelaar et al. 636–7), with humans and most primates among the microsmatic, and dogs and many other mammals among the macrosmatic.[57] For Pérez, this superior sensory ability led them to better reasoning of a sort, and a cognitive ability that surpassed even that of humans, who are not able to achieve what dogs can:

> And thus, the dog succeeds with this thinking that it does. With exhaustive and ordered meditation and well-concerted art, men would have great difficulty and not be able to do this to pull it off: dogs do this by their own nature (...) hating falsehood, they find the truth (...). And here are the dog's syllogisms, and how they make divisions to find the truth, and have certainty about where the hare or the deer goes. Philosophers do not spend many days dividing their propositions in dust by chance: and they write and explain each one with a plume or a stylus. And of three, since it is necessary that one of them be true, the other two, as lies, are discarded to the side, and they are killed, and in this way they define and conclude approving the force of truth in what they have left. Well, these are the syllogisms that the dog do, not taught except by nature.
>
> (Y assi con esta consideración que el Can haze, viene á acertar. Lo qual con mucha difficultad, los hombres con meditación prolixa de orden y arte bien concertada, no compondrian ni harian: lo qual los Canes de su propria naturaleza hazen [...] aborresciendo la falsedad, hallan la verdad [...] El aqui sus syllogismos del Can, y como hazen sus diuisiones, para hallar la verdad, y tener certidumbre por do va la liebre, ó el cieruo. Por auentura no gastan los Philosophos muchos dias, diuidiendo sus proposiciones en poluo: y escriuen y señalan con vna pluma ó vn puntero, cada vna: y de tres, como sea necessario que la vna sea verdadera, las dos proposiones como mentirosas las echan á parte, y las matan, y assi diffinen y concluyen allegar se á la fuerça de la verdad, en aquella que dexaron. Pues estos son los syllogismos que el Can haze, no enseñado sino por natura. [44–5])[58]

And yet, as the citation demonstrates, for Pérez, this reasoning – if we can call it that – is not learned but "by nature." Pérez states that the behaviour is unlearned, that is, instinctual in the sense of hereditary or vestigial. An independent question arises that is also unanswered, as to whether the term "by nature" carries with it any connotation that the reasoning is not *conscious*, that is, that the dog is not aware of what it is "thinking."

For Pérez, the canine sensory ability is related directly to an intellectual one that is, strikingly, described in gratuitously anthropomorphic terms. For this most extreme ability, the author employs the "as if" hypothetical that he had not used until now: "the dog finds the prints of the hare or of the deer until ... [he sees] some crossroads made up of paths and roads that go off in many ways: since he has not seen any other sign, and [the animal] does not appear on those roads ... the dog pauses: he tries and thinks quietly to himself, *as if* putting forth a syllogistic expression, by taking a whiff with sagacity" (el Can halla la pisada de la Liebre, ò del Ciervo, que hasta que ... algunas encruzijadas que haze de sendas y caminos, que van á muchas partes: como no aya visto mas señal, ni parezca por aquellos caminos ... se detiene en si: y trata y piensa entre si mismo, *assi como* echando una voz syllogistica con sagacidad de tomar el olor; 43, emphasis added).[59]

Unpacking the implicit understanding of canine cognition in this passage, although part of the claim is beyond that which can be determined empirically, significant scientific research today suggests that some of the observations tend towards accurate descriptions. For instance, Pérez distinguishes the superior olfactory abilities of dogs well before modern anatomical studies showed that dogs have about ten times the number of olfactory sensory receptors as compared to humans (Herz 22), in addition to important morphological differences, like the large snout and quadrupedal movement. These physiological distinctions in turn lead, we now know, to dogs' ability to detect odours at a small fraction of the substance concentration relative to humans.[60]

Pérez bases some of his assertions not on Aristotelian theory or authority, as would most philosophers in his day, but on his own reflections and on the empirical observation of animals' behaviour. In doing so, he imbues the animals with a kind of reasoning that seems, indeed, strikingly human. First, the animal seems to reflect on the information he has gathered from olfaction, in what is a resemblance to Darwin's anecdotal cognitivist observation about pausing and thinking. Second, Pérez refers to the syllogism, the most famous term from Aristotle's logic in his theory of inferences, which is based on two premises and which generates further knowledge from the premises. Indeed, the syllogism is the construction par excellence, which Luis Vives had referred to unmistakably in the chapter entitled "Reason" in *De anima et vita* as a human-only modality, in his claim that "animals do not begin with A to move to B in order to learn C." Without referring to any philosophers in particular, Pérez also singles out the philosophical context against which he is writing: "Dogs, without doctrine from anyone except their natural instinct, form and make syllogisms which all of the philosophers of Athens could not undo" (Canes, que sin doctrina de alguno, sino su instincto natural pueden formar y hazer syllogismos que todos los Philosóphos que fueron de Athenas, no puedan deshazerlos, ni entenderlos, ni quantos agora sean; 43). While Pérez does not name him specifically, there may be an allusion here to Chrysippus (c. 279–206 BCE), the Greek philosopher who is rumoured to have explained that his dog could think with syllogisms. As fanciful as this may sound to some readers, and despite the fact that Chrysippus and Pérez came to this view on canine logic through anecdotal cognitivism rather than the scientific method, current research may prove them right! Indeed, based on a 2007 study on dogs by Agnes Erdohegyi et al., philosopher of animal cognition Kristin Andrews concludes that "[i]t turns out that dogs might be able to act in the way Chrysippus described," that is:

> Exclusion reasoning [which] requires reasoning in terms of the disjunctive syllogism:
>
> 1 A or B
> 2 Not A.
> 3 Therefore, B. (Andrews 108)

In Pérez's text, the adverbial construction, "with sagacity," points to the dog's highly discriminatory sense of smell and intelligence, which is tied directly to the syllogistic: while *sagaz* and *sagacidad* can still be used today to refer to a highly developed sense of smell, the term can also point to an attribution of something like "wisdom." According to Covarrubias's *Tesoro de la lengua castellana o española* (1611), "sagaz" in fact bridges the gap between the literal sense of smell and an ability to discern, referring specifically both to a dog with a great sense of smell, and metaphorically, "Refers to the astute and prudent man" (Tomase por el hombre astuto y prudente; 1421).[61] While for Covarrubias this meaning of the word seems metaphorical, cognitive theories of embodiment take such metaphors as more meaningful than merely symbolic, as indicating the way in which humans, or other animals possibly, think about the world given the bodies they consist of. Cognitive linguist Iraide Ibarretxe-Antuñano analyses such a use of smell as an embodied metaphor, based on her comparison of English, Spanish, and Basque,[62] and identifies the same idea that Covarrubias identifies as one of the embodied olfactory metaphors, that is, to sniff out. The olfactory superiority of canines as highlighted in these texts imbues these animals with a certain grandeur that is linked to their cognition, in which there is a clear relationship between the working of their senses and the working of their minds.

Other writers in the early modern period were less reliant than Luis Pérez on authority and observed carefully the behaviour of certain non-human animals, and yet still came to a similar conclusion that they could infer quite unproblematically that the animals were engaging in some forms of advanced thinking. Works based largely on careful observation for a practical purpose are dedicated to explaining how to breed, raise, care for, and train certain species of animals. There is an increasing empiricism indicative of a modern scientific tendency in such writings. Other early modern hunting and husbandry authors thought about animals' minds in order to explain complex behaviours and also linked their sensory apparatus to their thinking.

For instance, a century later, Martínez de Espinar notes that his observations on canine sensorium and cognition specifically made him question what he had learned from natural philosophical sources "and conjoin it with experience" (juntarla con la experiencia; 9).[63] He insists, then, on trusting his experience and his senses rather than received information, a trend that was increasingly common in sixteenth- and seventeenth-century Spain.[64] Despite the increased reliance on observation, Espinar comes to similar conclusions about the senses, emotions, and intellect of dogs. As noted, it is typical of these treatises to privilege dogs' sense of smell in particular. Indeed, he dedicates an entire chapter to dog olfaction, quite hyperbolically described, and relies on the "impossibility" that humans could compete, an idea also mentioned by Pérez (above): "Among animals, the one with the best sense of smell is the dog; this, along with his knowledge, allows him to do things that seem impossible and that do not fit in a beast" (Entre los animales, el de mayor olfato es el perro; esto, junto con su conocimiento, le hace hacer cosas que nos parecen imposibles y que no caben en un bruto; 67).[65]

All non-human animals, for Martínez de Espinar, are – by logical necessity, rather than by experience – beasts or brutes lacking reason. Somewhat paradoxically, they are able to perform tasks that "seem impossible" in a reasonless being. This notion, to "seem impossible," thus points to a kind of paradoxical thinking about dogs, a tension also noticed earlier in Martínez de Espinar's discussion of deer. On the one hand, they are devoid of reasoning; on the other hand, they behave as if they have reason. This imposition seems like his own self-measuring against the possibility that he is engaging in gratuitous anthropomorphism. That is, the observer is tempted to ascribe reason to the dog and the deer, since the animal behaves in a manner consonant with human behaviour in a similar context, and thus, the (natural) anthropomorphic tendency alluded to in my introduction, a kind of magical thinking, leads him to ascribe advanced reasoning skills, and more particularly, what today we call Theory of Mind, which includes a well-founded belief that other humans have reason. Other descriptors in his first paragraph point to additional human-like characteristics, at least on the surface: they "learn what we teach them"; they are "obedient" and "diligent"; they have "knowledge" (*conocimiento*), through their olfaction;[66] and ultimately, they can be "very astute."

Martínez de Espinar links reason with seeing, while paradoxically attributing to dogs a kind of reason linked to smell, similar to Luis Pérez's evocation of the olfactory syllogism. While they do not possess the human faculty of speech, good hunting dogs communicate information to their masters in subtle ways; indeed, some even "dissimulate." Dissimulation, *a fortiori*, requires knowledge of what others are likely to be thinking, and thus some form of Theory of Mind. Regarding how some dogs will subtly signal where the prey is with their muzzle, "some do this *with so much dissimulation* that if the hunter does not understand it, only by a miracle will he find the prey" (algunos lo hacen tan *disimuladamente*, que si el cazador no los entiende, por maravilla verá la caza; 229, emphasis added). However, the very best hunting dogs "speak" more clearly: "There are others who circle and stop against the wind, pointing it out: these are the best, that clearly *tell* the hunter where it is" (Otros hay que rodean y se paran con el viento, señalándola; estós son los mejores, que fijamente *dicen* al cazador dónde la tienen; 229, emphasis added).[67] That this kind of hunting on the part of the dog involves knowledge is implicit in how Martínez de Espinar speaks about dogs who do this poorly, dogs who suffer from a lack of knowledge: "There are others who do an about turn and stop against the wind: most of the time, these ones don't know what they are doing" (Otros hay que dan media vuelta y se paran con el viento; éstos las más veces no saben lo que hacen; 442).

From the above, it is clear that Martínez de Espinar distinguishes differences among conspecifics, and he makes this point explicitly. Indeed, dogs are like humans because within both species, not every one is identical; rather, he argues, there are individual differences among members of both species: "Thus it is evident that neither men nor animals are all of one constitution" (pues es evidente que los hombres ni animales no son todos de una misma complexión; 68). (The implication, once again, is that most other animals, like sheep, are one and the same.) The dog also has its own "will" (*voluntad*) or in contemporary terms, intentional agency, but according to Martínez de Espinar, the dog's obedience can be made to overcome it, that is, the dog can learn. They are "brutes" with free will who can learn, and the learning seems to help them overcome their brutishness! After describing the tenacity with which a dog will stick to the scent it was taught to track, he muses on the nature-nurture question: "Good instruction can do so much that it overcomes nature even in those without reason" (Tanto puede la buena enseñanza, que vence el natural aun en los irracionales; 68).

Comparing dogs' vision with their olfaction, Martínez de Espinar writes that "their knowledge based on olfaction is so true that they can separate the animals [heads of sheep] knowing the one that they are following, even if she gets into a group of a thousand; this they do not achieve with sight, since, *as reasonless,* they lack this knowledge, and avail themselves of nothing other than their olfaction" ([e]s tan verdadero su conocimiento en el olfato, que apartan las reses, conociendo la que siguen, aunque se meta entre mil de ellas; esto no lo consiguen con la vista, que, *como irracionales,* les falta ese conocimiento, y no se valen de otra cosa que del olfato; 67, emphasis added). It is here that he provides a different understanding, one relying implicitly on Scholasticism (despite his contention that what he purports is based on experience): "como irracionales," he calls them. He also distinguishes them more explicitly from humans, who are "capable of understanding": "God reserved knowledge of things for man alone, and for this reason he made him capable of understanding" (el conocimiento de las cosas le reservó Dios sólo para el hombre, y para eso le hizo capaz de entendimiento; 68).

There is a tension in Martínez de Espinar between his explicit claims and his implicit assumptions: The excellent sense of olfaction, when described in detail, is indeed very similar to excellent sight, because it allows for the discrimination of one thing from another similar one: "the hound has no difficulty in knowing and dividing one animal from another by smell, just as, by sight, a man would know and divide a white thing from among other black things" (el sabueso no halla dificultad en conocer y apartar una res de otra por el olfato, como con la vista conociera, y apartara un hombre una cosa blanca entre otras negras; 68). Thus, olfaction works in dogs as does sight in humans. Yet a bias from Aristotelianism that taught that sight was the "most noble of the senses" seems simultaenously to operate in his thinking.

Horses

In many respects like hunting dogs and lapdogs, horses were prized animals that were often highly trained and interacted with humans in a variety of collective activities, including warfare and hunting parties. They are so implicated in European concepts of nobility that the words for "knight" in Catalan, Dutch, French, German, Italian, Portuguese, and Spanish all derive from the word for "horse." Like dogs, horses were often given names, and depicted in the paintings of the most illustrious rulers and patrons (see fig. 16). Once again, the mode of interaction seems determinative of the kinds of ways that writers on topics of hunting and husbandry anthropomorphize horses. Luis Pérez makes the task of demonstrating a link between the way in which humans considered dogs and horses quite effortless, since his tome is decidedly on both dogs and horses: *Del can y del caballo*. While he states that he writes on dogs first and foremost because they are even better animals, he does not shy away from extolling the virtues – based largely on cognitive capacity – of *Equus ferus caballus*.

Pérez constructively anthropomorphizes the emotions of horses and their understanding, often drawing on martial interactions between the horse and the enemy; their whinny is an indication of "happiness" (alegría; 120); they charge at armed men "daringly" (con osadia) and with a "boiling heart" (coraçon heruiendo; 120); the horse understands the symbolic sounds of organized warfare, and their sensory modalities are attuned to their emotions: when the horse hears the trumpet sound, he becomes happy beyond measure, and "smells war" from afar (120); the horse also understands the noises and clamour of battle (120).

While Pérez seems to draw on some experiential information, much of what he says is to reinforce the notion that horses are important and great through references to textual sources (appealing to authority), including the Book of Kings, the legend of Bragante, the legend of Santiago, the Apocalypse according to Saint John, and the legend of the Cid. Often he simply lists that horses were participants in important battles, but occasionally he refers to some of their cognitive aspects: "the horse [Babieca] rode so purposefully and sensibly that he demonstrated well the courage of the person of his lord [El Cid]" (el Cauallo [Babieca] yua con tanto sentido y tan sesudo, que mostraua bien el valor de la persona de su Señor [El Cid]; 130). He also cites Pliny on a horse's loyalty and

Figure 16 Diego Rodríguez Velázquez's *Don Gaspar de Guzmán, Duke of Olivares.* Photo credit: Erich Lessing / Art Resource, NY.

love (132) and obedience (147), and on the ability of horses to "learn everything that they are taught" [toman todo lo que les enseñan (137)]; their affection and love for their masters is so great, Pérez claims, citing Suetonious, that their emotional state will change with their master's affect, even to the extent of crying (140–1). While emotional and caring, he stipulates that they are "deficient of reason" (no capaces de razon; 169). He gives advice on how old male and female horses should be when they mate, how to arouse the male horse with the scent of the female (160), and how to arouse her to mate by applying an onion to her "natural parts" (160); although he cites no authority on this, the idea is repeated through this type of literature, and links a sensorial experience (olfaction, touch) with the desire to mate. He also praises horses on the belief that a male horse and his mother will never mate, anthropocentrically applying a human cultural prohibition against incest to this species, contradicting Aristotle on the matter while siding with Marcus Terentius Varro (167). In training a horse, the trainer should be kind, and brush the horse gently, singing and whistling to him, and saying sweet and loving words (180–1), some of which seems to imitate the natural behaviour of wild horses to rub each other's necks as described by the ethologist Michel-Antoine LeBlanc (380–3).

Similarly, in the *Libro de los secretos de agricultura*, Agustí emphasizes the importance of the emotional well-being of horses, who are strong yet delicate creatures. The servant who cares for horses of breeding as well as workhorses must have nurturing characteristics: "he should feel love for the animals in his charge and not abuse them, rather he should teach them and instruct them with love in hand gestures, the movement of the rod, voice or call, and he should not make them work more than they are able, and he should groom them cheerfully every morning" (que tenga amor à los animales que tiene encomendados, y que no les maltrate, antes les deve enseñar, y adestrarlos con amor en el ademàn de la mano, meneo de la varilla, voz, ò grito, y que no se les haga trabajar mas de lo que pueden, y que los almoaze alegramente cada mañana; V., 327).

The importance not just of treating them well, but of showing them "love" – a detail that is emphasized through repetition of this word in the passage above – is interesting, for it suggests that these horses are like human family members, and is reminiscent of, while going beyond, Pérez's talk of love among and for dogs. Also, this interspecies variety of love is not the only kind that Agustí mentions for horses. These animals have significant emotional depth, as he mentions that they feel "love" for each other too: "you must be very aware of the love that one horse has for another, and according to that, place them in a nearby stable" (aveis de estar muy advertidos del amor que un cavallo lleva al otro, y segun aquello ponerlos en el establo cercano; 328). Similarly, a mare feels love for her young: "you shall let him graze with his mother, so that she is not worried about the foal's absence, because females frequently suffer from love sickness and desire to see their foal" (lo dexareis ir al pasto con su madre, porque ella no tenga cariño con la ausencia del pollino, que comunmente las hembras enferman de amor, y deseo de vèr su pollino; 329).

Unlike the ox who was to be castrated and then punished into obedience at the yoke, the horse is pampered as if he were a baby or child, and then treated almost like a young person who is shown the world and is expected to learn. The trainer begins by sensorially "caressing" the horse, not only with his hands, but also "with his voice" and while "acting lovingly" (acariciar con la voz ... con otros actos amorosos; 334). Gradually, in a fascinating take on the admonition to "ver mundo," the horse is supposed to be shown the world, including which aspects of nature are controlled by man as well as certain technological advances, as Agustí emphasizes the phenomenology of sensorial equid experience: "one should lead him *to see* coaches, carriages, carts, and a large number of pigs, horses, cattle, and goats, and make him pass by the dead lambs and other comestible animals, *observing* every day, all that has been said, until he becomes skilled in walking and riding, well assured at having *seen and heard* all of the aforementioned things" (se deve conducir à *ver* coches, carros, carretas, y grande numero de puercos, hacas, ganados, y cabras, y hazerle passar donde estàn los corderitos muertos, y otros animales de comer,[68] *observando* cada dia, todo que se ha dicho, hasta que esté diestro en el caminar, y andar, bien assegurado en el *ver, y oir* todas las dichas cosas; 335, emphasis added). Horses, indeed, for Agustí, clearly have their own intentions and agency, but in a good horse these can be made to align anthropocentrically with those of people: "he should conform to man's will" (se deve conformar à la voluntad del hombre; 332). Significantly, unlike Agustí's ox, there is no talk here of killing the horse and salting his flesh at the end of his life, although the flesh would be highly nutritious. Analysing the mode of interaction between the human and the animal, and the concomitant understanding of animal sentience through individuated contact, helps explain the author's and his society's bias towards permissible ox-eating on the one hand, and the tendency to view horse as something not highly edible, on the other, similar to the case of the dog.[69]

Agustí also expounds on other issues without significant empirical justification, but which are interesting as they show just how human-like some thinkers considered the minds of select non-human animals to be. However, this kind of anthropomorphism must be distinguished from the gratuitous type: For Agustí, the horses are not like humans simply because he is *projecting* humanity onto the animals (for instance, by having them speak or making them appear to feel in ways for which there is no evidence that they do), but rather, inferring, from actual horse behaviour, the emotional and intellectual processes that are going on.[70]

Beyond the emotions she feels towards her young, the mental processes of the mare's mind (as well as the minds of other non-human animals) are apparently similar to those believed to be in play for humans (however misguided these views were). Thus, just as it was commonly propagated in early modern medical discourse, that among humans, the thoughts of the mother during conception, and specifically information from her visual field, would bear directly on the qualities of the offspring that is conceived, this same kind of belief is held for horses, dogs, and unspecified "other animals":[71] "the colours that the horse looks at while conceiving will be those of the colt: you can experience the same with dogs and other animals" (los colores que miraràel cavallo al concebir tendrà el pollino: esso mismo podreis experimentar con los perros, y otros animales; 330). Thus, sensory perception, eyesight, is not only a part of cognition but of reproduction.[72]

For Martínez de Espinar, the Spanish horse is even superior to the dog, and is "the most noble among all animals" (nobilísimo entre todos los animales; 54). He explicitly compares the horse with other animals that work for humans, including the ox, the dog, the elephant, and the sheep, but "none are are equal to him" (no le igualan en el modo; 54).

In his lengthy description, Martínez de Espinar highlights certain positive cognitive features, contextually appropriate horse emotions such as anger, meekness, bravery, and faithfulness:

> courage towards enemies, meekness and of excellent reins for those who guide him (...) and if the situation arises, not only does he not fear the enemies nor the sound of the troops, but rather these embolden him and bring him joy, whinnying with gusto until he attacks the opposite squadron (...) finally they are so warlike that, tied up in their stables, in hearing the instruments of war, they become enraged and show themselves to be ferocious.
>
> (bravos para los enemigos, mansísimos y de linda rienda para quien los maneja [...] y llegada la ocasión, no sólo no teme a los enemigos ni el sonido de las tropas, sino que esto le embravece y alegra, relinchando con gran brío hasta cometer al escuadrón contrario; [...] finalmente son

tan belicosos, que atados en sus pesebres, en oyendo los instrumentos de guerra, se embravecen y muestran feroces. [54)

Finally, helping to make my point about how the mode of interaction leads to greater familiarity between animal and human, Martínez de Espinar alludes to the experience he has gained through his own direct contact with horses in remarking on "the fondness that I have for the horse (...) having crossed the countryside on him [the horse] for so many years" (la afición que le tengo [...] el haber seguido el campo en él tantos años; 55).

Conclusion

Whether animals were believed to be endowed with reason or not, the period treatises that deal with animal husbandry and hunting show that the sensorium played a large part in the lives of wild animals and the ones with whom people shared their lives (dogs, horses). In dogs (as well as in most wild animals), the dominant sense was smell, a sense that is directly related to their intelligence: It was the organizing sense of their lives, imbuing them with special powers and abilities well beyond those of humans, abilities which seem impossible not only "in a brute," but similarly impossible for a human to accomplish with a human's lesser sense of smell. Concomitantly, these treatise writers are in agreement that canine vision was weak, and as such, the hierarchical sensory powers of humans and dogs were inverted. For horses, the important senses were more broadly conceived, as smell, sound, and sight combined were all important. Like that of dogs, horse psychology was something to be understood and, like the horse itself, harnessed in order to maximally seek utility from the species for human benefit.

Through such intimate living and working conditions (including collaboration in massive hunts, with hounds and horses, against a solitary foe), between people and horses and dogs, feelings of empathy, sympathy, and even those of "love" could develop, feelings that were absent in the treatises vis-à-vis other animals that maintained a different mode of interaction with humans, that of farmed animal or hunted animal.

While philosophers used comparisons with animals to disclose what is unique about the human mind or soul, and fable authors deployed animals to moralize and entertain people, early modern animal husbandry and hunting treatise writers often engaged in anecdotal cognitivism and relied on folk animal psychology – based on observations and experience – with the practical intention of exploiting animals, in which providing an adequate explanation of how to treat domesticated animals so that they would hunt well, breed well, and work well on the farm was key. Regarding wild animals, these writers explained how best to track them using trained dogs, with what they knew about animal behaviour and thinking in order to trick the prey into capture or death. For certain animals, when human cognitive biases, speciesism, and/or anthropocentric utility did not favour such attention, animals were considered merely as flesh, labour, or a combination of these.[73] But a part of this attempt at control over other non-human animals involved various types of constructive anthropomorphizing and empathic intuitions about the animals' feelings and thoughts, recognizing their particular sensorial strengths and weaknesses while engaging in animal perspective-taking, ways of engaging animal minds that would one day lead to a more robust defence of animal rights.

There is little reason today to think that cows, deer, sheep, etc., are far less sentient than dogs or horses; the reasons why some animals were (and continue to be) regarded as less sentient are largely relational and due to anthropocentric interests, which guide human anthropomorphism and anthropectomy. The model of animal mind that individuals and societies generate relates to the evocation of empathy, or its lack, and therefore to the treatment of specific animal exemplars and often to their species more broadly. The elucidation of mind is therefore central to animal studies and the animal rights movement. It is helpful to think, with Charles Darwin, that species change occurs gradually and incrementally, views that posit that humans and many non-human animals are similar in many respects, specifically resisting post-structuralist tendencies such as those extolled by some pro-animal rights authors (including Few and Tortorici's introduction to *Centering Animals*) to suggest that animals are *entirely* different, proposing that it is an imposition on the concept of animal to "impose" agency, and question their intentionality. Indeed, agency is important for animal studies. Currently, there is a wide array of views on animal cognition, but this Darwinian tendency to see the connection to human mental states is still strong, and bolstered by notions of evolutionary continuity.

With the parameters of possibility for what thinkers thought explicitly and implicitly about the varieties of Iberian animals from the Middle Ages and through the seventeenth century, the next chapter turns to analysing the minding of animals under the aspect of novelty with the American encounter.

Chapter Three

Describing the Animal in New World Habitats

They are such friends of these little dogs that they will take of their own food and give it to them, and when they travel they carry them along on their backs or upon their breasts. And if they are ill, the little dog must be there with them for no other reason than their good friendship and company.

(Y son tan amigos destos perrillos que se quitarán el comer, por dárselo, y cuando van camino los llevan consigo a cuestas o en el seno. Y si están malos, el perrito ha de estar allí con ellos sin servirse dellos para cosa sino sólo para buena amistad y compañía.)

– José de Acosta, *Historia natural y moral de las Indias*[1]

In Part I, Chapter 50, Don Quixote evokes a mysterious scene in which he enumerates two series of animals, first aquatic and then avian. These animals can be distinguished by their radically different habitational parameters. There are those who live below us, in water or on its surface, and those who live above us, in the sky or treetops.[2] Each group of animals is meant to evoke wonder in the human perceiver of this aspect of nature. Don Quixote's "fish" below and the "birds" above, juxtaposed in this way,[3] bring to the fore conceptions about animal minds that were frequently tied to their habitats in the early modern period.

The birds above are beautiful "painted" creatures that adorn the trees and the skies, pleasing to human ears that they "entertain":[4] "[H]is ears are charmed by the sweet, untutored song of the infinite number of small, brightly coloured birds that fly among the intricate branches" (429) ([E]ntretiene los oídos el dulce y no aprendido[5] canto de los pequeños, infinitos y pintados pajarillos que por los intricados ramos van cruzando; DQ 1.50:584). A single reference to something potentially cognitive in the birds is their ability to sing. But the text clarifies that it is an inherited trait, and that it is, specifically, "unlearned" (*no aprendido*). The implication is that bird singing requires little or no thought, and is contrasted implicitly with the song of the human singer, who only through diligent study and practice learns how to sing. This conceptualization of birdsong invokes the Aristotelian view par excellence, that animal sounds are voiced yet non-discursive.[6] And while research has demonstrated that several bird species learn elements of language, bird calls in certain other species, such as in owls, are entirely inherited and require no learning.

Regarding "fish," the narrator posits even less cognition than for the birds. A few of the creatures move around on the surface of the water ferociously, evoking fear in the human who watches them ("animales feroces y espantables") while others are below and remain unseen: "is there any greater joy than seeing, before our very eyes, you might say, a great lake of boiling pitch, and in it, swimming and writhing about, there are many snakes, serpents, lizards, and many other kinds of fierce and fearsome creatures" (428) (se muestra delante de nosotros un gran lago de pez hirviendo a borbollones, y que andan nadando y cruzando por él muchas serpientes, culebras y lagartos, y otros muchos géneros de animales feroces y espantables; 584). The fish are treated merely in terms of their effect on humanity.

Cervantes's lists of fish and birds pertain to what I call "animal catalogues," sections of natural histories and similar works that separate animals by the habitat in which they live. Typically, authors of these catalogues discuss the animals' abilities and traits as well as their effects on, and utility for, human beings. The most famous classical example of this genre is Pliny's *Natural History*.[7] Pliny divides animals by habitat into those of the land, the water, and the sky, displaying the erudition and knowledge that he amassed through book-learning and first-hand experience as fleet admiral.

In the Middle Ages, the *Physiologus* and bestiary traditions transformed the Plinian catalogue into symbolic and decorative volumes that related animals anthropocentrically to Christian virtues and sins.[8] Early modern European animal catalogues, in contrast, often followed more closely in the line of the earlier tradition's writers. The best known work of this type, by Swiss naturalist Conrad Gessner, was published in five volumes. His encyclopedic *Historia animalium* (1551–8) followed Pliny's structure of dividing animals by the habitat in which they lived.

Following a "philological" approach similar to Pliny's, Gessner includes a wide range of information on the animals: descriptions, anecdotes, and classical vignettes (taken from Pliny as well as from other sources). Despite his training as a naturalist, most of the information he provides stems not from first-hand direct observation or study but from learned sources in the tradition of Renaissance humanism. Frank Egerton points out that the most innovative element of the *Historia animalium* is not the text itself but the many detailed illustrations of animals,[9] the most renowned of which – e.g., the rhinoceros – were created by one of Europe's greatest artists, Albrecht Dürer (see fig. 17). Indeed, Gessner published the first printed encyclopedic work containing a large number of high-quality images, which in many cases were drawn *ad vivum*.[10]

For reasons that will become apparent, Gessner's book deals problematically with animals from what the Europeans considered the New World even though it was published some six decades after Columbus's first voyage to the Indies. As historians Miguel de Asúa and Roger French propose, Gessner's method of commentary, like that of others in the humanist tradition, relied on philological information from classical as well as Renaissance sources. However, because of the newness of the American encounter – by definition, a newness that signals the absence of a long tradition – the New World animals could not be treated as main entries, but instead were relegated to appendices where the pictures stand out as the most interesting thing about them.[11] For instance, as Laurent Pinon explains, when Gessner discusses the armadillo and the guinea pig, "[t]he short chapters devoted to these two animals contain images and precise descriptions, but no ancient references, no discussion about their names, no philological section" (Pinon 256) (see fig. 18).[12]

In Spain, nonetheless, decades before Gessner's *magnum opus*, in the wake of the newly encountered "Indies" or Americas, a host of new animals, with which Europeans had only recently come into contact, were catalogued, described discursively, and illustrated.[13] Alongside these exotic animals, Spanish and *criollo* historians also detailed the successes and failures of exporting European animals, such as cows and pigs, to the colonies, animals that Gessner would mostly ignore. In the late fifteenth and early sixteenth centuries, many animals were being described for Europeans for the first time, often in first-hand official accounts meant for the consumption of the Spanish monarchs and other interested parties. Asúa and French have analysed exhaustively the extensive production of writings on animals in this period,

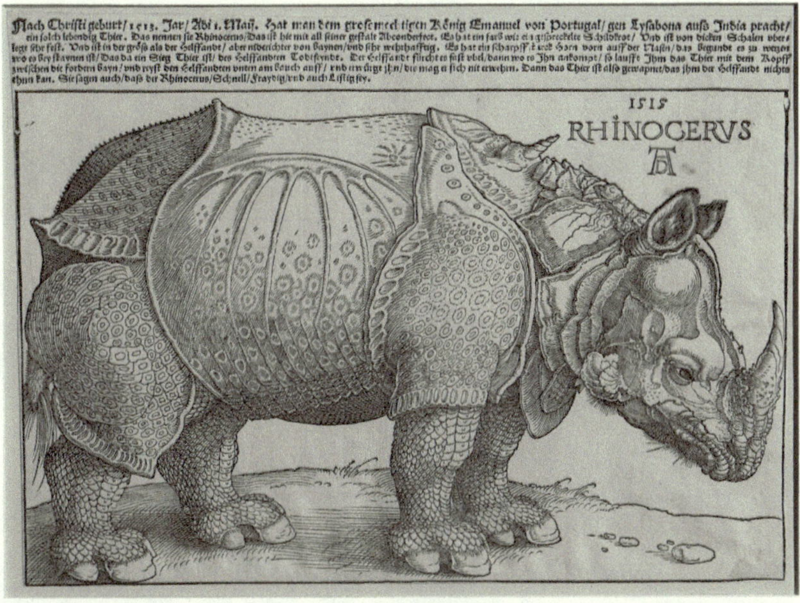

Figure 17 Albrecht Dürer's *Rhinoceros*. Photo credit: Erich Lessing / Art Resource, NY.

focusing especially on how Europeans explained and assimilated the newness of American animals (xiii–xv). In their letters as well as in natural and human histories, late fifteenth- and sixteenth-century writers wrote often of practical matters and about knowledge that they thought would help to sustain and expand the Spanish Empire. In these cases, the treatment of animals' minds often comes up in short asides where the mind can be gleaned mostly indirectly. These are the explicit and implicit aspects of animal cognition in natural historical writing on the Indies that interest me in chapter 3. I focus mostly on Gonzalo Fernández de Oviedo as the foremost and most in-depth author of this type of natural historical writing. I examine how animals were catalogued in his schema, and what ramifications these classifications, based on habitat, had for the conceptualization of animal cognition over the course of the sixteenth century and into the seventeenth. Oviedo (1478–1557), of aristocratic birth and education, Christian but with a somewhat secular orientation, served in a series of administrative positions for the Crown

Figure 18 Armadillo illustration in Conrad Gessner's *Historia animalium, Liber II*. Courtesy of the National Library of Medicine.

in Italy and Spain until his appointment as chief historiographer of the Indies. He embarked on several voyages starting in 1514, writing the lengthy *Historia natural*, which was mostly unpublished during his lifetime, publishing the brief *Sumario* (1526) along the way. I will also draw on other colonial sources including natural histories by Tomás López Medel (1520–82) and José de Acosta (c.1540–1600) as well as the *Historia de las Indias* by Bartolomé de las Casas (1484–1566).[14] Although primarily concerned with humans, the *Historia* of the "Defender of the Indians" also contains anecdotes and vignettes about non-human animals. In addition, I include material from texts that are primarily about Spain, when these mention American animals that were brought to Europe as well as when they discuss some European animals that were introduced in America. How did these Spanish and *criollo* authors conceptualize the minds of animals they had never before encountered? How do habitational parameter and mode of interaction contribute to human conceptualizations of these animals? What role did indigenous folkloric or mythological accounts play in the minding of these animals? I end the chapter with a short reflection on the minding of animals in the work of Bernardino de Sahagún (1499–1590). Sahagún was a Franciscan missionary who immersed himself in Nahua culture and language for the purposes of Christian proselytization during some sixty years. He documented and preserved elements and points of view of this culture in his manuscript, *The General History of the Things of New Spain* (*Historia general de las cosas de la Nueva España*),[15] which was created with the help of numerous indigenous informants. Despite the incredible differences between the European Christian world view assumed by Oviedo and others on the one hand, and the Nahua cosmology at the heart of Sahagún's on the other, universal human cognitive embodiment overrides these differences and explains the fundamental similarities in the minding of animals based on habitat and mode of interaction.

To investigate these and other questions concerning animal cognition, I arrange the sections below by differences in *habitational parameters*, along the lines of the divisions that some of the authors themselves followed in their catalogues (by realm or habitat), while also taking into account the *mode of interaction* between human and animal, which is not independent of the former.[16] While Marcy Norton proposes that there are primarily two European modes of interaction in the Americas – hunting and husbandry – I distinguish here additional modes, including "discovered" and "observed," which often involve different kinds of utility. This is especially true in the writing of Oviedo, who, as he explains, introduced previously wild animals into his living quarters or personal menagerie in order to study them and, at times, conduct experiments on them.[17] Another mode of interaction that will come up in the pages to follow is that of "being hunted by," which is, according to both Oviedo and Sahagún, the relationship of the indigenous peoples to certain snakes, jaguars, and other animals, who people may also reciprocally hunt.[18]

Terrestrial Animals of the Jungle and the Pastures

The early natural historical authors of Spanish America were a diverse group of individuals with varied training, expertise, and purpose. Yet all were influenced by the tomes of Aristotle and Pliny, of classical ways of conceiving and grouping nature. In this vein, their accounts of life forms are often structured in a hierarchical way, with plants and trees on one end of the spectrum and ferocious mammals at the other.[19] While several early voyagers, including Christopher Columbus, Americo Vespucci, Pedro Alvares Cabral, and Vicente Yáñez Pinzón, all relayed information, anecdotes, and legends about new animals to curious readers in the Old World,[20] Oviedo – appointed imperial historian of the Spanish Indies in 1523 – was the first to publish a lengthy first-hand natural historical description containing many of the newly encountered animals. Acutely aware of his importance, Oviedo draws attention to Pliny's lack of knowledge of the Indies in the *Historia*.[21] Like Pliny before him, and Gessner to come, Oviedo keeps to a traditional division of animals based largely on the habitats in which they live, rather than on what would centuries later become the norm, animal morphology.[22] Thus, Oviedo's chapters on the topic are divided into land animals, sea animals, and birds as well as on imported pasturing animals that were brought to the new habitat of America. In all things, Oviedo emphasizes that his is a veracious first-hand account, that he knows the things he speaks about directly, something that sets him against Peter Martyr (1457–1525), who in 1516 had published a questionable account of animals he had never seen (as he had never travelled to America), which included misleading details on animals.[23]

The division of Oviedo's animals into different habitats largely explains their cognitive minding, when mode of interaction is taken into consideration. Oviedo begins his chapter with a discussion of the jaguar, which proves to be a "ferocious" animal (which he calls "tiger"). He spends considerable time discussing whether it should be considered the same creature as the "tiger" described by Pliny, with whom Oviedo is well acquainted and whom Oviedo considers a rival of sorts.[24] With respect to cognitive factors, Oviedo's jaguars are treated mostly as emotional animals, not endowed with much thinking ability. While generally "fierce," they have a weakness, which is their (alleged) tremendous fear of dogs, and he explains how the emotion can be harnessed against them in hunting. This technique, repeated in other colonial histories, involves chasing the jaguar with hounds that bark and nip at the animal, until it hides in a tree. Once there, the hunter's task is made easy, as he can shoot the trapped jaguar, who is too afraid to descend. According to this minding, these fierce creatures predictably react to a stimulus with fear, demonstrating little or no thinking or agency, portrayed through the lens of implicit anthropectomy. While jaguars prove to be dangerous adversaries, Oviedo importantly distinguishes between how the Spaniards hunt them strategically and effectively, in contrast with how the indigenous people fall prey to the feline's hunting, a difference that could be read as an implicit judgment by Oviedo on the superiority of the Spanish over the indigenous people's abilities and culture.[25]

More so than the jaguar, the panther is described by Oviedo as a foe, a deadly animal that terrorizes villages by killing their people and animals. In a strange twist – unexplained by Oviedo – somehow the animal has the ability to block arrows from entering its flesh when it is aware that the arrows are coming.[26] While he does not theoretically consider the cognitive implications of this, the implicit kind of cognition that he describes is high, and involves intentional agency, self-consciousness, and higher reasoning. While this special ability is no doubt spurious, the passage does demonstrate how the mode of interaction with the animal (seeing it as an attacker in war) coupled with its habitational parameter (jungle treetops) may lead the author to conceptualize an animal as significantly more intelligent than what is conceived of as a more passive animal, even compared to that other noble feline, the "fearful" jaguar, which seemed to lack intentional agency and thinking.

Other animals that exhibit ferociousness are the wild boars (*puercos monteses*), who roam in packs. Again, however, they are easily hunted by the Spaniards.[27] Interested in the anthropocentric utility of these animals, Oviedo remarks that a hunter who is lucky will come across a female boar giving birth and thus be able to take her piglets from her, which he remarks "are very tasty" (tienen muy buen sabor; *Historia* 46; *Sumario* 100). Other than the emotion associated with ferocity, no cognition is posited. In sum, Oviedo's treatments of fierce terrestrial animals in the wild are often one-dimensional and limited to strong emotions.

The most interesting treatments of animals' cognitive faculties are for those exotic New World land animals that seem to hold little or no instrumental value for Oviedo, which makes them intriguing and worthy of study to him. They are beyond anthropocentrism. These animals arouse his curiosity, wonder, and other emotions.[28] Notably, while the habitat is the same – these terrestrial creatures also live in the rainforest – it is the mode of interaction that has shifted, no longer one of hunter-hunted, but rather a more disinterested relationship of observer-to-observed. Among these creatures, the anteater (*oso hormiguero*) and the sloth (*perico ligero*) stand out foremost. His descriptions reveal his sustained thinking about these curious non-ferocious animals. More to the point, whereas the boar piglets' flesh was merely "very tasty," the anteater meat arouses his "disgust" (*Historia* 47; *Sumario* 101), an emotional response that appears to come from culturally transmitted knowledge, rather than from having tasted the animals' flesh himself.

Oviedo relates that the first Spaniards to arrive in America, lacking food when their supplies dwindled, ate just about everything in order to survive.[29]

With the question of its being "food" literally off the table, and its anthropocentric utility undetermined, the mode of interaction between Spaniard and "strange" creature consists in observing and being observed, which results in a different kind of attention paid by Oviedo. As such, the *oso hormiguero* (literally, "bear who likes ants") is treated as more complex than were the boar and the piglets, now that the creature holds no direct exploitable value. Not only does the anteater display the emotion of cowardice (*cobarde*) but he also holds intentional agency ("desire" [*deseo*]), as he chooses to graze in different ways, an intellectual faculty that even the magnificent jaguar seemed to lack as she merely reacted to the fear-inducing dogs. Indeed, Oviedo is fascinated by the cognitive abilities of the *oso hormiguero,* a fascination revealed through his digressive analysis of the animal's ant-hunting practices. As he explains, anteaters take advantage of small structural weaknesses in otherwise formidably strong anthills that are as hard as "very strong mortar" (una muy fuerte argamasa). These weaknesses are imperceptible to the human eye, yet the anteater apparently understands how to exploit them: "He plies his trade upon the hidden ants, executing their death, in this way: he goes to the aforesaid anthill and, through a crack or fissure as fine as the blade-edge of a sword, he begins to use his tongue and, licking, he moistens that crack however small it is" ([T]iene esta forma de usar su oficio en las escondidas hormigas, ejecutando su muerte, que se va al hormiguero que es dicho, y por una hendedura o resquebrajo tan sutil como un filo de espada, comienza a poner la lengua, y lamiendo, humedece aquella hendedura por delgada que sea; *Sumario* 101). Oviedo's interest in the anteater is even more striking when he mentions how the animal led him to act, in his own attempt to reveal a "secret" of nature. Fascinated by the anteater's ability to breach the anthill, Oviedo tries to emulate this behaviour experimentally by having his men wield iron weapons against the ant colony's "mortar": "I have tested [the hardness of the mortar] and I have had [the anthills] broken open. I would not be able to believe how hard they are without having seen this myself, for even with pickaxes and iron bars they are very difficult to destroy, and in order to better understand this secret, I have had [the anthills] demolished in my presence" (lo cual yo he experimentado y los he hecho romper; y no pudiera creer sin verlo la dureza que tienen, porque con picos y barretas de hierro son muy dificultosos de deshacer, y por entender mejor este secreto, en mi presencia lo he hecho derribar; *Sumario* 101).[30] Not able to believe without seeing with his own eyes, Oviedo gains considerable respect for this non-human animal through the experiment, since the "mortar" was even harder than he had imagined it would be and it was difficult to breach even for his small army. Thus, a "useless" creature becomes an animal with a mind, worthy of Oviedo's time and careful attention, as the mode of interaction and the habitational parameters emerge as important factors related to this human's proto-scientific study of an animal's behaviour and capabilities. Such emphasis on the animal's actual mental characteristics is thus a psychological correlate to what Kathleen Myers has noted as Oviedo's attempt to capture the physical appearance of objects creating a "more empirical image ... [than the] schematic or conceptual idea" (Myers 66) typical of the Middle Ages.

The second "useless" land creature that Oviedo discusses is the sloth (*perico ligero*). Initially, Oviedo expresses only contempt towards it due to the animal's alleged laziness. The sloth, as its name in English still recalls, is anthropomorphically sinful. Oviedo calls it by various injurious, anthropomorphic names, including "stupid," "boring," "slow," and "scatterbrained":

> The sloth is the stupidest animal that can be seen in the world, and so sluggish and so slow in moving that to go the distance of fifty paces it requires an entire day (...) It moves that neck from side to side, as if scatterbrained, and its intention or that which it seems most to seek or desire is to cling to a tree or something it can use to climb high above the ground; and in this way, most of the time that these animals are found, they are taken from the trees, through which, climbing very slowly, they move hanging and clinging with those long claws.
>
> (Perico ligero es un animal el más torpe que se puede ver en el mundo, y tan pesadísimo y tan espacioso en su movimiento que para andar el espacio que tomarán ciencuenta pasos, ha menester un día entero [...] mueve aquel su pescuezo a una parte y a otra, como atontado, y su intención o lo que parece que más procura y apetece es asirse de árbol o de cosa por donde se pueda subir en alto; y así, las más veces que los hallan a estos animales, los toman en los árboles, por los cuales, trepando muy espaciosamente, se andan colgando y asiendo con aquellas luengas uñas. [103–4])

While Oviedo finds the animal morally sinful, he does not use the species as the medieval bestiary authors might, as merely a symbol of human sinfulness.[31] Instead, once again, Oviedo becomes fascinated by the animal's cognitive faculties, since he attempts to understand the sloth's intentional agency, just as he had for the anteater, and to a far greater extent than he ever did for the merely "furious" or merely "tasty" creatures. Despite his alleged contempt (or perhaps because of it), Oviedo reveals that he studied the animal assiduously by bringing one to his home to live with him for this purpose: "I have had one at home" (yo le he tenido en mi casa; *Sumario* 105). He reports, from first- and second-hand experimentation, that even violence would not make the sloth move any faster (104), suggesting that he tried to measure the effect of poking, prodding, or otherwise inflicting injury.[32] In fact, his disinterested engagement leads him to wonder about, describe in detail, and theorize yet another "useless" – yet interesting – quality the animal demonstrates. In a long, poetic flourish, Oviedo describes the sloth's strange and amazing voice and habit of "singing," singling out the animal's uniqueness:

> His voice is very different than that of any other animal in the world, for it is only heard at night and all night in continued song from time to time, singing six notes, one higher than another, always descending, such that the highest note is the first and from that one it goes down, lowering the pitch or sound, *as one who says, la, sol, fa, mi, re, ut*; so this animal says *ha, ha, ha, ha, ha, ha*. Without a doubt (...) had the first inventor of music heard this animal he could have had a better foundation for its establishment, because the aforesaid sloth *teaches us* the same thing by his six notes that can be understood by *la, sol, fa, mi, re, ut*.
>
> (Su voz es muy diferente de todas las de todos los animales del mundo, porque de noche solamente suena, y toda ella en continuado canto, de rato en rato, cantando seis puntos, uno más alto que otro, siempre bajando, así que el más alto punto es el primero, y de aquél baja disminuyendo la voz, o menos sonando, *como quien dijese, la, sol, fa, mi, re, ut*; así este animal dice *ah, ah, ah, ah, ah, ah*. Sin duda [...] oyendo a aqueste animal el primero inventor de la música pudiera mejor fundarse para le dar principio, que por causa del mundo; porque el dicho perico ligero *nos enseña* por sus seis puntos lo mismo que por *la, sol, fa, mi, re, ut* se puede entender.[33] [*Sumario* 104, emphasis added])

Building his own etiological myth – an uncustomary practice for Oviedo in this first-hand, often practical account of America – this hypothetical historiography credits the animal with creating the idea of singing and the musical scale,[34] providing these to the hypothetical human inventor of music![35] Connecting the sloth with the rich aesthetic practice of music, one with a long cultural history, and positing that humans have a merely mimetic role, this new myth, while not based in fact, gives significant weight to a complex cognitive behaviour of the sloth. While his interest and proto-scientific experimentation would seem more modern, Oviedo holds on to an aspect of the medieval bestiary tradition in that the animal is thought to "teach" humans something, in this case, music. Along with the anteater, the useless sloth displays a kind of immaterial utility, a prizing of novelty, knowledge, and wonder that sets him apart from the average animals that are used merely for food, skins, or trophies.

Other animals new to Oviedo and that impress him include the beaver, whose dexterity at sawing down trees "as if felling them with a saw" (como si con una sierra los derribasen) provokes wonder (*Historia* 55), and the *cozumatle* (which seems to be a wild cat),[36] which receives a greater level of attention to its cognition than the beaver: "a very cheerful animal that frolics about with those whom it knows" (muy alegre animal e retoza mucho con quien conosce; *Historia* 55). The verb "retozar" here, defined by Covarrubias as "to move oneself immodestly with joy and happiness, to make merry and to fawn over someone, as does a small dog when its mistress or master returns" ([m]overse descompuestamente con alegría y contento, por hacer fiesta y lisonjear a otra persona, como lo hace el perrico cuando viene de fuera su señora o su dueño; 1408), would indicate that, according to Oviedo, this animal happily and anthropomorphically engages with humans and becomes very excited and playful. It is not surprising, then, that among the many exotic specimens he brought or sent back to the Old World, he gave a cozumatle as a gift to one of his relatives, indicating that he thought the animal might easily be domesticated and kept in the home, like a pet (or collection piece): "I brought one of them to the city of Madrid in the year fifteen forty-seven and I gave it to an Asturian gentleman, a relative of mine" (Yo truje uno dellos hasta la villa de Madrid, año de mill e quinientos e cuarenta y siete años, e le di a un caballero asturiano, mi pariente; 55). These creatures, it seems, can be made to have a use, as Oviedo modifies the mode of interaction with the animal, from observer-observed to owner-collected (more on collected animals later in this chapter).[37]

One jungle genus stands out for its extreme intelligence for Oviedo, the first animals in the *Sumario* with which he seems truly impressed regarding their intellect. These are the various species of monkey, which he calls "gatos monillos" (literally, "little monkey cats"), who, not coincidentally, are not tasty to Spaniards, and apparently have little other anthropocentric utility.[38] Oviedo is particularly impressed with the imitative abilities of these "astute" animals who copy "in the same way" just what humans do, such as "break open an almond or a pine nut with a stone" or "throw a rock."[39] Apparently Oviedo is not the only one so impressed, because they are highly sought after in Seville, so much so that a multitude are brought back to Spain "daily."[40] For this reason, Oviedo recognizes that his implied reader in the Spanish hub will most likely be familiar with monkeys. Thus he relays only what he believes will be the most interesting information about them. He specifies that he is studying them in their natural American habitat, thus singling out his own importance and need for continued funding, and mentions things that he recognizes readers would "find it difficult to believe without seeing" (sin verlos, es dificultoso de creer; 51).

According to Oviedo, these monkeys have engaged in small battles with Spanish troops who are travelling through the jungle. They throw rocks at the men and, perhaps more surprisingly, aim and throw arrows that have missed the monkeys right back at the Spaniards.[41] In this vein, he relates a particularly comic story about Francisco de Villacastur, who lost several teeth like this.[42] Oviedo also claims that monkeys not only throw arrows back but will, remarkably, either break the arrows that have missed their mark or move them manually to a location higher in the trees out of the reach of the humans, "in such a way that they [the arrows] cannot fall down and be used again to injure them" (de manera que no puedan caer abajo para que los tornen a herir con ellas; *Sumario* 106). Such actions performed by the monkeys would certainly appear to demonstrate very high cognitive abilities, including concept understanding, self-awareness, intentional agency, and Theory of Mind as well as anticipation and avoidance of future action by others, what philosopher of animal cognition Kristin Andrews calls "mental time travel" (75). Indeed, Oviedo's folk animal psychology, while somewhat inexplicit and more focused on abilities that implicitly reflect cognition rather than theorizing the animal's mind, is quite a strong account of actual abilities in the case of monkeys, some of the closest relatives of *Homo sapiens*.

Other anecdotes that relate Oviedo's eyewitness experience show some highly self-aware and socially interactive monkeys. One tells of a monkey who was struck in the head with an arrow and who acted in a remarkable way. He was not mortally wounded, but as he was unable to remove the arrow, he had to live with a part of the arrow sticking out of his head. At first, his conspecifics came to his aid when he screamed, demonstrating an understanding of his communicative efforts and dire situation, as well as apparently demonstrating empathy. In addition, the other monkeys were curious, which they demonstrated by trying to touch the arrow. Unfortunately, this caused him even greater pain. Understanding – Oviedo implies – both his conspecifics' curiosity and their role in causing him greater pain with their handling of the arrow, the injured monkey then tried to control the way in which the others touched his half-arrow.[43] The injured monkey didn't like the way they were all touching him, so he took matters literally into his own hand: if they wanted to touch it, he would take their hand in his and guide it to the arrow gently. This is a very complex behaviour that involves an understanding of other monkeys' curiosity of his situation as well as his communicating a novel idea to his conspecifics. These animals' special abilities are treated like those of noble adversaries, akin to a duelling partner, and I would argue that such interest comes about in part because of the mode of interaction – the Spanish don't fear the monkeys, and they don't find the flesh enjoyable to eat, leaving the monkeys as a curiosity.[44]

While the arrow story and the previous monkey anecdotes may seem fanciful, the abilities and social intelligence that they adduce are in line with cognitive abilities that several primate species have been shown to hold. Indeed, recent scientific studies have shown primates to possess the ability to understand concepts as well as mind-boggling powers of calculation in order to survive and flourish amidst the complexity of their social groups of eighty conspecifics.

Focusing nuanced attention on the mode of interaction explains why some species are represented as possessing advanced cognitive abilities like Theory of Mind while others are not. When he writes about deer – a grazing forest and pasture animal in a hunter-hunted mode of interaction – Oviedo finds them easy to hunt (even easier than their cervid counterparts back in Spain), and states that he has killed them with bow and arrow (*Sumario* 99). Importantly, and somewhat predictably, he refrains from relaying any cognitive information on the species whatsoever. It is as if he does not consider them thinking animals.

In contrast, his rock- and arrow-hurling monkeys and his village-attacking panthers are quasi-human adversaries, not victims of the hunt. While he commented that the anteater was "disgusting" and piglets were "delicious," it is also of note that, for certain species, Oviedo does not consider the taste explicitly, nor mention having himself eaten the flesh, or having known anyone who has: monkeys, tigers, and jaguars all seem safe from the human harvesting of their flesh. These species are those that, for Oviedo, are the most like human warriors.[45] The higher yet limited conceptualization of their cognition corresponds both to their habitat and their human-to-animal mode of interaction.

In his *Natural and Moral History of the Indies* (*Historia natural y moral de las Indias*), José de Acosta does not treat many terrestrial jungle animals, yet he has a lengthy section on monkeys, reminiscent of Oviedo's fascination and treatment of these creatures in their natural habitat.[46] The significant and gratuitous anthropomorphism of Acosta's treatment attracts attention: after watching them in amazement ("me admiró"), this Jesuit priest, steeped in Aristotelian scholasticism, seems close to abandoning canonical ideas of human exceptionalism, of our being the only creatures on earth with reason and a soul. He starts by saying that "their agility and skill amaze because it *seems as if they have discourse and reason*, and their way of moving through the trees makes it seem as if they almost want to imitate the birds" (La ligereza y maña de éstos, admira, porque *parece que tienen discurso y razón*, y en el andar por árboles parece que quieren casi imitar las aves; 207, emphasis mine). Although he uses a hypothetical "as if" (parece que), he later states explicitly that he believes that monkeys understand human speech: "I do not think that there is any animal that perceives and adapts to human conversation as this class of monkeys" (no pienso que hay animal que así perciba y se acomode a la conversación humana, como esta casta de micos; 208). He also reiterates the "as if human" idea, but this time without a hypothetical, using the word "seem": "they do not seem to be brute animals but to possess human understanding" (no parecen de animales brutos, sino de entendimiento humano; 207). He marvels at how they work together in the jungle, grabbing each others' tails to assist getting across long spaces that they can't make in a single jump, in his appraisal, displaying human-like collective behaviour towards a common goal: "they support the others until they become linked – as I said – one to the tail of the other" (sustenta a los demás hasta que llegan asidos como dije, uno a la cola de otro; 207).

Indeed, primates are known to be extremely social creatures, although some of Acosta's evidence (holding on to each others' tails) seems like it may be spurious. It is no wonder that he is amazed, as he has also seen a monkey in the governor's house who could allegedly perform incredible tasks, some with anthropocentric utility. One monkey could go to the tavern for wine and pay for it, as a faithful servant: "as when they send him to the tavern for wine and put a coin in one hand and the jug in the other" (como en enviarle a la taberna por vino, y poniéndole en la una mano el dinero y en la otra el pichel; 207). In a comical turn, however, the monkey demonstrates his own intentional agency, not wanting to relinquish the items: "there was no way of taking the coin until they had filled the jug with wine" (no haber orden de sacarle el dinero hasta que le daban el pichel con vino; 207). As first-hand witness, Acosta also says that he saw this monkey drink wine immoderately: "And what is more, as he was a great drinker of wine (for I saw him drink, his owner pouring it to him from above), there was no touching the jug without his relinquishing it or giving permission" (Y lo que es más, con ser muy buen bebedor de vino [como yo se lo ví beber echándoselo su amo de alto], sin dárselo o dale licencia no había tocar al jarro; 208). In what seems like gratuitous anthropomorphism, the same monkey would also bother women who were made up nicely, as if the priest's patriarchal obsession about perceived female vanity were one and the same with the monkey's concerns: "if he saw women dressed in their finery, he would go and pull out their hairdo and upset and mistreat them" (si veía mujeres afeitadas, iba y les tiraba del tocado, y las descomponía y trataba mal; 208).[47] Ultimately, however, Acosta is somewhat anxious about this breaking down of the human/non-human binary and falls back on his religious world view, invoking a version of the *Scala Naturae*: "They recount so many things that, so as not to seem credulous of tall tales or so that others do not regard them as such, I believe it better to conclude this matter by only giving thanks to the Creator of all creatures, since only for men's amusement and humorous entertainment he appears to have made a kind of animal whose sole purpose is to be laughed at or to provoke laughter" (Cuentan tantas cosas, que yo por no parecer que doy crédito a fábulas, o porque otros no las tengan por tales, tengo por mejor dejar esta materia con sólo bendecir al Autor de toda criatura, pues para sola recreación de los hombres y entretenimiento donoso parece haber hecho un género de animal que todo es de reír, o para mover a risa; 208). In Acosta's text, then, the proper mode of interaction for monkeys – be it in service positions fetching wine from the tavern, as entertainment in their imitation and outlandish human-like behaviour – involves a master-to-servant one. While the monkey's flesh or skin serves no human purpose, there is still a strong anthropocentric utility. Since it does not involve killing the animals, this mode can lead to an appreciation of their cognitive features.

By way of contrast to both Oviedo and Acosta, and to illustrate further the point that mode of interaction involving anthropocentric utility of the animal plays a significant role in an author's animal minding, Tomás López Medel describes monkeys without anthropomorphizing and yet highly anthropocentrically. Their behaviour is described vaguely as "so audacious that it seems Nature had bred them to distract man from his sorrows" (tan hazañosos muchos de éstos que parece Naturaleza haberlo[s] criado para quita-pesares de los hombres; 177]), reminiscent of Acosta's iteration that they were created "only for men's amusement" (para sola recreación de los hombres). Unpacking Medel's statement, the monkeys have an emotional effect on humans, who enjoy watching the animals and who have their cares taken away (*quita-pesares*). Curiously, this does not increase Medel's empathy for the animals, nor does he attribute advanced cognitive features to them. The difference here is that Medel finds economic utility in dead monkeys. To be sure, in the same sentence he writes about how monkey skins make a beautiful lining for clothing. As is the case of Oviedo's tasty piglets, once humans identify a utility for dead animals, their cognitive features tend to become significantly less important. This is quite distinct from Oviedo's discussion of monkeys, where monkeys did not seem to have any utility to the Spaniards save perhaps for their purchase value as pets (better alive, and with interesting, amusing behaviours), and would be better categorized as admirable and playful adversaries (less like sword fighting and more like fencing) and to Acosta's, where the monkeys were potentially useful as servants or entertainers in the home.

Animals of the Pasture Lands

Most of the natural history authors follow Oviedo's lead and make a distinction between autochthonous herd animals of the Indies and those introduced from Spain. Since these animals – cows, pigs, etc. – were well known to Spaniards who were the intended readers of most of these works, it should come as no surprise, then, that little time is spent explaining their physical description or behaviour. However, even autochthonous herd animals of pasture lands tend to receive less attention to their cognitive faculties (i.e., practically none) compared to non-herd animals of the rain forest. Moreover, the cognitive abilities of herd-living, grazing animals – both autochthonous and imported – are conceived of differently than animals who are solitary or live in much smaller groups (many of which were examined earlier in this chapter). As will be seen, the habitational parameter of pastoral herd is predictive of a species being treated uncognitively, of lacking in mind.

In the *Historia,* Oviedo discusses the anthropocentric economic utility of such animals: the hides are good for leather (45), and he mentions the custom – widespread already in Europe at this time – of displaying deer heads as trophies, symbols of their hunter's value, which Oviedo calls "a show of status" (demostración de Estado; 45). He also mentions different kinds of sheep, recounting that Diego de Almagro gave him one in Panama to take back to Europe, but that it died at sea. Despite the fact that on the long voyage home, Oviedo certainly would have had time to observe the sheep's behaviour and infer its cognition anthropomorphically using animal folk psychology (as he did several times, including for the cozumatle, for instance), instead he informs the reader merely that it tasted good: "one of the best meats of the world" (una de las mejores carnes del mundo; 53). In other passages, Oviedo mentions other species of American herding animals that all seem to be cervids: *guacabitinax, guabiniquinax,* and the *taruco.* Indeed, none of these receive any treatment of their cognition. These species are mentioned only insofar as their flesh is tasty or not, how large the herds are (tarucos in "groups of thousands"), or how the indigenous hunt them.

Similar non-cognitive treatments of pasture animals abound. Argote de Molina was the author of a widely read "Discurso" on hunting, published alongside his 1582 edition of Alfonso XI's fourteenth-century *Libro de Montería.* Although his treatise is mostly concerned with Spain, he offers some information about hunting in America. Although he never travelled there, and therefore cannot serve as an eyewitness, Argote de Molina comments on what he has learned about the ease of hunting in America given the geographical conditions, and the number of people and animals. In his explanation, killing animals sounds more like gathering berries. In fact, he uses the verb "recoger" (to gather) to describe the action of hunting in America: "gathering all the animals placed before them" (recogiendo todos los animales que se les ponen delante; fol. 13r).

Commenting on a particular kill of this type that took place in 1551 (which he had heard about, "è oydo contar"), Argote de Molina remarks on the massive scale of the hunt, providing figures in the tens of thousands for certain animals, all the while anthropectomizing the animals:

> Gentlemen who happened to be in Peru in the year fifty-one [1551], in the province of Chicuytu in the Collao, when Don Francisco de Mendoza was Viceroy of Peru, told me about a hunting festival held by the Indians of Collao. A great number of them enclosed ten leagues of land in which *they killed twenty-five thousand guanacos and vicunas, three thousand foxes, and five hundred lions, and a great number of other animals.*
>
> (Estando en Piru, en el Año de cinquenta y vno [1551], en la Prouincia de Chicuytu en el Collao, Don Franciſco de Mendoça Viſorey del Peru, è oydo contar a Caualleros, que allí ſe hallaron en aquella ſazon, de vna fieta de Monteria, que ſe hizo por los Indios de Collao, cercando diez leguas de tierra, con gran numero dellos, en la qual *mataron veynto y cinco mil Guanacos, y vicuñas, tres mil Zorras mil, y quinientos Leones, in otro grandiſſimo numero de otros animales.* [fol. 13r, emphasis mine])

At first glance, his figures would seem rather Herodotus-like, exaggerated tales from far-off lands. However, judging from the fact that other authors, including José de Acosta, provide similar details for other hunts or fleets, the numbers may in fact be credible.

Discussing autochthonous pasturing animals in Peru – in particular "the alpacas and guanacos and llamas of Peru" (De los pacos y guanacos, y carneros del Pirú; 210) – Acosta mentions their utility as beasts of burden and as a food source. With respect to food, he has tried the flesh of all of these animals, and states his preference for the taste and texture of baby llama. Given this mode of interaction, it would not be expected that Acosta would elaborate on the cognitive capacities of these animals, and indeed, he says little about their intelligence. However, when he discusses these same animals in another context, Acosta does remark on some of their emotional aspects. His discussion of their capacity as beasts of burden (rather than *qua* food) is quite exceptional as compared to other Spaniards of his time, who tended to treat such grazing animals almost as automata, in the manner of Gómez Pereira, Descartes, or Malebranche, but without the philosophical rationale. Here the mode of interaction has changed, as has the habitat, since the herding animal is removed from its herd in order to employ it as beast of burden. I would argue that such animals are treated more cognitively because of this new context and mode of interaction.

Indeed, in this section of his *Historia*, Acosta seems bemused by the way that the "carneros rasosos" (llamas) comport themselves. He explains that they will suddenly stop, raise their necks, and stare at a person intently: "The llamas have a very funny gaze, because they stop in the path and crane their necks and stare at one very attentively, and they stay that way a while without moving, nor displaying any fear nor pleasure, such that the sight of their serenity makes one want to laugh" (Los carneros rasos tienen un mirar muy donoso, porque se paran en el camino y alzan el cuello, y miran una persona muy atentos, y estánse así tanto rato sin moverse, ni hacer semblante de miedo ni de contento, que pone gana de reír ver su serenidad; 211). His narration of the sequence of actions – *paran, alzan, miran, estánse* – seem intentional, and while they become objects of amusement ("gana de reír"), this meeting of the gaze – a deep look into the eyes of the other – hints that there is more. For Acosta, behind those non-human animal eyes there may lie reason, and if not, there is at the very least emotion. Llamas have an air of "serenity," and yet their minds are ultimately inscrutable.

The lives of these non-food animals are cheap nonetheless, where Spaniards are concerned. If the pack animals become suddenly scared and run off with their load, they may be shot and killed in order to safeguard the cargo: "Although sometimes they are suddenly startled and run away with their cargo up to the highest cliffs, and when it happens that they cannot be reached, they are shot at and killed with an arquebus so that the [silver] bars they carry are not lost" (aunque a veces se espantan súbito y corren con la carga hasta los más altos riscos, que acaece no pudiendo alcanzallos porque no se pierdan las barras [de plata] que llevan, tirarles con arcabuz y matallos; 211). In line with his Jesuit thinking, the indigenous peoples, for Acosta, have more patience than these trigger-happy Spaniards. Instead of shooting, they pay attention to the emotional life of the animal and go after "pacos" whom they consider "angry" or "bored" with their task; they wait by their side, speaking to them and touching them, implying that the indigenous believe that they are communicating with the pacos to some extent: "The Indians' solution in that case is to stop and seat themselves next to the llama and give it many caresses and coax it with flattering words until it calms down and gets back on its feet. Sometimes it may take some two or three hours of waiting for it to relax and calm down" (El remedio que tienen los indios entonces, es parar y sentarse junto al paco, y hacerle muchas caricias, y regalalle hasta que se desenoja y se alza, y acaece esperarle bien dos y tres horas a que se desempaque y desenoje; 212).

European Pasture Animals in America

Several authors before and after Oviedo discuss how European pasturing animals proliferate well in America. In chapter 9 of the *Historia general y natural,* Oviedo discusses "terrestrial animals brought from Spain" (animales terrestres que se trujeron de España; 38). They have done so well that their individual value has decreased in the context of supply and demand, and he lists the very low prices for purchasing these animals in America. Like their pasturing American counterparts, the European animals are conceived of as part of a mass. As such, no cognitive traits are provided. This is fairly typical of the way that European writers tend to treat animals raised as food, either in America or in Europe, even today. Oviedo also mentions a disturbing piece of information that will only worsen throughout the sixteenth century, noted in other natural historical accounts: European bovines have proliferated so easily in their new habitat, and have become so inexpensive, that they are slaughtered for their skins alone, which are exported to Europe for sale. The meat is left to rot. We can see here, already, the beginnings of the Anthropocene, in such profit-oriented, unecological, and unsustainable practices.[48]

Cows are not the only animals whose lives are cheap. According to Oviedo's assessment, it is more lucrative for farmers to grow sugar cane than to raise animals. Since keeping pigs is apparently anathema for growing sugar, those farmers who had animals abandon them, creating a population of feral ones. In fact, because of reckless and shifting European practices, the land has become overrun by feral pigs, cows, cats, and dogs.[49] Anthropomorphizing, Oviedo calls these now ferocious animals "fugitives" (bravos ... fugitivos; 38). They are "cimarrones" (38) – the same word that will be used to designate escaped human slaves in the Americas later in the century. There is a tinge of regret in some of what Oviedo writes, as he recognizes that Spaniards have ineluctably changed the countryside for the worse. When he talks about the feral rabbits – introduced originally by the Spanish as domesticated rabbits – he mentions how "harmful" ("dañoso") they are (38). Importantly, he also implies that the Spanish should have known better, that they should have learned to avoid the mistakes of history, since Pliny had written about this very problem, and since the Spanish had already had a similar negative experience with feral animals in the Canaries (38).

In his *Discurso*, which is mostly about hunting in Spain, Argote de Molina repeats much of what Oviedo says, but with greater detail.[50] These animals, which like Oviedo he too refers to as *cimarrones* (fol. 13v), are bulls and cows from Spain who have been so successful in reproducing, and are now in such abundance, that the human inhabitants have let them go wild. Once feral, they are still highly successful at reproducing, so much so that they are simply killed and skinned by locals. According to Argote de Molina, their flesh is left to rot because there is far too much to use. This, he argues, has led to an increase in the wild dog population. There is no thought in Argote de Molina's *Discurso* given to the mental life of these hunted herd animals, but the author expresses his own proto-ecological concerns. Their flesh was wasted because the animals were slaughtered for their skins to be exported to Spain. Written several decades later than Oviedo's *Historia*, he provides a perspective of how the problem adduced by Oviedo has only gotten worse. In a datum that is so large it may seem exaggerated, Argote de Molina – who resided in Seville – mentions all of the cow and bull hides that are brought back to his city and strewn along the banks of the Gualdalquivir, estimating that they amount to some two hundred thousand hides each year (fol. 9r).

Given a situation that José de Acosta understands as due to a lack of predators, especially on the islands, the sheer number of European animals is beyond measure and described hyperbolically as "innumerable": "now they have innumerable herds of horses, of cattle and cows, of dogs, of pigs" (agora tienen innumerables manadas de caballos, de bueyes y vacas, de perros, de puercos; 57). As he explains, corroborating claims by Oviedo and Argote, the rate at which they have reproduced has led to such overpopulation that the animals now "belong" to whoever wants to kill them: "And it has reached a point where the herds of cows no longer have any clear owners because they have multiplied so much. They belong to the first person to hamstring them in the forest or field" (Y es en tanto grado que los ganados de vacas no tienen ya dueños ciertos por haber tanto multiplicado, que son del primero que las desjarreta en el monte o campo; 57). Even more than Oviedo and Argote, Acosta describes what today we might call "an ecological disaster" with the waste left behind by those merely interested in the skins alone, which has led to an increase in the feral dog population who have become fierce like wolves: "The inhabitants of these islands [hamstring the cattle] to avail themselves of the hides for the hide trade, leaving the flesh there without eating it. The dogs have multiplied to such excess that they roam in packs and, having gone feral, they do as much harm to the cattle as if they were wolves, which causes great damage to those islands" (Lo cual hacen los moradores de aquellas islas para aprovecharse de los cueros para su mercancía de corambre, dejando la carne por ahí sin comerla. Los perros han en tanto exceso multiplicado, que andan manadas dellos, y hechos bravos hacen tanto mal al ganado como si fueran lobos, que es un grande daño de aquellas islas; 57–8). Acosta emphasizes these ideas, and adds a public health issue, "infection," reiterating his concerns about mass slaughter of animals in the chapter on "ganados ovejuno y vacuno": "They skin it and, carrying the hide to their home, they leave the meat behind, there being no one to use it nor want it because of the excess of it that there is: The excess on that island is such that they told me in some parts there was disease from the great quantity of rotting meat" (Desuéllanla y llevando el cuero a su casa, dejan la carne perdida por allí, sin haber quien la gaste ni quiera por la sobra que hay de ella. Tanto que en aquella isla me afirmaron que en algunas partes había infección, de la mucha carne que se corrompía; 198). It is important to note that, again, no cognitive details are provided for any of these animals save for "fierce"; they seem to be an innumerable mass of creatures that have no individuality or cognitive aspects worthy of note. While Acosta remarked on the curious and interesting emotions of the pacos in the context of pack animals, the same cannot be said of his remarks on the less exotic sheep and cows from Spain.

Like Argote, Acosta also remarks on the spectacle of seeing the skins of these innumerable creatures brought back to Seville, corroborating to some extent, Argote's astronomical estimate. Acosta refers more specifically than Argote to a fleet of ships from Santo Domingo that arrived in 1587 with 35,444 cow hides, and from New Spain with 74,350 cow hides. Emphasizing his first-person perspective, Acosta describes the spectacle of seeing tens of thousands of hides on Seville's riverbanks and how this evokes awe: "When they unload one of those fleets, the sight of the river of Seville and that sandy area where they put so many hides and so many goods is an amazing thing" (Cuando descarga una flota de estas, ver el río de Sevilla y aquel arenal donde se pone tanto cuero y tanta mercadería, es cosa para admirar; 198).

The wild terrestrial animals described in these European natural histories of the Indies come in various shapes and sizes and live primarily in two kinds of habitats, the rainforest, on the one hand, and the plains and mountains, on the other. This chapter has studied these habitats independently, in an attempt to disentangle to what extent habitat impacts the minding of the animals in question. While certain generalizations can be made about animals that live in the rainforest versus those that live in pasture lands and mountains, more importantly, the mode of interaction between humans and animals seems more determinative of the human recognition or attribution of sentience. The more dangerous animals of the rainforest, like the jaguar and the boar, are minded with emotions but do not hold significant intellectual interest for authors.[51] With regard to Oviedo, he is most interested in attributing cognitive ideas to animals for which he identifies no other purpose. These solitary rainforest animals are "useless": they don't have good flavour or valuable skin, and their labour cannot be easily harnessed, especially the anteater and the sloth. These animals, which because of their habitat and their way of being in the world do not offer any anthropocentric utility, become the greatest objects of Oviedo's fascination and, in this habitat, offer the most interesting cognitive cases.

In his history, Acosta is not systematic with animals, as is Oviedo, but it is through his writing that we can glean a European vs. indigenous approach to understanding the minds of pack animals – these are primarily herding animals of the pasture lands and mountains that are used for their labour transporting goods. According to Acosta, the Spaniards have no patience for these somewhat inscrutable creatures, and will resort to killing them, while the Indians attempt communication and persuasion, with their sounds and touching. Yet Acosta himself attempts to understand the mind of the paco, and provides interesting details, remarking on what seems like self-consciousness and intentional agency in the paco, in his curious image of the paco's gaze into the human's eyes. Once again, within the same or similar habitational parameter (e.g., the difference in how the paco is treated versus, say, the deer, as portrayed by Oviedo), the mode of interaction and the kind of utility that the animal provides for humans are what allow a greater scrutiny of the animal mind. Importantly, there is no evidence from cognitive ethology or evolutionary genetics that could show that a paco or an alpaca is more intelligent than, say, another member of the Artiodactyl order such as deer. In sum, grazing animals are looked at as a food source and tend not to be reflected on by their authors as having cognitive features. Rather they have physical features, ones that can be consumed, including flesh, wool, or skin. These observations help to expand the analytical tools of human-animal relationships vis-à-vis animal cognition: In addition to habitational parameter and mode of interaction, it is important to note the cultural issue of *who* is interacting with the animal – on the one hand, Spaniards, and on the other, the indigenous, who treat the creatures, in some cases, as sensitive and sentient.

Habitational Parameter: Water Creatures

By the mid-eighteenth century, more rigorous questioning of inherited categories about nature from the Greeks and Romans would famously lead to a more "Enlightened" classification system – Linnaeus's *Systema Naturae*, which is considered a hallmark of modern scientific systematization. Yet, in light of their encounters with certain aquatic species, colonial authors investigating the natural history of the Indies had already had occasion to question the stability of earlier inherited animal categories, which were based primarily on habitat. As delineated in the introduction to this book, even today we are in the grips of an archaic classificatory system to some extent, in which "fish" is the most formidable example. More than a taxonomic grouping of animals, it is a "folk category," as philosopher of science Colin Allen puts it (see introduction above). Such tensions within the category would eventually lead to the ejection of mammalian animals and reptilian forms from the category (a category that today still includes widely disparate species such as the coelacanth, the great white shark, and the tuna). However, this change was subtle and slow-going, begun in part when Old World eyes looked upon New World species that didn't seem to fit.

Well before the systematic taxonomic transformation, and the ejection of mammals such as dolphins from the concept of "fish," sixteenth-century naturalists were confronted with the problematic status of the manatees, whales, and alligators, which would have been, on Aristotelian and Plinean grounds, "fish." Regarding manatees, since they foraged on plants on the water's edge and stuck their bodies out of the water (a liminal species for the "water" habitational parameter), this left intact, for the most part, writers' prejudices about the sea *qua* habitat that were often determinative with regard to the mode of interaction and the adscription of (advanced) cognition to most "fish." It turns out that part of this questioning initially came about not so much as a scientific issue but as a cultural one, due to concerns that, if ingested during

Lent or other times that required abstinence of flesh, some of these sea creatures might not be "fish."[52]

Oviedo's classification of animals is highly anthropocentric, a classification that is implicitly expressed in terms of the species' practical interest to humans. The most common such situation is when the animals are presented as a food source for people. Nowhere is this more apparent than in his section on "los animales de agua" (marine animals).[53] In fact, the first noun of the first sentence of the first chapter on sea creatures conceptualizes them anthropocentrically with the word "food." Part proto-ethnography, part natural history, it reads as follows: "The most common *fare* of the Indians and that for which they have the most affinity are the fish of the rivers and sea" (El *manjar* más ordinario de los indios e a que ellos tienen grande afición, son los pescados de los ríos e de la mar; *Historia* 56, emphasis mine). Beyond discussing them as food, Oviedo mentions other aspects of fish, related to consuming them, such as how the Indians catch them, which species they fish for, and whether these fish are more or less healthful than Spanish fish in his view. Importantly, Oviedo is able to "testify" as to the taste of these fish, since he is a first-hand witness not only by sight but of gustation too, a distinction he makes explicit, in which he here goes beyond what Anthony Pagden has called "autopsy" in reference to Oviedo's insistence on eyewitness visual testimony:[54] "I have not only seen such fish but I have eaten most of them so as to be able to attest to their taste as well as their appearance in what I have been able to understand and consider in these matters" (no tan solamente en haber visto tales pescados, pero habiendo comido de los más dellos, para que también pueda en el gusto, como en la forma dellos, testificar lo que he podido comprehender e considerar destas cosas; 56). This is pertinent to a cognitive study of animals precisely because, as I argue, it is the conceptualization of the animal – through its habitat and mode of interaction – that leads to humans' view of the animal's cognition, including whether or not the animal is capable of suffering. In particular, if the animal tastes good, my hypothesis goes, the less likely the author is to be concerned about or to theorize the animal's higher cognition (including pain and suffering, which involve emotion, sensation, and self-consciousness).

As might be expected, then, most of the water creatures considered by Oviedo lack sentience in his conceptualization. For example, in his lengthy explanation of how to hunt sharks, he attributes no thought to them either implicitly or explicitly. The baited hook is placed in the water, and the shark goes for it in a way that Pereira or Malebranche might predict, as automatic, that is, as an automated reflex: "Following behind the ship, trailing the hook in the manner described, *the shark swallows it all as soon as it sees it*; and as it wants to make off with its quary, the hook pierces its jaw from the pull of the ship, catching the fish" (Pues yendo por popa, rastrando el anzuelo, segund es dicho, *como el tiburón lo ve, trágalo todo*; e como se quiere desviar con la presa, por tirar de la nave, atraviésasele el anzuelo e pásale una quijada, e préndele; *Historia* 61, emphasis added). Lacking in between the phrases about seeing and swallowing are any mention of thought, desire, emotion or intentional agency, grammatical and syntactical elements that are observed in Oviedo's description of certain other animals.[55] The fish are presented rhetorically as eating machines in what amounts to what I call "implicit anthropectomy," in which the writer is not actively (i.e., explicitly) denying human-like cognitive faculties of animals à la Malebranche (the explicit form would be "anthropectomy" *tout court*), but rather simply ignoring animals' possibilities for thoughts, feelings, or intentions. Such a view may have been informed by the Weltanschauung leading to the Marian miracles involving fish, moving creatures that were – in contrast to other types of animals in the miracles – lacking in all cognitive abilities.[56] I would argue that such views have held sway and still do, until extremely recently, and except in the cases of a limited scientific and philosophical audience.[57]

In the *Historia natural y moral de las Indias*,[58] Acosta's discussion of sharks (*tiburones*) goes even further than Oviedo's in this kind of automaton-creating implicit anthropectomy, and it implicitly shows how cognitive aspects of the observer influence the cognitive categorization of the animal in question, and in particular, of the way in which "fish" are considered the way they are because of the darkness of waters and the mystery surrounding them. For Acosta, sharks are awesome, terrifying creatures, and his description makes them sound like killing machines, that is, automata. At the level of image creation, the automatization works in the following way, and begins with an eyewitness account full of human emotion: When he saw one shark cut open, Acosta marvelled that among other things, they found "a big piece of the head of a cow with its entire horn" (un pedazo grande de la cabeza de una vaca, con su cuerno entero; 115).[59] In addition to these huge skeletal remains, which combine the long-dead cow with the recently deceased shark body within the same shark carcass, they also found metal objects, including a "big butcher's knife" and a "big iron hook." The shark's ingestion of these objects inspires awe in Acosta, emphasized through his use of polysyndeton ("and they pulled a big butcher's knife from its maw and a big iron hook, and a big piece of the head of a cow with its entire horn – and I still don't know if [they found] both horns" (le sacaron del buche un cuchillo grande carnicero y un anzuelo grande de hierro, y un pedazo grande de la cabeza de una vaca con su cuerno entero – y aún no sé si ambos a dos; 115). In another related anecdote on sharks, Acosta relates how some sailors marvelled at watching a school of sharks that devoured a quartered horse that they had hung there for their amusement, just above the water's surface. Acosta recognizes that the sharks have a strong sense of olfaction as they move towards the smell of the horse flesh and blood (tras el olor; 116); yet apart from this sensory observation, the sharks are portrayed as mere fascinating eating machines with no apparent cognition. Once again, as in Oviedo's description, just as in the Marian fish miracles, no room is left for anything but an automated response between the shark sensing the bait and the shark devouring it. To wit, Acosta engages in anthropectomy of these animals by not mentioning any thought processes or emotions, all the while instrumentalizing their teeth as machinery by comparing them metaphorically to razor blades (*navajas*).[60] The reader may wonder what thought processes I could possibly have in mind, since we all know that several species of shark are deadly creatures and we would not want to swim in waters that they inhabit. But we still might ask, did the sharks communicate to each other, did one inform the others about this appetizing horse flesh meal, and did they choose to eat this meal instead of another one? Were they gleeful at the taste of the blood? Were they concerned about predators? To be clear, I do not expect Acosta to ask these questions, but the fact that he does not has little or nothing to do with the actual measurable cognitive abilities of sharks; it has, rather, to do with the fact that they are believed to be "fish" and live deep under the water, and because the only time in which humans interact with sharks in the wild is to be hunted by them, to kill them, or to witness them coming to the surface to kill something else.

Oviedo's anthropectomy of animals considered "fish" extends to his disparaging of indigenous people for their (alleged) anthropomorphism of sea creatures, which makes his views of fish cognition somewhat more explicit than his implicit references to shark automatization. In his description of the "peje reverso" – most probably the species *Remora remora* (sucker shark), according to Enrique Alvarez López[61] – Oviedo scoffs at the idea that the "indios" attribute advanced linguistic abilities to this animal, which conflicts with his European view. According to Oviedo, the indigenous people act as if the *peje reverso* understands human language. The folk animal psychology of the indigenous, while most surely gratuitously anthropomorphic, seems like a good folk functional understanding that provides a technique for catching manatees and other sea creatures such as turtles, whereby they take advantage of the sucker shark's ability to attach itself to these animals and thereby reel in the desired animal. In order to achieve their goal, "the Indians speak many sweet words and give it many thanks for what it has done and for its work" (los indios hacen con dulces palabras e dándole muchas gracias de lo que ha hecho e trabajado; 66).

By virtue of this helping function, the *peje reverso* seems comparable to Europeans' hunting dogs, as an assistant in the hunt. Their mode of interaction to the sucker fish is different from the European one to this fish, not hunter-to-hunted but hunter-to-hunter assistant, which helps explain the highly developed cognition attributed to the animal. There is an important cultural difference here as we compare European and indigenous models of animal cognition. However, I would argue that at a deeper level, that of the human species, the relationship of human magical thinking is still dependent on the mode of interaction of the animal – the indigenous peoples have found a mode of interaction with fish that the Europeans have not, and it is based on this mode of interaction (i.e., their reliance on the sucker fish to catch other creatures) that they have minded fish accordingly as communicative, comprehending human speech, and having intentional agency. In this case, the indigenous peoples have fostered a communicative relationship and minded fish in a way that is atypical in European writing (and not common in Sahagún's indigenous-informed history either), which is a significant difference. Rather than adopt their anthropomorphism of the animal, Oviedo seems unnerved that the Indians "believe" that fish have thoughts and feelings. This leads him to a tirade on the Indians' apparent ignorance and misunderstanding of how the world works:

> This generation of Indians is so simple-minded that they wholeheartedly believe that the remora understands the human oration and all those words that the Indian says to motivate him before he sets him loose so that he'll latch on to the turtle or manatee or some other fish, and that it also understands the thanks he is given afterwards for what he has done. And

this ignorance comes from their not understanding that that is a property of Nature, since without saying anything to them it so happens many times in this great ocean.

(Es tan liviana esta generación de aquestos indios, que tienen ellos creído por muy cierto que el peje reverso entiende muy bien el sermón humano e todas aquellas palabras quel indio le dijo animándole, antes que lo soltase, para que se aferrase con la tortuga o manatí, u otro pescado, e que también entiende las gracias que después le da por lo que ha hecho. Y esta inorancia viene de no entender ellos que aquello es propiedad de la Natura, pues que sin les decir nada deso, acaesce muchas veces en ese grande mar Océano. [66])

Despite his insistence that the Indians are misguided in this instance of anthropocentric anthropomorphism, Oviedo himself is not immune to all anthropomorphizing for water creatures. Indeed, there is something about the whale that stands out to him, if only briefly and summarily. Oviedo relates that he and his comrades inferred that this animal had intentional agency and emotions, something they appreciated with their folk animal psychology but that is today borne out by decades of research, which has shown that certain species of whales most likely have their own language as well as dialects within that language.[62] Emphasizing his direct knowledge of the whale at sea,[63] he points to an event in which an adult whale approached their ship, along with a baby;[64] the large whale surfaced and showed part of its immensity; the men were scared by what might happen next, yet the whale did not attack and seemed "happy about the weather that was coming" as it left them alone: "and from what we could gather, this animal seemed happy about the weather that was coming, which soon turned into a gale or Westerly wind" (e a lo que podimos sospechar, este animal parescía que sentía leticia del tiempo futuro, que presto saltó en gran vendaval o Poniente; 58). This anthropocentric concern about the weather harks back to medieval beliefs in the bestiary such as the wise echinos fish in Latini's *Bestiary* (see chapter 1 above). Coincidentally, the wind that soon arrived was indeed the one that these very sailors had wished for, and which made their voyage speedier: "that wind served our purposes and sped our sailing, such that in a few days we arrived in the city of Panama" (el cual viento fué mucho a nuestro propósito e navegación, con que en pocos días llegamos a la cibdad de Panamá; 58). While this consideration of the whale's cognition is brief, it is significant for its anthropomorphizing, that it corresponds to a "fish" (*pex*). Importantly, they had this reflection about its cognition (as gratuitously anthropomorphic as it is) only once the "fish" came *out of* the water – that is, when it was, to a certain extent, within their own human *Umwelt*, in their human habitational parameter, visible from the ship above the water, rather than in the water's depths. Of course, as we know today, whales are mammals – more closely related to primates and canines than to a salmon or eel – and quite definitively no longer considered fish.[65] While Oviedo offers no reasoned argument to separate the whale from the "fish" category, he suggests some doubt as to its classification with his opening phrase, equivocating on the very question of whether all water animals are in fact fish: "a very large fish, or animal of the water, was travelling" (andaba un pex, o animal de agua, muy grande; 58). Reading this passage closely, Oviedo's reported observation that the whale was travelling with "su hijo" also makes it seem to him less like a fish and more like creatures that would one day become known as mammals.[66] By the end of the eighteenth century, whales and dolphins would no longer belong to the category of fish on morphological and functional grounds. Yet already, in Oviedo's casting doubt that the whale must be a fish, the taxonomical change was gradual, part of which is reflected in his anomalous assertion that this creature had thoughts of its own. After all, fish don't have thoughts or feel, or so goes the old wisdom that is pervasive even today. In fact, the belief that fish don't suffer is one rationale provided for why, during Lent, it is acceptable to eat them; land animals such as cows, sheep, and chickens were considered to have suffered and given their lives for the person who ingested their flesh,[67] whereas fish are not cognitively imagined in this way (see fig. 19).

But Oviedo's intuitive understanding of the concept "mammal" should not be overstated. In his chapter on sea lions (*lobos marinos*), for instance, he makes clear that he is aware that they breastfeed their young – making them similar to many of the land animals that he knows, including humans (all of which have come to be categorized as "mammals" in modern taxonomy) – and yet he continues to call them "pescado" (ch. 5). Similarly, when Oviedo discusses the manatee, his being the first non-mythological written account

Figure 19 Whale hunting in José de Acosta's *Historia natural y moral de las Indias*. Courtesy of the New Bedford Whaling Museum.

of this increasingly endangered Caribbean mammal, he notes the similarity of its taste with beef, but continues to call the animal "pescado" as well.[68]

For Acosta, the animal that causes him the most classificatory anxiety is the manatee. While writing about it in his chapter "On diverse fish and the Indians' ways of fishing" ("De diversos pescados y modos de pescar de los indios," 3.15:115),[69] Acosta explicitly calls the concept of "pez" into question, suggesting that the manatee does not in fact belong. Earlier encounters with the manatee had clearly treated the manatee as a fish. For instance, the physician Nicolò Scillacio described this "fish" that was "as large as cattle and it was eaten with relish because it tasted like veal – once its 'legs' had been removed" (qtd. in Asúa and French 8).[70] For Acosta, the fact that it tastes too much like veal is not a benefit but rather causes him angst ("casi tener escrúpulo"); but, like Oviedo and the whale, Acosta hesitates to call the manatee a fish unequivocally, because of the characteristics it shares with many of the land animals he knows (animals we know today are mammals) (see fig. 20):[71]

> In the islands called Windward – which are Cuba, Hispaniola, Puerto Rico, Jamaica – is found the fish they call manatee, a strange kind of fish – *if an animal that gives live birth to her children and has breasts and milk with which to raise them and grazes on grass in the field can be called a fish.* But in effect *it ordinarily inhabits the water* and that is why they eat it as fish. Although when I was in Santo Domingo I ate it one Friday and almost had qualms about it, not so much for the aforesaid as because in colour and flavor the pieces of this fish seemed to be not other than slices of veal, and in part, pork shank. It is as big as a cow."
>
> (En las islas que llaman de Barlovento – que son Cuba, la Española, Puerto Rico, Jamaica – se halla el que llaman manatí, extraño género de pescado: *si pescado se puede llamar animal que pare vivos sus hijos tiene tetas y leche – con que los cría – y pace en el campo.* Pero en efecto *habita de ordinario en el agua* y por eso le comen por pescado: aunque yo cuando en Santo Domingo lo comí un viernes casi tenía el escrúpulo, no tanto por lo dicho como porque en el color y sabor no parecían sino tajadas de ternera, y en parte de pernil, las postas deste pescado: es grande como una vaca." [115, emphasis mine])

The religious reason gives Acosta pause to reflect on species categorization, and ultimately consider if the animal is suffering. Unlike the whales, who live deep in the water and with which Acosta has little or no direct contact, the peaceful and languid manatee relates more closely than most "fish" to the human *Umwelt* in its edge habitat, making itself accessible to the human consideration of its circumstances.[72] While the classificatory anguish does not lead to a rich account of the manatee's mental life in Acosta, it does lead to something interesting in López Medel's *De los tres elementos: Tratado sobre la naturaleza y el hombre del Nuevo Mundo.*[73]

Medel's conceptualization of the manatee is widened by stories he has heard that have to do with indigenous traditions of pet-keeping. Long before the English "pet" became a category unto itself in Victorian England,[74] Spanish American colonial histories make clear that there was a tradition of pre-Columbian (indigenous) peoples interacting with animals in a pet-like manner, caring for them for no obvious

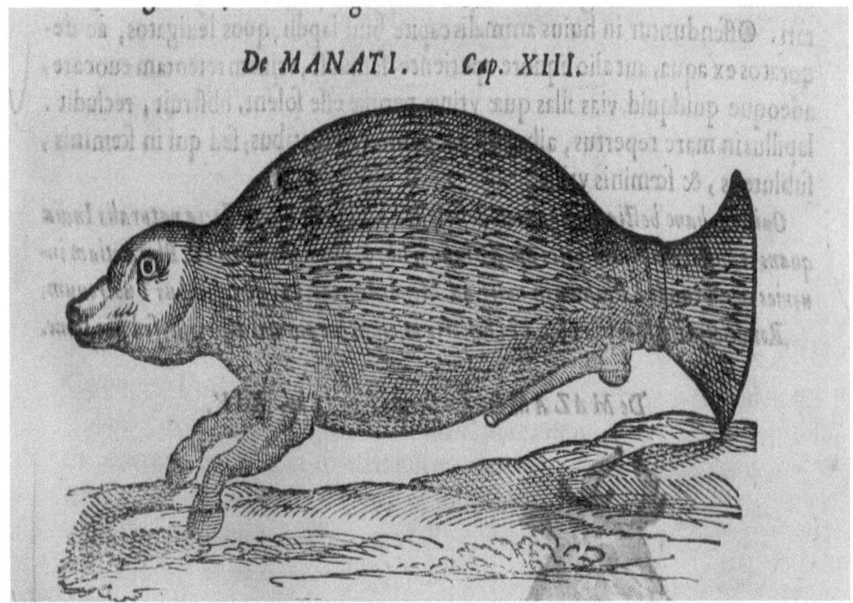

Figure 20 Manatee illustration in Francisco Hernández's *Rerum medicarum Novae Hispanae thesarurus*. Image from the Biodiversity Heritage Library. Digitized by the Getty Research Institute, Los Angeles (2975-262). Detail.

instrumental gain.[75] One of these particular cases comes across in the story about a manatee told by López Medel, in which an indigenous cacique of Hispaniola made something of a pet of a wild manatee.[76] In Medel's version, while the manatee did not live in the home (which would be impractical since it required a large body of water to survive), the cacique was fond of the manatee and had established a relationship with him since the animal was little. Medel notes that he called the animal by name, and fed him by hand, all common ways of treating a pet:

> The natives of the Indies say that this animal and fish is very tame and has much instinct. It is said of a cacique and lord of the island of Hispaniola that he had a manatee that he had raised since the animal was small in a great pool or pond of water and that, calling him by the name which he had given him, he came to him and *took from his hand* the plant that he used to give him to eat and, finally, he had him so tamed and trained that he

allowed himself to be touched by him and every time he called him, he left the water and went to the voice.

(Dicen los naturales de las Indias de este animal y pescado que es muy mansueto y de grande instinto. De un cacique y señor de la isla Española se refiere que tenía un *manatí* que había criado dende pequeño en un alberca o estanque grande de agua, que llamándole por el propio nombre que le tenía impuesto se venía para él y *tomaba de su mano* la hierba que le daba para comer y, finalmente, le tenía tan manso y avezado que se dejaba tratar de él y siempre que le llama salía del agua y acudía a la voz. [2.8:94, emphasis added on "tomaba de su mano"])

Like Acosta, Medel seems concerned about the animal's categorization, although he clearly calls the manatee "pescado," and never evinces worry that he might be sinning by eating its flesh on the wrong day. Nevertheless, he repeatedly compares the manatee to a cow, first with a general reference to its size as being like that of a calf (*ternera*), then noting that it is a grazing animal (*pascer hierba*), and finally describing the flesh as tasting like veal (*becerro*): "And before all is offered a certain species of fish that the Indians of the islands call *manatee*, and so the name has stuck among the Spanish; it is as big as a three- or four-month-old calf; it has four fin-like feet. It is commonly found in deep rivers and warm lands and not far from the sea; it climbs onto land to graze upon grasses, I mean those that it can reach near the water, and this is its principal sustenance" (Y ante todas cosas se ofresce una cierta especie de pescado que los indios de las islas llaman *manatí*, y con este nombre se ha quedado entre los españoles; es tan grande como un ternero de tres o cuatro meses; tiene cuatro alones a manera de pies. Hállase comúnmente en ríos caudalosos y en tierra caliente y no lejos de la mar; sale a tierra a pascer hierba, digo aquella que dende el agua puede alcanzar, y éste es su principal mantenimiento; 93; emphasis in original). Interestingly, he notes that the animal has four *alones*, which are *like* feet, demonstrating implicitly Medel's morphological observation that this sea creature has strong affinities to land-based quadrupeds.

In terms of reproduction, Medel is aware that the manatee reproduces "like a terrestrial animal" carrying a full-term baby in utero "like a cow her calf," rather than by laying eggs. He also distinguishes that male and female manatees have sexual organs, as he anthropomorphically writes that these are like human beings':[77]

Additionally, they relate two or three notable and strange peculiarities of the *manatee*: the first is that, whereas the other fish are conceived and formed in an egg and by way of oviposition, it is said that this animal is engendered like a terrestrial animal, being conceived and formed by generation in the belly of the female and being born once it is a fully formed animal, as a cow gives birth to its calf; secondly, it is said that it gives birth to two, a male and female. Additionally, Nature saw fit to distinguish the male and female sexual organs in this animal in the same manner as it did in humans.

(Item, refieren del *manatí* dos o tres especialidades muy notables y extrañas: la primera es que, como los otros pescados se engendren y fragüen de huevo y por vía de ovación, éste se dice que se engendra como un animal terrestre, concibiéndose y formándose por vía de generación en el vientre de la hembra y pariéndole a su tiempo animal formado, como una vaca su becerrito; lo segundo, se dice que pare ordinariamente dos y macho y hembra. Item, el sexu (sic) viril y femíneo en esta especie de animal pluvo a la Naturaleza distinguirle como en la naturaleza humana lo hizo. [94)])

That the manatee may be more sentient – judging from the cognitive awareness it shows in responding to the call and care of the cacique – or closely related to land animals like cows, does not of course necessarily mean that it is treated with any respect by Medel, who in other sections expresses no qualms about killing or eating just about any non-human animals, including dogs, and whose main implicit interest in animals is their anthropocentric use-value to humans, whether as a hide or a good meal.[78]

While the manatee in particular was a source of classificatory angst for later chroniclers of the Indies,[79] such was not the case for the author of one lengthy, systematic colonial natural history. For Oviedo, it is the iguana that serves this function for similar reasons. For Oviedo, the iguana[80] is a liminal animal that does not fit neatly into his categories. Indeed, a lot is at stake for Oviedo in this regard, insofar as it relates to human culture. This animal in particular gives him pause, not because he is disinterestedly classifying creatures and wants to get the classification right by some scientific standard, but, like Acosta, because of the religious implications of getting the classification wrong. In fact, the treatment of iguanas undergoes a subtle transition from "fish" to "animal," from Oviedo's earlier *Sumario* (1526) to his later *Historia* (1535). In the *Historia*, in talking about whether an iguana is a land animal or a sea creature, he says that "there are many men who do not know whether it is a fleshy animal or fish, or something in between, and they assign it to one group or the other (...) and even so they eat it in these parts, eating the animal on those days when meat is proscribed, such as Fridays and Saturdays and during Lent and other days it is forbidden by the Church" (muchos hombres hay que no se saben determinar si este animal es carne o pescado, o como cosa neutral, la atribuyen al uno y al otro género [...] y aun así usan de él en estas partes, comiendo este animal en los días que no son de carne, así como viernes e sábado, e la cuaresma, e otros días prohibidos por la Iglesia; 32).[81] He finds them very ugly and digresses about cooking them and how boiling them produces a lot of fat, "like other fish," including turtles! Oviedo has some anxiety over liking this flesh, not only because of the potential for not observing the proscription on *carnis*, but because the animal is so ugly,[82] which he remarks on repeatedly: "This ugly and hideous animal, just as I have said, makes for very good food, and better than the very good rabbits found near Spain's Jarama River" (Este animal, tal cual he dicho, e tan feo e espantable, es muy buen manjar, e mejor que los conejos de España muy buenos jarameños; 33). Such ugliness is helpful in his avoidance of developing any empathy for the iguana.

Oviedo, Acosta, and also Medel grappled with the established category of "fish" that they had received in light of the new species they encountered. While for Oviedo it is the iguana and the whale that prove difficult for him to assimilate easily to the concept "fish" (*pez*), for Acosta and Medel the uneasiness comes when they are each confronted with the manatee.[83] In a classificatory system that did not take morphology as an important factor, like Pliny's and later Gessner's, the manatee falls into the category of fish only because of the habitat in which it lives. Yet, this animal, which has "arms" and looks, acts, bleeds (and, apparently, tastes) like a cow, and lived in direct enough contact with the water's edge to encroach on the humans' *Umwelt*, seemed to confound the distinction, something that might have serious cultural implications. While for Columbus, in his diary, manatees were still creatures of myth – trying to incorporate them into his inherited classificatory system, he related them to the Odyssean sirens or mermaids – for later natural historians, they were shocking animals that led to challenging the categorization of the natural world.

As seen in the examples above, animals that spend some time out of the water's depths – such as whales, sea lions, iguanas, and manatees – living on the surface or edge, are treated more in depth, as the humans interact with them not just to kill them or be killed; the gratuitously anthropomorphized sucker fish to whom the Indians speak can also be understood in this paradigm, in which the sucker fish act like assistant fishermen, and hence, interact with humans through a mode more commonly associated with hunting dogs and falcons. Given their habitational parameter, these animals have more of a possibility of a relationship with humans – whether a jovial pet-like relationship, or an antagonistic violent one. Even from the latter, we learn something about the interiority of an animal.[84] With this liminal water habitat, it is easier for the anthropocentric human to see the animal's lifestyle, etc., than it would be for a human to appreciate an animal of the deep. When something lives only in the deep, the human appreciation of the animal is severely limited; thus, for instance, Medel suggests nothing about the interiority of the *raya* or *sábalos* (Medel 102–3).[85] In contrast, there are even actual fish beyond the exceptional marine animals and lizards already noted above – dorados (probably the ray-finned fish, *Coryphaena hippurus*, known as "dolphin fish" or "mahi-mahi") – that Medel describes with a little cognition, precisely because their habitational parameter overlaps with human sailors', as they leave, for a time, the water's depths: the dorados are "tenacious in the fight and struggle involved in following a ship for two or three days" (pertinaces en esta lucha y contienda que acontece seguir un navío dos o tres días; 103–4) as they anthropomorphically hope to eat the food that falls from the boat and the boat slime. The fish are seen following the boat for days, and considered "tenacious" – which seems like an anthropomorphic projection. Yet, ironically, they lose their lives, because they are caught by the fishermen, and they are tasty: "and it is a very wholesome and tasty fish" (y es muy sano y sabroso pescado; 104).

The fish of the waters' depths are removed from our minds; they live in ways we cannot fathom at an intuitive level. We have limited folk psychology to understand them, especially before the advent of technologies that have allowed greater research of underwater animals (video, scuba gear, submarines). Indeed, we do not appreciate animals abstractly; we need to sense them, primarily with our vision, but also with our other senses,[86] whether these be fish or other species including aquatic mammals that rarely surface where humans can see them. These examples from Medel, Acosta, and Oviedo flesh out our understanding of earlier views of aquatic animals and can help us better appreciate how *Umwelt*-centric and human-embodied our view of "fish" cognition and value has been for centuries, in order to better appreciate the cross-cultural tendencies to implicitly anthropectomize these creatures. We turn them into *automata* not because of their actual lack of emotion, intelligence, or conscious awareness. All of these capacities are merely assumed to be negligible because most of "fish" existence lies beyond the sensorial bounds of our anthropocentric world.

Habitational Parameter: "Birds" in the Wild

Don Quixote's description of beautiful "painted" creatures that adorn the trees and the skies and "entertain" human ears (see the beginning of this chapter) accords well with the typical treatment of birds in the wild by colonial natural historians. Birds are often treated anthropocentrically as aesthetic objects that delight the human senses of sight and hearing. For Oviedo, birds offer aural decorations that please the ears with their variety: "nightingales and other birds sing marvellously and very melodically and have many different kinds of song" (ruiseñores y otros pájaros cantan maravillosamente y con mucha melodía y diferentes maneras de cantar; *Sumario* 121). Visually, the flight of parrots is inspiring; while those in captivity seem "clumsy" (torpes), in the wild "they all are very great fliers" (son todos muy grandes voladores; 109). Medel and Acosta, similarly, each single out a few bird species for their striking visual beauty, focusing on their feathers with hyperbole.[87] On the whole, these birds are not minded; they are non-cognitive entities.[88]

While most birds are pleasing to the eyes and ears, some are also often considered for their anthropocentric utility, as food or as another product or by-product for human consumption. Eating them or killing them may also have the benefit of avoiding anthropocentric harm in instances in which the species in question is perceived to be harmful to human societies in some way. In this vein, Oviedo comments on the taste of turkey (*pavo*), implying that it ought to be eaten. Meanwhile, he notes that parrots (when left unmanaged) are a problem for the Indians' food security: "they are very harmful for grains and things that the Indians sow for their sustenance" (son muy dañosos para el pan y cosas que se siembran para mantenimiento de los indios; *Sumario* 110). The implication is that this un-minded bird should be killed. Other harmful "birds" are bats, which bite people and can make them very sick, even to the point of death.[89] In fact, Oviedo says he himself was bitten. These creatures are not understood nor grouped as mammals until centuries later; they are considered scary and ugly, but at least edible for Oviedo (*Sumario* 112–13). Relishing the thought of eating bat meat, Oviedo comments on how some people like the taste of "the fat ones" and explains how they can be skinned (113). He notes that unspecified "nocturnal birds" (pájaros nocturnos) wage war against the bats: "a sight that cannot be seen without inspiring pleasure in whoever watches them" (lo cual no se puede ver sin mucho placer de quien los mira; 111), signalling his own emotional response of pleasure to the bats' demise. *Alcatraces* (gannets) are another bird that Oviedo treats at length, and he mentions how their fat can be used for high-quality lamp oil (115).

For Acosta, some flying animals are so "ugly" (feos) and of "so little use" (no sirven de otro oficio; 205) that they are conceived of merely as fertilizer, or guano. Acosta thus sums up the anthropocentric view of all "birds" as utility for humans, relying on a version of the Great Chain of Being, in which bird cognition plays no role whatsoever: "Not only is the flesh of the birds for eating, their song for enjoyment, their feathers for ornament and finery, but their very guano is also beneficial for the earth, all of which is ordained by the Supreme Maker for the service of man so that man will remember to be grateful and loyal to Him who does all things for his benefit" (De manera que de los pájaros no sólo la carne para comer y el canto para deleite, y la pluma para ornato y gala, sino el mismo *estiércol* es también para el beneficio de la tierra, y todo ordenado del Sumo Hacedor para servicio del hombre, con que el hombre se acordase de ser grato y leal a quien con todo le hace bien; 4.37:205, emphasis added). While I am broadly considering bats as "birds" (they are of course mammals) in the wild, regarding their habitat, it is pointedly clear that their more specific habitat – a dark cave – itself is most likely partially responsible for the human bias towards them, and the intuitive folk psychological understanding of them as ugly, fearsome, and useless. Unlike other liminal mammalian species such as whales and manatees, the colonial authors do not seem aware that bats bear live young like other mammals, and in distinction to birds.

Very occasionally the minds of these wild animals are treated in these natural histories. In distinction to the treatment of certain mythological "fish" with advanced cognitive abilities (see pp. 177–9), these birds are not supernatural, but are understood with folk animal psychology. For instance, Oviedo is fascinated by how the "crazy bird" (pájaro loco) builds its nest, suggesting that its name is ironic and indicates that it is not at all crazy: "truly no bird that I have seen in these parts is wiser and more astute nor has better natural instincts for raising its young free of danger" (en la verdad ninguna ave de las que en aquellas partes yo he visto muestra ser más sabia y astuta ni del tal distinto natural para criar sus hijos sin peligro; *Sumario* 119). Indeed, they build their nests in trees that are far apart from others "so that" monkeys will not be able to jump to their nest from another tree, as is their wont (125).[90]

Furthermore, he portrays the "crazy bird" as a wise animal, demonstrating future planning against a raid on the nest should the monkeys make it there:

> [I]n the event that monkeys climb the trees where those nests are, they have another clever trick they employ so that they do not eat their young. Those branches and straw or things with which they make these nests are very rough and thorny such that a monkey cannot touch them without hurting itself. And they are so tightly woven and strong that no man would know how to make them that way. And if the monkey wants to stick his hand through the hole of the aforesaid nest to take the eggs or young of this bird, he cannot reach them nor get to the bottom because as I have said they are longer than three or four hand spans and the arm of a monkey cannot reach the bottom of the nest.
>
> ([E]n caso que los gatos suban a los árboles donde aquestos nidos están, no les coman los hijos, tienen otra astucia grande, y es que aquellas ramas y pujas o cosas de que hacen estos nidos son muy ásperas y espinosas, y no las puede tomar el gato en las manos sin se latimar; y están tan entretejidos y fuertes, que ningún hombre lo sabría hacer de aquella manera; y si el gato quiere meter la mano por el agujero del dicho nido para sacar los huevos o los hijos pequeños de estas aves, no los puede alcanzar ni llegar al cabo, porque como es dicho, son luengos más de tres palmos o cuatro, y no puede el brazo del gato alcanzar al suelo del nido. [*Sumario* 120])

Thus, they demonstrate the cognitive ability known as "mental time travel," as they try to prevent raids by the monkeys.[91] Beyond that, like the anteater – a land animal that Oviedo is fascinated with – the crazy bird even has a technical superiority to humans, who could not achieve such results (ningún hombre, 120]. They are also socially intelligent and build their nests near each other such that they may "watch over" the nests of others (hagan la vela por todos; 120) and then sound the alarm (dan grandes gritos; 120) if they see monkeys, in what sounds like praise of their military-style defence strategy. Whereas all of these claims may sound hyperbolic, scores of recent studies in cognitive ethology suggest that these types of abilities, including strong social intelligence and mental time travel, are in fact qualities of many species of birds, especially corvids, jays, and parrots.[92]

Another species of bird, the goldfinch (*pintadillo*), also evinces nest-building planning and prowess. They build their nests in such a way that the monkeys will not attack. Here it seems that the birds, who themselves feel fear, use Theory of Mind on another species, intuiting that monkeys will fear falling in the water. As such, they build their nests on small branches over bodies of water: "for fear of the monkeys, these little birds always nest over the banks of the river or the seashore where the branches of the trees on which the nests are built bend down to the water if even a light weight is placed upon the aforesaid branches. And they make the aforesaid nests almost upon the tips of the aforesaid branches, and when the monkey goes along the branch it bends down and hangs into the water. And *the monkey will turn back out of fear* and disregard the nest for fear of falling" (estos pajaricos, de temor de los gatos [monkeys], siempre crían sobre las riberas de los ríos o de la mar, donde las ramas de los árboles alcancen con los nidos al agua con poco peso que encima de ellas se cargue, y hacen los dichos nidos casi en las puntas de las dichas ramas, y cuando el gato va por la rama adelante ella se abaja y pende al agua, y *el gato, de temor, se torna* y no cura de los nidos, por temor de caer; *Sumario* 120–1, emphasis added).

Also with respect to cognitive faculties, the "stupid bird" (pájaro bobo) stands out. This time the animal species name is not ironic and refers to apparent cognitive deficits: "These birds are so stupid and linger so long [on the masts] that they are often captured by hand with a lasso on the tip of a dart or other short shaft" (son tan bobas y esperan tanto, que las toman muchas veces a mano, con un lazo en la punta de un dardo u otra asta corta; *Historia* 69). It is interesting to note that the birds that are singled out for cognitive comment – *pájaro loco* and *pintadillo* on the one hand, *pájaro bobo* on the other – are judged smart or stupid on the grounds of their defence strategy, like human militias. Thus, it makes sense given Oviedo's martial world view (and with his inseparable human cognitive embodiment) that he should praise the stronger one in battle, that is, the one who survives and is not eaten. Accordingly, this explains why, of the three species, Oviedo only comments on the meat of the *pájaro bobo*: he doesn't think they taste particularly good, but when having little else to eat, the sailors will debone them and roast or stew them. As good soldiers, the other species are not caught or eaten.

In sum, very few birds are treated cognitively, and those that are singled out, if positive, are considered non-edible birds. Rather, most birds are aesthetic objects (visually or aurally) and/or have another use value for humans: if not food, then lamp oil, valuable feathers, or fertilizer. Others are just useless, ugly, or bad.

Habitational Parameter: Sharing the Hearth

In his *Historia de las Indias,* Bartolomé de las Casas was mostly concerned about the well-being of the indigenous peoples affected by the conquest. Yet he famously described certain non-human animals in this context, which sheds light on his early modern implicit views of animal cognition. In several sections, de las Casas mentions dogs as the faithful companions of the brutal, invading Spaniards. He laments that the Spaniards called the indigenous peoples "dogs," only to quip with morbid irony that they treated their dogs far better than they treated these people.[93] If only they treated them like dogs! In fact, he explains, they treated them more "like cats," animals that were typically abused in Europe at the time.[94]

Indeed, a reading of natural histories from the period supports de las Casas's pronouncement on the positive view and good treatment of dogs. Both among Europeans and among the indigenous peoples, domesticated canines held a privileged status in the colonial animal "kingdom," one to which the minding of these animals through human attentiveness to cognitive factors plays a decisive role. The particular abilities of dogs – as understood through anthropomorphizing folk animal psychology – are anthropocentrically interesting and sometimes useful. It is important, as will be shown, that their mode of interaction and their habitational parameters allow for the close fraternization with people.

As historian Abel Alves discusses in *The Animals of Spain,* there were two canines whom the conquistadors treated above all others, indeed, like people. First, there is the conquistador dog Becerillo, who could "distinguish friendly indigenous from enemies as if he were a person" (cognoscía los indios de guerra y los que no eran como si fuera una persona) and who sought aid "as if he had reason" (como si de razón tuviera; *Historia* 2.389, qtd. in Alves, *Animals* 155–6). Both counterfactuals (*as if he were a person, as if he had reason*) refer to human-like cognition that, for the writer, is remarkable and even uncanny. Second, Becerillo's son, Leoncillo, was also incredible: he not only reasoned but also exhibited what seemed like human emotions. As Alves writes, "[Leoncillo] is described in Spanish documents as a remarkable dog, who, in his life, exhibited great sorrow at human tragedy" (156). According to de las Casas, the Spaniards even learned some moral lessons from this dog, decreasing their barbarism when learning from Becerillo that an innocent old Indian woman should not be killed, in a passage that highlights the importance of olfaction in representing dog embodiment. He tells the anecdote about an old indigenous woman whom the Spanish soldiers ordered Becerrillo to attack in order to pass the time; but when she spoke to the canine in "her tongue" (su lengua), he listened, and instead of biting her, he smelled her and then marked her with his urine, interesting details that signal de las Casas's understanding of the dog sensorium. The dog becomes for the Dominican friar a moral example to the Spaniards.[95] However, this case is exceptional, and more typically dogs are instruments of terror in de las Casas's *Historia*. For instance, they spare no human lives when hunting down the peaceful native peoples of Jamaica, treating them as if they were wild brutes, with the use of fierce dogs. Terrified by the conquistadors' dogs, the people ran into their burning homes rather than be eaten alive.[96]

Having a Friend for Dinner

As should be clear from the preceding sections, the author of the *Sumario* and the *Historia general y natural* is only infrequently explicit about the cognition of non-human animals, and as would be expected for the type of writing and the historical period in which it was written, he rarely expresses moral cares for them. An important exception to this lack of moral concern arises when Oviedo talks about the *xulo*, a small, autochthonous dog found on La Hispaniola. In line with his description of other New World species – manatee, turkey, etc. – Oviedo describes the taste of *xulo* flesh. As Asúa and French correctly assert about New World animal descriptions generally, "native animals were, first and foremost, food. And much of the talk about animals in the early chronicles is, in the end, talk about food, hunting and cooking" (8). While this is true, Oviedo treats some food talk with noticeable reticence, suggesting a belief that he is committing a moral transgression. He couches his description of *xulo* flesh with reference to how Spaniards were forced to eat *xulo* on a previous expedition when they ran out of other food, an anecdote that leads him to muse on how, more recently, he and other Spaniards were served dog meat. How does dog taste? Not at all bad! In fact, Oviedo liked the flavour, at least for as long as he didn't know what it was: "But as food it is not to be turned down among those who customarily eat it (...) and I have eaten some of them and it is very good fare. And, truthfully, I had three or four bites of the one I ate, not thinking it was dog" ([P]ero manjar es para no desecharle los que le tienen en costumbre [...)] y he comido de algunos dellos y es muy buen manjar. Y a la verdad, de aquel que yo comí, fueron dos o tres bocados, e no pensando que era perro; *Historia* 30).[284] Despite the appeal to his taste buds, Oviedo is quite disgusted with himself for having eaten dog flesh: "Truthfully it pained me to have eaten it, and I did not eat more" (En la verdad, a mí me pesó de haberlo comido, e no comí más; 30). So, he can't deny the fact that he ate it, but he wouldn't do it again. While the rationale for this remorse is not explicit, not only did he feel bad about eating *xulo*, but he emphasizes how he stopped as soon as he found out what it was that he was eating (no comí más). Furthermore, he reflects philosophically on how that which has been done cannot be undone, thus he cannot undo having eaten *xulo*. The question persists: why would a man with no personal relationship with these particular animals care if he has been a part of their death and ingestion? I would argue that the typical mode of interaction between humans and dogs makes this thinking imperative for Oviedo. As countless authors have observed since Antiquity, the dog is "man's best friend." And as animal rights advocate Jeffrey Moussaieff Masson has explained, we do not eat our friends (219).[97] This idea helps interpret Oviedo's apparent feelings of guilt towards unknown conspecifics of animals that were considered friends, feelings that are indirectly observed in Oviedo's somewhat lengthy circumlocutions and rationalizations about having tried dog flesh. Juxtaposed with this reticence, he notes that the indigenous eat *xulo* at celebrations, and that the most important person always gets the head: "they eat these dogs as the most precious and best fare of all, and no one eats the head if he is not *calachuni* or *teite*" (comen estos perros por el más prescioso e mejor manjar de todos, e ninguno come la cabeza si no es calachuni o teite; 30).[98] His signalling of their desire to consume dog flesh and their indifference to its disgust-evoking elements point to their radical difference from Europeans, which rationalizes Oviedo's moral indifference to the indigenous people's plight, and rhetorically helps in his depiction of them as subhuman, at least in the earlier *Sumario*.[99]

Dogs in the House

Beyond his discussion of the *xulo*, Oviedo considers another species of small dog from Tierra Firme called *gozque*, and the way in which the indigenous keep them in their homes impresses him.[100] Given these habitational parameters and this mode of interaction, the dogs are able to display behaviour for their human masters indicative of a rich cognitive life. This includes their ability to feel the highest emotion of all: love (*amor*). As Oviedo explains, "they show love for those who feed them by wagging their tails and leaping for joy, showing their wish to please those who feed them and whom they regard as their master" (muestran amor a los que les dan de comer, en el halagar con la cola y saltar regocijados, mostrando querer complacer a quien les da de comer y tienen por señor; *Sumario* 107). His warm and fuzzy descriptions, informed by his animal folk psychology, sound a lot like those any contemporary dog-lover would recognize. Yet, the passage contains internal tensions. On the one hand, the dog owners seem to love and take good care of these animals; on the other, however, they seem to indiscriminately harm or kill them without provocation, at least hypothetically ("aunque los maten"):

> In Tierra Firme, the arrow-shooting Carib Indians possess little toy dogs that they keep at home and they have all the colours of fur that dogs have in Spain. Some are shaggy and some silky-furred and they are mute, for they never bark nor yelp nor howl, nor do they cry out or moan although they are being beaten to death. They resemble little wolves but they are not, they are genuine dogs. And I have seen them killed without their protesting nor moaning, and I have seen them in Darien, brought from the coast of Cartagena, from Carib lands, as a trade item for which fishhooks are exchanged, and they never bark nor do anything aside from eat and drink. They are far more timid than ours, except with those in the home where they live.
>
> (En Tierra-Firme, en poder de los indios caribes flecheros, hay unos perrillos pequeños, gozques, que tienen en casa, de todas las colores de pelo que en España los hay; algunos bedijudos y algunos rasos, y son mudos, porque nunca jamás ladran ni gañen, ni aúllan, ni hacen señal de gritar o gemir aunque los maten a golpes, y tienen mucho aire de lobillos, pero no lo son, sino perros naturales. E yo los he visto matar, y no quejarse ni gemir, y los he visto en el Darien, traídos de la costa de Cartagena, de tierra de caribes, por rescates, dando algún anzuelo en trueco de ellos, y jamás ladran ni hacen cosa alguna, más que comer y beber, y son harto más esquivos que los nuestros, excepto con los de la casa donde están. [106–7])

Interestingly, these dogs are mute. They make no sound "even when they are being harmed seriously," which is a point that seems to fascinate Oviedo. They don't bark, whine, or growl despite aggression towards them. But why all the violence in this paragraph about these loving creatures?

Historian Marcy Norton proposes that some indigenous peoples had a more open concept of mode of interaction with animals than did Europeans. In this vein, she has pointed out clearly the example that dogs could become domesticated animals for companionship, but also, under some conditions, be used as a food source. Norton likens this flexible mode of interaction to the way in which human captives could become slave labourers, but also, under certain circumstances, some would wind up as adoptive family members raised as sisters and brothers:

> If "hunting" and "herding" can be fruitfully understood as primordial structures that organized society and ecology in Europe and became part of the colonial apparatus, then "adopting" was a primordial structure for much of human society and ecology in the Americas. This refers to pan-American practices of capturing and often taming wildlife for purposes ranging from providing food to companionship, a correlate of the Amerindian practice of destining some prisoners of war for death (and in some areas ritual consumption) and others for adoptive kinship. (Norton, "The Chicken or the *Iegue*" 22)

However, I find that the dog example is quite exceptional, and in fact dissimilar from the latter one involving human captives. Indeed, the *xulo* dogs were one and the same animals: one moment "pets," the next moment on a platter. Yet in the other case that Norton mentions, the humans diverged in their mode of interaction at the moment in which they were captured (i.e., slaves were not taken and made into family members years after they had already been treated by the same family as slaves or vice versa). Once they belonged to a family as kin, they were kin. With the notion of the more liberal concept resting on one sole non-human animal case, it is worth challenging the original idea that the indigenous "mode of interaction" concept is truly more flexible. Counter-examples would include cases in which Europeans were flexible. And indeed, Europeans sometimes held multiple modes of interaction with the same species of animal too (a horse may have been a workhorse, or one used in the hunt or in war). This would include anecdotes provided by Oviedo himself, in which he explains how Spaniards occasionally had to eat their own dogs because they otherwise would have starved to death. Admittedly, that extreme case might seem dissimilar in some respects, for in the case of the *xulo* dogs, the indigenous peoples are planning ahead for just such an occurrence of possible starvation; in contrast, the Spaniards make use of the dogs as flesh as a last resort.

Reminiscent of what Oviedo wrote about the "gozques" who live in houses, the *alcos* are a species of dogs that wag their tails, an action that is anthropomorphized to mean they are showing love. The indigenous peoples on La Hispaniola keep the *alcos* as domesticated animals, yet here the violence against the animals is absent. Acosta describes mutually loving human-animal relationships, and of humans who suffer for the sake of the dog, because they love the friendship and company offered by these non-human animals: "They are such *friends* of these little dogs that they will take of their own food and give it to them, and when they travel they carry them on their backs or upon their breasts. And if they are ill, the little dog must be there with them for no other purpose than their good *friendship and company*" (y son tan *amigos* destos perrillos, que se quitaran el comer por dárselo; y cuando van camino, los llevan consigo a cuestas o en el seno y si están malos, el perrito ha de estar allí con ellos, sin servirse dellos para cosa, sino sólo para buena *amistad y compañía*; 199, emphasis added). Note that not only are these dogs *not* food, but the first example that Acosta gives of human friendship towards them is that people give the dogs their human food. He seems somewhat surprised by this excellent humane treatment of animals, in which the animals are treated like babies and carried around "upon their breasts." Unlike the feelings that the Spaniards felt for Becerrillo and Leonillo, these *alco* dogs, had little other purpose, that is, the feelings towards them are not due to some anthropocentrically instrumental purpose; instead, they were, like pets, welcomed into the homes and treated like family.[101] Although no explicit cognitive details are provided about these animals, indirectly it can be inferred that they were receptive of the love they received and that they enjoyed being carried around like babies (the modern concept of "lapdog" comes to mind). This early idea of "pet" challenges the notion that the English invented the pet in the nineteenth century. Certainly there were earlier and widespread relationships in America and Europe of humans interacting with animals for no anthropocentric, material, instrumental purpose, both here among the indigenous peoples of La Hispaniola, as well as what can be gleaned from the isolated cases noted in chapter 1 on medieval Spain.

Some implicit cognitive features of dogs come out in these writings through contrasts and comparisons to other animals and humans. For instance, in his section on skunks (*zorrilla*) in the *Historia*, Oviedo writes about the effect of the animal's protective stench to ward off both dogs and humans. The reactions of both species are indeed quite similar, indicating some human-like cognition on the part of the dogs: "it exudes a stench so great and of such a kind that the dog instantly moves away from it and is left stunned, repulsed, frightened, and miserable looking at it; and he rolls about many times to rid himself of that pestilent stench that has adhered to him, and goes to the water if it is nearby to wash himself, and goes to extremes stretching and thrashing about frequently all day and night for two or even three days" (da de sí aquel hedor tan grande, y de tal manera, que el perro en el instante se aparta dél y queda como atónito, aborrescido y espantado y malcontento mirándole; y revuélcase muchas veces, por desechar auqel pestilente hedor que se le ha pegado, e váse al agua a lavar, si la hay por allí, y hace extremos tendiéndose y echándose muy a menudo todo el día y la noche e aun dos o tres días; 430). The dogs, it would seem, understand concept formation: they understand the cause and effect of the spray on them, as well as the cause-and-effect relationship required to know that water might be an agent that could potentially wash off a bad odour. Similarly, humans will spit and sneeze to get the stench out of their nose, and they will wash regularly for days: "spitting and sneezing many times, without expelling that stench from the nostrils with extreme disgust and such displeasure that for an entire day or even two or three they cannot forget it nor rid themselves of it, nor does anything they eat taste good although they wash and take smoke baths frequently" (escupir y estornudar muchas veces, y no se quitar de las narices aquel hedor con extremado asco y tal descontentamiento, que alquel día ni otros dos e tres no lo pueden olvidar ni desechar, ni sabe bien cosa alguna que comen, anque se laven e sahumen a menudo; 430).[102] For comparison, another animal that has a close mode of interaction with humans, the horse, seems just to take it: horses apparently just lose their appetite until the skunk smell goes away on its own; that is, they do not actively try to do anything to have the smell subside sooner. In this way, Oviedo's horses do not display any relevant cognitive faculties: "the horse forsakes eating until it has lost that disgust and repugnance" (el caballo aborresce el comer hasta que ha perdido aquel asco e mal hastío; 430). In contrast, Oviedo's dogs, whether autochthonous or imported, are highly intelligent creatures with rich emotional lives who deserve the special status they have.

Exotic Animals in Menageries and Palaces

Collected animals are often depicted in artistic representations of the sixteenth and seventeenth centuries. Among the most famous of these is the pentaptych known as "Allegory of the Senses" (1617–18) by Jan Brueghel the Elder and Peter Paul Rubens. In particular, their "Allegory of Sight" includes several live animals – lapdogs, a parrot, and a small monkey – and it illustrates the collecting of animals in Europe within a wider context of collecting paintings, sculptures, and scientific devices like the telescope (see fig. 21). While it is difficult to gauge the minding of the animals from these idealized depictions, the paintings speak of palace life with animals that add variety, colour, and exoticism, while praising what art historians Ariane Van Suchtelen and Anne T. Woollett have called "the princely culture of collecting," demonstrating the owner's importance and standing as collector.[103]

Since antiquity, prized gifts of exotic animals fed the desires of the most powerful nobles of Europe to boast amazing collections of living curiosities. In the Renaissance, provided they survived the long and difficult voyage back to Europe, animals from the Americas would count among the most prized of all, becoming what Asúa and French have called an "emblem of *dominium*" (201).[104] As historian Carlos Gómez-Centurión details, lions, jaguars, rhinoceroses, and other rare, exotic, and often ferocious creatures from Africa, Asia, and the Americas, were a symbol of royal magnificence, and collecting them was a practice continued into the modern era, for which important monarchs set aside parts of their palaces and estates. In Spain, the most important of these were in Toledo, Madrid, and Aranjuez. Outside of Europe, in Asia and in America, animals were also kept under similar conditions and for similar reasons, by other rulers. In pre-Columbian Mexico, menagerie collecting was practised most notably by Moctezuma II. As Asúa and French note on the palaces of Tenochtitlan, "Cortes' description in his Letters is famous for the palaces of Montezuma, which had been ornamented with magnificent gardens and ten pools with all kinds of waterfowl, salt water pools for the sea birds and freshwater pools for the river birds. Three hundred men were in charge of their feeding ... and there were also 'veterinarians' who attended the sick birds" (27). The live beings were housed in three sections: birds; wild terrestrial animals

Figure 21 Jan Brueghel the Elder and Peter Paul Rubens's *Allegory of Sight.* Copyright Museo Nacional del Prado / Art Resource, NY.

such as wolves and large felines; and a gruesome third section that held human captives with "physical handicaps" that Cortés referred to as "monstrosities" (28). Outside there were pools with aquatic birds, and presumably fish. This intercultural similarity – that rulers on multiple continents would collect exotic animals – suggests a cognitively embodied desire to collect and dominate other creatures, or at the very least, a human tendency to be fascinated by the rare and exotic. The menagerie or *casa de fieras*, as it was commonly known,[105] like its public offshoot, the modern zoo, cared for and displayed animals, allowing sightings and encounters for humans with animals that were either exotic, or rare, or far too dangerous with which to interact in the wild. Once the animal changes habitat in this way, I argue, the same animal's cognitive faculties may be conceived of and described differently.

The conceptualization of an animal from the wild may undergo significant change once it is housed in a menagerie. Why is it that the animal is generally portrayed as more sentient? I surmise that since the creature is exotic, it attracts attention. Once out of its natural habitat and moved into the new one, this change offers humans the opportunity not only to observe but also possibly to interact with the animal in a new way. Thus is borne the space to reflect on the behaviour and infer the animal's cognition more easily. Fed by humans, housed in different locales, and caged, tied, or otherwise held captive, the habitational parameters of these formerly wild animals have been transformed. So, too, with this new habitat, humans create a novel affordance, so to speak, potentially changing the mode of interaction to observer-observed (and concomitantly away from hunting and towards feeding and caring for). What effect do such changes have on the minding of these animals? Looking at a few cases of such captured animals reveals that these creatures are considered among the most sentient, even when the same species in the wild was not![106] Indeed, Oviedo's most sentient non-human animal of all is the captive jaguar. Both the habitational parameter of the animal and the mode of interaction between animal and human have changed significantly from the opening passages on animals whereby the jaguar was merely "furious" and "cowardly" (see the above section on terrestrial animals in the wild).

As one of the earliest and most extensive natural historical narratives of the Indies, Oviedo's is useful for assessing the effect of a change in habitational parameter on animal mindedness (while keeping the species constant). After having described how they are hunted in the wild, and how they are a great danger to the native population whom they frequently kill, Oviedo tells a lengthy and colourful vignette about a captive jaguar.[107] This animal had been given as a gift to Charles V around 1522 and was cared for by a Lombardian big cat tamer who had experience with African lions.[108]

From the start of this narrative, Oviedo is sceptical of the new human-animal relationship, inaugurated by the jaguar's change of habitat from jungle to menagerie, in which the animal becomes one of the King's curiosities. He refers to the danger of the powerful beast, which he suggests is inappropriately handled. To emphasize his point rhetorically, Oviedo contrasts the strength, ferocity, and malice of the jaguar with the weakness of the cord with which the animal is being held: "each day he would become stronger and fiercer, doubling in malice (...) Despite all of this ... this hunter or teacher [i.e., the tamer]... had already taken him out of the cage and had him very domesticated, tied with a very thin cord" (cada dia habia de ser mas recio e fiero e doblarsele la malicia [...] Con todo ... este cazador o maestro ... le habia ya sacado de la jaola e le tenia muy domestico, atado con muy delgada cuerda; *Historia* 41). The trainer acts as if the jaguar were benevolent, but Oviedo sees malice in the creature. He admits his own terror at the thought of this (formerly) wild animal on display, in which we can glimpse some of Oviedo's minding of the animal, which differs from the trainer's anthropomorphic minding (according to Oviedo's view). For one, the trainer seems to believe in the goodness and affection of the jaguar; in contrast, Oviedo understands the jaguar as having what today could be called Machiavellian Intelligence,[109] tricking the tamer about his own violent intentions and fooling the tamer into complacency. This poor comprehension of the real cognitive features explains why the Lombardian would restrain a dangerous beast merely with a "thin cord."

From Oviedo's perspective, the tamer's problem stems from engaging in gratuitous anthropomorphism, whereby he confounds the trainer-animal relationship by confusing it with the father-son familial bond. He refers to the non-human animal as his "son" (mi fillolo; 41), while claiming that their relationship amounts to something as complex as what is entailed in the concept of friendship (*amicitia*). Ironically, however, Oviedo himself engages in anthropomorphism that is similarly gratuitous. Indeed, in his estimation, the non-human animal is very deliberately and actively tricking the Italian into a state of false security. The jaguar is "mumbling under his breath" (murmuraba entre dientes; 42). While Oviedo's minding demonstrates some cognitive capacities that tigers most likely have (intentional agency, emotions, memory), it is not within the bounds of credulity to imagine that the animal is capable not only of human speech, but of dissimulating his speech and intentions (mumbling under his breath). At stake for Oviedo, then, is not that the Italian engages in gratuitous anthropomorphism per se, but that the trainer's very own Theory of Mind is faulty in not recognizing the jaguar's true self, as an antagonist with Machiavellian Intelligence. The trainer's faulty Theory of Mind leads him to believe that the animal is "grateful" ("you think that he is grateful for what you teach him" [vos pensáis quél agradece lo que le enseñáis; 42]), in which he attributes to the mind a gratuitously anthropomorphic emotion. In contrast, Oviedo warns that the animal is just waiting for his chance: "trusting in his friendship, you may draw near to scratch him as you do now and he will tear you apart" (confiado vos de su amistad, os lleguéis a rascarle como agora lo hacéis, y él os haga pedazos; Oviedo, *Historia* 42), in which he ironically contrasts the trainer's gentle "scratching" of the animal (*rascar*) in the present, with the jaguar's ferocious "tearing apart" of the trainer in the future, a carefully crafted rhetorical contrast reminiscent of the inappropriate thin leash/dangerous animal image he created earlier. What the tamer has done, for Oviedo, is unnatural. The very idea of changing the habitat and altering the mode of interaction is wrong. It would seem that a wild beast cannot be made a tame one, for his essential nature is to devour, and to act cruelly. For Oviedo, then, the human-animal mode of interaction, at least for certain wild species, ought never to change: "the truth is that *these animals are not meant to live among people,* given that they are ferocious and by their nature indomitable" (48) (en la verdad *estos animales no son para entre gentes,* segund son feroces e indómitos a natura; 42).[110] In these cases, nature is immutable.

Oviedo quips cleverly that tamers of such "ferocious" animals are themselves beasts, since by their actions and beliefs they betray their own lack of reason. His whole vignette stands out as quite literary, rhetorically designed to make himself, the narrator, look wise. In particular, only Oviedo could predict that the relationship between tamer and jaguar would end in a short time with the violent death of one of them. His prediction is borne out in little more than a week, we learn, when the jaguar dies under suspicious circumstances, about which Oviedo implies that the trainer has killed the animal after a "dispute" about the training regimen. The Lombardian, whom Oviedo "quotes" in his own tongue – a detail that adds additional "literary" flair and colour through an attempt to create verisimilitude, while displaying Oviedo's linguistic superiority for knowing both Spanish and Italian – had thought the jaguar was "my little child and an angel and I will make him work miracles" (mi fillolo, e un anzolo e lo ferró far miracule; 41). However, for Oviedo, there are no miracles of this sort, no angels among the beasts of nature. While they posses advanced cognitive features including Theory of Mind and Machiavellian Intelligence, their cognition is geared towards cruelty and devouring.[111] His use of the term "indomable" (literally untameable) for the jaguar's "nature" make the trainer's professional *raison d'être* both illogical and untenable.

And yet, large felines continued to be prized possessions among monarchs, and their new mode of interaction was not only one of menagerie inhabitant. At least as far as intentions, some big cats, and this jaguar in particular, were also supposed to be hunting companions. Collecting animals and having a group of hunting animals were not mutually exclusive activities. Indeed, as the tamer explains, his long-term plans included travelling to the Indies to capture and return to Spain with "five or six of these smaller ones" (cinque o sei de quisti piu picolini; *Historia* 41–2) so that his king would have a hunting team worthy of an emperor.[112]

As Oviedo predicted, the relationship between the trainer and the jaguar came to an abrupt end. For this animal, there was a forced change of habitat but no permanent change in mode of interaction, as he was killed by a person as if he had been hunted in the wild. In contrast, another anecdote told by Argote de Molina demonstrates better the fluidity between certain habitational parameters and modes of interaction, and concomitantly, between modes of minding the same animal, in different contexts. To wit, back in Spain, an African lion that was on exhibit as an exotic animal at court escaped and found herself "in the country near the road from Alcala" (al campo camino de Alcala), "half a league from Madrid" (media legua de Madrid; fol. 11r). While she would have been fed, kept safe, and proudly prized at court, once she finds herself outside the palace confines, she returns to being a "wild animal," and as such, she is hunted as one; cognitively, she is merely ferocious: "as the lionness had bled out from the sword wound, losing much of her fury, she ended up surrendering to the greyhounds" (como la Leona estuuiesse dessangrada de la herida de la Espada: perdida mucha de su furia, se acabo de rendir a los Lebreles; fol. 11r). Soon, the lioness is cornered, stabbed by a servant in the snout, and then set upon by a hunting dog. Interestingly, the detail of the hunting dog's name, Leonel, is given, which distinguishes the dog in his hunter-to-hunting companion relationship from the lion in her hunter-to-hunted one. Leonel almost kills the nameless lion, but he dies in the attempt, and the men go in for the kill and stab her to death (fol. 11r). Although once a prized and pampered possession in the royal menagerie, the wild lion dies an anonymous death that fails to mark any cognitive feature other than ferocity.

In addition to such dangerous animals, as mentioned earlier in another context, monkeys and parrots were among the most common animals brought back to Europe, and Oviedo expounds on the cognitive faculties of these creatures in captivity. Oviedo's section on "papagayos" is extensive, and he reports that among the many exotic items he brought back to his prince were many parrots. Commenting on their cognitive profile, he notes that the parrots "spoke very well" (hablaban muy bien; *Sumario* 109), highlighting their imitative capacity. Interestingly, Oviedo also draws explicit attention to their change in habitat, from wild jungle to captive in the hearth, and he makes the point that that such a change affects the appearance of their cognition and behaviour. Now, here (*acá*), they "speak very well," but in the wild what was important about their behaviour was that they flew elegantly (and no longer do), and paired in couples: "These parrots, although they seem very clumsy here, are great fliers and always go about by two and two, in pairs, male and female" (Estos papagayos, aunque acá parecen torpes, son todos muy grandes voladores, y siempre andan de dos en dos, pareados, macho y hembra; 109). As reviewed in an earlier section on birds in the wild, current comparative psychological research on certain bird species indicates that indeed they are highly cognitive animals and that their speech is not merely "parroting" but actually conveying ideas to each other (and in some instances, in captivity, to humans). Again it is the change in habitational parameters that leads to a different mode of interaction, which then leads to the minding of these animals as more cognitively interesting than if they had been left in the wild.

Bernardino de Sahagún: A Reflection on Non-European Sources and Human Embodiment

For a somewhat different take on animals from the Indies, I turn briefly to Bernardino de Sahagún's *Historia general de las cosas de la Nueva España*. The penultimate book of Sahagún's twelve-volume *Historia* (the most acclaimed version of which is known as the *Florentine Codex*)[113] is devoted to animals, plants, and rocks and minerals. As a figure whose work would become known as a precursor to anthropological methods, Sahagún relied heavily on Nahua informants who responded to questionnaires about the various species he mentions. Despite the radically different underlying assumptions about the nature of the universe – a Christian theological view in Oviedo and Acosta versus the Nahua cosmology in Sahagún – many of the same kinds of animal minding occur, pointing to some universal cognitive qualities in humans as they anthropomorphize and anthropectomize other creatures in the natural world, based on habitat and mode of interaction.

Part of these similarities may of course be due to Sahagún's world view, which permeates at least the organizing principles. As modern editor Manuel Barbero Richart notes, although informed by Nahua knowledge, and written bilingually in Spanish and Nahuatl, the overarching structure of the *Historia* is hierarchical, and follows a classical European paradigm in the manner of Aristotle or Pliny, which is not surprising given his Franciscan learning. Compared to Pliny or Oviedo, the portion of his work devoted to natural history is brief, as Sahagún's comprises only Book 11, where he discusses "The properties of animals, birds, fish, trees, herbs, flowers, metals and stones, and colours" (De las propiedades de los animales, aves, peces, árboles, hierbas, flores, metales y piedras, y de los colores; 219), starting from most important, to least in Sahagún's world view. Although the text is full of Nahua practical and cosmological knowledge gathered with the help of informants, some scholars have considered there to be an underlying Western way of structuring this culturally hybrid history in the manner of the *Scala Naturae*, in that the most important items come first: divine issues, then human concerns, followed by animals, plants, and finally rocks. Among the animals, these are structured hierarchically too, with land animals coming before "birds," which come before "fish." For the most part, and in line with the European appraisals of sentience discussed earlier, the salient cognitive elements of the animals follow this pattern: land animals are presented as among the most sentient, intelligent, or emotional, while the avian and fish species are mostly non-sentient. While I cannot treat Nahua cosmology in depth for reasons of focus and space, I point to the following examples of animal minding in Sahagún's *Historia* as further evidence of the human minding of animals based not on their intrinsic cognitive capacities but on their mode of interaction as it interplays with their habitat.

Among the most sentient jungle animals is the jaguar, which, like Oviedo, Sahagún calls "tigre." Once again, the jaguar is described here in gratuitously anthropomorphic terms as "noble," "a prince and lord of other animals" (noble y dizen es príncipe y señor de los otros animales; 221). Thus, in Sahagún, as in Oviedo's history, the jaguar takes the role that the lion had in Old World histories in imitation of Pliny. In fact, Sahagún's text is even closer to Pliny's for holding on to the gratuitously anthropomorphizing metaphor of royalty. The jaguar takes care of itself, in a human-like manner, one sign of which is bathing. Sahagún is also impressed by the feline's great eyesight – superior to that of humans – which allows it to see in the dark and to notice minuscule things. In a description that may owe something to Oviedo's vignette of the monkey (see above), the jaguar catches the arrows of hunters and breaks them with his mouth and paw. While Sahagún is rarely explicit about cognitive faculties, his anthropomorphic descriptions show a highly intelligent animal that demonstrates intentional agency, and appears to use Theory of Mind to prevent hunters from reusing their arrows. For Sahagún, the jaguar holds concepts, is self-conscious and aware of humans, indeed thinking about what they are thinking. To wit, the animal hiccups, with a deviant Machiavellian Intelligence-inspired plan: "in order to bring fear and terror, and to make the hunter falter" (a propósito de ponerle temor y miedo y desmayarle el corazón; 222), that is, with self-conscious awareness and knowledge of how to induce fear in other species.

Another animal with gratuitously anthropomorphized intelligence is the coyote (*coyotl*), which is "sagacious" (sagaz) and "diabolical" (diabólico; 225). For Sahagún, the coyote has an incredible memory as well as a drive to wreak vengeance, and will do so on any hunter who takes away what the coyote is trying to hunt. In this vein, Sahagún tells a long anecdote in which a man comes across a coyote and a snake, locked in a deadly hold, and the man chooses to help the coyote. The legendary vengeance is turned around, and this animal is forever grateful to the man, offering him two roosters, using a head gesture to communicate with the man that he should take the offering; the animal then follows the man home, and later continues to bring him offerings. While the similarity to the tradition of Saint Jerome and the grateful lion is striking, the story finds its roots in indigenous mythology, and is structured similarly not because of direct influence but rather because of the way that the embodied human mind interacts with the natural world and narrativizes in a literary way, regardless of what continent humans are on.[114]

Some of Sahagún's animals are more explicitly anthropomorphized, along with human features; he describes them frequently as "like a person" (como persona; 230), for instance. Among these, the monkey is the most similar, because of physical characteristics: "They have hands and feet like those of a person" (Tienen manos y pies como persona), "They have a face that is almost like that of a person" (Tienen cara casi como de persona; 230). Of course, research into evolution hundreds of years later would prove such folk understanding to be true; and the special closeness of one primate species' DNA to human DNA has now been the basis for an orang-utan's *habeas corpus* case in Buenos Aires, as explored in the introduction. Behaviourally, too, monkeys are like humans: "they eat like a person" (comen como persona; 230), and "they sit like a person" (siéntase como persona; 231). Sahagún's description of the monkey incorporates aspects that are similar to those of Oviedo, as he also tells that these animals throw objects at people who pass by: "They throw stones and sticks at people going by" (arrojan piedras y palos a los caminantes; 230). For all of their quasi-humanity, however, this does not lead to significant empathy on the part of Sahagún. On the contrary, hunters use the monkey's own curiosity combined with their desire for warmth against them, tricking them into capture by setting a bonfire, to which monkeys come and sit with their babies. However, the fire is a trap, and contains an exploding stone that soon hurls embers and ash everywhere, leaving the monkeys dumbfounded, blinded, and separated from their young, who are captured and raised as companion pets.[115]

Sahagún also tells of the opossum (*tlpacuatl*), who does not seem as intelligent as these other animals but is still anthropomorphized explicitly. From his description, the animal seems highly emotional. Its primary behavioural similarity for Sahagún is the way it cries: "tears come forth from its eyes like those of a person" (sálenle las lágrimas de los ojos como a persona; 229). Females cry when captured, and then cry even harder when their young are taken away (229). While not detailed explicitly, the purpose of the capture seems to be to keep the animal as a curiosity rather than to kill it for food. The emotional life of the opossum is not rich, but it is intense. It is worth nothing that the only aspect of her cognitive life that the reader is made aware of – crying for loss of freedom or loss of her young – comes to the fore because of the direct mode of interaction between humans and this animal, in which she is robbed by the human. It is beyond Sahagún's purview to wonder what other emotions she might have, or how these might be expressed.

Sahagún mentions one animal that is highly cognitive, the *ocotochtli*. Its physical description makes it sound something like a lynx, but the vignette is clearly apocryphal from a natural historical point of view, and the species would be best understood as mythological, not referring to an animal observed in the natural physical world.[116] Yet the description is interesting, for it raises the possibility in this section, which is concerned primarily with actual animals in the natural world, that non-human animals may have a rich cognitive life as well as interesting and effective, complex modes of interspecies communication. To wit, while no claim is made of this animal's communication with humans, the ocotochtli's voice is anthropomorphized as "like a soprano" (como tiple; 226), reminiscent of Oviedo's singing sloth, the mythological creator of music. The ocotochli is very successful at hunting – whether the prey be non-human animals or human beings – and is said to share its kill with other creatures of the rain forest. Its howls are heard far away, after which jaguars and other animals "understand that they are being called to eat" (entienden que son llamados para comer; 227). Even stranger details about this communicative creature emerge, as it exudes generosity, self-knowledge, planning, and an attempt not to harm other beings (except for the prey): Being a most generous creature, and knowing that its own tongue is venomous to others, it eats of its own kill only after all the other animals – who have been summoned by the ocotochtli – have had their fill, such that they do not suffer from the poison in its tongue. This most devious, intelligent animal is, like Oviedo's adversaries, an enemy of humans, since it preys on them, which may explain his intellectual reverence – based, in this case, on an *alleged* mode of interaction, reversing the typical hunter-to-hunted to hunted-to-hunter. While fancifully, fantastically, and gratuitously anthropomorphic, the image of the ocotochtli that emerges can be understood similarly to real animals, such as the menagerie jaguar elaborated upon by Oviedo, and shares a common human-cognitive (anthropocentric) reverence based on the (alleged) mode of interaction: when humans are hunted by land animals, the animal must be intelligent indeed.

Regarding herding animals, we can again see similarities to the minding of animals in the strictly European texts. Sahagún mentions by name only autochthonous animals of the Aztecs. His descriptions are physical (size of head, size of ears, etc.). His description of the *tlacaxólotl*, for instance, includes the size of its body ("bigger than a large ox" [mayor que un gran buey; 223]), size of its head, and size of its teeth. Also, it is tasty (su carne es de comer; 223). When he explains that it is hunted with bow and arrow, he mentions a practical cognitive element vis-à-vis this mode of interaction: "This animal does not fear people" (Este animal no teme a las gentes; 223).[117] Despite the indigenous or mestizo source of the information, Sahagún's grazing herd animals are, like Oviedo's and Acosta's, not minded, which can be accounted for in large respect as explained above by the habitational parameter and mode of interaction.

Much of what he says about "fish," from the perspective of how they are minded, is also similar to European accounts. First of all, the "animales del agua" are implicitly less important in the hierarchy according to their placement after "animales" and "aves," mimicking some versions of the *Scala Naturae*. In Sahagún's categorization, fish form a heterogeneous group that includes a Nahuatl classificatory group, "fish" (michin), along with other diverse animals that spend significant parts of their life in the water, not unlike the sixteenth-century European concept of "pez" (fish). Regarding cognitive knowledge of the animals in question, there is little of interest in Sahagún's mention of what seem to be fish proper (today's designations of bony fish, cartilaginous fish, ray-finned fish, etc.), which are divided by size into two subcategories: small (*michin*) and large (*tlamichin*). He observes little about them, other than their basic body shape, size, and surface, as well as whether they are edible:

> The fish found inland are similar to those of Castile. They are called *michin*. Their tails, which are cleft or bifurcated, are similar and so are the fins and the scales, and [they are similar] in that their bodies are wide and their necks thick and in that they are swift and slip from the hands. The fish of the sea are called *tlacamichin*, which means "big fish," "fish that swim in the sea," and they are good to eat. These big fish eat the little ones.
>
> (Los peces de esta tierra son semejantes a los de Castilla [y] llámanse *michin;* son semejantes en la cola, que la tienen hendida u horcajada, y también en las alillas y en las escamas, y en tener el cuerpo ancho y el cuello grueso, y en ser ligeros, y en que se deslizan de las manos. Los peces de la mar se llaman *tlacamichin* que quiere decir peces grandes, peces que andan en la mar, que son buenos de comer; estos peces grandes comen a los pequeños. [259])

While we cannot know for certain to what extent Sahagún's tract is infused by his Spanish world view and how much was provided by his Nahuatl-speaking informants, the morphosyntactic and lexical information does seem to demonstrate that the Nahua folk concept of "fish" was indeed quite similar to the European one. Once again, this leads credence to the idea that humans conceptualize that which lives in the water habitat differently than non-water habitat animals.[118] Other animals that are classified as "michin" by the indigenous include eels (*coamichin*, "which means 'snake fish'" [que quiere decir culebra pez; 259]) and turtles (*chimalmichin*, "which means 'buckler fish,' because their shells are round like a buckler" [que quiere decir, rodela pez, porque tiene redonda la concha como rodela; 259]),[119] *totomichin*, "bird fish" (ave pez; 259) (which is actually a bird that swims: a penguin), *papalomichin*, "butterfly fish" (pez como mariposa; 260), and *ocelomichin*, "tiger fish" (pez como tigre; 260). In none of these cases in which an animal is understood as "michi" does the author mention any cognitive faculty. Thus Sahagún's treatment corresponds perfectly to that of "fish" in the medieval literary genres examined in chapter 1 as well as in European natural historical writing.

While there is no actual liminal creature for Sahagún of the sort that, for Oviedo, Acosta, and Medel, led each of them to call into question the category of "fish" (iguana, whale, or manatee), there is a lengthy digression in the section on "animales del agua" that departs from the rest of the straightforward and brief accounts of different fishes. These animals (which are not "michin") clearly have a mythological rather than natural historical origin. Although they are included among these other actual aquatic animals, without any separation, the gratuitously anthropomorphized descriptions speak for themselves.

The *ahuitzotl* is a malevolent and treacherous mythological animal with a penchant for human flesh that beguiles and hunts its prey in uncanny ways.[120] In terms of physical characteristics, it is a dog-like creature yet lives mostly in the water; it is anatomically distinct, in that it has a tail "like a human hand" that it uses to grasp and drown its prey (see fig. 22). In the lengthy explanation of the ahuitzotl, there is no point at which Sahagún expresses any doubt as to the veracity of the account of this creature. Did he believe the informants that such a creature truly existed? Did he include it because it was anthropologically interesting? Because it plays an important role in Nahua cosmology? It is hard to say, except that his inclusion of it is somewhat anomalous in a work that often attempts to present accurate information about animal and plant species.[121] It is interesting to see just how highly cognitive and gratuitously anthropomorphized this creature is in the mediated indigenous world view of the *Florentine Codex*. It is an animal that lives mostly in "the deep wellsprings of the waters" (los profundos manatiales de las aguas; 264) and yet surfaces and even takes to land at significant moments, where it partially shares the human *Umwelt* – it is a liminal, fantastic creature that lures humans away from their habitational parameter to die underwater where their bodies are altered irreparably. After luring people into the water, the ahuitzotl has the ability to stir up the water and wind, whereby it takes them to the depths to drown them and horrifyingly eats their eyes and fingernails.[122] The creature has peculiar desires and a penchant for the human: When it feels the urge to kill, the ahuitzotl lures people using Machiavellian Intelligence. First, it gathers many fish together[123] to lure humans who will want to fish them. Then, once the people have arrived, the ahuitzotl stirs up the water and drowns its victim. As a capricious alternative, the ahuitzotl sometimes uses another means to lure people, a method which demonstrates its liminal status, how it is does not truly belong to the class of "fish": it chooses to walk on land and simulate the cry of a human

Figure 22 A detail of an ahuitzotl from the *Florentine Codex*. Florence, The Biblioteca Medicea Laurenziana, ms. Med. Palat. 220 f. 223r. Reproduced with permission of MiBACT. Further reproduction by any means is prohibited.

child. As Sahagún writes, "it began to cry like a child" (comenzaba a llorar como un niño; 265), another simile reminding the reader of the animal's hand that was "like a human hand." When some unsuspecting person tries to help the "child" in need, the creature takes advantage of this kindness and kills the prey![124]

Apart from the ahuitzotl, only one other water animal has significant cognition for Sahagún. Once again the animal is gratuitously anthropomorphized. This is the water serpent, which he seems to group with the ahuitzotl not because it is a mythological creature but because of the common characterological trait of guile (*astucia*), a word he repeats emphatically. The serpent is "very monstrous in its ferocity and deeds (...) The notable guile of this snake or serpent: to hunt people it has a notable guile" (muy monstruosa en ferocidad y obras [...] Notable astucia de esta culebra o serpiente: para cazar personas tiene esta culebra una astucia notable; 266). Like a human hunter who may employ

Machiavellian Intelligence to outsmart prey, Sahagún's water serpent, just like the ahuitzotl, lures people to a lagoon by *putting* fish there manually; when people come to catch the fish (governed by their predictable human desire for an easy catch), the snake either attacks them right away or tracks them through the forest by olfaction and kills them later. Remarkably, the way in which the luring fish are simply "placed" in the lagoon relies on their complete and implicit anthropectomy; they have been turned into automata, strikingly in the same manner in which fish are treated in the *Cantigas'* miracles, where Mary seals the hole in a sinking boat with fish to save her worshippers (see chapter 1).

The accounts of these two water creatures – the ahuitzotl and the water snake – provide descriptions of highly sentient creatures who are capable not only of avoiding death at the hands of humans but of outsmarting humans and hunting them. Both entries share a high dose of irreality, although it is not clear from the text where Sahagún's belief in these creatures' capabilities begins and ends, and to what extent he recognizes them as mythological.[125]

While incorporating aspects of indigenous and European traditions, Sahagún similarly provides many details about the physical characteristics of birds, including a good many drawings (see fig. 23).[126] His description focuses on the varied intense colours and lengths of their feathers: "diversos generos de aves, de pluma rica y colores diversos, que se llaman xiuhtototl y quetzaltototl (...) y xiuhtototl, y tlauhquechol; 289).[127] He also demonstrates his understanding that the indigenous peoples distinguish between feathers found on one part of the body and feathers on another part. Some are more beautiful than others: "The feathers that grow from its tail are called *quezalli* (and) they are very green and resplendent, they are as wide as the leaf of a cattail ... (and) they shine very beautifully ... The headdress that this bird has on its head is very beautiful and resplendent" (Las plumas que cría en la cola se llaman *quezalli* [y] son muy verdes y resplandecientes, son anchas, como unas hojas de espadaña ... [y] resplandecen muy hermosamente ... El tocado que tiene en la cabeza esta ave es muy hermoso y resplandeciente; 234). Whereas the emphasis is on the visual beauty of the feathers, as in other natural histories,[128] Sahagún's text differentiates itself by the myriad cosmological beliefs about birds, some of which involve supernatural cognitive abilities. Such is the case of the *acitli*, a bird with the ability to raise the tides in order to escape (243), and of the *atotoli*, a formidable adversary that can call on the wind to destroy the indigenous peoples who hunt it in their canoes (242).[129] In addition, birds are

Figure 23 A detail of a quetzalhuitzili from the *Florentine Codex*. Florence, The Biblioteca Medicea Laurenziana, ms. Med. Palat. 220 f. 178v. Reproduced with permission of MiBACT. Further reproduction by any means is prohibited.

also used for food, something about which he comments frequently; for instance, the *totollin* is described as something like a chicken, about which he has little to say except that "they are good to eat, the best meat of all the birds" ([s]on de muy buen comer, la mejor carne de todas las aves; 258).

Finally, regarding "man's best friend," Sahagún's *Historia natural y moral* has a section on "The dogs of this land" (Los perros desta tierra),[130] which represents a point of view on dogs that is anomalous in comparison to the other texts studied here. Not only does Sahagún not say any of the typical things about dogs (best friend, intelligent, etc.) that one would find in typical European-authored texts, but his description of dogs includes a first-person assessment of how delicious they are to eat. Sahagún especially likes the dogs called "tlalchichi": "they are very good to eat" (son muy buenos de comer; 232), he writes. This comment seems somewhat incongruous in light of the tlalchichi illustration, which makes the animals look very cute (see fig. 24). Whereas

Figure 24 A detail of a dog from the *Florentine Codex*. Florence, The Biblioteca Medicea Laurenziana, ms. Med. Palat. 220 f. 171r. Reproduced with permission of MiBACT. Further reproduction by any means is prohibited.

there may be a tendency to "not eat one's friends," ultimately it appears that such a tendency can be countered. Importantly for the assessment, however, the dogs' place is no longer the home, and the interaction is no longer that of pet, and the minded cognition (of the tlalchichi in particular) as a result is null.

With respect to animals being moved from one habitat to another, Sahagún describes briefly how both monkeys and parrots behave in captivity, introduced into the hearth habitat.[131] Monkeys are easily tamed, he says, joke around (especially "with women"), and ask for food by extending their hands and screaming, demonstrating similar cognitive capacities to those described by Oviedo and Acosta. In contrast, most birds seem to have few cognitive capacities for Sahagún. There is, however, one type of parrot, the *cocho*, who is able to change habitat, is docile, and is able to learn many things that would seem to signal significant cognition: "There is another kind of parrot that they call *cocho* (...) This bird sings and talks and speaks any language that they teach it. It mimics other animals. It responds saying what they say, singing what they sing. It is very docile" (Otra manera de papagayos hay que llaman *cocho* [...] Esta ave canta y habla y parla cualquier lengua que le enseñen; arrienda a los otros animales, responde diciendo lo que dicen, cantando lo que le cantan; es muy dócil; 238). It is the change in habitat that allows for these cognitive appraisals – borne out by scientific study (see introduction) – in which real cognitive abilities of parrots are observed.

Conclusion

This chapter has emphasized the importance of habitat to the mindedness of animals. Interesting test cases for the assertion of habitational import are the examples in which the species remains constant while the habitat changes, as in the case when animals are taken from the wild and placed into the home, the palace, or the menagerie. Something happens to the animal when the habitat changes: it often gets a mind. This can be gauged by the writing of naturalists: in almost all cases, the animal that was previously treated with implicit anthropectomy or with only a hint of emotion is now treated, in the new habitat, as a cognitively rich creature, endowed anthropomorphically with all manner of human intellectual abilities. For the most part, the animal's intelligence is treated with greater respect. Various factors account for this, only some of which have to do with the animal's actual cognition. Certainly, animals with specific cognitive features – especially those bred to be socially adapted to humanity, such as dogs – are selected for the home because of their cognitive features (that the lapdog likes to be petted, for instance). But for completely wild animals, like the jaguar, the change in their mindedness is remarkable. Contrasting the writing on the same species of animal but in different habitational contexts in this way demonstrates that the new mindedness of the animal comes about precisely because of the habitat change. In these cases, the animal is brought into the home or menagerie because it is exotic, even when it is not a good fit. As the case of Oviedo's captive jaguar demonstrates, it is only through this close contact with the animal that humans are likely to use folk animal psychology to understand the animal anthropomorphically.

Thinking more broadly about the divisions of habitational parameters in chapter 3, we see confirmed that certain animals that remain out of sight entirely – most "fish" – are literally out of mind and entirely anthropectomized, regardless of any actual abilities. Bishop Berkeley's famous question about the falling tree comes to mind: If a fish were to exhibit significant intellectual abilities at the bottom of a dark ocean where no person perceived it, did it really do those things? It seems that the anthropocentricity of humans tends to have us answer this question negatively. Richard W. Bulliet has noted a similar phenomenon relating to other animals, in his work on today's "postdomestic" communities in which killing of non-human animals is rampant and yet "people live far away, both physically and psychologically (...) never witness the births, sexual congress, and slaughter of those animals" (qtd. in Few and Tortorici 26–7).[132] In today's postdomestic societies, cows, pigs, and chickens have become, like the fish of the sea, removed from human habitational parameters. The historical case of "fish" is instructive in this light, for when the particular species lives at the border of a human *Umwelt* – surfacing to the top of the water as does the whale, helping to catch other creatures as does the suckerfish, feeding on plants alongside the edges of the shore as might a manatee in La Hispaniola – then humans may begin to see the animal a different way and ponder its intellectual abilities.[133]

These many examples make a strong case for the importance of habitational parameter to the minding of animals. Assessing the early testimonies of encounters with animals, Asúa and French conclude that "the image of the animals ... was formed on the basis of their expectations and beliefs, language playing a not insignificant part in its construction" (24). But as these chapters have shown, what we might call the "mental image of the animals" (how they are minded) is not solely formed on culturally generated expectations, beliefs, and language, but on categories that are more fundamentally human. Asúa and French attempt to demonstrate that what they call "Western mental categories" are not exhibited in Sahagún's *Historia*. I would only partially agree, and with a different explanation.[134] They demonstrate that Sahagún's animals are "humanized" and, "as in Western fables and folk tales, they exhibit distinctive personalities," for instance, that the coyote is "cunning, astute" (44). As I have demonstrated, Oviedo, Acosta, Medel, and Bartolomé de las Casas all engage in anthropomorphism of certain animals in specific contexts, the greatest example of which is Oviedo's captive jaguar, which demonstrates all manner of human cognitive capacities, and yet is an attempt to explain the thinking of the actual animal to the best of Oviedo's ability, rather than, say, represent a kind of symbolic meaning, as in the bestiary tradition or the fable tradition, as I laid out in chapter 1. The minding of animals speaks to the way that the human mind tends to categorize other animated forms and engage in different kinds of anthropomorphism based largely on where the animal lives; and in cases where folk animal psychology has been developed for practical reasons, the anthropomorphic understanding of the animal mind can be fairly accurate, what I have called "constructive anthropomorphism."[135]

However, habitat alone is never entirely separated from the actual cognitive abilities nor the mode of interaction between human and animal. As I have shown, animals that tend to be considered good eating to a particular society are less likely to be considered as richly cognitive. While we hear of the jaguar being brought to the menagerie (taste unknown), we don't read the same about the baby wild boar, which is most certainly also a highly intelligent species. Human self-interest in the food source is generally enough to preclude discussion of intellect. That Oviedo only eats dog meat when he doesn't know what he is eating demonstrates the importance, to humans, of assessing an animal's cognitive capacities only after judging it an appropriate food source or not.[136] And the many examples show how that anthropocentric utility (food, skin, labour) will trump further investigation and curiosity about an animal's mind in most cases. Better not to appreciate the animal's sentience if you're going to ingest its flesh. After all, as Moussaieff Masson maintains, most people do not want to eat their friends.

Chapter Four

Embodying Animals: Cervantes and Animal Cognition

[T]he difference in mind between man and the higher animals, great as it is, certainly is one of degree and not of kind. We have seen that the senses and intuitions, the various emotions and faculties, such as love, memory, attention, curiosity, imitation, reason, etc., of which man boasts, may be found in an incipient, or even sometimes in a well-developed condition, in the lower animals.

– Charles Darwin, *The Descent of Man*

In Cervantes's writing, we find all of the throughlines concerning animals found in the preceding chapters: Some human characters believe animals to be symbolic, ripe with meanings that bear specifically on their own life and aspirations;[1] some animals think and speak like people, provoking awe in spectators; still others are mentioned only insofar as they serve as food or property, apparently lacking any thought or feeling; finally, a significant number are treated more circumspectly, with the considerable respect that is due to minds that are complex but never fully fathomed. In subtle ways, Cervantes presents animal emotion, thought, understanding, and intentional agency, developing what I term "animal embodiment." Cervantes opens up in fiction a world of possibilities for minding animals, creating nonhuman characters that – like many of his complex human characters with whom they often interact – merit the reader's consideration, reflection, and empathy.

Cervantes portrays the sensorium, emotions, and intellect of nonhuman animals throughout *Don Quixote* and other works with various anthropomorphic techniques, with emphasis on perspective-taking, while, for the most part, eschewing gratuitous anthropomorphism as revealed in many episodes including that of the lion (2.17). At this turning point of early modernity and the creation of the first modern novel – characterized by its dialogism featuring interactions among complex individuated characters – and amidst the rapid increase of both humanistic inquiry and empirical scientific study, Cervantes ushers in the modern paradigm of the human-animal relationship, in which constructive anthropomorphism leads to embodied animal cognition, navigating human experiences of real animals alongside the history of writing on animals from the Middle Ages onwards. The lasting impact of this paradigm will be explored briefly in the present work's epilogue in modern fictional authors including Paul Auster. Before that, this chapter studies several key questions in Cervantes: How are the minds of animals similar to and different from the minds of humans? What are the contexts, modes of interaction, and habitational parameters in which animals differentiate themselves as cognitive beings for Cervantes? What do the actions of animals tell us about their mental states and sensorium? How are depictions of human-animal interactions important to uncovering animal sentience? Often through the use of perspectivism, Cervantes engages these questions to explore that which can be revealed amidst ambiguity, uncertainty, indeterminacy, and complexity. I will survey a range of cases to make these points, from the gratuitous anthropomorphism of "The Colloquy of the Dogs" ("El coloquio de los perros") to the subtle animal perspective-taking in the episode of the cats (2.46), to an example of constructive anthropomorphism in the close relationship between the goatherd Eugenio and his goat, and to verisimilar non-human animal cognitive embodiment in the case of El rucio and Rocinante.

Implicit Anthropectomy and Gratuitous Anthropomorphism in Cervantes

Don Quixote is replete with all manner of animals, mostly autochtonous ones from the Iberian Peninsula. Adrienne Martín has drawn out the way in which Cervantes's novel recaptures for us today the way in which animals were an important part of the fabric of human existence and daily life: for farming, for transportation, for protection, for companionship, and more (Martin 448). Drawing attention to the variety of animal species involved and the activities in which they engage, Abel Alves concludes that "*Don Quixote*'s animals are the animals of Spain in literary microcosm" (*The Animals of Spain* 58), focusing importantly on those relationships between humans and animals that demonstrate interspecies emotional bonds.

Yet it is also true that the majority of the animals that briefly grace the novel's pages are not considered for their sentience, emotions, or perspective, nor are they presented as creatures of human moral concern. Instead, these are the animals exploited by human characters only for labour, entertainment, and food, and their ignorance of animal sentience reveals well the epoch's lack of concern with the well-being of most animals.[2] The treatment of these creatures is easily categorized under an anthropocentric world view, such as Hernán Calvo's in his *Libro de Albeytaría* (1557), following Aristotle: that animals exist to serve humans. The idea that "man" was a more perfect being and therefore had a right to exploit lower beings was widely disseminated in the era and was an important component of what is often known as the Great Chain of Being.[3]

While Martín and Alves have pointed out how many of the nonhuman animals in *Don Quixote* are used as food, labour, or entertainment for humans, I first build on their work by exploring in part *how* this lack of anthropomorphism takes effect, an examination of what I term "implicit anthropectomy" in which a writer or character is not actively denying human-like cognitive faculties of animals à la Malebranche (the explicit form would be "anthropectomy" *tout court*), but rather simply ignoring animals' possibilities for thoughts, feelings, or intentions.[4] Later, I turn to the polar opposite of such characterizations, examining Cervantes's most gratuitously anthropomorphized creations, with a focus on animals that speak or otherwise evince the highest functioning of human intelligence.

A. Implicit Anthropectomy

When asked what can be served for dinner, the last innkeeper in *Don Quixote* reports grandiloquently, as if reciting from a Renaissance natural history, on the various kinds of animals that he can put on the table to offer his guests. They are divided by their broad habitational parameters: "the inn was stocked with the birds of the air, the fowl of the earth, and the fish of the sea" (844) (que de las pajaricas del aire, de las aves de la tierra y de los pescados del mar estaba proveída aquella venta; 2.59:484). While this is most definitely a hyperbole (in fact, his pantries prove as bare as Camacho's wedding was overflowing with food, much to Sancho's disappointment), the innkeeper finally extols the one dish that he can serve, "cow heel" (*uña de vaca*), prepared with garbanzos and back bacon. The dish is so good, in fact, it cries out in Spanish, "Eat me! Eat me!" (¡Cómeme, cómeme!). It turns out that unreasoning animals do speak after all! That is, cooked flesh speaks in the only way that animals who have been anthropectomized can communicate, synaesthetically through smells, to the embodied olfaction of diners who await with open "ears." The world view evinced by the innkeeper suggests that wherever they come from in the world – air, land, or water's depths – animals exist for human consumption. The food speaks only through prosopopeia, a specific kind of literary anthropomorphism that has nothing to do with the animals' actual cognition.[5]

Although not as suggestive of a global assertion on the value of animals as the innkeeper's natural historical outlook, there are many other instances in which implicit anthropectomy is at work, in discourse that suggests a similar Weltanschauung. For instance, the reader is not invited to think about the mind of the goat(s) that is boiling in the stew of the goatherds, which the narrator describes simply as "certain pieces of dried goat meat that were bubbling over the fire in a pot" (75) (tasajos de cabra [...] hirviendo al fuego; 1.11:153). Sancho is drawn to the food, as is often the case, by the smell, as the text explains that "[he] followed the aroma coming from certain pieces of dried goat meat that were bubbling over the fire in a pot" (se fue tras el olor que despedían de sí; 1.11:153). Asking about the sentience of the goat that made up this particular stew is admittedly reading against the grain. But the scene is odd because the goatherds are preparing a meat dish of the very animal they herd, when their idealized literary counterparts of sixteenth-century pastoral romance, a genre on which Cervantes frequently draws, are almost exclusively vegetarian.[6]

Likewise, the hundreds of dead animals mentioned at Camacho's famous and incredible wedding feast have been elaborately prepared or are waiting to be made into food. They are presented as inert, edible things, already skinned or plucked, bereft of even a hint of cognition: "they contained and enclosed entire sheep, which sank out of view as if they were doves; the hares without their skins and the chickens without their feathers that were hanging from the trees, waiting to be buried in the cauldrons, were without number; the various kinds of fowl and game hanging from the trees to cool in the breeze were infinte" (584) (así embebían y encerraban en sí carneros enteros, sin echarse de ver, como si fueran palominos; las liebres ya sin pellejo y las gallinas sin pluma que estaban colgadas por los árboles para sepultarlas en las ollas no tenían número; los pájaros y caza de diversos géneros eran infinitos, colgados de los árboles para que el aire los enfriase; 2.20).[7] The animal foodstuffs at the wedding are similar to both the "pieces of dried goat meat" and the "cow heel" because their odours communicate to Sancho, whose high regard for his own olfactory prowess is thematized throughout *Don Quixote*.[8] Indeed, before the reader is given the full description of all the foods, it is Sancho who predicts that the wedding will be grand, based on the odours he distinguishes in the morning air: "if I'm not mistaken, there's an aroma that smells much more like a roasted side of bacon than reeds and thyme: by my faith, weddings that begin with smells like this must be plentiful and generous" (583) (si no me engaño, sale un tufo y olor harto más de torreznos asados que de juncos y tomillos: bodas que por tales olores comienzan, para mi santiguada que deben de ser abundantes y generosas; 2.20:186). Thus, as in the previous example, a good smell of meat is airborne and precedes Sancho's eating the food. As in the example of the "cow heel," where garbanzos were secondary, the meat is privileged again in this case by Sancho, who appraises the wedding as a grand affair precisely because it will be meaty, not vegetarian – it smells "more like a roasted side of bacon than reeds and thyme." With hundreds of dead carcasses around – clearly an excess of food and an abundance of meat – neither the narrator nor any character suggests that too many animals have been killed. In fact, no animal is ever killed before the reader, and no thought is given to how they were slaughtered or processed, images which might readily involve demonstrating their suffering and emotions; rather, the animals are presented as already dead and ready to cook or in the process of being cooked.

In non-food contexts as well, the thoughts and emotions of animals are ignored through implicit anthropectomy in which case the animals may more easily and actively be killed without moral considerations. It is not just the innkeeper and Sancho who view cows, pigs, fish, game birds, and virtually all animals (except dogs, horses, donkeys, and humans) in this way.[9] In the famous episode of the armies of sheep (DQ 1.18), Don Quixote himself slaughters a number of animals. Unlike Luis Pérez's imaginings of the mental life of the hunted deer and the hunting dog discussed above in chapter 2, in these Cervantine sheep, the reader is not invited to think about their thoughts. Are the sheep as afraid as was the wild hare who was being hunted in 2.71?[10] Do the surviving animals become disturbed at the slaughter of their offspring, siblings, or parents? The reader is not invited to reflect or think about the animals' sensory experience, such as, for instance, the affective importance of smelling the deceased's blood.[11] While the particular situation is dialogical and perspectival, as are many episodes, an additional perspective that the reader is asked to consider here is not that of a surviving animal but of the shepherds, who are angry over the damage and loss of their property (1.18:224).[12] This view of animals as mere property is quite common in *Don Quixote*.[13] It is also the case of the herded bulls who trample Don Quixote and Sancho in DQ 2.58. While the knight does not attack the bulls, and they are the offenders in this case, the bulls are probably off to certain death in the short term, used in fairs and celebrations of the time that were precursors of the modern bullfight.[14]

Several animals mentioned in the text do not seem to have any higher cognition save for a single, simple emotion. For instance, the Vizcayan's mule in DQ 1.8 is an example of an animal whose mental state is only briefly considered and demonstrates a certain lack of cognition, an animal who seems to behave automatically according to the narrator: "And so he waited for him, shielded by his pillow, and unable to turn the mule one way or the other, for the mule, utterly exhausted and not made for such foolishness, could not take another step" (64) (Y así, le aguardó bien cubierto de su almohada, sin poder rodear la mula a una ni a otra parte; que ya, de puro cansada y no hecha a semejantes niñerías, no podía dar un paso; 1.8:137). Later, the mule transparently expresses the emotion of fear according to the narrator, running away from the battle between Don Quixote and Don Sancho de Azpetia, in an action that also seems automatic: "and the mule, terrified by the awful blow, began to run across the field and, after bucking a few times, threw his rider to the ground" (69) (y la mula, espantada del terrible golpe, dio a correr por el campo, y a pocos corcovos dio con su dueño en tierra; 1.9:145). The mule experiences an emotion, but it is simply fear, and it leads to the simple action of running away in fear, without reflection. While the mule and some other animals are singled out very briefly in this way, they are mere actors, never developed as individual characters; they are treated as exemplars of a mass or type, for instance, a "bad rental donkey." These animals are much like those that belong to the habitational parameter of the barnyard as portrayed in Herrera's *Agricultura general* and other works of this type, where animals seem bereft of thought, with extremely limited cognitive faculties, creatures who must be helped along by humans who can exploit them for profit. Their minds seem not worth thinking about.

B. Gratuitous Anthropomorphism

On the other end of the spectrum of cognitive representations, there are several special animals that appear to possess cognitive abilities far surpassing those of ordinary animals. These gratuitously anthropomorphised creatures are uncannily human or even superhuman. And yet their cognitive powers are suspect vis-à-vis their verisimilitude, questioned from within the text. In terms of modes of interaction and habitational parameters, these vary, and yet all of these animals have a close relationship with humans.

Don Quixote: Maese Pedro's Puppet Show

In DQ 2.25, Don Quixote and Sancho encounter Maese Pedro[15] and his "large tailless monkey with a rump like felt but a face that was nice-looking" (624) (mono, grande y sin cola, con las posaderas de fieltro, pero no de mala cara; 2.25:235). This primate earns money for his master by responding in a special way to verbal questions posed by humans who are surprised by this strange ability. Maese Pedro alleges that the monkey "knows" things from the past, as well as from the present, but he limits the claims on the monkey's foreknowledge: "this animal does not respond or give information about things to come" (624) (no responde ni da noticia de las cosas que están por venir; 2.25:235). The type of knowledge in his memory, therefore, while uncanny in a non-human animal, is therefore within the bounds of verisimilitude for what a human might possess (after all, Maese Pedro *does* have this information, though the source of it is concealed).[16] Of course, this is all a ruse, similar to the "magical" head that will later "speak" to Don Quixote at the house of Don Antonio Moreno in Barcelona, which Enrique Fernández has called an "anthropomorphic contraption" likened to "dehumanizing mechanization" (Fernández 127). For Fernández, drawing on similarities to the mechanical head episode, the monkey behaves like an automaton (127). While I do not disagree with his emphasis on mechanization and the many similarities between this and the talking head episode, the monkey is certainly more than an automaton, even without the gratuitous anthropomorphism.

The process of "answering" the questions is as follows, and through its analysis, we can gauge the actual abilities and the monkey's implicit, if limited, thinking: "And he hit his left shoulder twice with his right hand, and the monkey leaped onto to it, put his mouth up to his ear, clicked his teeth together very quickly, and after doing this for the length of time it takes to say a Credo, gave another leap down to the floor" (625) (Y dando con la mano derecha dos golpes sobre el hombro izquierdo, en un brinco se le puso el mono en él, y llegando la boca al oído, daba diente con diente muy apriesa; y habiendo hecho este ademán por espacio de un credo, de otro brinco se puso en el suelo; 2.25:235).[17] Without knowing more detail, the cognition of the macaque appears to consist in his ability to (a) recognize a specific tapping signal after which (b) he responds with a memorized, fairly complicated patterned physical response, which involves (i) jumping onto his master's shoulder, (ii) putting his mouth near Maese Pedro's ear, and (iii) making his teeth chatter quickly. Konrad Gessner's description of primates ("Apes") comes to mind here, as he describes them as "much given to imitation (...) and have been taught to leap, sing, drive Wagons (...) and are very capable of all humane actions" (Gessner 2). Moreover, citing a host of classical authorities, Gessner finds them, quite anthropomorphically, a somewhat immoral breed, "given to ... deceits, impostures and flatteries" (2). Indeed, this monkey is involved in a deceit, used by the impostor Maese Pedro, to fraudulently gain the money of the credulous. In addition to the necessary components of monkey cognition for the animal's actual behaviour (learn, memorize) within the story, characters believe that he is able to speak to Maese Pedro reasonably, coherently, and knowledgeably (and about content he would have no business knowing), which is of course far beyond what monkeys were thought to be able to do in the early modern period, or what they can do in the actual world.[18]

Rather than an automaton, the imaged whispering super-monkey seems to transgress the laws of nature, sharing characteristics of the animal, the human, and the supernatural: He holds an animal body and behaves much like an animal (jumping on things), yet allegedly communicates with human language using conventions for secrecy (whispering in the ear of his master), all the while holding superhuman powers in his ability to tell the "truth" about things of which he should have no prior knowledge.[19] Don Quixote and Sancho, for instance, are very surprised when the monkey reveals in detail who they are, with their exact names and information about their pasts. In line with thinking of the era, Don Quixote suspects that the devil is involved and he points this out to Sancho: "[he] must have made a pact, either implicit or explicit, with the devil" (626) (debe de tener hecho algún concierto con el demonio; 2.25:237) as he marvels as to why Maese Pedro has not been charged by the Inquisition (626).

Of course, since the disguised Maese Pedro already knows who Don Quixote and Sancho are, he has simply feigned having learned all of this from the monkey. When the veils of deceit and dramatic irony are ultimately lifted for the reader, the narrator reveals Cervantes's implicit view of monkey-ness: The monkey does communicate with Maese Pedro, but does not "know" any concept; instead, he merely responds to a stimulus with a learned response. In this case, the representation of the animal points specifically to a lack in animals, that which makes them *less* than human, cognitively, for he lacks the ability to comprehend and communicate complex statements (this primate, it seems, responds only to hand gestures and simple commands). But monkeys are extremely complex creatures. Current researchers have examined the mind-boggling complexity of monkey and ape social networks, and have posited notions of concept-formation that the animals must possess in order to make correct distinctions for survival. "Monkeys and apes live in complex social groups and must master a formidable calculus if they are to survive and reproduce" (Seyfarth and Cheney 379). Within these groups, individuals must distinguish among individuals, all of whom are in a linear dominance hierarchy based on matrilineal kin relations. "In a group of 80 animals, each individual confronts 3160 different dyadic combinations and 812,160 different triadic combinations. In other words, free-ranging monkeys and apes face problems in learning and memory that are not just quantitatively but also qualitatively different from those presented in the typical laboratory experiment" (Seyfarth and Cheney 382–3).[20] Maese Pedro's monkey, on the other hand, does not seem to know much at all. Through the use of gratuitous anthropomorphism, Cervantes carries out the monkey's anthropectomy.

The Trials of Persiles and Sigismunda

Other Cervantine animal characters who possess the ability to speak are the talking wolves who appear twice in *The Trials of Persiles and Sigismunda*. Rather than the deceptive gratuitous anthropomorphism of Maese Pedro,

Cervantes presents here actual gratuitous anthropomorphism, drawing on centuries of fantastic wolf-lore and werewolf stories and beliefs, and early modern Spanish fear of wolves.

In the first wolf example, Antonio recounts a story about how he found himself on a remote island full of wolves. To his great surprise, one of them speaks fluent Spanish:

> [O]ne of them ... I swear it's true ... told me with a clear and distinct voice and in my own language: "Spaniard, go away and look elsewhere for your fate, unless you wish to die here torn apart by our claws and teeth; and don't ask who it is telling you this, just thank Heaven you've found mercy even among wild animals." (36–3)
>
> ([U]no dellos – como es la verdad – me dijo en voz clara y distinta, y en mi propia lengua: "Español, hazte a lo largo, y busca en otra parte tu ventura, si no quieres en ésta morir hecho pedazos por nuestras uñas y dientes; y no preguntes quién es el que esto te dice, sino da gracias al Cielo de que has hallado piedad entre las mismas fieras." [1.5:77])

The reader learns little else about the talking wolves here, nor why this particularly moral wolf would come to warn Antonio of the lurking violence, because Antonio heeds the animal's advice and abandons the island out of fear. Soon, however, Cervantes weaves the talking wolves back into the novel with a story told by Rutilio.

Whereas Antonio saw and then heard the first wolf speak, the order of sensation is reversed for Rutilio, and at first he believes he hears a woman's voice in the dark, whose "honesty" is immediately called into question: "'You're in a place, my friend Rutilio, where no one in the whole human race will be able to harm you.' After saying this, she began to embrace me in a manner less than modest" (47) ("En parte estás, amigo Rutilio, que todo el género humano no podrá ofenderte." Y diciendo esto, comenzó a abrazarme no muy honestamente; 91). Pushing her away, her figure comes into visual focus, and he is shocked and terrified to learn that she is a wolf: "I pushed her away from me and saw, as nearly as I could make out, that I was being embraced by something in the shape of a wolf, the sight of which chilled my soul, confused my senses, and undid my great courage" (47–8) (Apartéla de mí con los brazos, y como mejor pude, divisé que la que me abrazaba era una figura de lobo, cuya visión me heló el alma, me turbó los sentidos y dio con mi mucho ánimo al través; 91). Rutilio intuits that this is a demonic creature and reacts violently, after which it becomes clear that the wolf can only speak because of black magic:

> But as it often happens that during the greatest dangers the slight hope of conquering them draws desperate strength from the spirit, what little hope and strength I had put a knife that by chance I carried in my clothes to my hand, and with fury and rage I drove it into the chest of the woman I thought was a she-wolf. Falling to the ground, she changed back from that shape and I beheld the wretched sorceress dead and bleeding. (48)

> (Pero, como suele acontecer que en los grandes peligros la poca esperanza de vencerlos saca del ánimo desesperadas fuerzas, las pocas mías me pusieron en la mano un cuchillo, que acaso en el seno traía, y con furia y rabia se le hinqué por el pecho a la que pensé ser loba, la cual, cayendo en el suelo, perdió aquella figura, y hallé muerta y perdiendo sangre a la desventurada encantadora. [1.8:91])

The woman's return, upon dying, to her human form demonstrates that the wolf-shape had been a demonic appearance only.[21]

The wolf's cognitive abilities (including speaking Spanish) are suspect, but in a different way than Maese Pedro's monkey.[22] Thus, while this non-human animal speaks in human language, rationally and coherently, this representation is not assumed to be representative of any animal cognitive processes, but it is possible only because the wolf was actually a magically metamorphosed human. As with the monkey, a specific cognitive lack on the part of typical exemplars of these animal species – the inability to articulate complex ideas in human language – is thematized explicitly in this representation. The only way that animals can perform such human abilities is through false appearances and/or demonic magic. In these cases, it is not the animals' cognition per se, but rather their lack of cognition, that is represented: They speak and reason only because they are human or due to a human trick.

"The Colloquy of the Dogs"

The novella "The Colloquy of the Dogs" depicts a more lengthy and complicated case of gratuitous anthropomorphism. The reader does not have to infer the dogs' sentience since they reveal in dialogue through direct speech their deep knowledge of customs, history, literature, philosophy, religion, and more, in great detail. It is particularly ironic that, of all twelve *Exemplary Novellas* (1613), "The Colloquy of the Dogs" – with its canine protagonists, Cipión and Berganza – is an actual colloquy, written in dialogue form as if it were a theatrical script, requiring speech from its protagonists in a way that the eleven third-person novellas do not. The fictional author of the "Colloquy" (Campuzano, the protagonist of the novella "The Deceitful Marriage") assures his interlocutor that he has merely put down in writing what he overheard one night, using direct speech in order to avoid all of the allegedly tedious repetition that comes about through reporting indirect speech (i.e., "he said," "she said," etc.). Because of this, and in contrast to the narratives of the bewitched wolves' demonic anthropomorphism and the monkey's pseudo-anthropomorphism, the "Colloquy" does not reveal an ultimate omniscient view concerning the abilities of the talking dogs from which we can gauge, with certainty, their ontological status within the fiction. However, in this consideration of animal cognition, I question to what extent these talking dogs are more than only apparently animal and to what extent speech itself is the main characteristic that defines them as human-like.

The dialogue begins in medias res and thematizes how amazing it is that the dogs are suddenly able to speak, and then continues on to discuss their past lives. It is suggested then, by the text, that they were more fully canine before the sudden unexplained metamorphosis when they acquired this human faculty. Are we are able to glean, from the dialogue itself, what their thinking was like before they had the capacity to speak? If they were fully canine beforehand, the reader should be able to apprehend this from the text, through their differently embodied modes of perception and understanding. However, given the overarching similarity between the way the dogs think in the present of the novella and the way the dogs thought beforehand (as reflected in their retelling of their pre-speech experiences), I will argue that Berganza and Cipión have been gratuitously anthropomorphised throughout and have largely always had humanly embodied minds, not canine minds, even though they have the outwardly appearance of dogs.[23]

That is not to say that they do not behave *like* dogs in some ways. Certainly, they are presented partially with some zoocentric concerns and from a dog's perspective some of the time. The most obvious of these is that Cipión and Berganza walk on all fours (see fig. 25). Other narrative elements concur too with the life of a domesticated dog. Some of these demonstrate Berganza's understanding of his different modes of interaction with humans: Berganza is at one point tied to a leash; he

Figure 25 A chapter illustration of *Coloquio de los perros.* Cushing Memorial Library & Archives, Texas A&M University.

eats like a dog[24] and refers to having gnawed on a bone;[25] on occasion, he barks (323);[26] he carries human food in his mouth like the dog in the Aesopian fable;[27] he provides labour to humans by protecting sheep in the manner described by Herrera;[28] finally, Berganza talks about biting as a form of attack and uses his teeth to drag a body.[29]

However, alongside these images informed by canine perspective-taking are descriptions of what a dog does from a mostly human perspective. Importantly, as we ascertain from period treatises by Luis Pérez, Hernán Calvo, and others, it was widely known in the era that dogs had a much greater olfactory sense and relied more on smell than sight, which was contrasted directly with humans, whose most noble sense, sight, was dominant. Such ideas held contemporaneously with Cervantes have been borne out by neurological and cognitive science research. For dogs and other macrosmatic animals, smell plays a much greater role in perception than in microsmatic humans, and dogs' noses have a much higher number of smell receptors while at the same time possessing significantly fewer pseudo-genes relating to olfaction.[30] Humans, in contrast, have trichromatic rather than bichromatic vision, possess a large visual cortex, and overwhelmingly rely on sight as our most important sense. In turn, our embodied cognitive experience naturalizes this in language, where transculturally, embodied metaphors dealing with the visual are by far predominant.[31] Prima facie, if a story were to depict dog embodiment well, it would rely heavily on the olfactory rather than on the visual. And yet, both in the frame story time (since speaking ability), and in the narrated past events that occurred earlier (supposed dog life *sans* speech), it is the visual that is privileged, as if the visual were the most important sense to interpret the canine *Umwelt* as it is for Homo sapiens. Put in other terms, Berganza's underlying conceptual understanding is not simply anthropocentric, it is predominantly human at the level of embodiment. He does not "see" the world the way a dog or a horse would, but for the most part as a human would. A cognitive analysis demonstrates that Berganza's underlying conceptual understanding is predominantly anthropocentric and human, indeed much like Don Quixote and Sancho's, and less like Rocinante's, which will be explored in a later section of this chapter.[32]

Like most human beings and fictional human characters, Cipión and Berganza rely primarily on the strongest of the human senses, sight. Olfaction is not even a close second; rather, hearing fills that role. These "dogs" *see* the world the way humans see the world, both literally and metaphorically. Berganza's embodiment does not show the reader what it would be like to be a dog as much as it shows what it would be like to be a person who is acting like a dog, much like Rutilio's "shewolf," who, for instance, wants to mate preferentially with a human being, demonstrating thoroughly anthropocentric desires. Indeed, Berganza uses the verb "ver" [to see] in the first sentence of his biography:[33] "I seem to recall that the first time I saw the light of day was in Seville, in the slaughterhouse there" (454) (Paréceme que la primera vez que vi el sol fue en Sevilla, y en su Matadero; 302). With all of the aromas of blood and guts that might be of interest to a canine in a slaughterhouse – with cows and other animals being dismembered for their meat – it is striking that the first thing that came to Berganza's mind is what he was looking at. He then goes on to describe his first master as "a hardy lad, thick-set" (454) (mozo robusto, doblado; 302), that is, only in visual terms. Later, when he finds the *amo*'s girlfriend, he anthropocentrically mentions how he raised his eyes to find her and then describes her visual appearance as beautiful, once more using the verb "ver": "Raising my eyes, I saw a very pretty young woman" (456) (alcé los ojos y vi una moza hermosa en extremo; 304). Anthropocentrically, and culturally appropriate in the context of Christian Spain, he focuses on the state and colour of her hands, which are described in visual terms: "clean, white hands" (456) (manos limpias y blancas; 304). In fact, the verb "ver" appears more than twenty-five times in the novella (not to mention many other visual references without that specific verb).

Beyond direct references to sight and the visual, Berganza's conceptual understanding is also almost entirely human, as he partakes of the same sight-privileging metaphors that humans do.[34] In their groundbreaking *Philosophy in the Flesh: The Embodied Mind and Its Challenge to Western Thought*, George Lakoff and Mark Johnson investigate the embodiment of human mind and thought, analysing Western philosophy from the point of view of cognitive studies.[35] They argue that concepts not only need a human mind to hold them, but are themselves body-oriented and recur across cultures; that is, the human understanding of ourselves and the world comes about the way it does only because of the commonalities shared by the bodies we consist of.[36] There is no direct access to a reality beyond species-specific categorization, no reducible fully objective perspective. The reasons why such accounts are cross-cultural and multilinguistic is that they are based on evolutionary changes to our species that we hold in common as humans. Given these specific, innate features and the kind of physical world we inhabit, all humans will share certain early developmental experiences regardless of where they are brought up. A prime example explored in depth by Lakoff and Johnson are "primary" and "secondary" metaphors, cognitive structures that rely on these innate and developmental features and produce important consequences in the structure of reality as adduced by human thought and reflected in natural languages. As an example, consider the concept of "More Is Up" and its corollary "Less Is Down," both of which are found in many languages including English and Spanish. These particular cognitive concepts are not mere linguistic accidents, but arise due to cross-domain pairing; that is, the early neural association between the subjective judgment of quantity (regarding obtaining more of something, such as a liquid) and the sensory-motor experience of verticality that is produced by pouring or seeing someone else pour something into a container. As the volume of liquid rises, there is more in the container. As the liquid is consumed, there is less and less, while the vertical column gradually goes down. Such pairings, of which there are at least two dozen, become what Lakoff and Johnson call, "primary metaphors" (46–56). These are simple metaphorical pairings that people tend consciously not to understand as metaphors because they are so basic. In turn, Lakoff and Johnson argue, "secondary metaphors" use these simple, primary metaphors as building blocks "like atoms that can be put together to form molecules" (60). The primary metaphors form the schema for other thoughts, leading to secondary metaphors like "prices are rising" or "the stock market crashed" in which ultimately "more means up" and "less means down" (47–8).[37] These cognitive metaphors correspond specifically to "cross-domain pairings" in which concepts are taken from a sensory-motor source domain (usually involving sight) and paired with a target domain from subjective experience. Such cross-domain pairings, learned in this way, correspond to permanent neural connections, which extend across the brain between the relevant sensory-motor area (source) and the subjective experience area (target), thus establishing the "inferential structure" for experience (56–7). Lakoff and Johnson rely on J. Grady's 1997 dissertation (UC Berkeley) for their list of twenty-four primary and secondary metaphors, in which only one has to do with olfaction, as will be detailed below.[38] If a dog were to express him- or herself in dog language, there is every reason to believe that the embodied metaphors would be olfactory, not visual, corresponding to the odour-rich *Umwelt* and excellent olfactory capabilities of canines.

Yet in the "Colloquy," the two protagonists consistently employ precisely these types of embodied visual (i.e., human) metaphors mentioned by Lakoff and Johnson. For instance, Berganza uses the verb "ver" [to see] metaphorically to mean "to know" or "realize," as in the phrase he utters, "Seeing what was going on" (477) (Viendo lo que pasaba; 325). His friend Cipión does the same when he categorizes an occurrence as "never before seen" (461) (jamás vista; 309, 346) with the metaphorical meaning of "new," that is, "not previously known." Along these same lines of cognitively embodied metaphors, the negative corollary of the metaphor "seeing is knowing" is that *not seeing is being deceived* and *covering up is deceiving*. Images of this type abound in the novella: falsehoods are "covered over with a show of virtue" (473) (cubiertas con la capa de la virtud; 321); the truth can be "lost in the gloom" (473) (quedar a escuras; 321); and Cipión uses a synaesthetic secondary metaphor involving what are clearly his dominant senses – sight and sound, not olfaction – in which he says "I wouldn't want the sunrise to find us lost in the shadows of silence" (485) (no querría que al salir del sol quedásemos a la sombra del silencio; 333).

Furthermore, Berganza even talks ekphrastically about painting in the description of the witch Cañizares, focusing on her physical appearance: "I will now describe [her body] to you as best I can. She was over seven feet tall, and nothing but a bony skeleton covered with swarthy, hairy, weather-beaten skin" (495) (la cual te la pintaré como mejor supiere. Ella era larga de más de siete pies; toda era notomía de huesos, cubiertos en una piel negra; 344).[39] The description he proffers involves height, thickness, and colour, but absolutely nothing about her smell.[40] Finally, his emotional state is not determined by typical dog stimuli but by sight alone: "it really scared me *to find myself* shut up in that narrow room with that body in front of me" (495) (me dio gran temor *verme* encerrado en aquel estrecho aposento con aquella figura delante; 344, emphasis added).[41]

These dogs see the world largely through human embodied understanding that is almost entirely anthropocentric because their cognition has been gratuitously anthropomorphized, modelled on human cognition, not on that of canines (which would be caninocentric). This point might seem uncontroversional – of course talking animals are anthropomorphized. Such a retort would miss the important point that the dogs' human understanding does not simply come about with their apprehension of human language. As I have shown, their sight-dominated conceptual understanding is true not only of their current, rational, speaking selves in the present, but also, and more importantly, also true of the "dogs" who they were, their anterior selves before they had the ability to talk. The primary evidence for this claim is my analysis of Berganza's memories, which are peppered primarily with visual anecdotes, understood through humanly embodied metaphors, and contain anthropocentric concerns for the most part. Also, several critics have observed that Berganza's autobiographical account, his various occupations, and his attitude have much of a picaresque (human) quality, beginning with his problematic upbringing followed by a series of violent experiences and an array of employment venues that reveal many facets of a hypocritical society.[42] Following this narrative set-up, anthropocentric concerns abound as do examples of human conceptualizations, including Berganza's insistence on Christian morality, his racial slurs about blacks and Moriscos, and his and Cipion's knowledge of the classics. For instance, elaborating on the immorality of the slaughterhouse's boss, Berganza laments how readily that man would kill another person as if he were merely a cow, overvalorizing the worth of an unknown man's life over that of a non-human animal in a moralizing, anthropocentric manner.[43]

But the old Berganza is not entirely embodied cognitively as a human. While one would expect there to be many references to olfaction in a novella all about dogs (if they were supposed to actually be dogs, as some critics have maintained),[44] there is one direct smell perception mentioned. While singular, it is befitting of a dog's sensory experience, emphasizing as it does canine olfaction:

> [T]he aroma of bacon had wafted into my nostrils that left me giddy with delight. Tracking down the bacon by following my nose, I found it in a pocket of those breeches. That is to say, on discovering in that pocket a most excellent piece of ham, I snatched up the breeches and took them out into the street in order to get the ham out and enjoy it in peace and quiet. Once on the street I devoted myself, with great gusto, to devouring it. When I returned to the room, I found the Breton loudly demanding – in a mixed and bastardized lingo, although he made himself understood – that they give him back his breeches, because he had fifty pure gold escudos in them. (477)

> ([L]legó a mis narices un olor de tocino que me consoló todo; descubríle con el olfato, y halléle en una faldriquera de los follados. Digo que hallé en ella un pedazo de jamón famoso, y por gozarle y poderle sacar sin rumor saqué los follados a la calle, y allí me entregué en el jamón a toda mi voluntad, y cuando volví al aposento hallé que el bretón daba voces diciendo

en lenguaje adúltero y bastardo, aunque se entendía, que le volviesen sus calzas, que en ellas tenía cincuenta *escuti d'oro in oro.* [325])

In this case, Berganza has clearly identified, through olfaction alone, a piece of bacon that is hidden from view in a pocket of the Breton's breeches. Once identified, as he explains, he uses reason to put in motion a plan using clear grammatical figures for instrumentality: "I snatched up the breeches and took them out into the street in order to get the ham out and enjoy it in peace and quiet" (477) (por gozarle y poderle sacar sin rumor saqué los follados a la calle; 325). This olfactory ability demonstrates that Berganza has a strong canine-like sense of smell – not only can he detect the bacon without the assistance of another sensory organ, but he can pinpoint its location in a pocket. The affective importance of smell is brought to the fore as the smell comforts him. Yet it is strange that this is the one and only reference to direct smell experience in the novella.[45] Furthermore, unlike in the *Quixote*, we do not find any primary or secondary embodied metaphors associated with olfaction.

As in the case with the *Quixote*'s whispering monkey, as well as those of the *Persiles*'s talking wolves, there is likely a trick or transformation here in the "Colloquy," one that is never overtly revealed to the reader and about which we can only ever speculate. The dogs are aware that their ability to speak is unusual for themselves and that the ability may be time-limited. Berganza and Cipión may be literary characters invented by Campuzano, the protagonist of the framing novella, "The Deceitful Marriage" ("Casamiento engañoso"), or alternatively, they may be his syphilitic hallucinations.[46] While the ultimate ontological status of the dogs is not determined conclusively in the novella or its larger frame, the colloquy's speakers' highly developed sentience is suspect because their embodiment privileges human rather than animal sensory perception in almost all cases. In contrast to Martín, for whom Berganza "understands the world in many canine ways" (entiende el mundo de muchas maneras caninas; 462), I think it is more productive to view Cipión and Berganza as representations of humans acting like dogs, or humans transformed through witchcraft into dogs.[47] Could it be that these dogs now see the world through human understanding because they have been transformed into speaking, reasoning creatures and have left therefore their dog-embodiment behind? That hypothesis is not satisfactory since their sight-dominated conceptual understanding is true not only of their current present selves. Indeed, most of the examples I have mentioned above relate to Berganza's recollections of his past experiences. The examples show that he clearly formed his memories as an embodied human, for instance, focusing on the lady's white hands or obsessing over the race and colour of some of the characters.[48]

These findings lead to a reading of the novella in its context following the "Deceitful Marriage": An analysis of the cognitive embodiment of these dogs, and the demonstration that gratuitous anthropomorphism is the mechanism through which they are animated, shows that Berganza and Cipión are not in fact much like dogs, but rather are the creations of a human who wanted to make the characters seem like dogs but who didn't have enough distance from his own sight-dominant conceptual understanding, and thus ended up portraying them as barking, four-legged humans. Thus, Campuzano is the author of this fictional dialogue, imagining what a dog's world would be like through his very human conceptual understanding. He writes a story that depicts talking dogs, but which are cognitively more like humans walking on paws. We do not learn what it is like to be a dog from this story, but what it is like to be a human acting like a dog. For the most part (all but one example), the representation of the animals' sensory modalities are human. This is in contradistinction to animals that Cervantes creates in other works. My reading of Campuzano as fictional author helps explain the preponderance of sight words and concepts, and the many references to the visual throughout the text (i.e., ekphrasis), at the expense of the olfactory, despite Campuzano's insistence in his prefatory comments to his interlocutor, the Licenciate Peralta, that he truly overheard this dialogue "in full possession of my senses" (443–5) (con todos mis cinco sentidos; 294). For the reasons delineated above, this turns out to be a hyperbole. I doubt it was with all five senses, but rather, as an analysis of the text shows, with *Homo sapiens*'s two most dominant senses, vision and hearing.

Animal Perspective-Taking and Modes of Embodiment

Beyond the two kinds of treatments analysed above (implicit anthropectomy and gratuitous anthropomorphism), the rest of this chapter examines the far more subtle representations of animal cognition that lie in between the two extremes. Cervantes relies on folk animal psychology and uses constructive anthropomorphism with zoocentric concerns and animal perspective-taking, entering the realm of "animal embodiment." Some of the animals may demonstrate "higher" thinking, yet not in an entirely human form nor with mostly anthropocentric concerns.

Don Quixote

The episode with the cats by which the retinue of the Duke and Duchess torture Don Quixote (2.46) suggests a brief but focused attention to the perspective and mental processes of felines, about which the reader ought to care. As Adrienne Martín has explained, *el episodio gatuno* is built around a combination of two early modern European cultural practices involving humiliation and torture. The first, known sometimes by its German name "Katzenmusik" (cat music), involved stuffing a group of cats into a bag in order to provoke their ire and the ensuing cat screeches, thereby creating a horrifying background "music" to accompany the spectacle of human humiliation known as *cencerrada* performed on cuckolds (Martín 455).[49] In the novel, the reader hears how the cats in the sack meow and scratch, but not explicitly of their pain or suffering, as they are pushed onto Don Quixote's face.[50] However, the narrator invites the reader to consider briefly the perspective and cognition of the one cat who literally gets out of the bag and who "sees himself" attacked by the knight.

This focus on an individual being, emphasizing the perspective of the cat towards Don Quixote, is quite similar to the way in which other human combatants of Don Quixote are presented:[51] "*finding himself* so hounded by Don Quixote's sword thrusts, *leaped* at his face and *sank* his claws and teeth into his nose" (756) (*viéndose* tan acosado de las cuchilladas de don Quijote, le *saltó* al rostro y le *asió* de las narices con las uñas y los dientes; 2.46:385). The cat here seems to react in a somewhat human way – "finding himself so hounded" (viéndose tan acosado) – before going on the offensive. Indeed, the gerund *viendo* and the verb *asir* in the preterite are also used to describe the Basque's actions in 1.9. But before labelling this gratuitous anthropomorphism (given the apparent emphasis on the strongest of human senses), it is important to reflect on the fact that with "viéndose," the text mostly suggests a moment of pause for reflection, not a literal focus on vision.[52] The idea that some non-human animals pause in the way that humans do before action was discussed by Charles Darwin as he developed his evolutionary continuity view in *The Descent of Man*. For Darwin, animals, like human beings, consider alternative actions they can take, a view that continues to attract significant followers from the worlds of comparative psychology and cognitive ethology. It is a moment of deliberation suggesting conscious awareness and thought and, in this case, self-awareness. In this cat's case, it is followed by swift action guided by implicit intentional agency. That is, the well-known self-defence strategy of cats, which some might consider an instinct, is not portrayed in a completely mechanistic way;[53] the cat does not scratch and bite Don Quixote *qua* automaton as Gómez Pereira, Descartes, or Malebranche would have it.[54] Rather, in a Darwinian way, the syntactical structure requires a brief moment of cognition on the part of the cat, whose counteroffensive is prompted by "seeing himself" under attack.[55] The strength of the attack on the cat by the man with the sword also plays a role in the cat's response. It is not just any attack that generates this counter-attack, but a strong offensive that he faces, emphasized with the adverbialized adjective "*so* hounded" (*tan* acosado; DQ 2.46, emphasis added). Under other circumstances, the language suggests, the cat might have *chosen* not to react quite this way, from which I conclude that, in this scene, Cervantes represents a form of animal intentional agency without gratuitous anthropomorphism.

The episode with a much larger feline invites questions of this animal's sentience too. In this particular instance (DQ 2.17), the reader has little direct access to what the lion is actually thinking, much like the way humans face non-human animals in the real world, without a common language. In a certain way, the lion's mind seems impenetrable. Yet, what is perhaps more interesting is that some characters first implicitly deny that the lion is thinking and then begin to think about his motivations (thinking about what the lion is thinking), affording the reader the same opportunity.

At the beginning of the episode, important but skeletal pieces of background information are revealed by the royal cart driver: Two lions, one male, one female, both famished.[56] From Don Quixote's own perspective, the lions are not particularly sentient, and as he challenges them in his act of insane bravery by demanding that the cart driver open the male's cage, he calls the felines "bestias," a term used in period treatises to mean that an animal specifically lacks "higher thinking" or "reason." Don Quixote hopes and expects that, with the cage open, the lion will rush out and attack him (see fig. 26). As in the episode of the cat who escaped from the bag, one of the *bestias* comes into focus through his challenge. Despite Don Quixote's own apparent beliefs in the animal's "bestial" instinctual behaviour, this non-human animal is individuated and becomes a character with a mind.

Other characters in the scene hold a similar belief to Don Quixote's that the lion will rush out and attack, but instead of hoping for this outcome as he does, they fear it. Thus, the carriage driver has egocentric concerns and only unlocks the lion's cage under duress, fearing that the lion will kill Don Quixote and then the (implicitly anthropectomized) mules who he needs to pull his cart (161). The country gentleman, Don Diego, who

Figure 26 *Don Quixote Offers Battle to the Lion*, a chapter illustration. Cushing Memorial Library & Archives, Texas A&M University.

is accompanying Don Quixote at this point, thinks Don Quixote is out of his mind ("softened his head and ripened his brains" [560]) (ablandado los sesos; 160); Sancho fears that the lions will kill Don Quixote and then everyone else including him, leading to his tears (162).[57] All four of these characters are certain that the lion will rush out of the cage and attack. Such certainty points to anthropectomy, for it implies that the lion cannot choose to do otherwise. That is, their implicit belief about the "beast" is that *it* has no thought process, that *it* will mechanistically charge out of the cage to kill Don Quixote. But the reader learns that these assumptions are wrong when that is not at all what happens:

> The first thing the lion did was to turn around in the cage where he had been lying and unsheathe his claws and stretch his entire body; then he opened his mouth, and yawned very slowly, and extended a tongue almost two spans long, and cleaned the dust from his eyes and washed his face; when this was finished, he put his head out of the cage and looked all around with eyes like coals, a sight and a vision that could frighten temerity itself (...) But the magnanimous lion, more courteous than arrogant, took no notice of either the childishness or bravado, and after looking in both directions, as has been said, he turned his back, and showed his hindquarters to Don Quixote, and with great placidity and calm went back inside the cage. (563–4)

> (Lo primero que hizo fue revolverse en la jaula, donde venía echado, y tender la garra, y desperezarse todo; abrió luego la boca y bostezó muy despacio, y con casi dos palmos de lengua que sacó fuera se despolvoreó los ojos y se lavó el rostro; hecho esto, sacó la cabeza fuera de la jaula y miró a todas partes con los ojos hechos brasas, vista y ademán para poner espanto a la misma temeridad. [...] Pero el generoso león, más comedido que arrogante, no haciendo caso de niñerías ni de bravatas, después de haber mirado a una y otra parte, como se ha dicho, volvió las espaldas y enseñó sus traseras partes a don Quijote, y con gran flema y remanso se volvió a echar en la jaula. [164])

When results do not follow expectations, the latter must be reconsidered, something that can be accomplished through a careful analysis of the lion's actions. The sentences are mostly in the preterite, and consist of a series of actions ("sacó," "miró," etc.), avoiding most explicit inferences about the lion's thoughts. What can be gleaned from this? First, it is clear that the lion is not in any rush to get out of the cage and that he takes his time, to stretch and wake himself up. In a not oft compared but analogous scene at the end of Part I, Don Quixote is let out of the cage to speak with the Canon of Toledo, at which point the first thing he does is stretch (1.49);[58] thus the lion's actions are a doubling of those of the main human character, who clearly possesses intentional agency. Some of the lion's actions may seem involuntary, especially the lengthy yawn. But like the smaller cat mentioned above, the lion also has a moment that we could only call reflection, as "he put his head out of the cage and looked all around" (sacó la cabeza fuera de la jaula y miró a todas partes). A few sentences later, the narrator emphasizes the reflective moment by repeating this idea, with different words, of the lion "looking in both directions" (mirado a una y otra parte). The repetition of this action-reflection, followed by the subsequent actions, again implies that the lion had a choice to make, and made it, expressing his intentional agency. The narrator tells us that the lion is not interested in "childishness or bravado" (niñerías ni de bravatas) and thus turns around and comically shows his hinder parts to the mad knight, then lies down again. While Cervantes may have selected these lion actions as a comical insult to Don Quixote – the hinder parts would be the least noble from the knight's perspective – Cervantes may have been familiar with lion behaviour and lions' individual differences,[59] or with debates about lion agency.

The narrator suggests that the lion may have other emotions beyond being furious, calling him "magnanimous lion, more courteous than arrogant" (generoso león, más comedido que arrogante), who moves with great placidity and calm (con gran flema y remanso). These seem to be anthropomorphising projections rather than descriptions of his interiority, which I believe the reader must infer. Their purpose may be irony. However, the term "generoso" also suggests that the lion chooses not to kill Don Quixote out of something like pity or clemency,[60] perhaps reminding the reader of the famous lion encounter topos, in the well-known story popularized in Pliny's *History* as well as in the hagiographic tradition surrounding Saint Jerome in which lions are gratuitously anthropomorphized and engage in implausible friendships with a human. Here, the fact that the lion "took no notice of ... the childishness" is a negative description, in which the narrator belittles the self-aggrandizing actions of Don Quixote, which are thus likened to trifles. To be sure, a potential meal for a hungry lion would be no "childishness" (niñerías).

That the lions have not eaten on this day is thus an important detail, and with it we have the outlines of the sixteenth- and seventeenth-century debate about animal sentience, which specifically raised the question as to whether animals deliberate and make choices, first taken up by Gómez

Pereira in his *Antoniana Margarita* (1554), and later by Descartes and Malebranche.[61] In fact, Pereira explicitly takes issue with Pliny's lion, which he attempts to rebut. When a lion does not kill a human, Pereira specifies, it is never by choice but rather because the lion is full: "The clemency of the lion from Getulia – Pliny, Book Eight, Chapter 16 – should not be attributed to the animal's heeding the captive's pleas. For, if that were the case, then it would be the normal state of affairs that lions always show clemency before such pleas, but that is not what occurs. What happened is that, barring other circumstances, the lion was stuffed" (La clemencia del león en Getulia – Plinio, libro octavo, capítulo 16 – no se debe atribuir a que el animal escuchó las súplicas de la cautiva. Pues, de ser así, lo normal sería que siempre se mostrasen clementes ante los ruegos – lo que no sucede. Lo que ocurrió es que, aparte otras circunstancias, el león estaba ahíto; 49, see also Alves, *The Animals of Spain* 42). While Pereira may be right in most cases that a hungry lion will charge a person, his claim that a lion who did not do this must be "stuffed" is an unfounded, rigid belief plagued by an unquestioned tendency to anthropectomy. Considering the Cervantine episode from start to finish, Pereira's schema is logically deficient and carefully countered by the narrator, since the reader knows that the claim is false and that the lions, in fact, "are famished" (van hambrientos; 2.17:160, my translation).[62]

Cervantes's reader is left face to face with the difficulty of scrutinizing the animal mind, a problem that endures in cognitive ethology to this day. In the absence of a common language between humans and the lion, we cannot know for certain why he chooses one thing over another. Yet we see him choose, once again in the Darwinian pause of intentional agency, looking one way and then the other before acting; the fact that he does not automatically rush out and kill Don Quixote, in opposition to what characters predict, suggests that the lion possesses richer mental processes, of reflection, intention, and emotion. Focusing clearly on one specific lion, offering some of the lion's perspective, and having him act in an unexpected way, Cervantes demonstrates, through subtle, constructive anthropomorphism, the complexity of the lion's mind. An individuated character is created, and while he does not speak – in fact, because of it – the lion is a most memorable one.

That non-human animals are unable to speak their mind to humans is a common thread in other animal episodes as well. In the story of the goatherd and his goat towards the end of DQ Part I, the reader is invited to think about this particular animal's cognition once again. With the goatherd chasing after her, the goat is scared and looks for protection among the people in Don Quixote's group. This goat, then, is presented as an individual (like the escaped cat or the male lion) favouring some form of anthropomorphism, rather than as one of a mass of animals (like the bulls, the sheep, or all the other cats still stuck in the bag), the treatment of which favours anthropectomy.

The goatherd first calls her "animal" ("alimaña"), which Covarrubias says generally refers to a rustic's domestic animal; but he also anthropomorphically attributes gendered human characteristics to her, calling her "my girl" (hija) and "my pretty" (hermosa), tags he more aptly would utter to a human female. The narrator does not state what the goat understands or knows, but suggests that there is some cognition about which we can infer: first, the goat stops among the people "as if" to find help. When the goatherd arrives, he grabs her by the horns, and speaks to her "as if she were capable of rational thought and speech" (432) (como si fuera capaz de discurso y entendimiento; 1.50:588). This counterfactual along with the narrative distance between the narrator and the goatherd here implies certainly that she is *not* capable of such understanding, that his behaviour is bizarre, and that he is engaging in downright gratuitous anthropomorphism. At first glance, then, the notion that the goat is sentient seems misguided.[63]

The goatherd is a parodic character, imaged on the typical literary shepherd from sixteenth-century pastoral romance such as *The Seven Books of the Diana* (*Los siete libros de la Diana*) (a tome that Don Quixote possesses in his library): a male voice, complaining eloquently of his unrequited love for a beloved female. Indeed, Eugenio's search for the goat involves the literalization of a fictional mode, in which the goatherd crosses the boundary between two fictional worlds:[64] between one fictional world modelled on the actual world (in which, as in the actual world, characters read chivalric and pastoral fiction and are aware that it is fiction) and another fictional world modelled on the pastoral fictional world (in which the people who take care of flocks spend most of their time talking of love and searching for their beloveds unaware that they belong to the realm of fiction). This goatherd's quest is thus akin to Don Quixote's own to resuscitate a fictional world, that of yesteryear's fictional chivalric heroes. The reader learns that Eugenio is in love with a human female, Leandra, a literary shepherdess par excellence, whose name literally echoes through the valleys since all shepherds are in love with her and continually call out her name (1.51:595). His feelings for the goat in 1.50 are imaged on his love for Leandra, and he explains self-consciously that he treats the goat as a surrogate for his beloved, about whom he is complaining. Eugenio's words thus reveal that he is self-consciously engaging in gratuitous anthropomorphism, and moreover that he treats the goat with a gender bias as he would any female human, relying on the time-honoured patriarchal formula of blaming females for their alleged moral weakness, paradoxically in light of their fortitude:[65] "And this was the reason, Señores, for the words and arguments I addressed to this goat when I arrived here, for since she is a female, I hold her in small esteem, though she is the best of my flock" (438) (Y ésta fue la ocasión, señores, de las palabras y razones que dije a esta cabra cuando aquí llegué; que por ser hembra la tenga en poco, aunque es la mejor de todo mi apero; 595). Just because Eugenio engages in gratuitous anthropomorphism, however, does not mean that the animal is not sentient.

The reader never learns directly what other characters think about her sentience. However, the narrator's perspective is prominent. As I pointed out above, the narrator uses a counterfactual to describe the goat's "rational thought and speech." Despite the negative implication of the counterfactual, a couple of pages later, the goat really seems to understand when Eugenio taps her on the back: "The nanny goat seemed to understand him" (433) (Pareció que lo entendió la cabra; 1.50:590).[66] These later words – with "seem" rather than "as if" – should make the reader reconsider the first utterance of the narrator: If at first the goatherd seemed laughable because he spoke to the goat "as if it were capable of understanding," now the narrator admits that the goat "seemed to understand" what he means.

Furthermore, I would argue that there are additional narrative clues for positing greater cognition on the part of the goat. Indeed, the situation is a doubling of an earlier scene from Part I, much like the characters' stretching in the episodes with the lion's cage and Don Quixote's cage. In fact, after Eugenio sits down, the goat lies next to him and she looks him right in the face: "she lay down next to him very calmly and looked into his face, *as if letting him know that she was listening to what he was saying*" (433, emphasis added) (se tendió ella junto a él con mucho sosiego, y mirándole al rostro *daba a entender que estaba atenta* a lo que el cabrero iba diciendo; 590, emphasis added). While Grossman translates "daba a entender" as "as if," the Spanish phrase has greater certainty than "as if" or "seems," and it could more literally be translated as "led one to believe." This calmed gaze into another's face, in which there is an emotional compenetration between two beings after a period of fear and excitement, is reminiscent of another quasi-pastoral episode: that of Cardenio, the "wild man," who, like the goat, had also wandered off into the mountains, and who, like the goatherd, complained of another "ingrata," Lucinda. Cardenio finds himself face to face with an unusually empathic Don Quixote, who gives Cardenio a long embrace, after which Cardenio spends a considerable time calmly looking at Don Quixote, face to face: "The other man ... allowed himself to be embraced, then stepped back, placed his hands on Don Quixote's shoulders, and stood looking at him as if wanting to see if he knew him" (182) (Después de haberse dejado abrazar, le apartó un poco de sí, y, puestas sus manos en los hombros de don Quijote, le estuvo mirando, como que quería ver si le conocía; 1.23:290).

By analogy, whether she understands the exact words or not, the goat seems to display empathy towards the goatherd. Like the episode of the lion, we know not exactly what she is thinking, but there are good indications that she has a significant emotional life, shows intentional agency and understanding, engages in limited communication with humans, and feels interspecies empathy. Cervantes's is a very different type of treatment of a goat, an animal marked in Herrera's *Agricultura* as one entirely lacking an intellectual life, whose "stupidity" is legendary.[67] Yet the story of Leandra is in no way a fable, whether Aesopian or Lybian,[68] for it lacks the gratuitous anthropomorphism that grants any and all human characteristics to non-human animals. This, in contrast, is a form of subtle, constructive anthropomorphism, avoiding the irreality of the talking animal, while eschewing the clearly wrong path of explicit anthropectomy. And it is more in line with current cognitive ethological appraisals of goats.[69] As is becoming clear, through constructive anthropomorphism, Cervantes endows these animal characters – cat, lion, goat – with individual minds, as they become, something more akin to non-human persons.

In treatises on husbandry and hunting, as well as in natural histories and books of an encyclopedic nature, the bonds between humans and dogs, and to a lesser extent between humans and horses, are stressed beyond all others as the most important interspecies relationships. As Marcy Norton explains, transgressions of such typical boundaries in effect for human-animal relationships were met with anxiety. Norton points to the case of Fernández de Oviedo's *Historia* where the author expresses his uneasiness about such transgressions while discussing the case of an unnamed indigenous man who lived, befriended, and hunted in the jungle with a group of feral pigs;[70] this association must have been particularly troubling for a Christian Spaniard like Oviedo, given the increasing importance of pork in the diet of Christians, who differentiated themselves by cuisine from the Jews and Moors.[71]

Yet, in Cervantes's *Don Quixote*, bonds with other animals are more common than bonds with dogs. The development of dog minds and relationships are practically non-existent in the *Quijote*. To wit, we learn nothing about Don Quixote's own dog, a greyhound, who is mentioned in the novel's famous first sentence but never again. Some hunters have dogs, and two dogs are mentioned in short vignettes in the Prologue to Part II, in which the dogs are terribly mis-treated.[72] But people's relationships with other species of animals are the norm in Cervantes's masterpiece. The case of Eugenio's goat is part of a larger phenomenon.

The Alderman's Donkey

Various individuals have an unusual fondness for particular and unusual non-human animal companions. One such is the alderman in the braying adventure ("episodio del rebuzno"), about grown men who have formed deep attachments to donkeys. The implicit propriety of such positive emotions towards donkeys is questioned and becomes a source of humour in the novel. While in fables and miracle stories donkeys sometimes appear in a positive light,[73] throughout the tomes on hunting, husbandry, and agriculture donkeys are typically reviled. Agustí's view of the donkey is typical, calling it "vile and despised animal" (animal vil y despreciado; 345). Thus, loving a donkey might seem quite absurd, seeing as it was considered a lowly and horrid animal. Unlike the horse, whose habitational parameter generally included close contact with humans on hunts and in wars through related modes of interaction, a donkey's place was generally working on a farm or as *merely* a pack animal.

Similar to the case of the goatherd and the goat, when the alderman's donkey goes missing, the alderman goes to great lengths to find him, not only because of the donkey's value, but for personal, affective reasons. His helpful friend, the other alderman, sees the donkey in the wilderness, but the animal is now unapproachable having become feral. The friend expresses compassion, as it appears that the animal has lost a lot of weight, described as skinny and negatively by what it doesn't have. Noting the animal's loss of weight, the second alderman uses an unmistakable *personal* pronoun (*le*), which could only be translated as "he": "I saw him this morning, without a packsaddle or any trappings, and so skinny it made me feel bad just to look at him" (621) (le vi esta mañana, sin albarda y sin aparejo alguno, y tan flaco, que era una compasión miralle; 2.25:230).

Thus, they attempt to find him. In so doing, the two aldermen reveal that they are considered experts in donkey communication, for not only can they recreate the sound a donkey makes, but they can also critique the donkey calls of humans using sophisticated terminology. In the same way that a connoisseur of wine would employ her particular skill with an appropriate vocabulary to discuss the nose or the finish, here the aldermen apply their specialized music vocabulary to an imitation donkey bray: "your sound is loud, your voice sustained, with the correct time and rhythm, your inflections numerous and rapid" (622) (el sonido que tenéis es alto; lo sostenido de la voz, a su tiempo y compás; los dejos, muchos y apresurados; 2.25:232).[74] Despite their skill at calling the donkey, by the time they find him, he has been killed by a wolf. This early death leaves the reader in the dark about the donkey's cognition and the donkey's perspective. The reader learns, however, what the aldermen think about donkey communication. Since they fool each other, unwittingly – each thinks that the other is the missing donkey who is braying – they must indeed be very good. Like practice at just about anything, this skill would have taken a significant investment of time and study. While the whole vignette and its later interruption into the main storyline with the warring armies is certainly meant to be humorous and perhaps serve as a critique of ridiculous reasons for going to war, it also centres the experience of the donkey and human fascination, affection, and folk psychology towards a non-idealized, unusual species, to which no tomes were ever dedicated in the era.[75] Vis-à-vis their thoughts on the donkey's cognition, the aldermen's assumption is that he would reply if he could: "the donkey will have to hear us and respond if he's in the woods at all (...) because if he hadn't been dead, he would have brayed when he heard us, or he wouldn't be a donkey" (621–2) ("no podrá ser menos sino que el asno nos oya y nos responda, si es que está en el monte [...] pues a no estar muerto, él rebuznara si nos oyera, o no fuera asno; 2.25:231–2). Indeed, they are right in that when the donkey does not answer, the reason for this is that he is already dead (of course, the reverse is not logically necessary). While they are sympathetic to the animal, and seem to enjoy donkeys, their view of his agency is quite limited – regarding communication, he would not have a choice but to reply.

There is of course another donkey who is more important than the alderman's. As a non-human animal character, he is second only to Rocinante in importance, appearing in a vast number of scenes, in close relationship with humans and alongside the single most important non-human animal in *Don Quixote*. Iconographically, both El rucio and his companion, Rocinante, are an integral part of the novel, and of the iconographical realizations of the Don Quixote story through the centuries, in painting, drawing, and statuary (see figs. 27 and 28). The embodiment of these two important equine characters is the subject of the last section.

Figure 27 *The History of Don Quichote. The First Part* title page. Cushing Memorial Library & Archives, Texas A&M University.

Figure 28 Bronze sculptures of Don Quixote and Sancho Panza in the Plaza de España in Madrid. Photo courtesy of Anne Nguyen.

Embodied Equids

Rocinante and Sancho's nameless donkey are two animals who are striking as a pair of animal friends, like Cipión and Berganza. However, unlike the dogs of the "Colloquy," the two main equids of *Don Quixote* are not gratuitously anthropomorphized.[76] Several scholars have commented on the relationship between the two equids,[77] Rocinante and El rucio, as will be examined below.[78] Regarding animal cognition, the narrator's explicit description of the deep equid "friendship" (*amistad*) provides grounds for acknowledging their sentience, while focusing mostly on behaviours rather than on cognitive abilities and properties or inner thoughts and feelings:

> for their friendship was so unusual and so firm that (...) [the author] writes that as soon as the two animals were together they would begin to scratch each other, and then, when they were tired and satisfied, Rocinante would lay his neck across the donkey's – it would extend almost half a meter on the other side – and, staring intently at the ground, the two of them could stand this way for three days. (528)
>
> (cuya amistad dél y de Rocinante fue tan única y tan trabada [...] y escribe [el autor] que así como las dos bestias se juntaban, acudían a rascarse el uno al otro, y que, después de cansados y satisfechos, cruzaba Rocinante el pescuezo sobre el cuello del rucio – que le sobraba de la otra parte más de media vara – , y mirando los dos atentamente al suelo, se solían estar de aquella manera tres días. [2.12:122])

Reflecting on their friendship, Martín calls this passage "one of the warmest and friendliest descriptions of the novel's equine protagonists" (459).[79] For Alves, the passage shows that Cervantes's equids love: "Cervantes' beasts understand, feel and love" (58). The deep bond between the two brings to mind Agustí's prescription in *Secretos de la agricultura* that it is good practice, when stabling, to keep a horse close to another whom he or she "loves," as he is concerned about their emotional well-being (328).[80] Given that their adventures with Don Quixote and Sancho keep them outside and on the go much of the time, the equids enjoy each other's company, often being spared the separation that would likely occur in most stabling settings. In *The Mind of the Horse: An Introduction to Equine Cognition*, comparative psychologist Michel-Antoine Leblanc discusses the horse as a "supremely social animal," which in the wild "never lives alone" (10.11). Drawing on recent studies, Leblanc views stabling as a hindrance to the emotional flourishing of horses and critiques the "arbitrary character of the constraints imposed on domesticated horses (such as confinement, social isolation, and relative inactivity)" that can "ultimately overwhelm their natural capacity to adapt"

(10–11). In Cervantes's passage, the freedom that the pair has to enjoy each other's company is thus ethologically salutary, and helps explain why these animals are flourishing emotionally.

Their well-being is not only caused by being together in each other's company, but also by the grooming behaviours in which they engage, which are mentioned by the narrator. The scholarly appraisals of the animals' emotions, by Alves and Martín, rely on constructive anthropomorphic inferences, based on explicit actions: "scratch" ("rascarse), "lay his neck" (cruzaba el pescuezo), "staring intently ... the two of them" (mirando los dos) rather than on explicit representation of the animals' thought processes.[81] Thus, in some respects, the narrator is relying on the same kind of description and narration of animal behaviour as that in which he engaged in the episode of the lion; the difference here is that the behaviours of Rocinante and El rucio are not ambiguous, and reasonable people can understand their feelings towards each other. Failure to do so would amount to blatant, unproductive anthropectomy. While not identical to human caresses, the animals' scratching each other, the crossing of their necks, as well as their maintaining of these postures for a lengthy period of time have broad correlatives in human actions based on emotion, which humans know intuitively and believe others to hold as well. Beyond such constructive anthropomorphism and folk animal psychology, ethological research shows that grooming behaviours performed on specific "preferred grooming sites" have a calming effect on horses, resulting in significant physiological benefits.[82] Grooming fills multiple functions, including cleaning and removal of parasites, establishing and deepening bonds, and avoiding potential aggressions (Leblanc 383). Contrasting social grooming in equids and in many primates, Leblanc notes that in the latter group, grooming involves the entire body and "thus appears especially to be related to hygiene" (383), whereas region-specific equine grooming is even more social and entails "a hedonic reward element designed to maintain the behavior" (383). This "hedonic reward" involves something similar to the neuronal release of endorphins in humans, documented in love, and in eating chocolate.[83] Cervantes's lengthy paragraph then – allegedly abridged for "decency and decorum" (528) – is an apt folk psychological appraisal of equine friendship that has been validated by contemporary cognitive science.

While early twentieth-century Hispanists recognized the importance of both Rocinante and El rucio in *Don Quixote*, in a 1968 essay, Montserrat Ordóñez Vila first argued that they should be considered "characters" outright "as beings with character and function that are specific to the literary work" (Ordóñez Vila 57), and she demonstrated that they were as meritorious as being called modern novelistic characters by the same criteria that Menéndez y Pelayo and Américo Castro had applied to Don Quixote and Sancho.[84] Ordoñez Vila provides an excellent case for the animals being almost omnipresent in the text, and also points to their suffering alongside the human protagonists, an idea on which I build. Much of the creation of character, I argue, stems from the careful treatment of the animals' sensation and cognition, through constructive anthropomorphism and folk psychology, of which suffering – that is, the experience of pain – is key. Indeed, both El rucio and Rocinante are cognitively embodied beings, showing species-typical functioning and individual personality, something achieved *without* gratuitous anthropomorphism. Their cognition is a complex, multifaceted representation in which consciousness, intentional agency, memory, and multiple emotions come together, and which is very much in line with what today is considered species-typical equine cognitive functioning.[85]

One of the most important aspects of cognition for cognitive scientists and philosophers of cognitive science is phenomenal consciousness, which is the qualitative nature of experience. As Kristin Andrews explains, paraphrasing Nagle, a creature has experience of phenomenal consciousness "if and only if there is something that it is like to be that creature."[86] Measures of phenomenal consciousness therefore have to do with qualia or awareness, and a paradigmatic measure of this, in scientific animal studies, is that of pain. Based on research by biologist Victoria Braithwaite and others, philosopher Gary Varner argues that vertebrates can probably all experience pain.[87] To come to this conclusion, Varner draws on research that shows that (1) the animal's skin has nociceptors (receptors in the skin that send a response to the spinal cord) and (2) that there is an anatomical brain structure in the animal, such as in the limbic and/or dopamine systems, that is involved after nociception has occurred (Andrews 63–5), both of which obtain in humans. Braithwaite has also studied several kinds of fish, tested in laboratory settings, to see if opioids such as morphine, which are known to decrease human pain, result in noticeable behavioural differences in animals that are subjected to pain, and indeed, they do (63). Taken along with other findings, this indicates that fish in fact experience pain. Importantly, since the experience of pain is also linked to human appraisals of a species's worthiness for empathy, Braithwaite and colleagues have undertaken this research into the pain of animals, in order to make people more aware that animals are suffering, that is, as Andrews puts it, "whether there is something it is like to be a hooked or suffocating fish" (63).[88] While the study of fish pain and consciousness in particular has been recent and somewhat controversial, the overwhelming evidence for vertebrates is no longer an issue of debate. As Andrews points out, at the Francis Crick Memorial Conference in 2012, participants signed "The Cambridge Declaration of Consciousness in Non-human Animals," which states that "convergent evidence indicates that non-human animals have the neuroanatomical, neurochemical, and neurophysiological substrates of conscious states along with the capacity to exhibit intentional behaviors. Consequently, the weight of evidence indicates that humans are not unique in possessing the neurological substrates that generate consciousness" (qtd. in Andrews 51).

For these reasons, it is significant that El rucio and Rocinante suffer the slings and arrows of the misfortunes of their masters, and suffer in various ways, sometimes indicating their pain with such "intentional behaviors." The slings, in particular, bring pain and along with it, the plausibility of phenomenal consciousness and awareness.

Both equids suffer in numerous scenes from physical and emotional pain. For instance, Rocinante, "whose back was almost broken" (que medio despaldado estaba; 1.8:130) is hurt after the windmills, an image that vividly evokes the scraped, tender flesh he would feel, and from which the reader may infer his pain, which is not made otherwise explicit. While some of the pain comes from accidents such as being thrown from a windmill's sail, the equids also suffer the malice of others, who are aware of their suffering and cause it deliberately. Alves points out the importance of the scene with the furze, highlighting the narrator's tender remarks about the "poor animals" who are helped by the knight and squire after they are thrown from their mounts:

> [T]hey rode with him to the city, and as they entered it, there were the Evil One, who ordains all wickedness, and boys, who are more evil than the Evil One; two of them who were particularly mischievous and impudent made their way through all the people, and one lifted the gray's tail and the other lifted Rocinante's, and there they placed and inserted branches of furze in each one. The poor animals felt these new spurs, and when they passed down their tails, they increased their discomfort to such an extent that they reared and bucked a thousand times and threw their riders to the ground. Don Quixote, enraged and affronted, hurried to remove the plumage from the tail of his nag, and Sancho did the same for his gray. (863)

([S]e encaminaron con él a la ciudad; al entrar de la cual, el malo, que todo lo malo ordena, y los muchachos que son más malos que el malo, dos de ellos, traviesos y atrevidos, se entraron por toda la gente, y, alzando el uno de la cola del rucio, y el otro la de Rocinante, les pusieron y encajaron sendos manojos de aliagas. Sintieron los pobres animales las nuevas espuelas, y, apretando las colas, aumentaron su disgusto de manera, que, dando mil corcovos, dieron con sus dueños en tierra. Don Quijote, corrido y afrentado, acudió a quitar el plumaje de la cola de su matalote, y Sancho el de su rucio. [2.61:508])

In terms of conscious awareness, anthropomorphizing the animals' reactions to the furze is scientifically sound and the appropriate thing to do, as they react with intentional behaviours, demonstrating their pain ("passed down their tails" [aprentando la cola] and "reared and bucked" [haciendo corcovos], which throw the riders to the ground). To fail to anthropomorphize constructively would be to engage in blind anthropectomy and result in an unscientific Malebranchian model of animal minds. Here and in other scenes, such as 2.64, as Ordóñez and others have pointed out, the animals' suffering is directly linked to their human riders'. After the final battle with the Knight of the White Moon (Caballero de la Blanca Luna), in which Don Quixote is defeated (2.64), the narrator describes first Don Quixote and then Rocinante: "They picked up Don Quixote, uncovered his face, and found him pale and perspiring. Rocinante had been so badly hurt that he could not move" (887) (Levantaron a don Quijote, descubriéronle el rostro y halláronle sin color y trasudando. Rocinante, de puro malparado, no se pudo mover por entonces; 2.64:535). This narrative technique sets up Quijote and Rocinante as two separate characters about whom the narrator feels obliged to comment, in parallel situations, and in experiences of pain.[89]

Pain and Communication

In addition to physical pain, the equids also seem to suffer from psychological pain, as interpreted by Sancho, who constructively anthropomorphizes their actions. While nociceptors are not known to be involved, and the neurological mechanism not yet understood, broad research on a number of animals leads many experts to believe that many, if not all, mammals (and perhaps other kinds of animals) feel psychological pain. Some research suggests that, if given a choice, many animals would choose to experience physical over psychological pain.[90] In the episode of the enchanted boat, Sancho and Don Quixote hitch the equids on land and then embark, at which Sancho becomes saddened watching the animals' reactions:

> [W]hen Sancho found himself some two *varas* onto the river he began to tremble, fearing that he was lost; but nothing caused him more grief than the sound of the donkey braying and the sight of Rocinante struggling to break free, and he said to his master: 'The donkey is braying because he is sorry about our absence, and Rocinante is trying to get free so that he can jump in after us. O dearest friends, stay in peace, and let the madness that takes us away from you turn into disappointment and bring us back to you!' And saying this he began to cry so bitterly. (648)
>
> ([C]uando Sancho se vio obra de dos varas dentro del río, comenzó a temblar, temiendo su perdición; pero ninguna cosa le dio más pena que el oír roznar al rucio y el ver que Rocinante pugnaba por desatarse, y díjole a su señor: "El rucio rebuzna, condolido de nuestra ausencia, y Rocinante procura ponerse en libertad para arrojarse tras nosotros. ¡Oh carísimos amigos, quedaos en paz, y la locura que nos aparta de vosotros, convertida en desengaño, nos vuelva a vuestra presencia!" Y en esto, comenzó a llorar tan amargamente. [2.29:263])

As an interpreter of equid sounds, Sancho anthropomorphizes the utterance that El rucio makes, which is described by the narrator as "roznar" and by Sancho as "rebuznar."[91]

While ethological research into donkey cognition is scarce, studies on the closely related horse, as well as on other farm animals, have shown that many animals have multiple meaningful calls.[92] Regarding horses, according to Leblanc, vocalizations can be broken down into seven main types – squeals, nickers, whinnies, groans, blows, snorts, and snores – and each of these can be further broken down into subcategories with specific contexts and meanings. Researchers have studied horse vocalizations for their acoustic properties in terms of frequency, duration, number of pulsations, and sound energy, and examined them contextually for how the horses use them.[93] If Sancho is right, El rucio is "saddened" (condolido) by their absence and probably emitting a groan or a whinny. For Leblanc, "groans appear to be the expression of mental conflict, suffering, or physical effort (...) With a bandwidth under 300 Hz, and very rapid pulsations, a groan may be followed immediately by a broadband, nonvoiced but audible supplementary exhalation"

(310). However, given the social context, it might also be a whinny, which "occur[s] especially during separation from group members at the moment contact is broken" (309).[94] Regarding Rocinante's actions, Sancho anthropomorphizes them constructively, understanding them as indicating that Rocinante is trying to free himself so that he may follow Don Quixote and Sancho, an unusual behaviour not mentioned at other times. Once again, without gratuitous anthropomorphism (e.g., Rocinante does not say he wants to be free in language), Cervantes uses the equids' actions, paired with the humanly embodied capacity for magical thinking and the tendency to use folk (animal) psychology, thereby constructing, through Sancho's perspective, a plausible reading of the animals' emotional pain.

There are other episodes of communication as well that are not always involved with pain. Communication between human and animal, and among the animals, is important to developing their portrayed higher-level cognition. In one example, Rocinante communicated through touch to the *señoras facas* "to communicate his need to them" (103) (comunicar su necesidad con ellas; 191). And Rocinante and El rucio demonstrated what ethologists call "synchronizing behavior" (when the horse whinneys and the donkey, in turn, sighs, in tandem, in 2.8), which does not necessarily refer to the "eye contact" that for humans is so important, but instead may involve other sensory modalities "that are salient and under voluntary control for that species" (Andrews 123). Unlike the speech of Balaam's talking donkey, the meaning of Rocinante's oral utternances is not immediately clear: Don Quixote interprets actions or sounds of Rocinante symbolically, but it is not always clear or unambiguous what these mean; the horse whinneys at one point, and may be expressing something, or may not be: "No sooner had Sancho said these words than the sound of Rocinante neighing reached their ears; Don Quixote took this as a very good omen and resolved that in three or four days he would undertake another sally, and after declaring his intention to the bachelor, he asked his advice as to the direction he should take on his journey" (483) (No había bien acabado de decir estas razones Sancho, cuando llegaron a sus oídos relinchos de Rocinante, los cuales relinchos tomó don Quijote por felicísimo agüero, y determinó de hacer de allí a tres o cuatro días otra salida, y, declarando su intento al bachiller, le pidió consejo por qué parte comenzaría su jornada; 2.4:69). Sancho too interprets the sounds of Rocinante and El rucio, in a scene in which, more importantly, the horse and the donkey may be communicating to each other, putting their sounds in alignment:

Don Quixote and Sancho were now alone, and as soon as Sansón rode away Rocinante began to neigh and the donkey to snort, and both knight and squire considered this a good sign and a fortunate omen; although, if truth be told, the donkey snorted and brayed more than the horse neighed, and from this Sancho concluded that his good fortune would exceed and go beyond that of his master. (503)

(Solos quedaron don Quijote y Sancho, y apenas se hubo apartado Sansón, cuando comenzó a relinchar Rocinante y a suspirar el rucio, que de entrambos, caballero y escudero, fue tenido a buena señal y por felicísimo agüero, aunque, si se ha de contar la verdad, más fueron los suspiros y rebuznos del rucio que los relinchos del rocín, de donde coligió Sancho que su ventura había de sobrepujar y ponerse encima de la de su señor. [2.8:92])[95]

Still other passages imply a need to communicate among these animals: El rucio acts as if he wants to speak in the episode of the Duke's people kidnapping Don Quixote: "[T]he same thing happened to Sancho, because as soon as he gave signs of wanting to speak, one of the men on foot goaded him with a barb, and the donkey, too, as if he wanted to speak as well" (906) (Y a Sancho le acontecía lo mismo, porque apenas daba muestras de hablar, cuando uno de los de a pie con un aguijón le punzaba, y al rucio ni más ni menos, como si hablar quisiera; 2.68:556).[96]

And in another scene, when Sancho talks to him, El rucio shows that he understands and then communicates by braying, thus verifying this understanding:

And there is more: it seems as if the donkey understood exactly what Sancho said, because he immediately began to bray, and so loudly that the entire cave resonated. "A famous witness!" Said Don Quixote. "I recognize the bray as if it were my own, and I hear your voice, friend Sancho. Wait for me: I shall go to the Duke's castle, which is close by, and bring someone who can rescue you from the pit where your sins must have brought you." (821)

(Y hay más; que no parece sino que el jumento entendió lo que Sancho dijo, porque al momento comenzó a rebuznar, tan recio, que toda la cueva retumbaba. "Famoso testigo," dijo don Quijote; "el rebuzno conozco como si le pariera, y tu voz oigo, Sancho mío. Espérame, iré al castillo del duque que está aquí cerca, y traeré quien te saque de esta sima, donde tus pecados te deben de haber puesto." [2.55:459])

Beyond Pain and Suffering: Emotions, Agency, Action

The equids feel a variety of specific emotions in appropriate contexts. While many non-human animals studied throughout the earlier chapters of this book were represented as having one emotion (such as the bull's rage in Cantiga 144), Rocinante in particular is portrayed as having a range of emotions including sadness, fear, joy, and fury, which lead to the development of Rocinante as a complex character.

The equids' emotions are portrayed implicitly, through actions, and explicitly, with descriptions. After the galley slaves have finished attacking Don Quixote and his retinue, the narrator describes the four characters – two humans and two non-humans – as all in it together:

> The donkey and Rocinante, Sancho and Don Quixote, were left alone; the donkey, pensive, with bowed head, twitching his ears from time to time, thinking that the tempest of stones had not yet ended and was still falling around his ears; Rocinante, lying beside his master, for he too had fallen to the ground in the shower of stones; Sancho, in his shirtsleeves [lit. naked] and afraid of the Holy Brotherhood; Don Quixote, grief-stricken at seeing himself so injured by the very people for whom he had done so much good. (172)
>
> (Solos quedaron jumento y Rocinante, Sancho y don Quijote; el jumento, cabizbajo y pensativo, sacudiendo de cuando en cuando las orejas, pensando que aún no había cesado la borrasca de las piedras que le perseguían los oídos; Rocinante, tendido junto a su amo, que también vino al suelo de otra pedrada; Sancho en pelota y temeroso de la Santa Hermandad; don Quijote, mohinísimo de verse tan malparado por los mismos a quien tanto bien había hecho. [1.22:276–7])

Of the four, the donkey's description is by far the longest and most complex: he is "pensive" (i.e., melancholic),[97] and his body language proves this as he droops his head; furthermore, El rucio shakes his ears every now and again, even though the pelting has stopped, because he "believes" (pensando) that the rocks have not stopped flying, in what seems like a traumatic fear response. In contrast, Rocinante's emotional state is not made explicit; he is described as just lying there, perhaps he is unconscious. Sancho is animal-like "naked" (en pelota),[98] and fearful (temeroso) of repercussions for having released the prisoners. Don Quixote is rationally and justifiably angry (mohinísimo) for being treated badly by those he helped escape.

In another episode at the end of Part I, from Sancho's perspective Rocinante is depressed (melancólico y triste) when Don Quixote finds himself caged.[99] While both of the "beasts" are portrayed as being melancholic (admitting to a level of conscious awareness that allows them to reflect on their sad predicament), Sancho later shows himself to be inconsistent with his second-order beliefs about animal cognition when he counsels Don Quixote to stop acting so depressed or melancholic (pensativo),[100] drawing an evidently false dichotomy between "beasts" and "men": "Señor, sorrows were made not for animals but for men; but if men feel them too much, they turn into animals; your grace should restrain yourself, and come back to yourself, and pick up Rocinante's reins, and liven up and rouse yourself" (521) (Señor, las tristezas no se hicieron para las bestias, sino para los hombres; pero si los hombres las sienten demasiado se vuelven bestias; vuestra merced se reporte y vuelva en sí y coja las riendas a Rocinante, y avive y despierte; 2.11:114). However, as the novel has previously demonstrated, "sorrows" were indeed also made for both Rocinante and El rucio. In fact, the text shows that the dichotomy is not so strong, and that humans and animals have much in common.

In the scene of the long caresses and grooming behaviour between Sancho's donkey and Rocinante that I mentioned earlier, the emotions of the animals are inexplicit, inferred through actions, and yet easily labelled by scholars (see Alves and Martín, mentioned above). Yet, in other passages, the narrator does not shy away from attributing emotional states directly to Rocinante,[101] in which cases the constructive anthropomorphism is the author's rather than the readers'. First, in the episode in which Don Quixote is standing on top of Rocinante while addressing the "princess" at the Inn (1.43),[102] the horse is described anthropomorphically as "melancholy and sad" (melancólico y triste), emotional states which correspond to his drooping ears ("with drooping ears" [383] [con las orejas caídas; 531]). An earlier scene in the *Quixote* holds contextual clues for unpacking this constructive anthropomorphism: the equation of Rocinante's depressed emotional state and its association with a downward bodily stance (droopy ears) is not only verified in the psychological literature in accounts of people suffering from depression as well as in the comparative psychological literature on dogs and horses, but it is striking in its similarity to the way in which Sancho had been described earlier, when he was depressed and physically exhausted after the vomiting episode that followed Don Quixote's embarrassing attack on the sheep herd (1.18:225). At that moment, Sancho is described in the typical position of the melancholic, associated famously with the drooping figure in Albrecht Dürer's *Melencolia I* (see fig. 29), as Sancho leans, in an explicitly "pensive" manner, with one hand on his cheek: "resting his cheek in his hand, in the manner of a man deep in thought (...) showing signs of so much sadness" (132) (con la mano en la mejilla, en guisa de hombre pensativo además [...] con muestras de tanta tristeza; 1.18:225). The drooping body might also be considered an embodied secondary metaphor (in the vein of Lakoff and Johnson) based on the idea that "down is bad" for the human author and the reader as well as for the horse.

Adding greater emotional complexity to the scene, another horse rouses Rocinante from his melancholic state. While passing by him – while carrying her human to the Inn – she sniffed Rocinante and thereby "caressed him" (hacer caricias); we might speculate that she understands his body language and that her gesture is meant to ameliorate his melancholy, although this added reading is not necessary for understanding Rocinante's mind. Returning the gesture, Rocinante makes an effort to smell the other horse. Cervantes whimsically anthropomorphizes Rocinante here:

> Just then, one of the horses of the four men pounding at the door happened to smell Rocinante, who, melancholy and sad and with drooping ears, stood unmoving as he held his tightly drawn master; and since, after all, he was flesh and blood, though he seemed to be made of wood, he could not help a certain display of feeling as he, in turn, smelled the horse who had come to exchange caresses; as soon as he had moved slightly, Don Quixote's feet, which were close together, slipped from the saddle, and he would have landed on the ground if he had not been hanging by his arm; this caused him so much pain that he believed his hand was being cut off at the wrist or that his arm was being pulled out of its socket. (383)

> (Sucedió en este tiempo que una de las cabalgaduras en que venían los cuatro que llamaban se llegó a oler a Rocinante, que, melancólico y triste, con

Figure 29 Albrecht Dürer's *Melencolia I*. Image copyright © The Metropolitan Museum of Art. Image Source: Art Resource, NY.

> las orejas caídas, sostenía sin moverse a su estirado señor; y como, en fin, era de carne, aunque parecía de leño, no pudo dejar de resentirse, y tornar a oler a quien le llegaba a hacer caricias; y así, no se hubo movido tanto cuanto, cuando se desviaron los juntos pies de don Quijote, y resbalando de la silla, dieran con él en el suelo, a no quedar colgado del brazo; cosa que le causó tanto dolor, que creyó, o que la muñeca le cortaban, o que el brazo se le arrancaba. [1.43:531])

Playing again with human-animal difference and sameness – indeed humans and horses are all literally made of flesh –the narrator employs standard moralizing Christian language to connote the metaphorical idea of being made "of flesh" (era de carne), moved as Rocinante was towards the non-spiritual.[103]

The representation of Rocinante and the unnamed horse – animals not endowed by the author with uniquely human abilities through witchcraft or other transformational means – sheds light on Cervantes's theory of horse cognition, which lines up in many ways with those of the treatise writers on this preferred animal. Indeed, Miquel Agustí even goes so far as to say that certain horses are "melancholic" (*Libro de los secretos* 333). In describing the characteristics to look for or to avoid in a horse, Agustí remarks that the horse should obey man's will and specifically warns about avoiding male horses that become distracted by the scent of a mare. For Agustí, "as [a man] mounts to ride, [the horse] should conform to the man's will and should not move ... due to the scent of any mare, pursuing her with fury" (se deve conformar à la voluntad del hombre, que le sube á cavallo, sin moverse [...] por ningun odor de jumenta, yendo à ella con furia; 333). Conforming "to the man's will" is something that Rocinante fails to do, since he chooses to sniff the other horse and leave Don Quixote tragicomically dangling by his wrist.

In the episode of the "señoras facas," which shares certain similarities to this horse-driven scene, Rocinante's actions are propelled by his intentional agency, which is interwoven with sensory perception and changes in emotional state as they would be in any complex being. Along with the importance of horse olfaction to Rocinante's *Umwelt* at an ethological level, Cervantes takes the horse's perspective in contrast to the anthropocentric "eye-to-eye view" or the abstract Spinozistic "view from eternity." Indeed, this is not a "view" at all, but a scent-to-smell relation of nose-to-hinder parts.[104] Cervantes's horses are embodied as equids in their sniff greeting, in a turn away from the anthropocentric concerns of many other animal depictions, including the two dogs of the colloquy who almost exclusively privilege sight and hearing over olfaction.

For embodied humans, smell usually remains in the background and comes to the fore only when a new and exciting scent is in the air. For macrosmatic animals, like horses and dogs, smell plays a much greater role in perception than in humans, and such animals have a much higher number of smell receptors and significantly fewer pseudogenes relating to olfaction. Inspired by constructive anthropomorphism and with ethologically correct information about horse anatomy and sensory perception gained most likely through close interactions with horses and the development of Cervantes's folk animal psychology, this move utilizes those intuitions and facts in efforts to capture, *pace* Nadler, the species-specificity of horse embodiment.[105]

The hand-dangling adventure outside the Inn is reminiscent of the earlier humorous scene in which Rocinante leaves his master, without permission, due to his sexual interest after smelling some nearby mares, who are personified as "the ladies" (103) (las señoras facas; 1.15:191) with whom he wishes to "pleasure himself" (103) (refocilarse; 191). The narrator sometimes claims that Rocinante is extremely obedient; but this is not true when we examine his narrated actions: Both of these sniffing scenes point to Rocinante as a less than ideally trained steed, but the portrayal follows *current* ethological descriptions of male reproductive behaviour: "Reproductive behavior, during the precopulatory phase: Stallions sniff the shoulder, flank, rump, or perineal area of the mare and also sniff traces of the mare's urine on the ground, frequently accompanied by flehmens" (Feist 1971; Keiper 1985; qtd. Leblanc).[106]

Cervantes makes clear the connection, for a male horse, between olfaction and the desire to have sex, understood with folk animal psychology, that is, with constructive anthropomorphism, with assumptions that human desire is similar to the horse's: "Rocinante felt the desire to pleasure himself with the ladies, and as soon as he picked up their scent he abandoned his natural ways and customs, did not ask permission of his owner, broke into a brisk little trot, and went off to communicate his need to them" (103) (a Rocinante le vino en deseo de refocilarse con las señoras facas, y saliendo, así como las olió, de su natural paso y constumbre, sin pedir licencia a su dueño, tomó un trotico algo picadillo y se fue a comunicar su necesidad con ellas; 191). The choice of the word "refocilarse" is the same one used in 1.16 to describe the mule driver's plan to have a tryst with the Inn's maid, Maritornes, thus pointing to affinities between the bestial and the human in desire.[107] It is important for the plot that both Don Quixote and Rocinante are beaten for making sexual advances to a female.[108] While Rocinante's psychology is quite transparent to the narrator, the minds of the mares who reject his advances are not, and the narrator infers what they are thinking and feeling based on their actions, with the verb *parecer* (to seem): "But the ponies, who apparently had more desire to graze than anything else, greeted him with hooves and teeth" (103) (Mas ellas, a lo que pareció, debían de tener más gana de pacer que de ál, recibiéronle con las herraduras y con los dientes; 191).[109]

Cervantes thus aptly illustrates how the sense of olfaction is of great importance to these non-human animals, and in particular to equids;[110] indeed, much more important than it is to human animals. The sniff-greeting scenes lie in stark contradistinction to the many scenes in *Don Quixote* where humans greet and gain embodied information from one other by looking each other over, shaking hands, hugging, or giving kisses. With regard to the horses, it points to olfaction as a stimulus that provokes an affective state, and is in line with contemporaneous knowledge and practices recommended in period treatises as well as common scientific knowledge of equine sense perception. Indeed, in *Libro de los secretos*, Agustí describes automated ways of arousing an "emotional" response in male and female horses. For a trepidacious male horse, Agustí suggests using olfaction to augment his desire to mate: "It is advisable to rub the mare's genitals with a sponge, and then place it in the nostrils of the horse, if he is not one quickly to leap, because this will move him" ("Conviene fregar la natura de la yegua con una esponja, y ponerla despues en las narizes del cavallo, si no fuere pronto al saltar, porque esso le moverà; *Libro* 329).[111]

These scenes of emotions, senses, action, and agency are laid out in a constructively anthropomorphic way, calling into question the anthropectomizing scientistic view that animals merely respond by instinct to stimuli, not choosing their actions.[112] In other sections that are less complex, Cervantes makes clear that Rocinante is given choices in some cases and that he makes them quite regularly: Rocinante, here and elsewhere, clearly acts upon his intentional agency on numerous occasions. Sometimes it is just briefly alluded to as in the second chapter of Part I: "Rocinante was in a hurry to get to the stable" (26) (Rocinante se daba prisa por llegar a la caballeriza; 1.2:82). The reader can infer it is because he wants to rest and eat hay. Early on in the adventure, in 1.4, the knight lets his horse pick the route and Rocinante does so. As Alves points out, the agency is sometimes left to the reader to decide – it is not what I term gratuitous anthropomorphism, which would not leave this open to interpretation. Other times, the agency is more clearly a choice that Rocinante is making, such as immediately following the episode with Andrés: "H]e arrived at a road that divided in four, and immediately there came to his imagination the crossroads where knights errant would begin to ponder which of those roads they would follow, and in order to imitate them, he remained motionless for a time, and after having thought very carefully, *he loosened the reins and subjected his will to Rocinante's, and the horse pursued his initial intent, which was to head back to his own stall*" (39) (En esto, llegó a un camino que en cuatro se dividía, y luego se le vino a la imaginación las encrucijadas donde los caballeros andantes se ponían a pensar cuál camino de aquéllos tomarían, y, por imitarlos estuvo un rato quedo, y, al cabo de haberlo muy bien pensado, *soltó la rienda a Rocinante, dejando a la voluntad del rocín la suya, el cual siguió su primer intento, que fue el irse camino de su caballeriza*; 1.4:99, emphasis mine).[113] On multiple occasions, Don Quixote lets Rocinante choose the path, such as in this case: "they remounted, and with no fixed destination, since it was very much in the tradition of knights errant not to follow a specific route, they began to ride wherever Rocinante's will took them; behind his will came his master's, and even the donkey's, who always followed wherever the horse led, in virtuous love and companionship" (157) (subieron a caballo, y sin tomar determinado camino, por ser muy de caballeros andantes el no tomar ninguno cierto, se pusieron a caminar por donde la voluntad de Rocinante quiso, que se llevaba tras sí la de su amo, y aun la del asno, que siempre le seguía por dondequiera que guiaba, en buen amor y compañía; 1.21:257).[114] It is worth noting that while the relationship between the donkey and the horse matures and is more intimate in Part II (just as is the one between Sancho and Don Quixote), this passage in 1.21 demonstrates that El rucio long held devotion to Rocinante.

In another instance, early on in Part I, when Don Quixote is returning to his town to attempt to follow the advice given to him by the innkeeper who knighted him, Rocinante does not choose the way,[115] but he does choose the pace, in another complex description of how his senses (feeling the reins), emotions, intentions, and actions are interrelated: "With this thought he guided Rocinante toward his village, and the horse, as if he could see his stall, began to trot with so much eagerness that his feet did not seem to touch the ground" (35) (Con este pensamiento guió a Rocinante hacia su aldea, el cual, casi conociendo la querencia, con tanta gana comenzó a caminar, que parecía que no ponía los pies en el suelo; 1.4:95). He walks "con tanta gana" (which might be translated as "with so much joy"), and speeds up.[116] As Don Quixote is guiding him home, meaning that they have reversed direction from the way they got to the inn, this indicates also that Rocinante must know where his town is located and understand that they are returning home. That is, he must remember, as Don Quixote does, where the town is located. Is this hard to believe? Without denying the possibility outright, the narrator resists the idea that Rocinante understands where he is going with the limiting phrase "as if he could see his stall" (35) (casi conociendo la querencia; 95), perhaps cautiously avoiding gratuitous anthropomorphism. Yet later in the chapter, the narrator says that "the horse pursued his initial intent, which was to head back to his own stall" (39) (el cual siguió su primer intento, que fue el irse camino de su caballeriza; 99). According to Leblanc, the comparative psychologist who is an expert on equids, horses do remember locations well. On horse memory, Leblanc explains:

> Horses, to take just one example, are capable of orienting themselves and heading to their home range, even though it may extend to several dozen square kilometers. They do not wander haphazardly in search of a watering hole that may be very far away from where they are feeding. Similarly, horses have not been observed to move randomly between grazing sites and their home range, but are able to localize sites that are more likely to offer the best food (...) [T]he young horse progressively forms a sort of mental cartographic representation of its home range – a cognitive map – by memorizing places, their relative positioning, and routes, in short, by familiarizing itself with its environment by means of visual and especially olfactory cues.[117] (59)

So, Rocinante knows where his town is, knows that he is heading home, and is happy to do so, and thus chooses a quicker pace than usual. Although in this instance Rocinante is not free to choose the path, he does choose the pace, travelling more swiftly than ordinarily. His desire to reach home, then, is implicit in the actions that he performs, and the reader would be wise to constructively anthropomorphize the psychology of this complex non-human animal.

In a directly opposite manner to Don Quixote giving Rocinante free reign, in the episode of the fulling mills, Sancho famously hobbles

Rocinante by hitching his feet,[118] unbeknownst to his master. Cervantes plays with the mind-control elements over animals of the biblical and the Marian traditions, when Sancho – who becomes like God – takes over Rocinante's agency by restraining him surreptitiously in the hobbling night scene: "'Oh, Señor, *heaven, moved by my tears and prayers, has willed Rocinante not to move*, and if you persist, and spur and urge him on, that will anger Fortune, and it will be, as they say, like kicking at thorns'" (144) ("Ea, señor, que *el cielo, conmovido de mis lágrimas y plegarias, ha ordenado que no se pueda mover Rocinante*, y si vos queréis porfiar y espolear y darle, será enojar a la fortuna, y dar coces, como dicen, contra el aguijón; 1.20:240, emphasis mine). Don Quixote falls for the trick, the narrator explains: "he thought it a good idea to be calm and wait, either for the dawn or until Rocinante could move forward, believing no doubt, that his situation was caused by something other than Sancho's labors, and so he said to him: 'Well, Sancho, since Rocinante cannot move, I am content to wait until dawn smiles upon us'" (144) (tuvo por bien de sosegarse y esperar, o a que amaneciese, o a que Rocinante se menease, creyendo, sin duda, que aquello venía de otra parte que de la industria de Sancho; y, así, le dijo: "Pues así es, Sancho, que Rocinante no puede moverse, yo soy contento de esperar a que ría el alba"; 1.20:241). Once Rocinante is freed, he shows renewed energy and agency in movement, as he plunges like a wild horse: "[he] very carefully unhobbled Rocinante and tied up his breeches. When Rocinante felt himself free, though he was not by nature high-spirited, it seems he felt offended and began to paw the ground because – and for this I beg his pardon – he could not prance. Don Quixote, seeing that Rocinante was moving again, took this as a favorable sign and believed it meant he should embark on the fearful adventure" (148) (con mucho tiento desligó a Rocinante y se ató los calzones. Como Rocinante se vio libre, aunque él de suyo no era nada brioso, parece que se resintió, y comenzó a dar manotadas, porque corvetas, con perdón suyo, no las sabía hacer. Viendo, pues, don Quijote que ya Rocinante se movía, lo tuvo a buena señal, y creyó que lo era de que acometiese aquella temerosa aventura; 1.20:246). Rocinante is not always obedient even with the spurs, and in the episode of the Galley Slaves, even when they are raining rocks on the protagonists, Rocinante refuses to obey Don Quixote: "[T]hey began to throw so many stones at Don Quixote that he could not even manage to protect himself with his shield, and poor Rocinante paid no more attention to his master's spurs than if he had been made of bronze" (172) ([C]omenzaron a llover tantas piedras sobre don Quijote, que no se daba manos a cubrirse con la rodela, y el pobre de Rocinante no hacía más caso de la espuela que si fuera hecho de bronce; 1.22:27).

Even Don Quixote's most important and somewhat rare victory, against the Knight of the Mirrors (El caballero del Espejo), is owed in large part to Rocinante's somewhat unexplained and special behaviour at that moment:

> Don Quixote, who thought his enemy was already bearing down on him, swiftly dug his spurs into Rocinante's skinny flanks and goaded him so mercilessly that, the history tells us, this was the only time he was known to have galloped, because on all other occasions he always ran at a pronounced trot, and with this unprecedented fury Rocinante reached the place where the Knight of the Mirrors was digging his spurs all the way into his horse without being able to move him the length of a finger from the spot where he had called a halt to his charge. (545)

> (Don Quijote, que le pareció que ya su enemigo venía volando, arrimó reciamente las espuelas a las trasijadas ijadas de Rocinante, y le hizo aguijar de manera, que cuenta la historia que esta sola vez se conoció haber corrido algo, porque todas las demás siempre fueron trotes declarados, y con esta no vista furia llegó donde el de los Espejos estaba hincando a su caballo las espuelas hasta los botones, sin que le pudiese mover un solo dedo del lugar donde había hecho estanco de su carrera. [1.14:142])

Furthermore, Sancho and El rucio typically follow Rocinante: "the donkey followed in Rocinante's footsteps since he did not like being without him" (642) (el rucio siguió las huellas de Rocinante, sin el cual no se hallaba un punto; 2.27:255).

In fact, while the narrator does not make this explicit, it is also Rocinante who drives the plot and helps find El rucio and Sancho, when they are stuck in the sinkhole after Sancho's governorship. Again, typical of the narrator, who tends to avoid explicit anthropomorphism, this agency is downplayed: "It so happened that he rode out one morning to practice and rehearse what he was to do during the combat he would soon be engaged in, and after spurring Rocinante into a charge or short gallop, *the horse's feet came so close to a cave that if he had not pulled hard on the reins, it would have been impossible not to fall in*. In short, Don Quixote stopped Rocinante and did not fall, and coming a little closer, and without dismounting, he peered into that deep hole, and as he was looking in *he heard someone shouting* inside" (819–20) (Sucedió, pues, que saliéndose una mañana a imponerse y ensayarse en lo que había de hacer en el trance en que otro día pensaba verse, dando un repelón o arremetida a *Rocinante, llegó a poner los pies tan junto a una cueva, que a no tirarle fuertemente las riendas, fuera imposible no caer en ella.* En fin, le detuvo, y no cayó; y, llegándose algo más cerca sin apearse, miró aquella hondura, y, estándola mirando, *oyó grandes voces* dentro; 2.55:457, emphasis mine). Whether through olfaction or hearing, it is at least plausible that Rocinante sensed that Sancho and El rucio – his dear friends – were nearby and moved towards them to be near (he is moved by olfaction in other cases, as mentioned).

Morality

One of the most controversial elements of animal cognitive studies is the extent to which animals may be understood to be moral beings. First, we need to make a distinction between moral agents and moral subjects. Today, while lay people may use moral language to describe the actions of a pet – for instance, "bad dog!" – most scientists and philosophers do not consider non-human animals moral agents, that is, beings who are capable of making moral judgments and being held accountable for them. In the Middle Ages and the Renaissance, as is now well known, this was not the case, and several scholars have documented the ways in which all sorts of creatures, regardless of their assumed level of sentience, were treated as culpable agents, and punished for alleged wrongdoing, in what by today's standards and my terms of analysis would amount to gratuitous anthropomorphism. To offer just one example from the historical archive, Martha Few and Zeb Tortorici explore the public burning of a turkey in Yucatán, in 1563, an act that accompanied the castration of the offending fourteen-year old boy who had been found guilty of bestiality with the turkey.[119]

While *Don Quixote* is indeed quite modern, the rustic Sancho engages in this type of animal *qua* moral agent thinking vis-à-vis Rocinante when he judges him perniciously for his attempted dalliance with the "señoras facas": "Your grace, see if you can stand, and we'll help Rocinante, though he doesn't deserve it, because he's the main reason for this beating. I never would have believed it of Rocinante; I always thought he was a person as chaste and peaceable as I am. Well, like they say, you need a long time to know a person, and nothing in this life is certain" (105–6) (Mire vuestra merced si se puede levantar, y ayudaremos a

Rocinante, aunque no lo merece, porque él fue la causa principal de todo este molimiento. Jamás tal creí de Rocinante, que le tenía por persona casta y tan pacífica como yo. En fin, bien dicen que es menester mucho tiempo para venir a conocer las personas, y que no hay cosa segura en esta vida; 194).

In another scene, the narrator juxtaposes Sancho's treatment of El rucio with El rucio's behaviour towards Sancho; without making the case explicitly, Sancho comes off as less moral than his donkey, who, it is implied, is a good moral agent. In the boar hunting scene in Part II, Sancho abandons El rucio out of fear: Sancho "*abandoned* his donkey, and began to run as fast as he could" (684, emphasis added) (*desamparó* al rucio y dio a correr cuanto pudo; 2.34:305, emphasis added). Sancho hides in a tree, and afterwards, when he is found screaming, El rucio is by his side: Don Quixote "saw him hanging upside down from the oak, his donkey beside him, for the gray did not *abandon* him in his calamity" (685, emphasis added) (viole pendiente de la encina y la cabeza abajo, y al rucio junto a él, que *no le desamparó* en su calamidad; 306, emphasis added). The reiteration of the preterite form "desamparó" with opposite valences and subjects points unmistakingly to the conclusion that El rucio treats Sancho better than Sancho treats El rucio. After this, the narrator comments on the "friendship and good faith" (685) (amistad y buena fe; 306) that they have between them (without explicitly commenting on the fact that Sancho had left El rucio alone).

While most modern thinkers no longer hold animals as moral agents in this way, many would agree that animals can be moral patients, that is, that humans have a responsibility to act morally towards them, given their characteristics. In addition to the bonds between them, both El rucio and Rocinante have important relationships with their corresponding humans.[120]

Don Quixote cares about Rocinante a great deal, and when he sends Sancho off on Rocinante to deliver his letter to Dulcinea, he tells the squire to treat his horse as if he were Sancho himself: "He mounted Rocinante, whom Don Quixote commended to his care, saying he should attend to him as to his own person" (204) (Y, subiendo sobre Rocinante, a quien don Quijote encomendó mucho, y que mirase por él como por su propia persona; 1.25:317). Likewise, but more emotionally, Sancho gives his donkey a hug and a kiss, calling him "companion" and "friend": "when he reached the gray he embraced him and gave him a kiss of peace on the forehead, and, not without tears in his eyes, he said: 'Come here, my companion and friend, comrade in all my sufferings and woes'" (807) (llegándose al rucio, le abrazó y le dio un beso de paz en la frente y, no sin lágrimas en los ojos, le dijo: "Venid vos acá, compañero mío y amigo mío, y conllevador de mis trabajos y miserias"; 2.53:444), The care he feels for the donkey makes him sad when El rucio suffers. For instance, when the donkey makes sounds of complaints after they fall in the sinkhole together, it "greatly distressed Sancho, especially when he heard the donkey moaning woefully and grievously, and no wonder, for he was not lamenting capriciously; in truth, he was not in very good condition" (817) (de lo que Sancho se congojó mucho, especialmente cuando oyó que el rucio se quejaba tierna y dolorosamente, y no era mucho, ni se lamentaba de vicio, que a la verdad no estaba muy bien parado; 2.55:455).[121] He later says that he would rather suffer personally than see a hair on El rucio's tail disturbed. At one point, Sancho must choose whom to help first, Don Quixote or El rucio, after they've both been injured, and while he wants to help El rucio– more for the emotional than the physical suffering the donkey is enduring – he helps Don Quixote out of loyalty because of his explicit oath. I quote the long passage in its entirety to demonstrate the tortured decision that Sancho must make:

> But as soon as Sancho had left his mount to assist Don Quixote, the demon dancer jumped on the donkey and began to hit him with the bladders, and fear and the noise, more than the pain of the blows, made the donkey fly across the countryside to the town where the festival was to be held. Sancho looked at his racing donkey and his fallen master and did not know which of the two problems he should take care of first; but, in fact, because he was a good squire and a good servant, love for his master won out over affection for his donkey, although each time he saw the bladders go up in the air and come down on his donkey's rump, he suffered the torments and terrors of death and would rather have had those blows fall on his own eyes than touch a hair of his donkey's tail. In this perplexity and tribulation, he reached Don Quixote, who was much more bruised and battered than he would have wished. (524)

> (Mas apenas hubo dejado su caballería Sancho por acudir a don Quijote, cuando el demonio bailador de las vejigas saltó sobre el rucio, y, sacudiéndole con ellas, el miedo y ruido, más que el dolor de los golpes, le hizo volar por la campaña hacia el lugar donde iban a hacer la fiesta. Miraba Sancho la carrera de su rucio y la caída de su amo, y no sabía a cuál de las dos necesidades acudiría primero. Pero, en efecto, como buen escudero y

como buen criado, pudo más con él el amor de su señor que el cariño de su jumento, puesto que cada vez que veía levantar las vejigas en el aire y caer sobre las ancas de su rucio, eran para él tártagos y sustos de muerte, y antes quisiera que aquellos golpes se los dieran a él en las niñas de los ojos que en el más mínimo pelo de la cola de su asno. Con esta perpleja tribulación llegó donde estaba don Quijote, harto más maltrecho de lo que él quisiera. [2.11:117–18])

Sancho would rather exchange places with El rucio in this instance, and receive the drubbing himself as a poking in the eye instead of having even a hair on his beloved animal's tail bothered. He later claims that he would never exchange El rucio for anything: "Well, the truth is I don't have a horse, but my donkey is worth twice as much as my master's nag. May God send me evil days, starting tomorrow, if I'd ever trade with him, even if he threw in four bushelweights of barley. Your grace must think I'm joking about the value I put on my gray" (534) (verdad es que no tengo rocín, pero tengo un asno que vale dos veces más que el caballo de mi amo. Mala pascua me dé Dios, y sea la primera que viniere, si le trocara por él, aunque me diesen cuatro fanegas de cebada encima. A burla tendrá vuestra merced el valor de mi rucio; 2.13:129).

Companionship: The Human-Animal Paradigm

As delineated above, the non-human friendship between the equids is complex and well-developed: it involves sensation, action, and intention, in which the animals caress each other,[122] and use their differently abled sensory modalities to seek out each other's company, indicating that they clearly enjoy being together. Finally, the narrator stipulates that they are a model of animal friendship. As such, the donkey and the horse become the "contant companion" of each another ("perpetuo compañero" 1.20:247), as well as of Sancho and Don Quixote, respectively.

Even more important than the bond between the two equines, or between Sancho and the donkey, however, is the relationship between Rocinante and Don Quixote through both parts of the novel. Indeed, unlike anyone else, Rocinante is there at the beginning with Alonso Quijano and is one of the novel's most important characters. As Mary Powers explains, "throughout the novel, the reader is aware of Rocinante's presence and becomes convinced of his fidelity and durability"

(520). He is named by Don Quixote,[123] who then prophetically speaks of the history of Rocinante and Don Quixote, as a pair of companions, in and beyond this story: "Fortunate the time and blessed the age when my famous deeds will come to light, worthy of being carved in bronze, sculpted in marble, and painted on tablets as a remembrance of the future. O thou wise enchanter, whoever thou mayest be, whose task it will be to chronicle this wondrous history! I implore thee *not to overlook my good Rocinante, my eternal companion on all my travels and peregrinations*" (25, emphasis added) (Dichosa edad, y siglo dichoso, aquél adonde saldrán a luz las famosas hazañas mías, dignas de entallarse en bronces, esculpirse en mármoles y pintarse en tablas, para memoria en lo futuro. ¡Oh tú, sabio encantador, quienquiera que seas, a quien ha de tocar el ser cronista de esta peregrina historia, ruégote *que no te olvides de mi buen Rocinante, compañero eterno mío en todos mis caminos y carreras*!; 1.2:80, emphasis added).[124] That Don Quixote is right about the importance of Rocinante in the real world speaks to the importance of Cervantes's experiment at embodying animals through constructive anthropomorphism.[125] As Don Quixote says, Rocinante is indeed a constant companion. Through Cervantes's complex, constructively anthropomorphic, and equid-centric treatment of the horse and the donkey, Rocinante and, to a slightly lesser extent, El rucio become largely realistic, fleshed-out characters – with their own species-appropriate *Umwelt* and perspective – about whom the reader knows and cares in a way that is unlike any non-human animal textual representation before them. Rocinante, in particular, will serve as a paradigmatic example of the human-animal friendship.

Unlike the horses in epic (such as the Cid's Babieca, who was chosen for his excellence in battle and only mentioned for the first time about halfway through the epic poem), Rocinante is far from perfect. As Powers argues, "[h]is uniqueness consists in defying the standards of equine acceptability, and in returning the affection of man and beast alike. If he often fails tests of grace and speed, it is unimportant" (523). Bearing the traces of his lack of pedigree as an old hack or *rocín* in his very name, Rocinante is not from a "good" breed of horses. However, what is important is that he is just as much an object of respect and compassion, not despite his lack of excellence, but, in fact, because of it. Just as the novel *Don Quixote* is unimaginable without Sancho, such is the way for Rocinante too. This is achieved not by having Rocinante talk or by the narrator providing his discursive thoughts formulated in complex human sentences.[126] Using constructive anthropomorphism that relies on folk animal psychology, and paying attention to the animal's *Umwelt* and nose-to-the-ground perspective, with respect to the interests and sensory modalities of horses, Cervantes evoked the companion animal's vicissitudes at the side of his master, and in his interactions and relationships with others as he suffers the slings and arrows of fortune, as well as the rare success, for some of which he is the plot-moving proximate cause.[127] Not even Sancho's body suffers as much when Don Quixote is injured. To wit, in the episode of the windmills, only one companion of Don Quixote is caught in the sails, flung through the air, and thrown crashing to the ground. In sum, Cervantes embodies Rocinante through a process of characterization that tends towards empathy – making Rocinante, first and foremost, imperfect, and then having him suffer as well as accidentally cause mishaps for others while not intentionally causing their suffering. By doing so, Cervantes pens a non-human animal character that, like the orangutan Sandra four centuries later, could be considered a non-human person, creating the paradigm in Western literature of human-animal companionship.

Epilogue

Minding Animals after Cervantes

"Father, father," he cried, "father, what are they doing? Father, they are beating the poor horse!"

"Come along, come along!" said his father. "They are drunken and foolish, they are in fun; come away, don't look!" and he tried to draw him away, but he tore himself away from his hand, and, beside himself with horror, ran to the horse. The poor beast was in a bad way. She was gasping, standing still, then tugging again and almost falling.

"Beat her to death," cried Mikolka, "it's come to that. I'll do for her!"

"What are you about, are you a Christian, you devil?" shouted an old man in the crowd.

"Did any one ever see the like? A wretched nag like that pulling such a cartload," said another.

"You'll kill her," shouted the third.

"Don't meddle! It's my property, I'll do what I choose. Get in, more of you! Get in, all of you! I will have her go at a gallop!"

– Dostoyevsky, *Crime and Punishment*

The close companionship between a human and an unidealized animal – Don Quixote and Rocinante, Sancho and El rucio – might have been what nineteenth-century Spanish author Leopoldo Alas was thinking about when he wrote the child- and animal-focused story for adults "Adiós, Cordera" (1892), in which two siblings, growing up motherless, rely on the nurturing of the farm's cow whom they affectionately name Lamb. This same relationship with its possibilities informed Nobel laureate Juan Ramón Jiménez' *Platero y yo* (1914), in which the poet travels with his donkey, Platero, around Andalusia. We also see a trace of Cervantes's human-animal friendship in Nobel laureate John Steinbeck's *Travels with Charley* (1962), about a writer who travels the country with his pet poodle in a truck aptly named "Rocinante." Likewise, Ana María Matute's short story "Fausto," about an unnamed girl in post–Civil War Spain who befriends a sickly cat whom she names after a scary guard dog she has met; like the girl, the cat suffers physically and emotionally from neglect and abuse. Also focusing on animal suffering, Guy de Maupassant's short story "Coco" (1884) treats the relationship of a wealthy farm mistress and her aged horse, Coco, which she keeps stabled and fed: "A very old white horse, which the mistress wished to keep until its natural death, because she had brought it up and had always used it, and also because it recalled many happy memories, was housed, through sheer kindness of heart, at the end of the stable" (2). Maupassant's horse is only slightly anthropomorphized: "his long eyelashes gave to his eyes a sad expression" (2). More importantly, the horse suffers, but not by accident like Rocinante, but rather due to the cruelty of a "brute" farmhand who is in charge of taking care of Coco, a boy who slowly kills the animal out of "revenge." The farmhand believes that taking care of the old animal is a waste of time and money: "The boy would fume, feeling an unholy desire to revenge himself on the horse. He was a thin, long-legged, dirty child, with thick, coarse, bristly red hair. He seemed only half-witted, and stuttered as though ideas were unable to form in his thick, brute-like mind" (2–3). Despite the boy's moral deafness, Coco tries to communicate to him by whinnying for food.

The general framework of *Don Quixote* also informs Paul Auster's novel *Timbuktu* (1999), in which a downtrodden poet, misunderstood by his society, and considered insane by his family and peers, sets out on a mission to improve the life of his companion animal. In doing so, Willy must take into consideration physiology and perspective, reflecting on Mr Bones's sensorial capacity and *Umwelt*, anthropomorphizing appropriately and considering the animal's thoughts and feelings. While I do not aim to provide a linear story of the direct influence of Cervantes's equids on Auster's canine, it is not a coincidence that one of

Auster's self-professed favourite authors is Cervantes: "one book that I keep going back to and keep thinking about it's *Don Quixote*. That's the one, for me. It seems to present every problem every novelist has ever had to face, and to do it in the most brilliant and human way imaginable" (Auster, in Capen 104).[1] For Willy, it is not enough just to feed and provide shelter for the non-human animal, he is curious and "fascinated" by this creature whose "nostrils were turned into suction tubes, sniffing up scents in the way a vacuum cleaner inhales bits of glass" (Auster 37). The human yearns quixotically to create for the dog an experience that, from the dog's perspective, would be an aesthetic one, and thus he attempts to realize "A Symphony of Smells":

> And if, as all philosophers on the subject have noted, art is a human activity that relies on the senses to reach that soul, did it not also stand to reason that dogs – at least dogs of Mr. Bones's caliber – would have it in them to feel a similar aesthetic impulse? Would they not, in other words, be able to appreciate art? (...) If dogs were beyond the pull of oil paintings and string quartets, who was to say they wouldn't respond to an art based on the sense of smell? Why not an olfactory art? Why not an art for dogs that dealt with the world as dogs knew it? (39)

Auster's reflection on the possibility of a non-human artwork is an outgrowth of Cervantes's sustained experiments with Rocinante and El rucio, whereby Cervantes anthropomorphized appropriately, considered the sensorial capacity and *Umwelt* of the equids, envisioned their thoughts, intentions, and feelings, and treated them with the respect owed to main characters of a novel. That a dog is the subject of Willy's proposed aesthetic experience relies on his strong feelings of affection towards his dog, his fascination with the animal's relationship to his canine *Umwelt*, and his intimate relationship with the non-human animal. Willy is aware that he has special knowledge of Mr Bones – knowledge he had never before had of any other animal – because of their shared habitational parameters and their close mode of interaction, one of companion animal to human caregiver:

> [U]ntil Mr. Bones came into his life, he had never had the opportunity to observe a dog's behavior at close hand, had never even bothered to give the subject much thought. Dogs were no more than dim presences to him, shadowy figures hovering at the edge of consciousness. You avoided the ones who barked at you, you patted the ones who licked you. That was

> the extent of his knowledge. Two months after his thirty-eighth birthday, all that suddenly changed. (36)

Like Cervantes's, Auster's is not a one-sided story of human love towards an animal, met with indifference from the animal. Rather, like El rucio and Rocinante, Mr Bones cares for his human companion and loathes the thought of separation from him. Devastated by Willy's demise, Mr Bones meets a number of masters who take him in for short periods of time, like Cervantes's Berganza in "The Colloquy of the Dogs." Ultimately abandoned and lonely, Mr Bones plays "chase the car" on a six-lane highway running back and forth, in what amounts to an act of suicide, a tragic ending to this novel about a dog for whom the reader has come to care deeply.

Insightful passages in the early modern hunting and husbandry tomes that rely on folk animal psychology, and the mindedness of the animals of the Indies in the natural historical works guided by human curiosity, were steps along the way to Cervantes's fiction, as was Montaigne's reflection on his cat's playfulness and the difficulty of assessing a non-human animal mind's content without a shared language. Although the narrators infer what Fausto, Cordera, Platero, and Mr Bones are thinking, these animals are not gratuitously anthropomorphized and hence do not speak human language, even if they have a tremendous capacity for understanding it.

The philosopher Thomas Nagel, in his work on the nature of consciousness, may be right that we will never *know* exactly what it is like to be a bat or any other non-human animal. But neither, for that matter, will we know exactly what it is like to be another person, at least not in Nagel's stringent sense. Yet we can come to know other beings, human and non-human, through close contact, respect, and, in the case of non-human animals, a disavowal of speciesism, treating the animal not just with compassion, but as an individual with a mind, employing appropriate levels of anthropomorphism. Many Western pet owners treat their dogs in this way, rewarding them for good behaviour, teaching them tricks, and showering them with affection. Such is also the way that cognitive ethologists and comparative psychologists have often gotten to know particular animals, in the wild and in the lab. Jane Goodall, Irene Pepperberg, Marc Bekoff, and others have spent thousands of hours with animals in research settings getting to know individual animals. Do the billions of anonymous cows, pigs, chickens, turkeys, and other animals raised through factory farming each year deserve more respect? Do they deserve to be treated ... like animals? As a mass, they almost surely never will be treated with respect. In Cervantes's Rocinante and El rucio, as in Auster's Mr Bones, Matute's Fausto, Alas's Cordera, and Dostoyevsky's unnamed horse from this epilogue's epigraph, it is by focusing on the individual animal – on his or her *Umwelt* and his or her sensorial experience, thoughts, and emotions – that empathy, care, and a moral attitude can be realized. In some sense, these stories bear a resemblance to the way in which marginalized people are treated in society and in books: as a mass, people are easily disparaged and dismissed, but as individuals they are more likely to be treated with humanity. We can see this with Agi Morati, the Islamic father of Zoraida, who – despite his religion, culture, and status as enemy of the Spanish Empire – becomes a human being worthy of respect in Cervantes's *Don Quixote*.

Once the research into the cognitive abilities of so many non-human animals becomes even more nuanced, an object of reflection by moral philosophers, and better assimilated by the public, it is possible that we will look back in horror at how so many animals were treated as mere property throughout history and today. A major step in recognizing this potential moral wrongdoing is carefully considering the *Umwelt* and the sensorial and cognitive abilities of non-human animals, and exploring through writing their consciousness, suffering, thoughts, motivations, and emotions. Cervantes did not take all of these steps alone, but we can credit him with putting the pieces together, thereby creating embodied non-human animal characters that are appropriately anthropomorphized, anticipating modern paradigms of the human-animal relationship as well as a philosophical notion of the non-human animal person.

Notes

Introduction

1 All translations are mine unless otherwise noted. In the case of literary criticism, newspapers, and other secondary sources, the text in the original language has not been printed.
2 "Advances in science and technology have allowed us to demonstrate that we share 99.4% of our DNA with this category of animal" (Los avances de la ciencia y la tecnología han permitido demostrar que con esa categoría de animales compartimos el 99,4% de los genes de nuestro ADN; Baggis 5).
3 "Captivity makes them experience a high level of stress and changes in their behaviour, including suffering from depressive states that can lead to death. Also, it has been demonstrated in some cases that these beings communicate with gestures, sounds, and expressions in sign language; that they maintain family bonds and lament the death of their own" ([E]l cautiverio los hace experimentar un alto grado de estrés y alteraciones en su comportamiento, pudiendo sufrir estados depresivos que los llevan a la muerte. También se ha demostrado que estos seres se comunican con gestos, sonidos y expresiones y a través del lenguaje de los signos, en algunos casos; que mantienen lazos familiares y lloran por la muerte de los suyos; Baggis 5–6).
4 Despite the court having recognized Sandra as a non-human person, the matter of the judicial remedy has been moved to the civil court system and the case was still in the courts at the time that this book went to press. For an overview of the relevant court cases and procedures, in Argentina and also in similar pending cases in the United States, see

Shawn Thompson's "When Apes Have Their Day in Court," *Philosophy Now* 111 (2015–16): 26–9.

5 Howard Mancing has been the driving force of introducing cognitive studies more broadly into Spanish literary and cultural studies. Simerka's excellent book is an in-depth analysis of Theory of Mind in a large group of early modern plays. In addition to Simerka and Mancing, Isabel Jaen and Julien Simon have recently edited an important collection of essays on the topic.

6 On cognitive ethology as a science, see the foundational essay by Dale Jamieson and Marc Bekoff, "On aims and methods of cognitive ethology," *PSA: Proceedings of the Biennial Meeting of the Philosophy of Science Association* (1992): 110–24. For more on Morgan's Canon – named after nineteenth-century psychologist C.L. Morgan who first enunciated it – see Andrews.

7 In the same essay, Montaigne also asks why we assume that the problem of interspecies communication lies with animals rather than us, and suggested that perhaps "The defect that hinders communication betwixt them and us, why may it not be on our part as well as theirs? 'Tis yet to determine where the fault lies that we understand not one another; for we understand them no more than they do us; by the same reason they may think us to be beasts as we think them. 'Tis no great wonder if we understand not them when we do not understand a Basque or the Troglodytes" (2.12:157).

8 The claim is made by John S. Kennedy (*The New Anthropomorphism*, Cambridge and New York: Cambridge UP, 1992), who is also one of the biggest critics of any form of anthropomorphism.

9 In *Why Only Us?*, Noam Chomsky and Robert Berwick suggest that a specific genetic change around three hundred thousand years ago accounts for human language and culture; however, as the authors concede, this is speculative. One cause of the lack of evidence (and the move toward speculation) is that the fossil record only indicates cranium size and contains no remnants of brain structure, as Thomas Shoenemann (2009) has indicated ("Evolution of Brain and Language," *Language Learning*, v. 59 [Suppl. 1]:162–86).

10 See Allen and Stephen J. Crowley (2008); Aberdein; (Luciano) Floridi, "Scepticism and Animal Rationality" 1997.

11 Habitational parameter involves the locations in and conditions under which the species generally lives. See Norton, "Animal (Spanish America)" 21; see Morgado García for habitational parameters ("Una visión cultural de los animales" 13–14).

12 Paradigmatically, this is human oblivion to the emotions and suffering of a group of animals.

13 Habitational parameter and mode of interaction are not independent variables; it is difficult or impossible for humans to have most other *modes of interaction* with a fish, given its habitat. My reflection on animal size and anthropocentric affordance was inspired by the Aesopian "Fable of the Lapdog and the Donkey," which I discuss in chapter 1. Here the size and (from a human point of view) cuteness determine to a large extent the possibilities and the limits of an animal's interaction with humans.

14 The renowned ethologist Marc Bekoff has also used this phrase as a title. We share the notion in common that minding is "caring," but his other meanings are quite different from my own. In *Minding Animals: Awareness, Emotions and Hearts*, NY and Oxford: Oxford UP, 2002, Bekoff writes, "I use the phrase 'minding animals' in two ways. First, 'minding animals' refers to caring for other animal beings, respecting them for who they are, appreciating their own worldviews, and wondering what and how they are feeling and why. The second meaning refers to the fact that many animals have very active and thoughtful minds" (xvi).

15 While I share with Kennedy the view that anthropomorphism is a human cognitive tendency, I do not agree with his view that anthropomorphic attributions of mind to non-human animals are misplaced. To be clear, I think anthropomorphism is an innate and embodied tendency that it is well-directed in the case of many complex organisms.

16 Here I allude to philosopher Thomas Nagel's famous essay "What Is It Like to Be a Bat?" in which Nagel concludes that because of such different sensory modalities it is impossible to know what it is like to be another kind of being, an idea with which I ultimately differ.

17 Kennedy is a strict behaviourist and believes that this kind of thinking, while natural, is entirely misguided. "Altogether, then, it seems likely that consciousness, feelings, thoughts, purposes, etc., are unique to our species and it is unlikely that animals are conscious. If we were entirely logical about it these probabilities would be enough to make us try to avoid descriptions of animal behavior. But we are not entirely logical about it, and we have to ask why scientists as well as laymen should be so addicted to anthropomorphic expression" (24).

18 Abel Alves has analysed the writing of Gómez Pereira, in addition to Sepúlveda's and Olivia Sabuco's for their views on animal feeling and intentions (*Animals* 45–50).

19 Beyond a literary device, many natural philosophers of the era would also have found the physical property of attraction to be a fundamental

element of cosmic unity underlying all of natural philosophy (see Tomas Nejeschleba, "The Theory of Sympathy and Antipathy in Wittenberg in the 16th century," *Acta Universitatis Palackianae Olomoucensis. Philosophica-Aesthetica 32; Philosophica VII*, Olomouc: Univerzita Palackeho v Olomouci [2006]: 81–91). The argument against animal rationality and its subterfuged rationale have a clear similarity with those proposed by Juan Ginés de Sepúlveda in the Valladolid Debate (1550–1) from the same decade, in which case a self-interested class of people (the *encomenderos*) wished to continue exploiting certain humans for slavery by denying their rationality, an argument which was countered famously by Bartolomé de las Casas, for which he gained the rubric "Protector of the Indians."

20 In his day, Descartes was accused of plagiarism, but in a letter from 1641 to Father Marin Mersenne, he maintained that he had never seen Gómez Pereira's tome. See Alves, *Animals* 7.

21 Historian of science Bertonoli Meli has demonstrated a resurgence in early modern vivisection (which had been practised in classical times by Galen and others); see also Alves, *Animals* 6.

22 "Hath not a Jew eyes? Hath not a Jew hands, organs, dimensions, senses, affections, passions? Fed with the same food, hurt with the same weapons, subject to the same diseases, healed by the same means, warmed and cooled by the same winter and summer, as a Christian is? If you prick us, do we not bleed?" (*Merchant of Venice* 3.1.58–64).

23 Hunting helps overcome aversions to killing animals or people that one might naturally have, specifically the embodied elements of learning to overcome aversion or the disgust reaction to blood and guts. See chapter 2 for more on Espinar.

24 Such as current factory farming, which takes place on an enormous scale of billions of animals each year. Even in the late twentieth century and into the twenty-first, certain philosophers have held not only that we can't know what animals are thinking, but that they don't have "intentional states" (see Davidson 1975, qtd. in Allen and Trestman ["Animal Consciousness"]).

25 Some very recent research has called into question the strength of dog olfaction vis-à-vis humans, such that this point requires some nuance: Indeed, research still shows that dogs have far superior olfactory perception than humans in what is now referred to as "orthonasal olfaction," which is what most lay people generally refer to as "smelling" or "sniffing." In this regard, some dogs can detect odours at a small fraction of the substance concentration of humans – hence the use

of dogs, for instance, to sniff out illicit substances such as drugs or explosives. However, humans are more discerning than dogs at a particular kind of smelling, known as "retronasal olfaction," which is a kind of olfaction that importantly forms part of the experience of taste or flavour. See Gordon Shepherd, *Neurogastronomy: How the Brain Creates Flavor and Why It Matters* (New York: Columbia UP, 2012), 19–27. Also, in a 2006 study published in *Nature Neuroscience*, Porter et al. tested whether humans would be able to perform "scent-tracking" in an open field in the way that dogs and other macrosmatic animals can, and found that humans were able to do this and that they improve over time with practice. Both species were tested on different substances (chocolate for humans, pheasants for dogs), and while the research found that humans can learn to scent-track reasonably well, nonetheless the paper refers to dogs' as having "greater scent-tracking ability" (n.p., online).

26 Covarrubias's separate entry for "Pescado" refers the reader back to "pez," and then clarifies the words for fishing and for fisherman: "PESCADO: Es todo género de pezes. Pesca, la que está en la red, o se ha sacado a la orilla fuera de la orilla fuera del agua. Pescador, el que tiene por oficio pescar. Proverbio: 'Pescador de caña, más come que gana.'" Note that Spanish makes a distinction about fish, lacking in English, akin to English's cow/beef distinction, in which "pez" is the animal in its habitat, "pescado" is the animal to be consumed.

27 The popularity of this view is strong even among those who consider themselves morally opposed to harming "sentient" animals. Hence the increasing popularity in the last twenty years of the term "pescatarian," which denotes people who consider themselves vegetarian but also eat fish or seafood. This tendency has led to a campaign by the animal protection group PETA for "pescatarians" to stop eating fish (http://www.peta.org/living/food/eat-fish/). Additionally, the term "cold-blooded" to refer to all fish is erroneous, since some "fish" regulate their body temperature.

28 Allen notest that, "[t]hus far I have followed many authors in using 'fish' generically as if this is a biologically appropriate category for making broad cognitive comparisons. In fact, it is something of a folk category (albeit a slightly scientifically-modulated category – for example insofar as it no longer contains whales and dolphins). Nevertheless, the group of organisms we intuitively call 'fish' comprises several taxonomic groups and huge number of species – approaching 32,000 currently, and given the rate of discoveries estimated to asymptote somewhere near 35,000" (Allen 32).

29 The term "paraphyletic" refers to an evolutionary group of organisms that are all descended from the same ancestor, but does not include all of the descendants. Since primates and humans, along with all other mammals, have a common evolutionary ancestor with the coelacanths, this makes the grouping of "fish" that are generally considered related to the coelacanths a "paraphyletic" one – the full evolutionary relationship of the coelecanths *includes* you and me even though they live in water and we live on land.
30 This piece in the *New York Times* is based on his 2016 book *What a Fish Knows: The Inner Lives of Our Underwater Cousins.*
31 See, for instance, the video of Mr G and Jellybean (AnimalPlace).
32 Ruiz Gómez 264. This is a fundamental distinction in my analysis of different types of fables in chapter 1.
33 How else to explain the widespread disregard for the poor treatment of animals in factory farming or the billions of "fish" that are caught in nets and left to die by asphyxiation on the deck of ships around the world to this day? See Balcombe.
34 For more on the distinction between these traditions, and how the Bestiary tends to be more symbolic than the *Physiologus*, see Voisenet.
35 This goat sucker bird is described by classical authorities including Pliny (*History* 10.56: 367).

1. Deploying the Animal in Medieval Miracles, Bestiaries, and Fables

1 See Eco et al.
2 Scenes of animal interpreting are common in epic literature; for instance, in the opening lines of Homer's *Iliad*, with the Greek forces suffering from a "foul pestilence," Agammenon asks Kalchas, who is "far the best of the bird interpreters," to explain the causes of Apollo's anger. Similar supernatural beliefs and actions are typical in medieval European epic as well as in the thirteenth-century Castilian *Poema de Mio Cid*, where the Cid and his men see two crows, one on the right as they are leaving Vivar, and another on the left as they are entering Burgos: "Crows flew across to their right as they were leaving Bivar, and as they drove down to Burgos, crows crossed to their left" (in *Poem of the Cid: A Modern Translation with Notes* by Paul Blackburn) (A la exida de Bivar, ovieron la corneja diestra / y entrando a Burgos ovieron la siniestra; 2.2–3). The poem tells the story of an unlucky past and foretells a bright future: "The Cid shrugged and shook his head: 'So we're thrown out of the country, well, cheer up, Fàñez!'" (Meçio mio Çid los ombros y engrameo la tiesta / "Albriçia, Albar Fañez, ca echados somos de tierra!").

3 "The animal is merely an instrument for understanding" (El animal es tan sólo un instrumento para la comprensión; 193).

4 *De doctrina christiana* 2.1.1.

5 Eco, 1989.

6 Cervantes writes, "el tiempo de Guisopete" which Grossman translates as "the days of Guisopete." Guisopete is most likely Sancho's garbled way of referring to Aesop, who was often called "Isopete" in medieval Iberia. See Donald McGrady, "Notes on Guisopete, Istoriado, and Other Aesopic Problems with Special Reference to Don Quijote," *Analecta Malacitana* XVIII.1 (1995): 127.

7 *Liber Man*. 3.10: 117–24.

8 Indeed, medieval texts reveal a deep engagement with symbolic animals. As historian of science Lorraine Daston has noted, symbolic use of animals was typical of the medieval period.

9 Cantimpré 4.I.194. See Nordenfalk.

10 "Myth and Reality in the Miracle of Cantiga 29" (1999). According to Kinkade and Keller, the "beasts were painted from live models" (53). While I am convinced that the artist used live models in this case, the assertion that they amount to photographic realism seems hyperbolic.

11 Alfonso X P.II, T.XVIII, L.XXI.

12 This is despite the commonly held notion that "pet" is a nineteenth-century Anglo-American construction, and that people cared little about animals in earlier times.

13 In turn, this is based on embodied conceptualization – e.g., we live *on* earth, not underwater – resulting in a plethora of anthropocentric and anthropomorphic valences (such as animal running, speaking, being healed, etc.) as part of the animal miracle. Furthermore, symbolic deployments of the animal are not the only kinds of valences in the Middle Ages. There are also proto-scientific naturalistic descriptions, which will be explored in this chapter.

14 Regarding my claim that they are not independent variables, it may be nearly impossible to have most other *modes of interaction* with a fish, given its habitat. The donkey and lapdog fable discussed later in this chapter demonstrates another form of dependent variable, in the size of the animal determining an appropriate habitat and from there its mode of interaction – e.g., the small size of the dog is a requirement for it to make use of the affordance of a lap, which then allows for the human-lapdog mode of interaction; the distinct size of the donkey determines that it is not apt for the lap space and hence not appropriate for that type of human-animal interaction, something that the fable lays bare.

15 A tendency we also see in hunting books, specifically those on falconing.

16 The treatise on falconry of Alfonso X's great grandson, Alfonso XI, survives, as does one by his nephew, Don Juan Manuel.

17 Kinkade and Keller mention "a passage in the Chronicles of the Kings of Castile [that] explains the presence of these animals in Spain [their FN 20]. The King of Ethopia [*sic*] sent them to commemorate the anniversary of the death of King Ferdinand, Alfonso's father" (10). Morales Muñiz discusses other medieval royals who collected lions, including Juan II of Castille and Carlos II and Carlos III of Navarra, who collected exotic animals alongside wolves and bears. See also Anna Adroer, and Carlos Gómez-Centurión's many essays on the topic of royal menageries in Spain, with emphasis on later seventeenth and eighteenth centuries.

18 This translation is mine. Except where noted, translations from the Cantigas are from Alfonso X, The Wise. *Songs of Holy Mary of Alfonso X, the Wise* trans. Kathleen Kulp-Hill.

19 Menéndez Pidal 228. About Cantiga 144, Menéndez Pidal writes about the poor bull and mentions that the *Partidas* prohibited prelates from "going to see ... bulls fight" (ir a ver ... lidiar toros; qtd. in Menéndez Pidal 228), pointing out that the good man did not want to see the bull fight, and that he didn't like it; thus, Mary saves a good man who did not want people to torture an animal.

20 Her control, and their mental life, can be explicit or inexplicit; in the *cantigas* her control is usually explicit.

21 This is another miracle performed at Mary's "Port" near Jerez (there are twenty-two miracles performed there, a site at which Alonso X had a church built according to this *cantiga*).

22 *Viajes por España*, qtd. in Ruiz Gómez 254–5. [Note: Ruiz Gómez quotes but does not give author, page numbers, or edition information on *Viajes por España* in his notes or bibliography; there are minor differences between his citations and mine. I cite directly from Rosmithal's relation (47–154) in *Viajes por España de Jorge de Einghen, del Barón León de Rosmithal de Blatna, de Francisco Guicciardini y de Andrés Navajero*, (ed. and trans. Antonio María Fabié (Madrid: Librería de los Bibliófilos, 1879)].

23 In the *Poema de Fernán González*, the miraculous boar hunt occurs in vv. 226–50. The story is also told in *Cronica General de Alfonso X*, 690, "The chapter on how fray Pelayo spoke with Count Fernand Gonzalez, and told him that he'd win in battle" (El capitulo de como frey Pelayo fablo con el conde Fernand Gonçalez, et dixol que el uençrie la batalla), and in "Romance del conde Fernan Gonçalez" by Lorenzo de Sepúlveda, which was published in *Romances nuevamente sacados de historias antiguas*

de la crónica de España (1580) and begins, "The good count, named Fernan Gonçales, the Lord of Castilla, was leaving Salas" (De Salas salia el buen conde / Fernan Gonçales nombrado; / señor era de Castilla).

24 Was the animal moved by God, the Virgin, or Saint Peter to that place? Did the animal know something special? It is not clear, but it is evident that the boar did not display typical behaviour.

25 For more on the Orphic tradition in art, see Toynbee (qtd. in Kinkade and Keller).

26 Not entirely out of compassion, as he has also been ordered to skin the mule, to make use of the hide, which can only happen when the animal is dead.

27 The text says that the Virgin kindly removed the witnesses from all doubt about whether it was the same mule that had been sick or not, but it is not explicit about how the mule thinks or is controlled.

28 The King loved this animal in part because of its intelligence (cleverness): "the King loved dearly and carried with him and cared for tenderly ... It did this [hunting birds in nests] and many other clever things, scampering and jumping, at which the king took great delight" (bestiola que muit' amava / el rei, que sigo tragia – e a que mui ben criava ... e tirava / con ela aves das covas ... / Pero esta outras cousas – muitas e bõas fazia/ trebellando e saltando, – onde gran prazer avia/aquel rei; 354:10–17).

29 In her translation, Kulp-Hill asserts that the king in this story is "Probably Alfonso X" (431n.2).

30 The section is now lost.

31 The idea of taming a wild lion is thematically linked to the ancient tradition – variants of which are found in Aesop – of the injured lion who seeks the help of a prey animal (human or mouse), and who later cares for the prey instead of predating (for instance, the life of Saint Jerome, retold in Lope de Vega's *El cardenal de Belén*).

32 In the *Cantigas*, God often causes the animal miracle; other times Mary directly causes it. In all of these cases, the animals are overpowered, controlled, and caused to venerate, unlike human protagonists in other *cantigas*, who appear to have free will.

33 Ruiz Gómez contrasts this view with that of Aquinas, who argued that animals could not go on to paradise: for the medieval theologian, dirty wild animals had no place in eternal salvation, thus their presence made no sense in Heaven (268).

34 As will be developed in later sections of this book, the notion that only humans have meaningful language is challenged by twenty-first-century research in cognitive ethology and comparative psychology – for

instance, recent discoveries have shown that certain species of parrots not only "parrot" (i.e., mimic) sounds, they create utterances that are meaningful to other parrots. The Aristotelian distinction of voice (φουη) versus articulate discourse (λογοσ) will be fundamental in my analysis of different types of fables.

35 The beginning of this cantiga reminds the reader of a biblical antecedent of divinely inspired animal speech in the story of Balaam's donkey (Book of Numbers 22.28). In Numbers 22.28, God (rather than Mary) "opened the mouth of the donkey, and it said to Balaam, 'What have I done to you, that you have struck me these three times?' Balaam said to the donkey, 'Because you have made a fool of me'" (NRSV).

36 Of course, animals do not have the same level of language and culture as humans. But current research in cognitive ethology and comparative psychology is revealing that some species of animals – in particular, parrots and parakeets – have much more complicated language and tool-making abilities in the wild than was previously known.

37 While the sheep may feel a bond with the woman, it is not made explicit. There is no evidence presented from the sheep's perspective, that the sheep has a better life being owned by the old woman rather than by the shepherd.

38 "A que faz o ome morto resurgir sen nulla falla, / ben pode fazer que viva outra morta animalla" (3–4).

39 For instance, we might hypothesize that the Virgin has taken over their "minds," but it is equally possible that she camouflaged the bait that the Moors were using so the fish didn't bite.

40 Cantiga 328, the miracle of Alfonso X winning lots of lands, has nothing to do with animals; but it serves well to illustrate how fish are conceptualized on the grounds of human embodiment, that is, in passing "in each of these rivers, there are very good fish"; the text merely mentions the availability, abundance, and tastiness, which are the essential characteristics of fish for the author. To be sure, land animals are briefly mentioned too: "The place lies in a very rich land, abundant in bread, wine, delicious fruit and fish and game" (398). But in other cantigas, non-fish animals are treated with additional cognitive qualities.

41 For more on the distinction between these traditions, and how the Bestiary tends to be more symbolic than the *Physiologus*, see Voisenet. See also Baldwin's introduction to Latini, *Medieval Castilian Bestiary* (vii–xxiii). The Latini is cited in the text as *Bestiary*.

42 While all writing is to some extent subjectively inflected and – due to the fact that it is of interest to at least one human – anthropocentric,

the bestiary writing of the Middle Ages features pronounced anthropocentricity, a kind of decentring of the animal that presents it primarily in terms of utility or meaning in human spheres.

43 Pliny describes the echinus as adhering to the bottom of ships to prevent them from moving in Book IX, section XLI of the *History*.

44 Different species of dolphins have varying expected survival rates in the wild, and a thirty-year estimate is fully compatible with a number of species.

45 Like humans, marine mammals of the cetacean order tend to have one offspring per pregnancy.

46 This idea will be developed further in chapter 3 on New World animals.

47 Relying on Saint Ambrose's authority on the subject of its evil and cruelty, "Saint Ambrose comments that this snake is the most cruel, pitiless and full of evil" (Et desta serpiente dize San Anbrosio que es la cosa mas cruel & mas sin piedat & mas llena de maldat).

48 "[O]f such a fierce nature (...) when she feels the pleasure of lust, she presses her teeth and cuts off the head. And when the young are in the belly of their mother and want to leave, they tear down and break open by force the belly of their mother and come out" (de tan fiera natura (...) quando ella siente el deleyte de la luxuria, aprieta los dientes & corta la cabeça. Et quando los fijos son en el vientre de su madre & quieren salir, derronpen & quebrantan por fuerça el vientre de su madre & salen fuera; 14).

49 This appraisal is consonant with that of Don Juan Manuel in his book on falconry, *El libro de la caça*.

50 For instance, in the early verses of the *Poema de Mio Cid*, where the Cid interprets the crows' meaning (anthropocentrically and subjectively) based on their location relative to his position.

51 An analysis of cognitive aspects of insects is beyond the scope of this book. It is worth pointing out, however, that Brunetto deals with some including bees. The bee is at once admirable for its engineering prowess, and imitable for its love of its king (which we know today is actually the hive's queen) (24–5).

52 Cross-modal perception involves interactions between two or more senses. Humans often assume incorrectly that animals are receiving the same sensory input as they are; another anthropocentric assumption is that an organism's sensory modalities will work in tandem (the way, for instance, our sight and hearing do), which is not necessarily the case.

53 He refers to the "bondat de su carne." Little is said of the "pavon" except that it tastes bad, and nothing is said of its cognition.

54 As this was written before the encounter with America, this is the real "India" and not what will later be called "las Indias," another prominent origin of parrots.

55 In addition to numerous research studies, Pepperberg also wrote a memoir about her long-time relationship with Alex, which spanned over three decades. Although many comparative psychologists were intially suspicious of her research findings, a significant body of research by other scientists has now corroborated many of Pepperberg's discoveries about parrot cognition.

56 Repeating Pliny's claim.

57 See the introduction for a discussion of "constructive" versus "gratuitous" anthropomorphism.

58 "[W]hen they hear the hunters' dogs that are chasing them, they head to the place of the other wind, so that their scent does not arrive to the dogs by the wind" (que quando oyen los canes de los caçadores que van en pos ellos, endresçan su carrrera a la parte del otro viento, por que el olor dellos non venga a los canes por aquel viento; 44).

59 See E. Téglás et al., *Current Biology* 22.3 (2012): 209–12.

60 "[A] very beautiful young virgin .... setting aside all cruelty, he rests in the lap of the young virgin and falls fast asleep" (donzella virgen muy fermosa ... dexando toda crueldat, echase en el regaço de la donzella & aduermese muy seguro; 57).

61 This is Stephen A. Barney's translation in Isidore of Seville (66). As Burrus and Goldberg point out in their modern edition of the *Esopete ystoriado,* Isidore of Seville's well-known definition of "fable" is included in the prologue to the anonymous Spanish translator's 1488 version: "fables are things not done but rather feigned, and they were discovered so that the feigned words of irrational animals would let be known, from one to another, the image and customs of men" (las fabulas son cosas non fechas, mas fingidas, & fueron falladas porque por las palabras fingidas delas animalias irracionales de vnas a otras la ymagen & costumbres delos ombres fuessen conoscidas; 2v; qtd. *Esopete* vii).

62 For instance, in the "fable of the rooster and the sapphire," which is found in LBA 1.387–9 among other places, the speaking sapphire complains to the unspeaking rooster that its tremendous value as a precious gem remains unappreciated.

63 Other purposes that Isidore mentions are entertaining the reader, as well as explaining something in the world (for instance, aetiological tales).

64 That is, with disregard to the evolution of human minds and bodies.

65 A fourth category could be constructed of animals that are not depicted as fable animals but in narratives that simply mention animals, such as the animals eaten in LBA. These are not part of the study because animals are not the protagonists and, since they are depicted as inert entities, they lack cognitive interest. The *Esopete ystoriado* is a Spanish version of *Aesop's Fables*; the translation is based in part on Steinhowel's Latin-German edition (1476–7) and a French translation by Julien Macho (Lyon, 1480), according to Burrus and Goldberg (vii–xiv). As Deyermond (177, 179, 254) points out, a long manuscript tradition invokes animals in broader *exempla* collections, for instance, parts of *Disciplina clericalis* (eleventh century), *Calila e Digna* (thirteenth century), and *Libro de los gatos* (thirteenth-fourteenth century) among others.

66 This is Isidore's fundamental definitional criterion.

67 If animals in the actual world do string together parts of language in meaningful utterances – a hotly researched and debated area of comparative psychology that has pointed to a few promising examples of more sophisticated language use among parrots and corvids – they most likely do so in a way that is very different from the way that humans do.

68 The moral of the mouse fable involves being happy with a poor table, because the rich one involves significant fear when the lady of the house walks in on the meal offered by the rich mouse, and the mice almost lose their lives.

69 In the CL and the LBA, there are no Lybistican-type (Type 1.b) stories, in which humans and animals interact, but in the EY, there are four.

70 I employ the term "animal-perspective taking" in distinction to "embodiment," the latter being a full-blown attempt at representing the animal's way of thinking and feeling, which also relies on differences in animal sensory perception and more. Embodiment draws on the use of theoretical knowledge and other insights into the animal's perspective, including physiology and sensory modalities.

71 An analysis of fables shows that the theme of freedom is common: in addition to the one currently being discussed, it is also foregrounded in the fable of the ox (below), in that of the bird who wants to avoid being netted and hence turns himself in, of the netted lion rescued by the mouse (above), and more.

72 While these particular moral concerns seem out of line with what a dog would care about, current cognitive science takes seriously questions about animal morality. See Andrews, chapter 7.

73 This technique is described in Herrera's *Agricultura general*, about which I talk more in chapter 2.

74 It is explicitly called "fabula." This fable is found in very similar versions in both the the LBA and EY, and in this case, I focus on the earlier one.

75 Perhaps the gardener has read too many fables like the one of the lion and the mouse and thinks the snake will be grateful for his assistance. Fernández de Oviedo makes a case, along similar lines, against the Italian feline tamer who befriends an American jaguar, analysed below in chapter 3.

76 The dénouement reveals the expected misogynistic resolution, with the "bad character" of the wife mended by her witnessing this display of pseudo-anthropomorphism, as she gets up from the table and ultimately brings her husband the water he has asked for.

77 Lack of comprehension of human speech can be deadly for animals in a similar vein in other works that develop this motif. In Lope de Vega's *Los comendadores de Córdoba*, the main character believes at the end of the play that he must cleanse his honour with blood after his wife and niece commit adultery with two men in their home, and does so relying on a somewhat similar hypothetical about animal-human interactions and language use. After killing the two pairs of lovers, he kills the servants for not warning him and then finally "the dog and monkey" because they too dishonoured him, he claims, by not "telling him" about the dishonour that was occurring in his household.

78 Translations into English of Ruiz Gómez and other secondary literature throughout are mine.

79 In a religious sphere, animals had fairly static cognitive valences, including moral ones, which were richly symbolic. When society became less religious than in these times, these cognitive qualities retained their moral valences without as much religion; this helps explain why Oviedo and others will refer to animals as "bad" or "good" (the former more than the latter).

2. Exploiting the Animal through Hunting and Husbandry

1 "[Don Quixote] realized that they were falconers" (653) (conoció que eran cazadores de altanería; 2.30:268).

2 In 1582, the aristocratic Argote de Molina published a thirty-five-chapter "Discurso" on hunting that he composed, alongside the three parts of a previously unpublished thirteenth-century anonymous treatise written at the behest of Alfonso XI. In one passage, Argote discusses circumstances

that make it difficult or impossible to communicate properly with the rest of one's hunting party (a situation described by Cervantes in the quote above); Argote points out that if it is too windy, it will be impossible to hear one another while hunting, and offers advice on what to do in such circumstances while pursuing an animal such as a boar.

3 As Murillo points out in a footnote to the word "venablo" (spear), Covarrubias's *Tesoro* explains that it was "a particular weapon of huntsmen in search of wild boars" (arma particular de monteros que van a caza de jabalíes; 1519).

4 On hunting, in *Lector Ludens*, Scham claims that Sancho objects to hunting on grounds of its brutality, in the discussion with the Duke (190). Scham suggests that, for Sancho, animals' suffering should be an object of our compassion (191). Unfortunately the quote he uses for support does not make this point convincingly. Scham (191–2) seems to rely on Margaret Greer's characterization of the hunt as "cruel" (Greer 205), where she writes that Cervantes juxtaposes the "cruel" hunt of the dukes with their pranks to critique them; but it is not clear from the text that the reader is supposed to find these scenes of hunting cruel. Scham discusses how "modern accusations of cruel sensibilities" of the era "overlook" the efforts made to reform (103–4); however, Scham fails to notice that those efforts were aimed at improving things for the humans, not the bulls. He mentions Cristobal Perez de Herrera's proposed reforms to Felipe II, who does critique "de ser los plazeres tragedias" (but this is all an anthropocentric concern; it's not about the bull, but about spectators taking pleasure in the risk and possible harm to the bullfighter). Also, note that the Duke evokes the topos of "hunting as good practice for war," but he doesn't mention the *blood* that was in Espinar.

5 There is a certain similarity to the way in which Sancho hides out here, and the way in which people hide from the bulls in certain texts, e.g., *Peribáñez*, where they are up on the boards (priest and women especially), and in Cantiga 144 about the bull, where everyone is hiding out and shooting the poor animal from above.

6 See chapter 3 on encyclopedic works in the line of Pliny, including Gesner's *Historiae Animalium* (1551), and in the New World bestiaries, by Fernández de Oviedo, Medel, Sahagún, and others.

7 While increasingly empirical, such works often dedicate a significant number of words to spurious-sounding connections between character traits and qualities like fur colour. In *Discurso sobre la montería,* Argote de Molina, for instance, talks of white and red dogs as being preferred for their superiority.

8 Folk psychology is used precisely because it has at least some success at prediction. Philosopher Daniel Dennett has argued that we would need something *better* than folk psychology in order to dismiss it, and the something better would have the need to explain why folk pscyhology works when it does work. See Griffin 10.

9 Humans often portray themselves as outsmarting prey. But in many cases they are also often outnumbering the animal.

10 In his recent book *Beyond Words: What Animals Think and Feel* (New York: Henry Holt and Co., 2015), Carl Safina attempts to have his readers appreciate the cognitive individuality of species like whales, in the wild, that are difficult to connect with for humans. Travelling with marine mammal biologist Kenneth Balcomb in a boat, he describes somewhat intimately how the individual whales are behaving, and what even attentive humans will miss: "This big one over here with the high, wavy dorsal fin is K-25 (...) He's after one large, isolated fish. He dives away (...) Somewhere down below, where their lives occur, a lot is going on. Into a realm where we cannot follow, they so easily slip away. *That* is my fear" (408–9).

11 Because of practical matters of habitat and danger, it remains difficult for cognitive ethologists to perform studies of larger predators in the wild.

12 Boars foam at the mouth. They make themselves angry and start foaming at the mouth in various circumstances, such as to protect their young.

13 The beginning of the paragraph clarifies that the horseman, in this case, was the young prince who would later become King Philip II.

14 Alves writes, "John Cummins, in his study of Medieval European hunting writes, 'The boar was hunted with varying degrees of dedication over most of Europe, but to judge by the surviving manuals and by its role in imaginative literature it was most valued in the Iberian peninsula and in Germany'" (*Animals* 117–18).

15 Maria del Valle discusses the public experiencing the danger and thrill vicariously in bullfights (el peligro ajeno) in an embodied way, with shouts; could it be that the public empathizes so much with the human combatant that there is no empathy left for the "enemy"?

16 More recently, a component of such traditional practices as Tordesilla's "Toro de la Vega" is the accompanying demonstration and outcry by opponents of animal cruelty, amidst significant, negative media attention; for instance, see "La derrota de Cachobo" in the daily *El País* (16 September 2015). In Toro de la Vega, the bull is let loose for the celebration and a Guardia Civil helicopter is used to keep track of its location as it sometimes runs away from the area where the organizers

want it to run and the animal makes its way into the area's industrial park. One person is supposed to be declared the victor against the bull, rather than this being the whole crowd's task to kill the animal. A significant segment of Spain's population now frowns on this activity, according to *El País*, and in two of Spain's seventeen autonomous communities, bullfighting per se has been outlawed (Catalonia and the Balearic Islands).

17 His aside on what makes a good "fiesta" brings to mind Friedrich Nietzsche's comments on the need for cruelty in festivals and how punishment is festive, which, not incidentally, is also the philosopher's reflection on Cervantes's masterwork: "I have pointed out, with cautious finger, the steadily increasing spiritualisation and 'divinification' of cruelty, which twines through the entire history of higher civilisation (and which, if taken in a deeper sense, even constitutes it) (...) when princely weddings and first-class popular celebrations were inconceivable without executions, tortures or an auto-da-fe; and when, similarly, an aristocratic family was inconceivable without a being against whom all were at liberty to direct the shafts of their malice and banter. We recall, for instance, the case of Don Quixote at the court of the duchess. In reading *Don Quixote* we modern readers experience a bitter sensation upon our tongues, almost a torture, and hence we should, for this very reason, appear very unintelligible and unfathomable to the author of it and his contemporaries. They read it with the very best conscience, as the most cheerful of books; they would almost – split with laughter. To see another suffer is pleasant; to make another suffer is still more pleasant – a stern dictum this is, but also a fundamental proposition, old, mighty, human, all-too-human, which, perhaps, even the apes would sign (...) No festival without cruelty: thus the oldest and longest history of man teaches us – and in punishment, also, there is so much that is festival!" *On the Genealogy of Morals*, trans. Walter Kaufmann (NY: Random House, 1967), Essay 2, 66–7.

18 This element of the slaughter is commonly referred to as *desjarretar*, called "hamstringing" in English.

19 A similar practice in a colonial context is described by Rodríguez Freyle in *El carnero* in which the townspeople enjoy some amusement at the expense of the raging bull who is bleeding to death: "They had brought a little livestock to the home of Juan Díaz so that they could kill a young bull; they hamstrung it; it was fierce and they had a bit of fun with it" (Habían traído a la casa grande de Juan Díaz un poco de ganado para de él matar un novillo; desjarretáronlo, era bravo y tuvieron con él un rato de entretenimiento; 306).

20 Horses will be treated in more detail later in this chapter. I offer this example as a quick comparison to the lack of cognitive detail for the furious hunted animal mentioned in the passage.

21 See also Pedro Fernandez de Andrada's *Libro de la jineta* (1599) and *Nuevos discursos de la jineta* (1616), and later Juan Enríquez de Cabrera's *Reglas para torear* (1683); see also Deleito y Piñuela 1988; Alves mentions bullfights, *Animals* 10fn8.

22 Argote de Molina, "Discurso," chap. 23 (fol. 7r).

23 "y alli lo matauan en el agua, o ſaliendo della lo alanceauan" (fol. 7v).

24 Argote de Molina, "Discurso," ch. 31, on Galician pit hunting (*buytron*).

25 Some field research suggests that deer really are better at evading hunters than wolves or bears because they have evolved to evade other forest predators. See Valerius Geist, *Deer of the World: Their Evolution, Behaviour, and Ecology* (Shrewsbury, UK: Swan Hill Press, 1999). Geist minds deer in similar ways to these early modern authors. Describing the evasion techniques of the mule deer, the animal's ability to instantly change direction during flight, he writes, "[t]he ability to change direction is important. It probably shapes much of the mule deer's attributes indirectly. It requires, theoretically, a *composed calculating* deer that remains *calm* even if a pursuing predator is close. Only then is an evasion by the deer *sensible*, for its departure in an unpredictable direction deprives the predator of a midcourse correction" (289, my emphasis). Geist also describes how mule deer move in what seem like random directions, which make them hard for him to locate during his research and, he reasons, harder for predators to hunt them (290). Also, DeYoung and Miller imply that deer have significant advanced cognitive skills and they include an anecdote about one particular deer who "successfully elude[d] trained hunting dogs by entering a ditch and remaining submerged with the exception of her nostrils, forehead and eyes" (319).

26 The term usually meant "stag" but could also metonymically stand in for any large hunted animal," including bear and boar.

27 See chapter 1, above, with examples from *El conde Lucanor* Ex. 5 and *LBA* vv.1437–44.

28 Other writers attribute "engaño" to the dog in certain circumstances: while Pérez generally praises dogs in *Del can y del caballo*, he also writes that the dog "is often deceitful and traitorous" (suele ser también engañoso y traydor) for wagging its tail to passersby as they approach only to bite them in the behind after they pass (50). Incidentally, this description of a dog's "engaño" does not sound like it was based on observation, but on sins more human: In this vein, Pérez also charges

dogs with being gluttonous (goloso) for eating dead things that will later make them vomit (and after which, they again eat the vomit); he also relies on Aristotle (Bk 9 of *Animals*) for calling dogs "envious" (because a dog will keep secret an herb that it eats and that it uses to purge itself, without anyone looking, going to extensive trouble to keep this secret; 51).

29 Primates were well known to imitate all actions, as mentioned by Covarrubias and a whole line of thinkers from Pliny onwards.

30 For instance, in the mouth of the Duke in Cervantes's *Don Quixote* and many years before that in the narrator's voice in Rodríguez de Montalvo's *Amadís de Gaula*.

31 For instance, in the chapter on boar hunting, he reminds the reader that "this action of killing wild boars on horseback is ... the most appropriate imitation of war" (ser esta acción de matar jabalíes a caballo ... la más propia imitación de la guerra; 280–1); he also praises the King for his excellence at this sport. Of course, Philip IV was no warrior in point of fact.

32 As mentioned in n.118, for Scham, Sancho's words on hunting betray a critique of the cruelty of hunting.

33 An alternative method of "caza de buey" is described by Argote de Molina. Using a fabricated, artificial blind that looks like an ox, "made of canvas on top of a light frame, the shape of an ox painted, with its head and horns" (hecho de lienço armado ſobre aros ligeros, vna forma de Buey pintado con ſu cabeça, y cuernos), the hunter hides in this, and then comes out unseen to kill the prey ("Discurso," ch. 33, fol. 12v). See Arrellano, whose short article on "caza de buey" explains a reference in a poem by Quevedo.

34 While this seems to be implied in the quote, and especially given the use of the word "escarmentar," this type of learning is known as "associative learning" in behavioural psychology, and (for behaviourists) does not require any thoughts or representations, or meta-cognition. My point here is not that associative learning requires mental representations but that Martínez Espinar attributes higher cognition to the animal anthropomorphically in this case.

35 I quote from the 1818 edition available on HathiTrust. The *Agricultura general* and *Obra de agricultra* were both published in 1513. It is interesting how this practice illustrates that reading rates in Spain were much higher than generally assumed for the early days of the printing press.

36 Some cognitive ethologists, like Marc Bekoff, dedicate their work to having the general populace recognize the sentience of many non-human

animal species; for instance, Bekoff has a column about animals in the popular journal *Psychology Today*.

37 See chapter 3.

38 Admittedly, this is not unique to how humans may perceive animals and is similar to gross stereotypes about people with certain racial or ethnic physical characteristics.

39 As an example of their stupidity, he points out that they are so sensitive to cold (*friolento*) that they allegedly group together and "they suffocate the little ones, and many times they even suffocate the big ones" (ahogan á los chicos, y muchas veces aun se ahogan los grandes; 503). He also explains the terrifying reason why people should never keep pigs in the house, claiming that they have been known to eat human babies: "often it happens that they eat the baby in the crib" (muchas veces contesce comer la criatura en la cuna; 499).

40 The story of this bird is told by Pliny (10.56), who implies that he doubts its veracity.

41 See chapter 3.

42 According to Daisy Freund, the UN's Food and Agriculture Organization's "Guidelines for Humane Handling, Transport and Slaughter of Livestock" explains that "[w]hen the animals are subjected to manhandling, fighting in the pens, and bad stunning techniques, the fright and stress causes a rapid breakdown of muscle glycogen. This lightens the color of the meat and turns it acidic and tasteless, making it difficult to sell, so it is usually discarded."

43 Farm animals are always considered in terms of their utility – usually as food that the animal provides, or other product that the animal produces; but in a couple of cases, the utility is purely aesthetic. Such is the case of the swan; he explains how to attract one to a pond, for beauty alone, as "it is a bird of great beauty, and taste" (es ave de grande belleza, y guſto). Agustí discusses peacocks in similar terms: "its beauty provides happiness and contentment" (su belleza da mucha alegría y contento; 381). In this, he follows in the tradition of Herrera, who explains how to plant and care for roses, for the aesthetic pleasure they bring to the household. Returning to the peacock, there is additional utility from its faeces, which are apparently good as a remedy for a particular ailment, yet the peacock is anthropomorphically described as "envious" (embidioso), a kind of black envy in fact, when the author explains that it will eat its own faeces in order to not let men benefit from them.

44 Agustí's male rabbits are such beasts that they are known to eat their young, and thus somewhat irrational. The explicit emotions mentioned

in the 700+ page tome are few and far between for farm animals. Mostly, he treats these animals as animated things, both when alive and dead. In a paragraph on pig salting, the pig doesn't seem like a live animal that is killed, but a thing throughout. In the first sentence, Agustí says that, for the sake of salting, on the day that the farmer wants to kill the pig, it should not drink. In the next sentence, the pig has been killed, with no thought given to anything other than how it will taste (351).

45 For a recent cinematographic treatment of this theme, see Richard Glatzer and Wash Westmoreland's *Still Alice* (2014), starring Julianne Moore.

46 On Chaser, see *Nova* documentary (PBS, 9 Feb. 2011).

47 Some of the details of his explanation are reminiscent of the fable of the bull who had too much spirit and was eventually slaughtered for its meat (see chapter 1).

48 In *The Mythical Zoo*, Boria Sax explores the poor treatment of donkeys in diverse texts including the Hebrew Bible, Aesop's Fables, and Apuleuis's *Golden Ass*.

49 And some have been baptised. In *The Mind of the Horse: An Introduction to Equine Cognition*, comparative psychologist Michel-Antoine Leblanc reviews the scientific literature on equids from which I will draw in this and subsequent chapters.

50 See the fable of the hunter and dog in LBA as a way that hunters did not treat their old dogs. LBA, 392, "Enxiemplo del galgo y el señor" (1357–68.392).

51 Rather, knowing a lot about the feelings and thoughts of sheep might lead one not to want to slaughter one.

52 Paintings of the era often portray hunting dogs and quarry, and sometimes display a large number of dogs in a hunting party (see Morales Padrón, "Los perros en la pintura," *Laboratorio de Arte* 5 [1992]: 270, 265–74).

53 According to Jaime Salazar y Acha, the "Monteros de la ventura" were also known as "monteros de la cuenta" in charge of some type of accounting (*La casa del rey de Castilla y León en la Edad Media* 319), thus I translate as "Accountant Hunters."

54 Argote de Molina provides a marginal reference to Luis Pérez's tome in his chapter on the fidelity of dogs (fol. 4v).

55 Humans are showing empathy by imagining the baby of the species, and also by referring to the young with the notion of "love"; as mammals, of course, cows and boar would also rear their young with breast milk; but such references are lacking in these manuals!

56 Those who have hunted with dogs over the ages may have made similar inferences about dog's possessing some sort of reason. Alves mentions the anecdote of James I of England, who reigned some fifty years after the

publication of *Del can y del caballo*, and who "used his own observations of his dogs to argue for a breakdown of boundaries between so-called instinct and reason" (Alves, *Animals* 14). Interestingly, this was probably by means of James's experience with hunting dogs, as it is for many of the treatise writers in Spain. James talked of "yelling arguments" that could not be "carried on without an exercise of understanding" (qtd. in Fudge 102–3, qtd. in Alves, *Animals* 14). Topsell notes that "Aelianus thinketh that Dogs have reason, and use Logick in their hunting, for they will cast about for the game, as a disputant doth for the truth, as if they should say either the Hare is gone on the left hand, or on the right hand, or straight forward, but not on the left or right hand, and therefore straight forward. Whereupon he runneth forth right after the true and infallible footsteps of the Hare" (111).

57 For more details and current controversy about whether humans' sense of smell has been underrated, see the introduction.

58 In addition to these amazing olfactory abilities, Pérez praises the dogs' memory and fidelity (45) and also states that dogs dream, just like all four-legged land animals (75–6).

59 Pérez frequently relies on authorities; he retells an anecdote told by Saint Ambrose about the murderous soldier from Antioch who killed a man whose dog was able to identify the murderer in front of a crowd of people, gripping him with his jaws until the man confessed (47–8). Some of the talk of the "syllogism" may be from authority, given that he does talk here about historical thinkers mentioned in these pages, "all the philosophers in Athens," Saint Ambrose as well as Aristotle.

60 Hence the use of dogs in contemporary society, for instance, to sniff out trace amounts of illicit substances such as drugs or explosives at airports. However, humans are more discerning than dogs at a particular kind of smelling, which is known as "retronasal olfaction" and is a kind of olfaction that importantly forms part of the experience of taste or flavour. See Gordon Shepherd, *Neurogastronomy: How The Brain Creates Flavor and Why It Matters* (New York: Columbia UP, 2012), 19–27.

61 In the twenty-first century we might call this ability "Olfactory Intelligence," which humans lack but which seems akin to human reason given the logical term "syllogistic" that he uses. Also, while Covarrubias says that the term used in this metaphorical sense is about humans (el hombre astuto), he uses the term in the metaphorical sense for animals too, for instance, in his entry on the chameleon ("Camaleón").

62 This is an embodied metaphor that previous smell researchers (specifically, Lakoff and Johnson, and Sweetser) have overlooked. For

Ibarretxe-Antuñano, the "metaphorical scope" of olfaction is not in fact any weaker than it is for other senses (30). See also González, (www3.uji.es/~gonzalez/neuroimage.pdf) and Annie Murphy Paul, "Your Brain on Fiction," *New York Times*, 18 March 2012, p. SR6.

63 The *editio princeps* was published in 1644.

64 See José Antonio Maravall on this trend in *Antiguos y modernos (Visión de la historia e idea del progreso hasta el Renacimiento)* (Madrid: Alianza, 1986), where he writes, for instance, on the medical doctor and humanist Francisco López de Villalobos: "The way to guarantee truth is to turn to personal experience, developed through philosophical principles" (El modo de garantizar la verdad está en acudir a la personal experiencia, elaborada por los principios filosóficos; 460).

65 Not all writers go as far as Pérez or Martínez de Espinar in explicitly imbuing these animals with a kind of reason or conceptual thinking.

66 "We see how they learn what we teach them, how quick they are to obey, particularly those of the hunt; the measures they take to search for the prey, sniffing and tracking" (Vemos cómo aprenden lo que les enseñan, que pronto son en obedecer, particularmente los de caza; las diligencias que hacen para buscarla, venteando y rastreando; el gran conocimiento que tienen en el olfato, donde jamás se engañan; 113).

67 Experimental research demonstrates that dogs indicate location of objects that are of common interest through a variety of mechanisms. Kaminzki and Nitzschner write, "Dogs have been shown to indicate the location of a target object by producing typical 'showing-behaviors' like e.g., gaze alternation towards the target location (Miklósi, Polgárdi, Topál, & Csányi, 2000). These types of signals are produced with persistence, which means that dogs will only stop producing them once they have acquired the target (Gaunet, 2010). This shows that these signals are communicative and referential signals produced in order to indicate the location to the human" (298).

68 Note in this context of horse learning and experience, the implicit understanding of animals being "de comer" (comestible) or not.

69 Horse meat is consumed today in Spain and other Western European countries more frequently than dog meat, but it is not available in abundance like that of cows, pigs, sheep, and chicken. Moreover, in the Middle Ages and Early Modern period, one is hard-pressed to find recipes for preparing horse meat, for everyday meals or for banquets. In Carolyn Nadeau's recent study, *Food Matters*, which analyses hundreds of recipes from many Iberian sources, there is not one recipe for preparing horse. Regarding its consumption today, an article in the Spanish newspaper

El País recommends eating horse meat for its nutritive value, and laments the lack of availability of horse meat: "In Spain, it is almost a taboo, it's a food item that is difficult to find" (Por qué debería comer carne de caballo, pero no puede; Elena Horrillo, *El País*. 9 June 2016. https://elpais.com/elpais/2016/06/03/buenavida/1464958980_166722.html. Web).

70 Stopping short, of course, of being scientific studies.

71 A long tradition upheld this belief in both animals and in women, from biblical and classical sources, most prominently in the story of Laban's sheep, which Jacob manipulated by showing them coloured poplar rods. See Genesis 30; Huet, 272n.8; on the use of this discourse against human miscegination in Spain, see Irigoyen García 62.

72 Agustí also describes more automated ways of arousing an "emotional" response in animals. As sight is important for conception and colour breeding, olfaction should be used to generate desire in the male horse: "Conviene fregar la natura de la yegua con una esponja, y ponerla despues en las narizes del cavallo, si no fuere pronto al saltar, porque esso le moverà" (329). Meanwhile, the sense of touch (heat sensation) can also be used to generate sexual desire in the female horse: "si acaso la yegua no quisiere sufrir el macho, conviene picar una cebolla, y fregarle la natura, que esso la calienta" (329).

73 In this respect, not much has changed in the last several hundred years. From a cognitive perspective, pigs are much like dogs, yet treated as edible, worthless, etc., because of speciesism and inherited cultural bias, in a hierarchical order well described by Serpell in his chapter that contrasts pets with domesticated pigs (3–21).

3. Describing the Animal in New World Habitats

1 All translations in this chapter were prepared by Robert K. Fritz unless otherwise noted.

2 In nature, of course, some aquatic birds both grace the water's surface and also dive below to catch prey.

3 I use scare quotes on "fish" and "birds" when these terms (*pescados/peces* and *pájaros*) do not accord taxonomically with today's categories; for instance, whales, which are mammals, were once considered "fish."

4 I translate "entretiene" as "entertain"; Grossman translates it as "charm."

5 *Diccionario de Autoridades*: "Aprendido: Sabido, adquirido con estudio" [Learned: Known, acquired through study] (translation is mine).

6 On this distinction, see introduction (above). For more on Cervantes's knowledge and ideas about music, see Gasta, who foregrounds how

(human) music is a learned tradition: "In Cervantes's Spain music was considered one of the foremost arts, and cultural elites aspired to learn to sing diverse genres and to play fashionable instruments. Music's special status was most visible in academic study: the two major universities in the peninsula, Salamanca and Alcala, both had chairs of music who instructed society's upper echelons in trendy polyphonic styles (Istel and Baker 435)" (357).

7 Books 8 through 11 are entirely devoted to animals.

8 See chapter 1.

9 Egerton 207.

10 Oviedo's work was earlier and contained many important illustrations, but the number and quality were limited in comparison to Gessner's. Kusukawa argues polemically that "ad vivum" should not always be interpreted as "from life," and that Gessner had many sources for the images, including textual ones; this argument is especially compelling when taking into consideration that some images are fantastic.

11 The Swiss natural historian includes few American animals in his *Historia animalium*; these incude the guinea pig, opposum, the *peje reverso*, and the llama. See Asúa and French 193–4.

12 Gessner's image of the armadillo is based on another image and a dried specimen from Germany while the guinea pig image is based on a live animal that he was sent by a friend from Paris (Pinon 256–7).

13 The terms "New World," "colonial," "Indies," and "Americas" are all imprecise and imperfect and I use them acknowledging this. Columbus went to his grave believing he had found a route not to a new continent but to Asia; later travellers, including Oviedo, would refer to the Indies but know that this was a new continent. The term "colonial" is problematic as these lands were not initially colonies. New World, as I mention above, is of course only "new" from the perspective of Europeans, and only to those Europeans who, after Columbus, recognized that they had arrived in what would come to be known as the Americas.

14 My selection of texts includes highly influential and lesser known works. As Asúa and French point out, Oviedo and Acosta were the most important texts on the subject: "people who had a serious interest in plants and beasts in the Indies read Oviedo and Acosta, those two stout, ponderous pillars upon which much of the early modern knowledge of American nature was built" (53). These were "the scholarly and authoritative works on the subject (...) the main avenues through which knowledge of the new animals reached Europe" (53–4).

15 The best extant version of this manuscript is known as the *Florentine Codex*, which is available in digitized versions on the Internet, as well as in a facsimile edition published in Italy.
16 See my introduction for "habitational parameter" and "mode of interaction," which I borrow from Morgado, "Una visión cultural de los animales," and Norton, respectively.
17 From his comments, it is clear that some of Oviedo's European friends and acquaintances in the colonies also studied these animals.
18 Varying the method, chapter 2 was divided primarily by mode of interaction, while chapter 3 is divided primarily by habitational parameters.
19 Thus, Oviedo begins his chapters on animals with "the most noble" one, the jaguar, which he calls "tiger."
20 Some non-voyagers, like Peter Martyr, wrote only second-hand information. See Asúa and French 1–5.
21 During the Early Modern period and especially in light of New World encounters with certain new aquatic animals, taxonomic categorization was at times challenged by Spanish colonial writers leading to an impetus for a renewed classification system, one which would eventually eject mammalian animals and some reptilian forms from the category. However, this change was slow-going, and due in part to animals that didn't fit entirely the mould – since they foraged plants on the water's edge and stuck their bodies out of the water (they were liminal species for "water" habitat). For the most part, writers' prejudices about the sea *qua* habitat were often determinative with regard to the mode of interaction and the adjudication of (advanced) cognition. Well before the scientifically informed change of whales, dolphins, and porpoises out of the fish category (in the eighteenth century), sixteenth-century colonial naturalists were already confronted with the problematic status of the manatee.
22 More recent notions that inform taxonomy today are evolutionary proximity and genetic relatedness.
23 See Asúa and French 57–62. In particular, Martyr's description of the manatee is seriously lacking, described as "a species of monster ... covered with scales instead of a shell" (*Decade* II.9 [1.263]; qtd. Asúa and French 58).
24 Beginning with a large feline, Oviedo's history is slightly different from Pliny's, who begins with the elephant, although he quickly moves to large felines and talks of them at length; Gessner in turn begins with the lion, so Oviedo's prefigures his.
25 Similarly, the "royal lions" (leones reales) of Tierra Firme are somewhat "cowardly"and will not attack unless they are under attack (something

that Oviedo claims is common to all lions). "In Tierra Firme there are royal lions, no more nor less than those in Africa; but they are somewhat smaller and not as brave, on the contrary they are cowardly and flee; but this is common among lions, which do no harm if not pursued or attacked" (En Tierra-Firme hay leones reales, ni más ni menos que los de Africa; pero son algo menores y no tan denodados, antes son cobardes y huyen; mas aquesto es común a los leones, que no hacen mal si no los persiguen o acometen; *Sumario* 9) . While all of these felines are "ferocious," the "brown lions" (leones pardos) are more so: they are "swift and ferocious" (veloces y fieros; 98).

26 According to Oviedo, as a panther was terrorizing a village and ravaging people and animals, the Indians shot at the animal with many arrows, but only the first one got through the animal's skin; somehow she was able to block all other arrows from penetrating her flesh implying some conscious attention on the part of the panther because Oviedo says, once alerted to the threat of the arrows, the animal was able to defend herself. Nevertheless, the panther bled to death from the first wound, and was left hanging from a leg by a *lazo* (*Historia* 42).

27 Oviedo describes the best way to hunt them (from a few feet up in a tree) (*Historia* 45; *Sumario* 99).

28 Oviedo's "interest" in the piglets is their taste; I use the term "disinterested" here and elsewhere not as a synonym for "uninterested" but rather to describe a non-utility-based interest. Akin to disinterestedness, some (lucky) animals are not rivals for food sources (like wolves) nor a food source for humans (like cows), nor are they "fun" to hunt (like panthers or bulls).

29 "The flesh of this animal is unclean and tastes bad; however, as the misadventures and needs of the Spaniards in those parts, at the beginning, were many and very extreme, they did not forego trying to eat it; but this food was abhorred as soon as some Christians tried it" (La carne deste animal es sucia e de mal sabor; pero como las desaventuras e necesidades de los españoles en aquellas partes, en los principios, fueron muchas e muy extremadas, no se ha dejado de probar a comer; pero hase aborrescido tan presto el manjar, como se probó por algunos cristianos; *Historia* 47; *Sumario* 101).

30 In this passage Oviedo uses the plural direct object pronoun "los" and the singular direct object pronoun "lo" though the antecedent in each instance is "anthills." I have rendered "lo" as "[the anthills]" (plural) for consistency.

31 Of course, the name in English as well as the more modern name of the sloth in Spanish, "perezoso," retains that link to the animal's potential symbolism.

32 Contemporary studies of animal pain have also inflicted suffering on some animals purposefully to ascertain if they are feeling pain. The results of Oviedo's experiment, we can surmise, would be inconclusive, as to the root cause of why the animal was not moving more quickly.

33 "Without a doubt, it seems that, as I said in the chapter on armadillos, such an animal could be the origin or inspiration for making the protective armor of a horse" (Sin duda me parece que así como dije en el capítulo de los encubertados, que semejantes animales pudieran ser el origen o aviso para hacer las cubiertas a los caballos; *Sumario* 104).

34 Oviedo refers to the hexachord, which was the medieval precursor to the seven-note diatonic scale that is most prominent in Western music. He is probably referring to eleventh-century musical theorist and pedagogue Guido of Arezzo's six-tone mnemonic for singers, ut, re, mi, fa, so, la, in descending (reverse) order. "Ut" was traditionally the first syllable in early solfège, replaced in the seventeenth century with "do." See Palesca and Pesce.

35 This is also a fabular way of thinking, that animals provide an example for humans.

36 "It is the size of a household cat in Spain; and it has hair like like that of a Gallician marten on its body, and its belly is somewhat reddish. The backside of the knee joints of the legs serve as its heels, and its feet are long, and its claws are hard but not harmful. It has a narrow head and a long snout, and many thick teeth. They live in Tierra Firme, and have a long plump tail like a cat but it is longer than a cat's, and parts of it have different hair: the hair on its back is of one colour and the hair on its belly is of another, and it has a fine appearance. It is a very tame animal, if not angered, because once angered it bites hard, especially over food" ([E] s tamaño como un gato de los caseros de España; y tiene el pelo como marta gallega en el cuerpo, y en la barriga tira a bermejo. Las corvas de las piernas son el calcañar, y el pie largo; y tiene uñas recias, pero no nocivas. La cabeza tiene muy aguda, e luengo el hocico, e de muchos e espesos dientes. Háylos en muchas partes de la Tierra Firme, e tienen la cola luenga e rolliza como gato, pero más larga que gato, e a trechos, toda ella diferenciada en el pelo: que el un trecho es de la color y pelo del lomo, e el otro trecho del pelo de la barriga, e paresce bien. Es animal muy manso, si no se enjoa, porque enojado, muerde reciamente, en especial sobre la comida; *Historia* 55).

37 Unfortunately, we don't learn about the success or failure of the transplantation of the cozumatle to Asturias. Barrera-Osorio relates the gift of the cozumatle to the desire of European collectors for marvels

(121) while Gerbi sees the gift of the cozumatle as one of many examples of Oviedo's strategy of trying to convince his reader of his descriptive accuracy as chronicler of the New World (390).

38 Before Oviedo, Columbus had also called the monkeys "gatos," following the Spanish and Latin editions of Marco Polo's *Travels*, where they are called "gatos paules"; Enciso's *Suma de Geografía*, presented to King Charles in 1518 used the term "gatos rabudos" (see Asúa and French 6, 17). These are most likely golden marmosets, which resemble lions (Asúa and French 22).

39 Recent studies in archaeological evolution have demonstrated that monkeys learned and passed down this ability.

40 The importation of monkeys to Europe through Seville was so widespread in the first half of the sixteenth century that these animals needed no comment about their physical characteristics. In the *Sumario* (1526), Oviedo writes, "In that land there are monkeys of so many kinds and so much diversity, that one could not write in a short space an account of their different forms and their innumerable pranks, and since every day they are brought to Spain, I will not occupy myself in speaking of them except for a few things" (En aquella tierra hay gatos de tantas maneras y diferencias, que no se podría decir en poca escritura, narrando sus diferentes formas y sus innumerables travesuras, y porque cada día se traen a España, no me ocuparé en decir de ellos sino pocas cosas; 105). Gessner also expressed amazement at the abilities of "apes," similarly impressed by how they are "much given to imitation (...) and have been taught to leap, sing, drive Wagons (...) and are very capable of all humane actions" (2). Similarly, both Medel and Acosta, mentioned later in this chapter, are also fascinated in their own ways by monkeys.

41 This type of imitative learning, from humans to another animal, has been experimentally studied and documented in dogs and monkeys; see Fugazza.

42 That the vignette is comical and leads only to lost teeth rather than a deadly end is key to Oviedo's treating the monkey as an innocuous (non-deadly) creature, that is, it is important for the mode of interaction.

43 "And after many of them had touched the arrow, as he saw that they gave him more pain and no relief, he put one hand on the feathers and the other on the arrowhead, and as soon as the monkeys who came to touch the arrow on one side or the other extended a hand, the injured monkey released the arrow and took the hand of the other and guided it gently to touch the arrow, otherwise he would not allow it to be touched" (Y después que muchos dellos le tentaron la saeta, como él vido que le

daban más pena e no algún remedio, puso la una mano en las plumas e la otra en el hierro, e al que venía a le tocar la saeta por el un lado o por el otro, así como extendía la mano, soltaba él [the injured monkey] la saeta e tomábale la mano al otro e levábasela pasito a tentar la saeta, o no se la dejaba tocar; *Historia natural* 51).

44 To some extent, they are a curiosity as the battle results in comicalness and broken teeth rather than death. These cognitive qualities might have gone unnoticed were they not important to understand for practical reasons, in that the animals were captured for profit selling them as exotic companion animals back in Europe. While Oviedo's monkeys are described with significant cognition, and their humanness is brought to the fore, in Medel's treatment, their activities are described without anthropomorphizing although very anthropocentrically: he describes their behaviour vaguely as "so audacious that it seems Nature had bred them for man's amusement" (tan hazañosos muchos de éstos que parece Naturaleza haberlo[s] criado para quita-pesares de los hombres; 177). The monkeys have an emotional effect on humans, who enjoy watching them as they take humans away from their cares (*quita-pesares*); and yet, this does not increase his empathy for the animals: in the same sentence, Medel talks about how their skins make a beautiful lining for clothing. This is quite distinct from Oviedo's discussion of monkeys, where they did not seem to have any utility to the Spaniards, and would be better categorized as adversaries.

45 Indeed, Oviedo doesn't mention the taste of human flesh either, presumably because he hasn't tasted it, which is something that, for Oviedo and others, differentiated the Spaniards from some groups of indigenous peoples. One exception to the ferocity/taste dichotomy stands out: he mentions the bear in his discussion of the *beori* (tapir) (*Historia* 42–4); the bear is a very dangerous animal for him and yet he mentions the taste; however, this may be because the bear is already considered food for him. He also mentions a Spaniard in Mantua (Francisco de Gonzaga) who has domesticated bears and fattens baby bears up at his palace (43).

46 Given the much later date of composition of Acosta's history, it remains highly probable that he read Oviedo's.

47 In the 1611 *Tesoro*, under the entry for "mona," Covarrubias links the expressions "mona triste" and "mona alegre" to two kinds of hangovers in humans, based on the alleged proclivity of monkeys to drink alcohol and to react in one of two different ways when drunk (1293).

48 Elinor G.K. Melville's important book *A Plague of Sheep: Environmental Consequences of the Conquest of Mexico* studies how the transport of European grazing animals as a food source to the Americas made possible the success of the Spanish in taking over Mexico.
49 Dogs have become worse than wolves, he says (*Historia* 38).
50 Argote had deep roots in Sevillian court life and since he was writing in the 1550s, he most surely was familiar with the well-known writings of Spain's "Historian of the Indies."
51 A later section of this chapter examines the jaguar in a new habitat, the menagerie, in which the animal's mindedness will be remarkably complex.
52 The underlying biases of this idea are based on the erroneous assumption that fish do not suffer, hence why they can be eaten by Catholics at these important liturgical times.
53 The idea that sea creatures should be thought of primarily, or even solely, as a food source is captured in the English term "seafood," a non-taxonomic category that includes a disparate grouping of creatures that live in the water (muscles, lobster, octopus, etc.), conceived of, anthropocentrically, as human food.
54 See Pagden's chapter "The Autopic Imagination" (83) in *European Encounters with the New World.*
55 For instance, in his explanations of animals that have thought or desire, like the anteater. For more on this issue of pausing versus not pausing before action, see my discussion (chapter 4) of Darwin's continuity view and the cat who got out of the bag in Cervantes (*Don Quixote* 2.46).
56 See chapter 1.
57 As Balcombe has noted, few people consider the net fishing of billions of fish each year a cruel form of harvesting them; since the fish on the decks of these boats are slowly suffocating to death, it is plain for Balcombe that most people simply are not aware and don't appreciate their suffering, despite significant evidence that fish feel pain and are self-aware.
58 Acosta treats the realm of fish similarly to Oviedo and others, but is more explicit about how the world of fish is a world apart from the world of humans and land animals. Indeed, "only the Creator could declare their species and properties" (sólo el Hacedor puede declarar sus especies y propriedades; 115).
59 "I marvelled at the incredible voracity of the sharks" (De los tiburones y de su increíble voracidad me maravillé; 115).
60 "I saw the quarter-part of a nag hung for amusement very high above a pool made by the sea and within moments a group of sharks came

after it, drawn by its smell. And, so that the merriment would be of greater enjoyment, the meat of the nag did not touch the water but was suspended above it by I don't know how many handspans and all around it leapt this rabble I speak of. In one mid-air attack they cut meat and bone with a bizarre swiftness, and in this way they cut off the shank of the nag as if it were a stalk of lettuce, for those teeth of theirs are like razor blades" (Yo vi por pasatiempo echar colgado de muy alto en una poza que hace la mar, un cuarto de un rocín, y venir a él al momento una cuadrilla de tiburones tras el olor, y porque se gozase mejor la fiesta, no llegaba al agua la carne del rocín sino levantada no sé cuántos palmos, tenía en derredor esta gentecilla que digo, que daban saltos, y de una arremetida en el aire cortaban carne y hueso con extraña presteza, y así cercenaban el mismo jarrete del rocín como si fuera un troncho de lechuga, pero tales navajas tienen en aquella su dentatura; 115–16).

61 Qtd. in Alvarez Pelaez 546n.34. Columbus had also remarked on the *peje reverso*. See Asúa and French 6.

62 For more on current whale studies, see the introduction, above.

63 *Historia* II.13.2, ballenas. Oviedo differentiates himself from Pliny, who says they are the biggest animals: "But I cannot speak so freely regarding the size or greatness that he attributes to them, for I have not measured them nor seen them on land" (Pero yo no puedo tan libremente hablar en la mensura o grandeza que él les da, proque no las he medidio ni visto en tierra; 57). He's merely seen them in the sea, alive and coming at him! Oviedo is making my point about affordances and scale; when an animal is too large, there can be no affordance because of size differentials; the scale is literally unfathomable.

64 He refers to the adult whale with a masculine pronoun, but most likely, it would have been the mother travelling with the offspring, not the father. Writes Oviedo: "a very large fish or animal of the water was swimming and from time to time it reared up above the water; and what it showed above the water, which was its head and two arms and from there below part of its body, was much taller than our caravel and its masts. And raised in this manner it threw itself mightily upon the water and did the same again soon thereafter. But it did not blow any water from its mouth, but instead made the waves upon which it fell leap violently. And a child of this animal, or an animal similar to it but much smaller, did the same, always turning away from the larger one. And the sailors and those who traveled in the caravel said they judged them to be a whale and calf. The arms it displayed were very large and some said that whales do not have them; but what I saw is what I have said because

I traveled onboard the caravel. And present there was Father Lorenzo Martín, canon of the Church of Castilla de Oro, and the shipmaster and pilot was Joan Cabezas, and also there was a gentleman, the aforesaid Sancho de Tudela, with others who happened to be there, and they are still alive and can attest to the same, because in such matters I never wanted to forgo the provision of witnesses. In my opinion, I estimated each arm of that animal to be twenty-five feet in length, and the arms to be as thick as a barrel. And the head greater than fourteen or fifteen feet in height, and the head and body wider than double that. And as it raised itself high what it revealed was more than five times that of a man of average height" (andaba un pex, o animal de agua, muy grande, e de rato en rato se arboraba; e lo que mostraba fuera del agua, que era la cabeza e dos brazos, e de allí abajo parte del cuerpo, más alto era que nuestra carabela e sus másteles mucho. E así levantado, daba un golpe consigo en el agua, e tornaba a hacer lo mismo desde a poco espacio. Pero no lanzaba agua, por la boca, alguna, puesto que al caer, hacía saltar asaz de las ondas sobre que caía. Y un hijo deste animal, o semejante a él, pero mucho menor, hacía lo mismo, siempre desviándose del mayor. E a lo que los marineros e los que en la carabela iban, decían, por ballena e ballenato los juzgaban. Los brazos que mostraban eran muy grandes, e algunos decían que las ballenas no los tienen; pero lo que yo vi es lo que tengo dicho, porque iba dentro en la carabela. E allí iba el padre Lorenzo Martín, canónigo de la iglesia de Castilla del Oro, y el maestre e piloto era Joan Cabezas, e allí iba asimismo un hidalgo, dicho Sancho de Tudela, con otros que allí se hallaron, e son vivos, que podrán testificar lo mismo, porque nunca querría en semejantes cosas dejar de dar testigos. A mi parescer, cada brazo de aqueste animal arbitraba yo que sería de veinte e cinco pies de luengo, e tan gruesos los brazos como una pipa. E la cabeza mayor que catorce o quince pies de alto, e más ancha, ella y el resto del cuerpo, de otros tantos. Y levantábase en alto, y era lo que mostraba, más que cinco estados de un hombre mediano en alto; 58).

65 Even though the term "fish" is not a homogenous taxonomic category, it now excludes mammals, which are a taxonomic designation; see the introduction.

66 The whale stood out in another colonial natural history too. Acosta also recounts an awe-inspiring story of an indigenous man battling against a whale on the whale's turf, that is, in the water, which he did not see first-hand but which is trustworthy as it was related from "expert people" (personas expertas): As the whale is being stabbed repeatedly through its breathing hole, he describes the animal's emotional response ("rabidness"

and "fury"), interpreting its jerky movements "as if it were crazy with anger" until beaching itself where a group of fellow hunters await it for slaughter ("The whale bellows and strikes the sea, raising heaps of water, and it plunges in with fury and leaps again not knowing what to do in its rabidness (...) [I]t turns about this way and that as if crazy from anger until finally it moves closer to shore" (Brama la ballena y da golpes en la mar, y levanta montes de agua, y húndese dentro con furia y torna a saltar, no sabiendo qué hacerse de rabia (...) [D]a vueltas a una parte y a otra como loca de enojo, y al fin se va acercando a tierra; 3.15, 117). The wonder and irony of this hunt arise from the size differential between the one "indio" and the "whale as big as a mountain" (3.15, 117). While Acosta's narration often refers to the whale as "ballena," he interchanges this term with the word "pez," the latter also being the common word in the explanation of the illustration of this hunting method of straddling the whale to "fish" it. There is scant empathy for these animals, which today we know are highly sentient and intelligent mammals, with the largest brains of all creatures on the planet, since, it would seem, the animals live in the deep, and Acosta has no direct experience of them, he only hears about them being "fished" and eaten as "fish" (*pez*).

67 What is stake here and in other cases then is the real possibility of committing a sin by eating meat (*carne*) on a day when Catholics are supposed to avoid it (whereas "fish" is and was completely permissible). See Michael Foley, *Why Do Catholics Eat Fish On Friday?* (New York: Palgrave Macmillan, 2005). For the sake of Lent, the church ruled that lizards were "fish" – these creatures have in common "cold-bloodedness" that makes them dissimilar enough from human beings generally, and before Christ's Passion in particular, for them to be comestible.

68 Columbus may have been describing manatees when he writes in his log, in a mythological vein, that he had sighted three "mermaids" near the island of Hispaniola (qtd. in Asúa and French 4; qtd. in Few and Tortorici 6). See also González Echevarría (*Celestina's Brood* 112) on the manatees as sirens.

69 He also treats fishes, sharks, whales, and caimans.

70 Scillacio, "De insulis meridiani atque indici maris nuper inventis," 91 (*Raccolta di Documenti e Studi pubblicati dalla R. Commissione Colombiana pel quarto centenario della scoperta dell'America*, Roma 1893, qtd. in Asúa and French 7). As Asúa and French point out, Scillacio taught at the University of Padua and never left Europe; for his 1494–5 pamphlet, written in Latin, he relied on accounts from "travelers who had accompanied Columbus" (7).

71 Acosta is either mistaken about this grazing on land (*pace en el campo*) or he means that the manatee remains in the water and eats the plants at the water's edge.

72 The manatee was a mammal possibly unknown to Pliny, and certainly unknown to the American explorers. Columbus mentions "mermaids" in his journal; as González Echevarría notes in *Celestina's Brood*, Peter Martyr popularized the findings of American animal discoveries in Europe (102).

73 Medel studied Canon Law at Alcalá, and held various administrative posts including governor of Yucatán 1552–3; he also held posts in Guatemala and Colombia. Medel wrote the text after his stay in Colombia, which began in 1557, but the date of composition is unknown. The only extant manuscript of *De los tres elementos* is a copy from the eighteenth century.

74 Scholars of Victorian British literature have written about the "invention" of the pet during this period. Kreilkamp writes, "Here's a riddle: what invention of eighteenth-century England develops, in the course of the nineteenth century, into a major instance of and vehicle for the culture's high valuation of sympathy and domestic life, and becomes known, worldwide, as a quintessential embodiment of English identity and a national self-image founded on an idealized vision of home? If the genre of the novel probably comes to mind, the modern domestic pet also fits the bill. If England became known as a nation of shop-keepers, it was also preeminently associated with long novels and beloved pet animals, two cultural forms which, I argue, developed not just in parallel but in tandem" (87). Building on the work of Harriet Ritvo and others, Kreilkamp's claim is based on the defensible idea that animal cruelty became a moral outrage in England during this period: "A major transformation occurred around the turn of the nineteenth century as a country which had been strongly associated with sports involving cruelty to animals such as bull-baiting and cock-fighting, came increasingly to define itself – led by Evangelicals and middle-class reformers – by opposition to such cruelty" (Kreilkamp 98; see also Ritvo 141).

75 In some cultures, as Marcy Norton has explained, domesticated animals were kept as pets but used as food in case there was a shortage; she explains this as a non-binary manner in which to interact with animals.

76 This is a version of a story told long before by non-travelling European Peter Martyr. Medel probably learned of this story through Martyr's *Decades of the World*, which of course came much earlier than Medel and provided additional information about the Cacique and the water

animal: "This particular manatee was a pet of the chieftain Caramatexius and lived in Lake Guarabo, near the 'palace' of its master in Hispaniola. Caramatexius caught it when it was very young and fed it daily with roots over twenty-five years, until it grew big. Matum – as the pet manatee was called – answered to the sound of its name and ate from the hands of sympathetic humans. It would play and wrestle gently with the 'chamberlains' of the king and attracted the attention of natives who were amazed at the sight. Yet it would shun Spaniards, because once a young Christian miscreant hand thrown a pike at it. Matum was even able to transport people across the lake on its back: people said that it had once carried ten persons from one shore to the other, all of them singing and enjoying themselves. The marvels of the lake of Baie or the boy-carrying dolphin of Arion," says Martyr, "are not as admirable as this aquatic creature of the Indies" (qtd. in Asúa and French 58–9, translation is theirs). Note that Asúa and French use the word "pet" without historicizing it in their translation of the passage from Martyr. While various peoples and groups of peoples have treated animals *as pets*, the term "pet" is clearly from modern English and is somewhat anachronistic in a Renaissance context.

77 Medel goes on to tell a similarly anthropomorphizing story, another one that involves an animal recognizing a human voice. It is also a water animal, which he calls a *cocodrilo*. In his vignette, a group of youngsters, having tamed the animal, would play with it by taking turns riding it in the water: "In a similar vein, Some Spanish conquistadors from the province of Cartagena of the Indies attest to a crocodile that makes its den in the Rio Grande de la Magdalena next to a village located on the banks of the same river. [This crocodile] was so trained and tamed that when the boys came to the banks of the Rio Grande that passes by there and called to it by a certain name they had given it, it came out from the depths of the river to the surface of the water and came to the shore where the boys were and with complete docility consented to let them mount it and it carried them and swam all over the river, from one part to another, until it returned to the land where it accepted the food they gave it which consisted of fish and other similar things" (Semejante a esto es lo que algunos españoles conquistadores de la provincia de Cartagena de las Indias afirman de un crocodilo que, en el río Grande de la Ma[g] dalena, junto a un pueblo que en la costa del mesmo río está poblado, tenía su manida, el cual estaba ya tan acostumbrado y mansueto que, llegándose los mochachos a la ribera de aquel río Grande que por allí pasa y llamándole por un cierto nombre que le tenían impuesto, salía de

lo hondo del río a la superficie del agua y se llegaba a la orilla a donde estaban los mochachos y con toda mansedumbre consentía que subiesen en él y los llevaba nadando por todo el río, a una parte y a otra, hasta que le encaminaba para volverse a tierra y rescebía la comida que le daban de pescado y de otras semejantes cosas; 94–5). There is a suggestion that the crocodile possesses intentional agency and concept understanding in the way he describes how it "consented" to having the children ride him; additionally, it was the crocodile who determined where to travel. For Medel, the example demonstrates the value of training, through repetition, perhaps extrapolating what he must have known of dog or other animal training through folk animal psychology. Thus, implicitly, the wild crocodile, for Medel, is capable of the requisite cognitive capacities for intellectual abilities and emotional control appropriate for behavioural training. However, this type of appreciation does not make Medel more empathetic towards the plight of these animals. In fact, in a separate anecdote, Medel relates how he amused himself once, passing time by killing several baby crocodiles for no other reason than because he merely had nothing else to do: "Having gone down the river fed by Lake Nicaragua and being on the seashore waiting for sailing weather, I saw a brood of little crocodiles on the banks of the shallows of a river that emptied into the sea, and *to amuse myself I began killing the little lizards with a stick* and casting them out of the water" (Bajando yo por el desaguadero de Nicaragua, estando en la orilla de la mar esperando tiempo para navegar, ví una lechigada de crocodilos pequeñitos a la orilla y lengua del agua de un río, que por allí entraba en la mar, y comencé por *holgarme con un palo de matar de aquellos lagartillos* y echarlos fuera del agua; 97). He also envisions the role of parent as protector for the offspring, like a human parent, when explaining that the mother (or father) came after him after the uncalled for violence: "In my distraction, a male or female lizard, which was probably their mother, charged at me so violently that if I had not quickly retreated, alerted by a boy that was with me, it would have possibly done me some harm" (estando descuidado, arremetió hacia mí de dentro del agua un lagarto o lagarta, que debía de ser su madre, tan desaforadamente que si no me tuviera afuera presto, avisado por un mozo que conmigo iba, fuera posible hacerme algún daño; 97).

78 He narrates how the indigenous hunt the manatee, the uses of its flesh (for lard and meat), and its morphology in his view: "and as it comes ashore on the banks of the river to graze, the Indians lie in wait for it and when it exposes itself they shoot arrows or other similar projectiles at it. Good lard is made from the manatees and, put in a marinade, its meat tastes like veal

and many would be fooled into believing it to be so. It has no scales nor any shell, but rather a hide like a dolphin's. The manatee's mouth, lips, and head are like that of a bull calf. The hide is very tough and has some hairs and it has a short, wide tail, like a carpenter's adze; it is somewhat long and plump" (y saliendo a las orillas de los ríos para pascer y alcanzar hierba los indios le aguardan y en descubriéndose le ti(e)ran o con flechas o con otros semejantes tiros. Hácese buena cecina de los *manatís* y la carne de ellos, echada en adobo, paresce de ternera y muchos se engañarían con ella. No tiene escama ni concha alguna, sino cuero como tonina; tiene el *manatí* la boca, bezo y cabeza como un becerro; el cuero muy recio y algunos pelos en él, y tiene la cola muy corta y ancha, a manera de azuela de carpintero; es algo largo y rollizo; 93–4).

79 Both Medel and Acosta discuss compuctions over eating this "fish" on Lent.

80 He might be discussing the "marine iguana," which hunts exclusively under water and is a good swimmer-diver.

81 Like many of the other species he is interested in, Oviedo says that he has had iguanas living in his home, and even after observing them, he does not understand what they eat.

82 Darwin also found the iguanas of the Galapagos extremely ugly.

83 Anita Guerrini notes that some French anatomists studied the dolphin, in the context of Pliny, and saw it was "what we would call a mammal" (59).

84 For instance, about the adult crocodile who wants to protect her young whom Medel kills.

85 Nor of the whales whom the indigenous dive down to net.

86 That the word "pet" is metonymical for touching the animal is a telling etymology.

87 For instance, Medel writes, "there is a kind of bird that is as big as a magpie that has very long, beautiful, and varied feathers with many marvelous colours" (hay un género de pájaros de tamaño de una urraca, de muy lindas plumas y muy largas y variadas, con muchos y maravillosos colores; 39); he explains that the Indians are interested in their beautiful feathers, and will catch the bird, just pick a few and then release it so that in subsequent years they can take more. Acosta talks especially about the feathers of birds and relates their uncommon beauty, and aesthetic utility: "The macaws are birds that are larger than parrots and are similar to them: they are prized for the diverse colours of their feathers which are very handsome" (Las guacamayas son pájaros mayores que papagayos y tienen algo de ellos; son preciadas por la

diversa color de sus plumas, que las tienen muy galanas; 4.37:204). He discusses feather art of Indians as well, rich in colour, and which create a *trompe l'oeil* ("one could not judge by looking if they were the natural colours of the feathers or if they were painted" (que la vista no pudiese juzgar si eran colores naturales de plumas, o si eran artificiales de pincel; 4.37:204), and which "is of an unparalleled beauty" (son de extraña hermosura; 4.37:204).

88 Captive parrots – these same parrots but with a new habitat – are treated in the section on captive animals. Along with monkeys, the importation of parrots to Europe through Seville was extremely widespread in the first half of the sixteenth century.

89 Like "fish," "bird" is a somewhat capacious category that may include animals, like bats, that are not birds according to modern taxonomical categories.

90 Commenting on the mico, he suggests they feel fear of the animals on the ground, and demonstrate forethought and logic in their tree-travelling behaviour: "[T]hey make their nests in unoccupied trees or those that are isolated from the rest because the cat monkeys are used to going from tree to tree and jumping from one to another without descending to the ground for fear of other animals, except when they are thirsty and descend to drink when they will not be disturbed. And that is why these birds do not want nor tend to nest except in a tree that is somewhat distant from the rest. They make a nest that is as long as or longer than a man's arm that resembles a sack that is wide at the bottom and narrows towards the top where it is hung and where they make a hole to enter the sack that is just big enough for the aforesaid bird to fit" (H]acen sus nidos en árboles desocupados o apartados de otros, porque los gatos monillos acostumbran irse de árbol en árbol y saltar de unos a otros, y no bajar a tierra, por temor de otros animales, sino es cuando han sed, que bajan a beber, en tiempo que no puedan ser molestados. E por eso estas aves no quieren ni suelen criar sino en árbol que esté algo lejos de otros, y hacen un nido tan luengo o más que el brazo de un hombre, a manera de talega, y en lo bajo es ancho, y hacia arriba de donde está colgado, se va estrechando y hace un agujero por donde entran en aquella talega, no mayor de cuanto el dicho pájaro puede caber; *Sumario* 119).

91 As mentioned in the introduction, mental time travel refers to "[t]he ability to project oneself mentally either backward or forward in time, which allows one to remember past events or envision future events" (Andrews 188).

92 See the introduction.

93 "[I]n recompense for their services and labors, they paid them in lashes and beatings; and no word could be heard from their lips but 'dog'" ([E]n remuneración de sus continos servicios y trabajos, era muchos azotes y palos, y otra palabra no oían de su boca sino perro; 6).

94 "[A]nd would that it please God that they treated them as they do their dogs, for they will not kill a dog for a thousand gold coins but think nothing of stabbing to death ten or twenty Indians when they feel like it and testing their strength or the blades of their swords for sport as if they were killing cats" ([Y] pluguiera a Dios que como a sus perros los trataran, porque no mataran un perro por mil castellanos y no tenían en más matar diez y veinte indios cuando se les antojaba, a cuchilladas, y probando, por su pasatiempo, las fuerzas, o los filos de las espadas, que si fuera matar gatos; 6). On the abuse of cats in Europe, see Martin 455–6.

95 "In the Indies, whenever the Spaniards brought dogs they always used to throw the Indians they captured to them, men and women, either for the dogs' amusement and to make them more ferocious or to strike more fear into the Indians that they would be ripped apart. They once agreed to throw an old woman to the aforementioned dog and the captain gave the old woman a piece of paper telling her, 'take this letter to some Christians' that were a league distant from there, in order to later set the dog loose once the old woman was no longer among the other people. The Indian happily takes the letter believing that on the way she could escape the clutches of the Spaniards. Once she had departed and been underway for some time away from the other people, they set the dog loose. As she saw the dog come so ferociously at her, she sat on the ground and began to speak to it in her language: 'Master dog, I am going to take this letter to the Christians; do not harm me, master dog.' And she extended her hand, showing him the letter or paper. The dog stopped very docilely and began to smell her and it lifted a leg and urinated on her in the way dogs are wont to urinate on a wall. And thus he did her no harm at all. Amazed at this, the Spaniards called the dog and leashed him and freed the sad old woman so as not to be more cruel than the dog" (Siempre acostumbraron en estas Indias los españoles, cuando traían perros, echarles indios de los que prendían, hombres y mujeres, o por su pasatiempo y para más embravecer los perros o para mayor temor poner a los indios que los despedazasen. Acordaron una vez echar una mujer vieja al dicho perro, y el capitán diole [a la mujer] un papel viejo diciéndole: "Lleva esta carta a unos cristianos," que estaban una legua de

allí, para soltar luego el perro desque la vieja saliese de entre la gente; la india toma su carta con alegría, creyendo que se podría por allí escapar de manos de los españoles. Ella salida, y llegando un rato desviada de la gente, sueltan el perro; ella, como lo vido venir tan feroz a ella, sentóse en el suelo y comenzóle a hablar en su lengua: "Señor perro, yo voy a llevar esta carta a los cristianos; no me hagas mal, señor perro," y extendíale la mano mostrándole la carta o papel. Paróse el perro muy manso y comenzóla de oler y alza la pierna y orinóla, como suelen hacer los perros a la pared, y así no la hizo mal ninguno. Los españoles, admirados dello, llaman al perro y átanlo, y a la triste vieja libertáronla, por no ser más crueles que el perro; 203–4).

96 Along the lines of these attack dogs, horses were also used as instruments of warfare by the Spaniards, and were treated as individuals. As Asúa and French point out, Bernal Díaz enumerates and describes each of the sixteen horses that his crewmen brought to Mexico (27). From the perspective of the conquered, the Michoacans noticed the working relationship between the horses and their riders, observed that the animals obeyed what seemed to be verbal commands, and believed that the horses understood human speech. See the *Chronicle of Michoacán*, c.1540, qtd. in J.H. Elliot, *Spanish Conquest* 173, qtd. in Asúa and French 27, fn. 9.

97 The conclusion to *The Pig Who Sang to the* Moon is entitled "On Not Eating Our Friends" (219–38).

98 When faced with new species that didn't neatly fit into old categories, or came into contact with similar species but with different traits, early modern Spanish historians and naturalists were led to re-evaluate the inherited categorization of animals, as a precursor to modern scientific method. For instance, Oviedo is fascinated by the muteness of the *xulo* dog, proposes a hypothesis, and tests it. While his hypothesis was not particularly apt, he successfully proved that it was wrong because he tested it, way back in the 1520s. His hypothesis was that the dogs were silent because of something on the island so he removed one from the island brought it to the mainland: He proved conclusively that taking the dog off the island did not suddenly give it voice!

99 Oviedo is perhaps the colonial author who is most critiqued by de las Casas.

100 Oviedo calls them "gozques," although the definition of this term, according to *Autoridades*, is "A small dog that is only good for barking at those who go by or those who enter the house" (Perro pequeño, que

solo sirve de ladrar a los que passan, o a los que quieren entrar en alguna casa), which would not apply if they are actually mute. Covarrubias also singles out the barking as a significant feature of the gozque, which according to the *Tesoro* is a small mixed-breed dog that "barks all night long" (ladran toda la noche). If mute, Oviedo's gozques would not have the protective function of warning that others "want to enter a house" and would serve only as as a pet or as a potentional food source.

101 According to Scillacio's pamphlet about the New World , the indigenous would eat the mute dogs when there was a food shortage (Asúa and French 8).

102 Note that the same number of days is used here and earlier – this is a rhetorical strategy that implicitly links the company of dogs and humans.

103 Most likely commissioned by the Archdukes Albert and Isabella, the five senses paintings soon came into the possession of the Spanish royal family and were listed in the 1636 inventory of Madrid's Royal Alcázar (Woollett and Suchtelen 94).

104 The two African lions with which Don Quixote interacts in 2.17 are being delivered by the cartdriver to the Spanish King as a gift from the General of Orán. For more on this episode, see chapter 4.

105 In Spanish, the terms *casa de fieras* (house of beasts) and *coleccion de animales* (animal collection) were used; the word "menagerie" came into English through French only in the early 1700s.

106 However, most texts do not contain much on the cognition of these collected animals – for instance, Bernal Diaz's description of Moctezuma's animals is mainly a catalogue.

107 Oviedo calls the animal, variously, "tigre" or "ochi." From the description, it is clearly a jaguar, not a tiger.

108 The vignette is told in both the *Sumario* and the *Historia natural*, but it contains more details in the latter.

109 Machiavellian Intelligence is a form of Theory of Mind used specifically to deceive and manipulate (see Simerka 81).

110 This view happens to coincide with the Humane Society of the United States' current thinking toward large cats; the HSUS lobbies for a complete ban on interactions between humans and large cats, because they are likely to lead to acts of violence and harm to animals, humans or both. See http://www.humanesociety.org/news/magazines/2016/05-06/exotic-pets.html.

111 This is, indeed, very unlike Pliny and others, who tell tales of dangerous wild animals who remember the human who helped out, eternally grateful for the favour.

112 For a robustly imperial-sounding compliment, he refers to his King as "Caesar" and admits also to Oviedo that he hoped to be recompensed for his achievements with a title of nobility.

113 The volume was unknown until it was discovered in Florence in the twentieth century. The large format manuscript of approximately 1,500 folios is left-column Spanish, right-column Nahuatl with illustrations throughout. The way in which the animals are divided in Book 11 seems clearly European: "de los animales" (land animals), "de los aves" (birds), "de los animales del agua." There are some anomalies: for the chapter entitled "animales del agua," the page headings say "de los peces." And when the author discusses fish, for instance, the first section is on fish that one would find in Castile and in America. As the book progresses, the organizing principle of the work is not as clear: after fish, Sahagún interjects what he knows about the armadillo (a land animal), then discusses river fish, lizards, and later more fish, frogs, caimans; finally, there are some amphibious mythological animals.

114 For a convincing cognitive theorization that the human mind essentially organizes experiences along certain models that can be called "literary," see Turner.

115 "To capture them they use the following trick: they make a great fire where these animals are found and they surround it with ears of corn and in the middle of the fire they place a stone called *cacalótetl*. The hunters of the quarry hide or burry themselves and when the monkeys see the fire and smell the smoke, they soon come to warm themselves and to see what kind of thing it is; and the females bring their young on their backs and they all soon sit around the fire, warming themselves. And when the stone grows hot, it discharges a deafening blast and casts embers and ashes on the monkeys. Frightened, they make to flee and leave their little ones here and there; nor do they see them for they go about blinded by the ash. Then the hunters suddenly rise up and take the little monkeys in their hands and they raise them and tame them. These animals are easily tamed. They sit like people. They fawn over the women; they joke about with them. They demand food by extending their hands and they scream" (Para tomar estos usan de este embuste: hacen una grande hoguera donde andan estos animales, y cércanla de mazorcas de maíz, y ponen en el medio del fuego una piedra, que se llama *cacalotetl*, y los cazadores de esta caza escóndense, o entiérranse, y como ven el fuego los monos, y huelen el humo, vienen luego a calentarse y a ver que cosa es aquello, y las hembras traen sus hijos a cuestas, y todos se asientan luego alrededor del fuego, calentándose; y como la piedra se calentó da un tronido grande, y derrama

las brasas, y la ceniza sobre los monos y ellos espantados dan a huir, y dejan sus hijuelos por allí, ni los ven, porque van ciegos con la ceniza; entonces los cazadores levántanse de presto y toman a manos los monicos y críanlos, y amánsanlos. Estos animales fácilmente se amansan; siéntase como persona, cocan a las mujeres, búrlanse con ellas, y demandan de comer extendiendo la mano, y gritan; Sahagún, *Historia* 231).

116 On the legend of *onzas* and other kinds of cougars or lynxes that are mythological, legendary, semi-legendary, see Alvarado Reyes (http://www.scielo.org.ar/scielo.php?script=sci_arttext&pid=S0327-93832008000100015).

117 He also describes the *coyámetl*, which he says is very similar to the "Castilian pig" (puerco de Castilla), and he explains what it looks like and what it eats (227). Deer are also a subject of his book. He remains exclusively physical about their description, including the taste of their flesh, and remarks about what they feed on ("they graze on herbs and leaves of the trees" [pacen las hierbas, y las hojas de los árboles; 231]).

118 See my introduction, where, drawing on Allen and others, I discuss how the concept "fish" is not a scientific taxonomical category despite the elimination of marine mammals from the grouping.

119 As observed earlier in this chapter, Oviedo too mentions the turtle as a kind of "fish."

120 Another creature that allegedly hunts humans preferentially – like the legendary or mythological cat-like *ocotochtli* – is gratuitously anthropomorphized in a special way.

121 There is yet more implicit discursive evidence that this animal is considered mythological by the author – it is a unique being, not one of many, not male and female like other species, etc.

122 The rest of the body is left, uneaten, a detail which speaks of the ahrizotl's cosmological role.

123 As in the medieval Virgin stories, it is unclear what the process is by which the *ahuitzotl* gathers these fish, which seem completely anthropectomized. See chapter 1.

124 The animal is protected by the god Tlaloc, and an old woman who caught one was told to put it back where she found it! (265–6). Also, note the similarity between this description and that of Peter Martyr who mentions a "ferocious animal [in Cumaná], the size of a dog, came down to town and roamed the empty streets wailing with so human a voice that the people, assuming it was a crying child, came out of their houses, only to be killed by it" (qtd. in Asúa and French 61).

125 To demonstrate better what I mean by Sahagún's lack of questioning of this creature's existence, I can contrast it with Medel's account of

the "pexe tierra," a kind of eel that digs into the mud – in which Medel explicitly says we should not believe the stories about it: "The common people, who do not know or do not want to consider things inwardly and think of them in terms of their causes, are accustomed to gathering miracles and marvels where there are none or making them out to be greater than they really are" (El vulgo, que no sabe o no quiere considerar las cosas interiormente y tomallas dende sus principios, suele amontonar milagros y maravillas donde no las hay, o hacerlas mayores de lo que ellos realmente son; 105). He goes on to tell about a sixteen-foot-long sea monster that could walk on two feet and had hands, feet, and dual (human) sexual organs, with the head, neck, ear, and mouth of a dog, a creature the reader is clearly not supposed to believe in. The jungle was (and is) a dangerous place for a human to be, and many of the creatures he describes more cursorily – like tigers (jaguars) – would kill Indians regularly, according to Oviedo at least. The properties and cognitive capabilities of *ahuitzotl* and the water serpent seem to stand in for Sahagún as the danger of the forest more broadly, representing in an unreal way the real danger of the forest that conflates with the real dangers of the water. Medel here critiques exaggeration and perhaps gratuitous anthropomorphism.

126 Figure 23 provides an excellent example of an illustration of a hummingbird (*quetzalhuitzilin*, 238).

127 As like fish and the suffix "michin," most birds contain the suffix "tototl," which standing alone means "bird" in Nahuatl.

128 If we take Bernal Diaz's often exaggerated account as accurate in this regard, he too suggests that Moctezuma also found birds primarily beautiful. According to the Spanish historian, the Aztec king had ponds stocked with fish and numerous aquatic birds, as well as a whole menagerie wing devoted to birds.

129 Other birds with special mythological powers are the *tenitztli* (243) and the *acuitlachtli* (245), which may not actually be a bird but is in the bird section.

130 Sahagún, *Historia* 38.

131 In America, this is assumed, since he spent most of his life there.

132 See also Bulliet 3.

133 These unique cases of special animals like the *cocho* or the captive jaguar are like today's viral YouTube videos that depict special animals. With the knowledge and abundance of information we have today, we can see that there are many special animals, so many in fact as to make one doubt their uniqueness, and rather to posit that many of their conspecifics, observed under similar conditions and contexts, might

easily perform similar behaviours. Reading them in conjunction, we can see that special animal phenomena (e.g., the "pet" manatee from La Hispaniola mentioned earlier) are all over the place, and perhaps not so special after all.

134 They write that Sahagún's section on animals "immediately calls to mind that we are no longer dealing with Western mental categories" (Asúa and French 43).

135 Furthermore, in making a different argument, Asúa and French happen to provide examples that Oviedo engages in what, in another context, they would have called "humanizing" and what I call "gratuitous anthropomorphizing." However, when the author's assessment is negative, as in the cases of the sloth and anteater, the historians chalk it up to personal autobiographical factors, rather than on a non-European world view as they held in the case of Sahagún's anthropomorphizing (it can't be a non-European world view in Oviedo of course). Specifically, they relate Oviedo's negative appraisal of the sloth and the (partially) negative appraisal of the anteater to his biography and profession: "The world of the *adelantados* valued reckless action and physical prowess. Oviedo was not only shocked by the 'laziness of the sloth' he was also disgusted by the timid habits of the anteater, which he qualifies as 'cowardly and defenseless'" (66). Clearly both "laziness" and "cowardly" are anthropomorphisms, yet in these cases Asúa and French do not qualify them as such, because they are looking for another type of explanation. The authors miss the point about the *mode of interaction* here; Oviedo would not be disgusted by a sheep, although it could also be called "cowardly" and "defenseless." The difference, as I have shown above, is that these animals have no use value to humans. It's certainly not that he wants all animals to be like *adelantados* – he likes to eat his piglets after all!

136 "And I arrived to find certain friends of mine eating a very fat one that had been well roasted and basted or slathered in lard and garlic, and it did not taste bad; rather, when my companions saw that I began eating with such pleasure and enthusiasm, one of them said, 'Sir, it would not be a bad idea if we took some of these dogs with us since you find them so tasty'" (E llegué donde ciertos amigos comían de uno muy gordo e muy bien asado e untado o lardado e con ajos, e no me supo mal; antes, de ver aquellos compañeros que yo con buen gusto e aliento entraba en ello, uno dellos dijo: "Señor, no será malo que nos llevemos de aquí algunos perros déstos, pues que también os saben"; 30).

4. Embodying Animals: Cervantes and Animal Cognition

1 See chapter 1, where I mention the scene in DQ 2.71 to introduce the topic of animal symbolism. In addition to the scene mentioned there, there are several other examples of the knight interpreting animals symbolically, for instance: "All that could be heard in the town was the sound of dogs barking, which thundered in Don Quixote's ears and troubled the heart of Sancho. From time to time a donkey brayed, pigs grunted, cats meowed, and the different sounds of their voices seemed louder in the silence of the night, which the enamored knight took as an *evil omen*" (509, emphasis added) (No se oía en todo el lugar sino ladridos de perros, que atronaban los oídos de don Quijote y turbaban el corazón de Sancho; de cuando en cuando rebuznaba un jumento, gruñían puercos, mayaban gatos, cuyas voces de diferentes sonidos se aumentaban con el silencio de la noche, todo lo cual tuvo el enamorado caballero a *mal agüero*; 2.9:99–100, emphasis added). Other symbolic uses are, for instance, the explicit references to medieval bestiary-style symbolism: "No one should think that the author digressed by comparing the friendship of these animals to that of men, for men have learned a good deal from animals and have been taught many important things by them, for example: from storks, the enema, from dogs, vomiting and gratitude; from cranes, vigilance; from ants, foresight; from elephants, chastity; and loyalty from the horse" (529) (Y no le parezca a alguno que anduvo el autor algo fuera de camino en haber comparado la amistad de estos animales a la de los hombres; que de las bestias han recibido muchos advertimientos los hombres y aprendido muchas cosas de importancia, como son: de las cigüeñas, el cristel; de los perros, el vómito y el agradecimiento; de las grullas, la vigilancia; de las hormigas, la providencia; de los elefantes, la honestidad; y la lealtad del caballo; 2.12:123). On at least one occasion, Don Quixote rejects the opportunity to interpret foreboding animals symbolically, perhaps because of his strong desire to partake in the mission; this is right before he descends into the Cave of Montesinos, where the narrator points out the symbolic value of the dark birds and how Don Quixote must not be very superstitious: "and so he put his hand to his sword and began to slash and cut the thicket at the mouth of the cave; with the clamor and din, an infinite number of huge crows and rooks flew out of it, and there were so many flying so quickly that they knocked Don Quixote to the ground; *if he were as much of a soothsayer as he was a Catholic Christian, he would have taken this as a bad omen* and refused to go down into such a place. At last he stood, and seeing that no more crows

or other nocturnal birds such as bats, which had come out along with the crows, were flying about ... he began to lower himself down to the bottom of the fearful cavern" (602, emphasis added) (así, poniendo mano a la espada comenzó a derribar y a cortar de aquellas malezas que a la boca de la cueva estaban, por cuyo ruido y estruendo salieron por ella una infinidad de grandísimos cuervos y grajos, tan espesos y con tanta priesa, que dieron con don Quijote en el suelo; y *si él fuera tan agorero como católico cristiano, lo tuviera a mala señal* y escusara de encerrarse en lugar semejante. Finalmente, se levantó y viendo que no salían más cuervos ni otras aves noturnas, como fueron murciélagos, que asimismo entre los cuervos salieron ... se dejó calar al fondo de la caverna espantosa; 2.22:209, emphasis added).

2 Much as today, the vast majority of domesticated animals in the United States – several billion cows, pigs, and chickens primarily, and more than half a trillion "fish" – are slaughtered as an unindividuated mass, at the same time that, according to recent statistics, over half of American households have a pet dog that is surely treated much better. Serpell points this out in chapter 1 of *In the Company of Animals*.

3 As Alves points out, for Aristotle the incapability of animals to reason or hold abstract principles justified human domination of them, just as it was used as justification for the domination of "natural slaves" and of women by men (Alves, *Animals* 13).

4 Westerners frequently complain about dogs being bred for human consumption in other parts of the world, or about the Arctic seal hunt, yet they are not terribly bothered by the raising and slaughter of pigs. In Kantian terms, we could say that those who engage in implicit anthropectomy are treating animals as "mere means." For Kant, people should never be treated as "mere means" since they are "ends in themselves." I am applying Kant's term beyond his own use: Kant did not believe that non-human animals had Reason, for which they were not "ends in themselves" nor accorded the same respect as humans.

5 On this phrase as an embodied metaphor, see Wagschal 155.

6 As Poggioli explains, writing on the pastoral literary tradition, "[t]he shepherd does not need to grow wheat like the farmer, or prey on wildlife like the hunter. He is a vegetarian on moral as well as on utilitarian grounds, choosing to live on a lean diet rather than on the fat of the land" (5).

7 Another example of a herded animal whose sentience is not considered, like the sheep, are the six hundred pigs in DQ 2.68, whom the reader gets to know only from the noise they make, "grunting and snorting" (904) (el gruñir y el bufar; 2.68:553). We know only the perspectives of the narrator

and the characters who are trampled: the former calls them "unclean animals" (904) (animales inmundos; 2.68:553) while the characters are "[thrown] into confusion" (904) (en confusión; 2.68:553).

8 For instance, in the scene with the Tomé and the wine. On Sancho's excellent sense of smell and taste, see Wagschal.

9 There are a few cases of dead donkeys, but not dead horses – no dog or horse is ever killed or eaten in the novel, but there are multiple dead donkeys whose carcasses show that carrion eaters have devoured them.

10 This scene is analysed, in the context of medieval symbolic interpretations of animals, in chapter 1.

11 In contrast, the reader is often told of fears or desires of human observers of Don Quixote's violence, for instance, Sancho and the lion-keeper, the lady and the Basque, etc.

12 "Saying this, he rode into the midst of the host of sheep and began to run at them with his lance as fearlessly and courageously as if he really were attacking his mortal enemies. The shepherds and herdsmen guarding the flock came running, shouting for him to stop, but seeing that this had no effect, they unhooked their slings and began to greet his ears with stones as big as fists (...) they hurriedly gathered their flocks together, picked up the dead animals, which numbered more than seven, and left without further inquiry" (230) (Esto diciendo, se entró por medio del escuadrón de las ovejas y comenzó de alanceallas con tanto coraje y denuedo como si de veras alanceara a sus mortales enemigos. Los pastores y ganaderos que con la manada venían dábanle voces que no hiciese aquello; pero viendo que no aprovechaban, disciñéronse las hondas y comenzaron a saludalle los oídos con piedras como el puño (...) recogieron su ganado y cargaron de las reses puertas, que pasaban de siete, y sin averiguar otra cosa se fueron; 1.18:223).

13 From the point of view of Animal Studies, Martin analyses the various functions that animals played in Spain and in *Don Quixote*, noting that "This novel in particular contains a very high number of real animals (...) In addition, there are alimentary animals, such as those that turn Camacho's wedding into a Rabelaisian feast" (452, translation mine).

14 For more on early bullfighting and bull-baiting, see chapter 2.

15 Maese Pedro is of course the picaresque character and escaped felon Ginés de Pasamonte from Part I, but in disguise.

16 As Enrique Fernández suggests, this is indeed a "cunning" limitation on the monkey that will not jeopardize Maese Pedro's trick (127); I would add that since what he states does not involve foretelling what will occur, it is also carefully not against the Church's rules against prognostication.

17 While the species of monkey is not specified, it is called "large" (grande), yet is small enough to jump up on Maese Pedro's shoulders: "[he] jumps onto his master's shoulders and goes up to his ear and tells him the answer to the question, and then Master Pedro says what it is" (624) (salta sobre los hombros de su amo, y, y llegándosele al oído, le dice la respuesta de lo que le pregunta, y maese Pedro la declara luego; 234). With the narrator's specification that the monkey has no tail, it is likely that this is a Barbary ape (macaque), which has only a small vestigial tail (these animals still inhabit Gibraltar); the smallest of the "apes" that are truly "tailless" (family Hominidae) is the chimpanzee – but a full-grown adult male would be too large and heavy to jump up on his shoulder.

18 As mentioned in chapter 3, Oviedo knew that monkeys did not speak human languages, and the rare mentions of a monkey speaking were exceptional anecdotes.

19 Unlike Rocinante, this special monkey has no name, he is simply "the soothsaying monkey" (623) (el mono adivino; 233).

20 A great deal more cognitive research has been done on apes and monkeys. For instance, Vauclair demonstrates categorization abilities in baboons, in levels of increasing abstractness, including "concepts" (239).

21 For Forcione, these encounters are examples of a pervasive "lawlessness" (61); reading the stories of animal-related demonic possession together, Forcione sees Berganza's Cañizares as an "amplified version" of the Persiles' story of Rutilio: Rutilio watches over the cadaver of the witch-wolf and then "experiences a symbolic death and a metamorphosis into an animal state, when he dons the skins which he finds on the hanging corpse, and, reduced to muteness, spends three years amusing the barbarians" (143n.19).

22 The image is in line with the kind of reasoning about the monkey that Don Quixote himself had surmised in the 1615 novel, i.e., that such a creature would have to be demonic.

23 Unlike the representation of Rocinante's embodiment, which in my appraisal is very horse-like, that of the two dogs in "El coloquio" seems more human when looked at from the standpoint of cognitive embodiment. Such a claim is controversial, since it is common among Cervantes scholars to hold that these dogs are really like dogs.

24 An exception to his eating like a dog is when Berganza says that he ate salad, using a counterfactual: "which I ate as if I were a person" (468) (la cual comí como si fuera persona; 316).

25 "[F]or ever since I could gnaw at a bone I have wanted to be able to talk" (453) (Desde que tuve fuerzas para roer un hueso tuve deseo de hablar; 301).

26 "Despite all this, even if my food was taken away, my barking could not be stopped" (475) (Con todo esto, aunque me quitaron el comer, no me pudieron quitar el ladrar; 323).

27 "My master taught me to carry around a basket in my mouth" (456) ([M]i amo me enseñó a llevar una espuerta en la boca; 304). See above, chapter 1, for my reading of the Aesopian dog who drops the meat. Beusterien rightly points out that Berganza is an exemplary dog in this regard, in that, unlike in fable versions of the dog who carries meat in his mouth, Berganza does not try to eat it (42).

28 "[T]he proper and natural function of dogs is to stand guard over livestock" (457) ([E]l natural oficio de los perros guardar ganado; 305).

29 "I ... attacked my own master, knocking him to the ground" (483) (Arremetí con mi propio amo … di con él en el suelo; 331).

30 In macrosmatic mammals, smell is of much greater importance, a distinction that is easily quantifiable: for instance, dogs have about ten times the number of olfactory receptors as humans do, which means that canines can detect smells in concentrations that are 100 million times lower than we can (Herz 20–2). Humans also have a much higher number of "pseudo-genes" related to olfaction than do dogs and other macrosmatic species. A pseudo-gene is a DNA sequence that is a remnant of some gene, but which is no longer functional. The percentage of olfactory pseudo-genes among dogs is fifteen, whereas for humans the percentage is about sixty-five (Herz 24). Typical species-specific vision, in contrast, is tri-conal in humans, and bi-conal in dogs and horses, such that one main difference in the senses of sight is that the colour vision of typical members of these species is akin, but not identical, to that of humans with green/red colour blindness (Marshall and Arikawa). "Horses, dogs, some primates and barracuda, on the other hand, have only two spectral classes of photoreceptors, and may be likened to red–green colour blind humans in performance; they are dichromats." See Marshall and Arikawa.

31 On human embodied metaphors and the dominance of visual over other kinds of metaphors, see Lakoff and Johnson, *Philosophy in the Flesh* and *Metaphors We Live By*.

32 There is also significant evocation of empathy towards Berganza, which can be detected when he tells the stories of how he was abused or mistreated, and even in the fear response he has of the witch, but I would suggest much of the empathy is anthropocentric, towards Berganza *qua* human animal, as I will explain.

33 This privileging of their sight overshadows the reference to Berganza's superior olfactory skills, which are in fact scarcely mentioned.

34 This is one of the visual primary metaphors that Lakoff and Johnson describe in their view of human embodiment.
35 Many of the ideas in Lakoff's and Johnson's book were first introduced in less developed form in their *Metaphors We Live By*.
36 Clearly, there are also differences among humans that may be cultural, historical, and/or physiological (which are not directly addressed by Lakoff and Johnson). However, such differences do not appear to negate the commonalities of our most fundamental and basic cognitive structures (particularly, primary and secondary metaphors).
37 While they may sound similar, such basic cognitive metaphors are not the same as "lexicalized" or "dead metaphors," a term used in literary studies, philosophy, and linguistics to designate any metaphor in a particular language that has become such an ordinary part of language that it no longer seems metaphorical (i.e., "table leg").
38 More recently, Ibarretxe-Antuñano has argued that the number of secondary metaphors involved with olfaction is in fact much greater, and she lists up to nine. While I agree with Ibarretxe-Antuñano that Lakoff and Johnson's, and also Sweetser's, secondary metaphorical understanding of olfaction is overly narrow, I think that her own list is too broad. As I will demonstrate below, historical analyses of great works of literature like *Don Quixote* can provide evidence for claims of cognitive metaphoricity, and in this case, my analysis of *Don Quixote* will demonstrate that Lakoff and Johnson's view is overly restricted. Two of Ibarretxe-Antuñano's other olfactory categories are found in *Don Quixote*.
39 Note that Berganza uses the verb "pintar" (to paint), which Grossman's translates less visually with "describes."
40 Other metaphors that both dogs use have to do with techniques in fine art; repeating the sense of the *darkness is lack of knowledge* conceptual metaphor, Cipión uses the phrase "dimly ketched out" (my translation). Grossman translates more idiomatically "roughly sketched out" (502) for "bosquejado en sombra" but the element of darkness is missing from her translation. In contrast to the dog-like references, the human conceptualizations abound, and there are even more examples of human conceptualizations from Berganza's insistence on Christian morality, to his racial slurs about Africans and Moriscos, to Cipion's knowledge of the classics.
41 Note that Cervantes uses the verb "to see myself" (*verme*) metaphorically, but Grossman translates as "find myself."
42 See especially Sobejano; Avalle-Arce; González Echevarría, "Life and Andventures of Cipión"; and Forcione. Aylward summarizes these and other similar views.

43 "But nothing astonished me more, nor seemed worse to me, than seeing how these butchers kill a man as readily as they kill a cow; for at the drop of a hat, as easy as one-two-three, they slip a yellow-hafted knife into a person's belly, as if they were adminstering the death blow to a bull's neck" (455) (Pero ninguna cosa me admiraba más ni me parecía peor que el ver que estos jiferos con la misma facilidad matan a un hombre que a una vaca; por quítame allá esa paja, a dos por tres meten un cuchillo de cachas amarillas por la barriga de una persona, como si acocotasen un toro; 303).

44 Beusterien treats Cipión and Berganza as dogs, whether they be humans transformed into dogs or actual canines; their speaking does not detract from their being dogs, drawing on a theoretical approach from Cary Wolfe, "Flesh and Finitude: Thinking Animals in (Post)Humanist Philosophy," *SubStance* 117.37.3 (2008), 8–36; for Beusterien, Cervantes does not limit speech to humanity, and he notes that there is no explicit mention that the dogs are speaking a "human" language. Critiquing Forcione's interpretation in *Cervantes and the Mystery of Lawlessness*, which views the animals' eventual loss of speech as returning to "the dark silence of animality" (221, qtd. in Beusterien 38), Besteurien writes "[b]ut, at the beginning and end of the dialogue, when the dogs extol the wondrous benefits of language, the praise is never delineated as 'human.' In contrast to the Ovid story, Berganza and Cipión – whether they be humans metamorphosized into animals or just animals – have the power to speak on one special night. Cipión and Berganza are not mute, like the stag in Ovid or ass in *The Golden Ass*. In contrast to Périer's dog dialogue and other anthropocentric recuperations of the Acteon story, Cervantes never mentions that the dogs have consumed or incorporated a human tongue in order to speak (even though they demonstrate superb linguistic wit and amazing poetically-charged rhetorical turns). In short, while he praises language, Cervantes does not espouse *human* exceptionalism with respect to language" (38). Of course, literary critics routinely look at what fiction says beyond what an author explicitly "mentions" or doesn't mention. Indeed, with closer scrutiny to how the dogs talk, Berganza's humanly embodied visual secondary metaphors counter Beusterien's claim at an implicit level, as do many other details, such as the fact that no scientific study has ever found that dogs speak what could be called a language (whereas there is significant evidence of language among whales, dolphins, and certain bird species; see my introduction). Beusterien's interpretation makes an excellent case for the need for more cognitive science in animal studies, because distinguishing

clearer categories of the cognitive capabilities, sensory modalities, and *Umwelts* of different kinds of animals (*Homo sapiens*, *Canis lupus*, etc.) would help avoid such claims. My emphasis on the sensorial-cognitive faculties underlying the assumptions and practice of speech, in the manner that Berganza and Cipión use speech, demonstrates that this type of speech is in fact human and tied to the human body through cognitive embodiment. While my essay focuses on early modern thinking about animal thinking, my approach relies on an insight from contemporary theories of cognitive embodiment, and in particular to Lakoff and Johnson's *Philosophy in the Flesh*.

45 There is a second olfactory reference in the "Coloquio," but it is abstract and counterfactual, referring to how a dog might use olfaction as a means of gathering information: "And each morning I would return to the herd, after finding no wolves, nor even a trace of any. I would be out of breath, dead tired, and totally worn out, with my feet torn and bleeding from the thorns. And each time I would find, amid the herd, either a dead sheep, or a ram with his throat slashed open and half eaten by wolves" (462) (a la mañana volvía al hato, sin haber hallado lobo ni rastro dél, anhelando, cansado, hecho pedazos y los pies abiertos de los garranchos, y hallaba en el hato, o ya una oveja muerta, o un carnero degollado y medio comido del lobo; 310). In this other example, Berganza refers to the activity of searching for a wolf who has allegedly killed the sheep that he is supposed to be protecting – however, the wolf is no wolf, but a man in wolf's clothing. Since there is no wolf to smell, Berganza's experience marks the absence of olfaction; it is an explicit non-smell, indicated with a preposition and a conjunction of negation ("after finding *no* wolves, *nor* even a trace of any" [*sin* haber hallado lobo *ni* rastro dél]).

46 El Saffar discusses the question of uncertainty at length (32–4).

47 See Wagschal 159n.37.

48 The sensory verb "oler" (along with its synonyms) occurs with little frequency in this novella about a pair of canines, while visual information nonetheless abounds. The novella consists in fact of a similar sensory setup and experiential world as *Don Quixote*, in which sight and hearing (especially through language) dominate over the other senses, except with two dogs (instead of two humans) as main characters; thus, "El coloquio de los perros" conflicts with what we know about the relative importance and functioning of olfaction and sight in canines according to current scientific knowledge. Indeed, the colour vision of dogs is extremely weak, but while a dog could certainly see "white," a dog would not see yellow, and hence would be unable to articulate a thought

or memory based on colour difference pointing out the following scene: "for at the drop of a hat, as easy as one-two-three, they slip a yellow-hafted knife into a person's belly, as if they were adminstering the death blow to a bull's neck" (455) (a dos por tres meten un cuchillo de cachas amarillas por la barriga de una persona, como si acocotasen un toro; 303). Similarly, the discrepancy between "rojo" and "morado," which is of such importance in the *memory* of Berganza, would have been imperceptible and meaningless to a dog, a bichromat with two types of cones (and many fewer) rather than three as in humans; dogs have one sensitive to blue and the other to greenish-yellow, meaning that anything looking like yellow, orange, or red, is not going to be easily differentiated except by brightness (Horowitz 128). "His Holiness the Pope enters dressed in full pontifical regalia, along with twelve cardinals, all of them clad in purple, because when the action occurs at this point of my play it is the time of a *mutatio caparum*, when the cardinals exchange their scarlet robes for purple ones. It is therefore entirely appropriate, in order to observe the proprieties, that these cardinals of mine come out all dressed in purple. And this is a detail very much in keeping with the spirit of the play" (503) (Sale Su Santidad del Papa vestido de pontifical, con doce cardenales, todos vestidos de morado, porque cuando sucedió el caso que cuenta la historia de mi comedia era tiempo de *mutatio caparum*, en el cual los cardenales no se visten de rojo, sino de morado; y así, en todas maneras conviene, para guardar la propiedad, que estos mis cardenales salgan de morado; y éste es un punto que hace mucho al caso para la comedia; 351).

49 For more on this "music" and *cencerrada*, see Martin 455–6.

50 I concur with Martin, who observes, "it is worth noting that nothing is expressed about the abused cats" (456).

51 For instance, the *vizcaíno* in 1.8–9. With respect to the cat, note the use of the gerund form of "ver," followed by the use of the preterite, and the the verb "asir" ("[he] sank his claws and teeth into his nose" [756] [le asió de las narices; 385]). Similarly, when he is first differentiated from the rest of the travelling party – right before he challenges Don Quixote – the *vizcaíno* is presented in a dependent clause with the gerund form of the verb "ver," followed by a main clause in the preterite, and even the use of the same verb, "asir," in the main clause: "One of the squires accompanying the carriage was a Basque, who listened to everything that Don Quixote was saying; and *seeing* that he would not allow the carriage to move forward but said it would have to go to Toboso, the squire *approached* Don Quixote and, *seizing* his lance" (63, emphasis added) (Todo esto que don Quijote decía escuchaba un escudero de

los que el coche acompañaban, que era vizcaíno; *viendo* que no quería dejar pasar el coche adelante, sino que decía que luego había de dar la vuelta al Toboso, se *fue* para don Quijote y, *asiéndole* de la lanza; 1.8:135, emphasis added). This is a common way that Cervantes makes an individual stand out from a group.

52 Note that Cervantes uses the verb "ver" (to see), but Grossman translates less visually, providing the sense of what the metaphor means, "finding himself." While cats are macrosmatic, like dogs and unlike primates, they have particular strengths in night vision, with significantly greater percentage of rods (for night vision) than humans (some estimates are of 600–800 per cent more rods).

53 In contrast, the Basque's rental mule, in 1.9, is an example of an animal whose mental state is only briefly considered and which demonstrates a certain lack of cognition, an animal who seems to behave automatically according to the narrator: "And so he waited for him, shielded by his pillow, and unable to turn the mule one way or the other, for the mule, utterly exhausted and not made for such foolishness, could not take another step" (64) (Y así, le aguardó bien cubierto de su almohada, sin poder rodear la mula a una ni a otra parte; que ya, de puro cansada y no hecha a semejantes niñerías, no podía dar un paso; 1.8:137). Later, the mule transparently expresses the emotion of fear according to the narrator, running away from the battle between Don Quixote and Don Sancho de Azpetia, in an action that also seems automatic: "and the mule, terrified by the awful blow, began to run across the field and, after bucking a few times, threw his rider to the ground" (69) (y la mula, espantada del terrible golpe, dio a correr por el campo, y a pocos corcovos dio con su dueño en tierra; 1.9:145). Similarly, in terms of automated response, the episode of the donkeys suggests that donkeys have little choice but to bray when they hear braying; Sancho reinforces this in his own reminiscences: "when I was a boy, I used to bray whenever I felt like it, and nobody held me back, and I did it so well and so perfectly that when I brayed all the donkeys in the village brayed" (641) (cuando muchacho, que rebuznaba cada y cuanto que se me antojaba, sin que nadie me fuese a la mano, y con tanta gracia y propiedad, que en rebuznando yo, rebuznaban todos los asnos del pueblo; 2.27:255). In the case of another rental mule, that of the barber and priest in 1.29, its cognition is opaque as it lifts its feet (perhaps to complain) and knocks off Maese Nicolás' disguise; it is not made clear why the mule does this (except that it is not supposed to do what it is doing, and it is a "bad" animal).

54 See introduction above for more on animals qua *automata* and on Darwin's view. As Alves explains, Malebranche was an adherent of Cartesianism who went beyond Descartes in positing that "animals feel no pleasure or pain" (Alves, *Animals* 8). Before both Descartes and Malebranche, Gómez Pereira had also denied feelings and emotions to non-human animals (Alves, *Animals* 7–8).

55 In this case, a human verb of embodiment is used, but "to see" is also an appropriate one for the cat in this situation since Don Quixote is attacking the cat with a sword.

56 "They're male and female; the male's in the first cage and the female's in the one behind, and they're hungry now because they haven't eaten today" (560) (Son hembra y macho; el macho va en esta jaula primera, y la hembra en la de atrás; y ahora van hambrientos porque no han comido hoy; 2.17:160).

57 "Sancho wept for the death of his master: this time he believed there was no doubt he would fall into the clutches of the lions" (562) (Lloraba Sancho la muerte de su señor, que aquella vez sin duda creía que llegaba en las garras de los leones; 2.17:162).

58 After stretching, Don Quixote heads toward Rocinante and talks to him: "The canon took one of Don Quixote's hands, although both were tied together, and on the basis of the knight's promise and word, they let him out of the cage, and he was infintely and immensely happy to find himself free, and the first thing he did was to stretch his entire body, and then he went up to Rocinante" (422–3) (Tomóle la mano el canónigo, aunque las tenía atadas, y debajo de su buena fe y palabra le desenjaularon, de que él se alegró infinito y en grande manera de verse fuera de la jaula. Y lo primero que hizo fue estirarse todo el cuerpo, y luego se fue donde estaba Rocinante; 1.49:577).

59 Relying on traditional ethological accounts, one reason for the lion's lack of interest in Don Quixote could be that "Lions are active primarily at night" (Shaller 24) and the novel's actions occur during broad daylight. Also, Dunston et al. attest to significant individual differences among male lions, amounting to "personality," assessing "behavioural variations and consistencies in daily activity, social and hunting behaviour" and noting varying degrees of boldness among individuals in different contexts.

60 The term "generoso" is somewhat ambiguous here and does not help to resolve the human vs animal characterization. For Covarrubias in the *Tesoro de la lengua castellana o española* (1611), the term "generoso" applies to "considerada su persona sola, tiene valor y virtud, y condición noble,

liberal, y dadivosa," but it could also mean of good stock, as in "Cavallo generoso, el castizo de buena raza" (968).

61 See the introduction for more on Pereira, Descartes, and Malebranche.

62 This vignette from Pliny was obviously well known, and can be found also in Gessner's *Historiae Animalium*. In Topsell's English version of Gessner's book, he adds more detail to the story as well as noting that Romans believed it to be true, so much that they had inscribed on the "great Roman Palace" verses about this: "Iratus recolas, quam nobilis ira leonis; / In sibi prostratos, se negat esse feram" (Topsell 365). Robert Favreau (623) documents this, with slightly different orthography, and notes that it can be found in Henzen et al. (624n.59). Apparently, Roman senators were supposed to consider this before taking office.

63 The goatherd's anthropomorphizing is in the opposite direction of the initial view of the lion, in which case all characters assumed that the lion made no choices but just reacted by attacking.

64 On theories of fictional worlds, see Pavel, *Fictional Worlds*; Ryan, *Possible Worlds*; and Martínez-Bonati, "Towards a Formal Ontology of Fictional Worlds."

65 When faced against their own wishes by multiple suitors. Sor Juana Inés de la Cruz famously deconstructed masculine hypocrisy in her poem "Hombres necios," for instance, "Siempre tan necios andáis / que, con desigual nivel, / a una culpáis por crüel / y a otra por fácil culpáis."

66 Alves has also drawn attention to how the goat has understanding (Alves, *Animals of Spain* 86).

67 Herrera 361; see chapter 2 above for Herrera's anthropectomy of farm animals including goats.

68 See chapter 1 for this distinction.

69 For instance, in "Nonhuman Mind-Reading Ability," Marthe Kiley-Worthington (3) contends that goats are among species that are excellent at Mindreading.

70 On the Europeanness of this hierarchy in the era, see Norton, "Chicken." Norton points out the case of an unnamed Indian man mentioned by Oviedo in his *History* who lived with, hunted with, and became friends with feral pigs in the jungle, hunting other pigs who did not belong to their group. Norton observes Oviedo's uneasiness with the transgression of the typical European boundaries in effect for human-animal relationships, which reserved a special bond to human-dog and human-horse interactions.

71 Nadeau connects the expulsions of 1492 and 1609 to Christian culinary preferences: "as the Crown sought to unify a nation under one religion ... [p]ork's position in the early modern period is a clear example of how

food preferences carry hegemonic identity. And even after Spain's imperial presence faded, ham continues to inform Spain's cultural identity" (111).

72 These animals are not so much characters in the novel as illustrative examples in the prologue.

73 The boy in the medieval *cantiga* loves the donkey, an affection that is not only condoned but promoted by the father who tries to protect his son's feelings when the animal dies.

74 In a later section of this chapter, I review recent research on the cognitive ethology of equids, including their modes of communication. Interestingly, the alderman's terminology is not that far off from current acoustical analyses of equid calls.

75 Unlike, for instance, the many entire books devoted to horses and dogs, or both, like Pérez's *Del can y del caballo*.

76 The only exception to this treatment is outside of the main narrative, in the preliminary poems that precede the novel's first chapter which purport to demonstrate that Don Quixote has become a legend and in which Rocinante is portrayed with personification.

77 Equid is the name of the taxonomical family of the mammalian class that includes zebras, horses, and asses, all of which are closely related; they belong, with rhinoceros and tapirs, to the taxonomical order of "odd-toed ungulates," also known as Perissodactyls. Other ungulates, more distantly related, belong to the order of "even-toed unglates" (Artiodactyla), a group that includes cows, sheep, goats, deer, giraffes, hippos, and pigs, among others.

78 I refer to Sancho's donkey as "el rucio" or "El rucio" throughout. Although some English readers may be used to the name "Dapple" (a moniker given to him in Cohen's broadly divulged Penguin translation), in the Spanish original the donkey is specifically contrasted with Rocinante for lacking a name; the narrator refers to him by various terms, including "el rucio" (grey one), which is what Sancho says he calls him.

79 It is interesting to note that in *Libro de albeytería*, Hernán Calvo warns of "caballos que son muleros" (124) and how to rid them of what he considers a serious problem; but Calvo explains that the *muleros* are male horses that want to mate with "mulas," so the case may not be very similar.

80 To be sure, Agustí is only talking about horse-to-horse relations, and my use of this as inter-equine horse-to-donkey relationship goes beyond what Agustí says. In fact, Agustí is against interspecies relationships: he warns against them, and of the dangers of the "caballo mulero." (Despite

their both being equids, the interspecies arrangement is unusual in literature, save for the fable.)

81 The narrator also makes inferences based on the behaviour of the animals, in a similar way to Luis Pérez and other treatise writers on dogs and equines.

82 The most important is the lowering of the heart rate, which indicates the calming effect: "imitation of grooming resulted in a substantial decrease in cardiac rate of 11.4 percent on average in the eight adult horses and 13.5 percent on average in the eight foals for the preferred site, whereas the same stimulation applied to the nonpreferred grooming site had no effect, which suggests that grooming the preferred site did have a calming effect on the groomed individual. Finally, in discussing why the calming effect is limited to a particular site on the body, the authors find it likely that the parasympathetic part of the autonomous nervous system is involved, noting that the ganglion stellatum, which is the most important ganglion in the horse, is close to the preferred grooming site and that it is known to be linked to major efferent cardiac pathways." As Leblanc points out, these preferred grooming sites correspond to places that veterinarians had long been using acupressure to help calm nervous horses (380).

83 "A large part of this activation is opioidmediated, accompanied by activation of the serotonergic neurons in the raphe nuclei section of the reticular formation" (Leblanc 384). A study by S.D. McBride, A.J. Hemmings, and K. Robinson ("A preliminary study on the effect of massage to reduce stress in the horse," *Journal of Equine Veterinary Science* 24.2 [2004]: 76–81) cited by Leblanc notes that these same neural mechanisms, activated by acupuncture and massage, can lead to decreased heart rate (Leblanc 384).

84 "Along with their masters, they jump out of the pages of the book towards us, with a highly defined form and performance" (Ordoñez Vila 58).

85 The treatment of El rucio as a sentient being is especially remarkable in light of societal bias against donkeys; the reader will recall from chapter 2 that Agustí does not merely anthropectomize donkeys as he does most other farm animals, but he singles out the donkey as a "vile and despised animal" despite its being "necessary" on the farm for the kinds of service it can provide (345).

86 See the introduction to this book.

87 Vertebrate is a taxonomic classification of subphylum, consisting of all animals with a backbone, and includes all mammals, birds, reptiles and many fish. Also among invertebrates, there is evidence that cephalopods (octopus, squid, and other similar animals) also feel pain.

88 A recent article in the *New York Times* by cognitive researcher Jonathan Balcombe argues that humans should not eat fish because they feel pain that many humans ignore. Balcombe writes that "a half trillion fish" are caught in nets in the world each year and are mostly left to suffer through painful suffocation atop boats. Importantly, as mentioned in the introduction, philosopher of cognitive science Colin Allen has demonstrated that the very term "fish" is not a scientific, taxonomic category, but more of a folk category, and that it contains a heterogeneous collection of creatures, some of which are importantly different in terms of their sentience and ability to feel pain – a tuna is not the same as an eel or a minnow.

89 This is by no means an exhaustive list of examples of their physical pain. Another is, for instance, when Don Quixote and Sancho are attacked by the "troop of 600 pigs," Rocinante is named twice: "The large grunting herd came running in great haste and confusion, and without showing respect for the authority of either Don Quixote or Sancho, they ran over them both, destroying Sancho's stockade and knocking down not only Don Quixote but Rocinante for good measure. The herd, the grunting, the speed with which the unclean animals ran past, threw into confusion and to the ground the packsaddle, the armor, the gray, Rocinante, Sancho, and Don Quixote" (904) (Llegó de tropel la extendida y gruñidora piara, y sin tener respeto a la autoridad de don Quijote ni a la de Sancho, pasaron por cima de los dos, deshaciendo las trincheras de Sancho y derribando no sólo a don Quijote, sino llevando por añadidura a Rocinante. El tropel, el gruñir, la presteza con que llegaron los animales inmundos puso en confusión y por el suelo a la albarda, a las armas, al rucio, a Rocinante, a Sancho y a don Quijote; 2.68:553).

90 "Based on a range of scientific studies (many of them horrific and unconscionable), we know that emotional harm actually hurts more than physical harm, and that animals will 'choose' physical suffering over emotional suffering, if forced to pick. McMillan cites an experiment in which an electrified grid was placed between a puppy and a person to whom the puppy was socially attached. The puppies crossed the grid, despite being shocked the entire way, to be reunited with their social contact. In another electrified grid experiment, mother rats were separated from their infant pups. The mother rats consistently chose to cross the grid and retrieve their pups, one by one, and return them to the nest, despite being shocked the whole way there and back. One mother rat crossed the grid 58 times before researchers terminated the test. McMillan also mentioned the well-publicized case of a cat named Scarlett who ran into a burning building five times to rescue her kittens, despite

severe burns to her face and head. These animals are willing to suffer physical pain to alleviate emotional suffering" (Pierce: https://www.psychologytoday.com/blog/all-dogs-go-heaven/201204/emotional-pain-in-animals-invisible-world-hurt).

91 In the *Tesoro*, Covarrubias only has an entry for *rebuznar*, which he defines as follows, comparing the donkey's sound to that of a horse: "[Braying] is the typical sound of a donkey, just as whinnying is that of the horse, from the Latin *rudere*; the braying sound is the voice of the donkey" (Es propio del asno, como del caballo relinchar, *latine rudere*; rebuzno, la voz del asno). The subtleties and multiple types of sounds among members of an individual species as noted by Leblanc were clearly not apparent to Covarrubias. The *Diccionario de Autoridades* (1727–39) says that "roznar" is a synonym for "rebuznar" but also can be more of a chewing and cracking food sound: "The chewing or eating by animals of hard things, making noise with their teeth as the things breaks" (Mascar o comer los animales cosas duras, haciendo ruido con los dientes al romperlas).

92 "A variety of studies have also shown that, among different species of farm animals, a mother (cow, goat, sow, or hen) and her offspring recognize each other by their vocalizations (Walser, Hague, and Walters 1981; Walser 1986; Kent 1987; Barfield, Tang-Martinez, and Trainer 1994; Weary, Lawson, and Thompson 1996)" (Leblanc 308).

93 The breakdown is remarkably similar to the two aldermen's comments on tone, duration, etc., quoted above in the previous section.

94 A whinny generally comprises three phases, beginning at a high pitch, like a squeal, continuing with a more or less rhythmic vocalization, and ending with lower-frequency sounds similar to nickers. Whinnies are the longest vocalizations, lasting an average of 1.5 seconds. These three types of vocalizations also appear to involve individual recognition cues (see Tyler 1972; Ödberg 1974; Wolski et al. 1980; Lemasson et al. 2009; Proops et al. 2009).

95 Here we see the thinking of Don Quixote rubbing off on Sancho, who begins to interpret animals symbolically.

96 In another example, equids seek each other out for companionship: "[W]ithout saying a word, the squires went to find their animals, for by this time all three horses and the donkey had smelled one another and were standing close together" (541) (Pero, sin hablar palabra, se fueron los dos escuderos a buscar su ganado; que ya todos tres caballos y el rucio se habían olido y estaban todos juntos; 2.14:137).

97 As I will elaborate a little later, the term "pensativo" (literally, "thoughtful") is used contextually to mean "melancholia" in the sixteenth and seventeenth centuries.

98 Grossman translates as "in his shirtsleeves," but *Diccionario de Autoridades* states that "en pelota" means "completely naked" (vale totalmente desnudo).

99 "'Even so,' replied Sancho, 'for your greater ease and satisfaction, it would be a good idea for your grace to try to get out of this prison, and I promise I'll do everything I can to help your grace out and back on your good Rocinante, who also seems enchanted, he's so melancholy and sad'" (421–2) ("Pues con todo eso," replicó Sancho, "digo que, para mayor abundancia y satisfacción, sería bien que vuestra merced probase a salir de esta cárcel; que yo me obligo con todo mi poder a facilitarlo, y aun a sacarle de ella, y probase de nuevo a subir sobre su buen Rocinante, que también parece que va encantado, según va de melancólico y triste"; 1.49:576).

100 This is the same term used in Part I to describe El rucio's mental state, which in this case leads Don Quixote to give Rocinante what amounts to too much freedom, according to Sancho: "Don Quixote was thoughtful as he went on his way (...); these thoughts distracted him so much that, without realizing it, he dropped the reins, and Rocinante, sensing the freedom that had been given to him, stopped at every step to graze on the green grass that grew so abundantly in those fields. Sancho brought his master back from his preoccupations" (521) (Pensativo además iba don Quijote por su camino adelante (...) y estos pensamientos le llevaban tan fuera de sí, que, sin sentirlo, soltó las riendas a Rocinante, el cual, sintiendo la libertad que se le daba, a cada paso se detenía a pacer la verde hierba, de que aquellos campos abundaban; de su embelesamiento le volvió Sancho Panza; 2.11:113).

101 As the only animal with a real name, Rocinante stands out as special.

102 While Don Quixote has his wrist tied in Maritornes's trap and is balancing with his feet together on top of his steed, Rocinante responds in kind when one of the four travellers' mares smells his hinder parts.

103 For González-Echevarría, Rocinante's unfortunate beating in the other scene where he is "in love" with the *yeguas* is an example of how Cervantes critiques the socially constructed laws that attempt to channel desire ("El prisionero del sexo" 15).

104 The etymology of the term "perspective" demonstrates its very anthropocentricity – privileging the dominant sense of humans – for it contains the root word "specere," to look, "to look at closely," which came into Latin with the study of optics. Typical of human embodiment, our thinking about abstract concepts, like eternity and truth, are visually inspired, hence Spinoza's "sub specie aeternitatis" is often translated as "from the perspective of eternity."

105 Gessner writes of another macrosmatic animal something similar about greetings: "They even smell to the hinder parts of one another, per adventure thereby they discern their kind and disposition of each other in their own natures" ("Of Dogs," 109, Topsell's edition).

106 In the seventeenth century, Calvo's *Libro de Albeyteria* offered remedies for a horse who has bad habits and goes off after the smell of females. Calvo is particularly adamant about horses that are "aficionados de mulas" and tells a vignette of a man who was murdered because his horse was attracted to female mules, the knowledge of which was used against him by certain enemies to render his horse useless and hence the man defenceless.

107 As Ramírez and Rodríguez have pointed out, the scene takes place in the dark. Deprived of the hierarchically privileged "noble" vision due to the lack of light, Don Quixote seems to become more animal.

108 The señoras facas episode of 1.15 is not an isolated one, but integrated and has an effect on the plot. Rocinante is so injured, for instance, that Don Quixote, also injured, must travel on donkey-back for some time; the "excesses" of Rocinante – noting his agency – are later referred to in thinking back to the pasage, as Sancho recalls what happened "yesterday": "I feel worse than I did yesterday when the Yanguesans, because of Rocinante's audacity, committed the offense against us which you already know" (117) (estoy peor que ayer cuando los gallegos, que, por demasías de Rocinante, nos hicieron el agravio que sabes; 1.17:207–8). The episode is also remembered by Sancho in Part II, Chapter 2, when he asks Sansón Carrasco if the scene made it into the "history" about Sancho and Don Quixote's adventures that Carrasco has read, expressing it thusly: "'Tell me, Señor Bachelor,' said Sancho, 'is the adventure of the Yanguesans mentioned, when our good Rocinante took a notion to ask for the moon?'" (475) ("Dígame, señor bachiller," dijo a esta sazón Sancho, "¿entra ahí la aventura de los yangüeses, cuando a nuestro buen Rocinante se le antojó pedir cotufas en el golfo?"; 1.3:61).

109 For Sancho, this behaviour on the part of Rocinante is reprehensible, as he considers him a "person": "I never would have believed it of Rocinante; I always thought he was a person as chaste and peaceable as I am" (105–6) (Jamás tal creí de Rocinante; que le tenía por persona casta y tan pacífica como yo; Part I, ch. 15, 194).

110 There are other examples of the importance of Rocinante's olfaction to his being, including the scene in which Rocinante and El rucio display their sociality with the two horses of the Knight of the Forest and his squire: "for by this time all three horses and the donkey had smelled one another

and were standing close together" (541) (ya todos tres caballos y el rucio se habían olido y estaban juntos; 2.14:137). Their sociability is at odds with the enmity of the humans who are about to fight.

111 According to Agustí, the sense of touch (heat sensation) can be used to generate sexual desire in an unreceptive female horse: "if perchance the mare does not want to endure the male, it is advisable to cut an onion and rub her genitals [with it], indeed this will heat her up" (si acaso la yegua no quisiere sufrir el macho, conviene picar una cebolla, y fregarle la natura, que esso la calienta; 329). Topsell's edition of Gessner's work has similar but distinct suggestions also involving olfaction and touch: "for the male, give him the tail of a Hart burned, mingled with wine, and anoint therewithal his stones and genital member, and so shall the dull Stallion be more prone to venery; also there is a kind of Satyrium, which they give to them in drink, or the power of a Horses stones: likewise if the female refuse, take shrimpes beaten soft with water (as thick as hone) therewithal touch the nature of the Mare in her purgation, and afterwards hold it to her nose; or else take Hens dung mixed with Rozen and Turpentine, and anoint the secrets of the Mare, which shall so far increase her lust, as it cureth the lothsomenefs better than the shrimps, and increaseth lust (...) And so if none of these means do prevail with her, they do rub her secrets with a Nettle, and that causeth her to suffer the Horse to enter" (235). There is also an automated response to certain smells that provoke immediate labour: "if a Woman in her flowers, toch a Mare with foal (or sometime do but see her) it causeth to cast her foal, if that purgation be the first after her Virginity: In like manner if they smell of the snuffe of a Candle, or eat Buck-mast or Gentian" (236).

112 I employ the term "scientistic" pejoratively in lieu of "scientific" here; I value and rely on science and the scientific method; I take issue with limiting and overly reductive approaches that overlook evidence that is more difficult to categorize and test scientifically, in the name of science.

113 This is also, therefore, an indication of Rocinante's memory and knowledge, of where his stables are located; memory will be looked at in a later example.

114 Also in 1.23, "But since no person appeared in that desolate and rugged place whom he could question, his only concern was to move on, following no other path than the one chosen by Rocinante, which tended to be the one the horse could travel most easily, and always imagining that there was bound to be some extraordinary adventure waiting for him in the thickets" (177) (Pero como por aquel lugar inhabitable y escabroso no parecía persona alguna de quien poder informarse, no se curó de más

que de pasar adelante, sin llevar otro camino que aquel que Rocinante quería, que era por donde él podía caminar, siempre con imaginación que no podía faltar por aquellas malezas alguna extraña aventura; 284).

115 In another variation on the choices that he makes, in which Rocinante does as he pleases, there is another example in which Don Quixote has not given his expressed consent. In this example, Don Quixote is melancholic (*pensativo*) and Rocinante felt the freedom and stopped to eat the green grass, taking advantage (from Sancho's perspective) to feed as he liked: "sensing the freedom that had been given to him, [Rocinante] stopped at every step to graze on the green grass that grew so abundantly in those fields" (521) (sintiendo la libertad que se le daba, a cada paso se detenía a pacer la verde hierba, de que aquellos campos abundaban; 2.11:113).

116 Cohen translates "with so much zest" and Grossman "with so much eagerness." These are adequate translations yet they fail to capture something in the word "gana" indicating joyfullness. Covarrubias in his 1611 dictionary equates "con gana" with "experiencing joy" (tener gozo).

117 There is neuronal evidence for this view based on brain analysis: "Moreover, as is now known, the mammalian brain contains place cells, particularly in the hippocampus (O'Keefe and Nadel 1978), and head direction cells found in areas anatomically and functionally related to the hippocampus (Taube, Muller, and Ranck 1990), which provide neuronal support for such a representation. This explanatory model also takes into account the capacity of domesticated horses to return to the stable after unseating their rider in familiar environments, aside from the olfactory cues supplied by the stable itself when the winds are favorable" (Leblanc 59).

118 Sancho's motivation is based on his fear of being alone in the dark, and he doesn't want Don Quixote to leave him there to investigate the loud, mysterious noises.

119 According to the legal record, the turkey was imprisoned and then died of its injuries (because of the boy's actions) four days later; Few and Tortorici assert that the turkey would have been killed at the castration if it had not died of its injuries (*Centering Animals* 1–2).

120 In fact, Sancho considers both El rucio and Rocinante persons (personas).

121 El rucio, his donkey, is "his constant companion in good fortune and bad" (149) (perpetuo compañero de sus prósperas y adversas fortunas" (1.20:247).

122 For evidence of love among these "amigos," and also their "albedrío": "leaving Rocinante and the gray, the two constant companions and

friends, free to wander wherever they chose to graze on the plentiful grass that abounded in the meadow" (843) (dejando a su albedrío y sin orden alguna pacer del abundosa hierba de que aquel prado estaba lleno a los dos continuos compañeros y amigos Rocinante y el rucio; 2.59:483–4).

123 As Mancing points out, the epic tradition of naming horses (for instance, El Cid's Babieca) is not followed in the chivalric romance tradition where horses tend not to be named; however, the authors of the Italian chivalric epic tradition named their horses (Mancing, "Rocinante" 618).

124 As Worden has argued, the first illustration of *Don Quixote* is in fact by Cervantes himself, through the ekphrasis in Part I Chapter 9, in which both Rocinante and Sancho's donkey appear (here called *asno*): "At the mule's feet was a caption that read: *Don Sancho de Azpetia*, which, no doubt, was the Basque's name; and at the feet of Rocinante was another that said: *Don Quixote*. Rocinante was so wonderfully depicted, so long and lank, so skinny and lean, with so prominent a backbone, and an appearance so obviously consumptive, that it was clear with what foresight and accuracy he had been given the name Rocinante. Next to him was Sancho Panza, holding the halter of his donkey, and at its feet was another caption that said: *Sancho Zancas*, and as the picture showed, he must have had a big belly, short stature, and long shanks, and for this reason he was given the name Panza as well as Zancas, for from time to time the history calls him by both these surnames" (68) (Tenía a los pies escrito el vizcaíno un título que decía: *Don Sancho de Azpeitia*, que sin duda debía de ser su nombre, y a los pies de Rocinante estaba otro que decía: *Don Quijote*. Estaba Rocinante maravillosamente pintado, tan largo y tendido, tan atenuado y flaco, con tanto espinazo, tan hético confirmado, que mostraba bien al descubierto con cuánta advertencia y propiedad se le había puesto el nombre de Rocinante. Junto a él estaba Sancho Panza, que tenía del cabestro a su asno, a los pies del cual estaba otro rótulo que decía: *Sancho Zancas*, y debía de ser que tenía, a lo que mostraba la pintura, la barriga grande, el talle corto y las zancas largas, y por esto se le debió de poner nombre de *Panza*, y de *Zancas*; que con estos dos sobrenombres le llama algunas veces la historia; 1.9:144). In the last chapter of Part I, the narrator alludes to parchments that reveal more of the story and have illustrations, where Rocinante also stands out as the most important animal: "In this box he discovered some parchments on which, in Gothic script, Castilian verses celebrated many of the knight's exploits and decribed the beauty of Dulcinea of Toboso, the figure of Rocinante, the fidelity of Sancho Panza, and the tomb of Don Quixote,

with various epitaphs and eulogies to his life and customs" (445) (En la cual caja se habían hallado unos pergaminos escritos con letras góticas, pero en versos castellanos, que contenían muchas de sus hazañas y daban noticia de la hermosura de Dulcinea del Toboso, de la figura de Rocinante, de la fidelidad de Sancho Panza y de la sepultura del mismo don Quijote, con diferentes epitafios y elogios de su vida y costumbres; 1.52:604).

125 Pollos Herrera, a veterinarian, compares the representation of Rocinante and El rucio in *Don Quixote* by Cervantes, and in Avellaneda's continuation, concluding that Cervantes knew more about horses and donkeys than Avellaneda (see "Rocinante y El rucio en el *Quijote* de Avellaneda").

126 An early prototypical relationship between human and equine is Balaam's Donkey (Numbers 22.28), mentioned in chapter 2 of this book, but in that case the donkey is abused by Balaam, and the donkey is gratuitously anthropomorphized, questioning Balaam as to why he is being beaten.

127 As Mancing demonstrates with examples from the Renaissance onward, Spanish writers were already depicting theory of mind in complex ways. Early modern Spanish texts are prototypical of the modern novel in large respect because the characters demonstrate a level of psychological complexity unprecedented in prior narratives, specifically of the kind that is privileged in definitions of the modern. In *Don Quixote*, Cervantes does not limit himself to the human but involves a scientifically plausible complex animal mind as well.

Epilogue

1 Urbina cites a web location that is no longer functional. However, the transcript of the interview between Auster and Stephen Capen is available as Capen, "*The Futurist Radio Hour*: An Interview with Paul Auster" (100–5), published in a collection of interviews entitled *Conversations with Paul Auster*.

Works Cited

Aberdein, Andrew. "Logic for Dogs." *What Philosophy Can Tell You about Your Dog*. Ed. Steven D. Hales. Peru, Il: Open Court, 2008. 167–81. Print.

Acosta, José de. *Historia natural y moral de las Indias*. Ed. Edmundo O'Gorman. México: Fondo de Cultura Económica, 1962. Print.

Agustí, Miquel. *Libro de los secretos de agricultura, casa de campo, y pastoril*. 1626. Barcelona: Juan Piferrer, 1722. Web.

– *Llibre dels secrets de agricultura, casa rústica y pastoril*. Barcelona: Esteue Liberôs, 1617. Print.

Alas, Leopoldo. "¡Adiós, Cordera!" *¡Adiós, Cordera! y otros cuentos*. Madrid: Grupo Planeta, 2010. 249–62. Print.

Alfonso X, King of Castile and Leon. *Songs of Holy Mary of Alfonso X, the Wise: A Translation of the Cantigas de Santa María*. Trans. Kathleen Kulp-Hill. Tempe, AZ: Arizona Center for Medieval and Renaissance Studies, 2000. Print.

Allen, Colin. "Fish Cognition and Consciousness." *Journal of Agricultural and Environmental Ethics* 26.1 (2013): 25–39. Print.

Allen, Colin, and Marc Bekoff. *Species of Mind: The Philosophy and Biology of Cognitive Ethology*. Cambridge, MA: MIT Press, 1999. Print.

Allen, Colin, and Michael Trestman. "Animal Consciousness." *Stanford Encyclopedia of Philosophy*. Summer 2015. Web.

Alvarado Reyes, Ernesto. "The Legend of the Mexican Onza." *Mastozoología neotropical versión online*. Scientific Electronic Library Online (SciELO) Argentina. June 2008. Web. 2 November 2016.

Álvarez Peláez, Raquel. *La conquista de la naturaleza americana*. Madrid: Consejo Superior de Investigaciones Científicas, 1993. Print.

Alves, Abel A. *The Animals of Spain: An Introduction to Imperial Perceptions and Human Interaction with Other Animals, 1492–1826*. Boston: Brill, 2011. Print.

– "The Sanctification of Nature in Marian Shrines in Catalonia: Contextualizing Human Desires in a Mediterranean Cult." *The Sacralization of Space and Behavior in the Early Modern World: Studies and Sources*. Ed. Jennifer Mara DeSilva. Farnham, UK: Ashgate, 2015. 161–76.

Andrews, Kristin. *The Animal Mind: An Introduction to the Philosophy of Animal Cognition*. New York: Routledge, 2015. Print.

Arellano, Ignacio. "Bueyes De Caza: Una Referencia De Quevedo." *La Perinola. Revista de Investigación Quevediana*10 (2006): 339–44. Print.

Argote de Molina, Gonzalo. *Libro de la montería que mando escreuir el muy alto y muy poderoso rey don Alonso de Castilla y de Leon, vltimo deste nombre / Acrecentado por Gonçalo Argote de Molina*. Sevilla: Andrea Pescioni, 1582. Fondos digitalizados de la Universidad de Sevilla. N.d. Web. 16 October 2016.

Ari, C., and D.P. D'Agostino. *Journal of Ethology* 34 (2016):167. Web.

Asúa, Miguel de, and Robert French. *A New World of Animals: Early Modern Europeans on the Creatures of Iberian America*. Burlington, VT: Ashgate, 2005. Print.

Auster, Paul. *Timbuktu: A Novel*. 1st ed. New York, NY: Henry Holt, 1999. Print.

Avalle-Arce, Juan Bautista. "Cervantes Entre Pícaros." *Nueva Revista de Filología Hispánica* 38.2 (1990): 591–603. Print.

Aylward, Edward T. *The Crucible Concept: Thematic and Narrative Patterns in Cervantes's Novelas Exemplares*. Madison, NJ: Fairleigh Dickinson UP, 1999. Print.

Baggis, Gustavo Federico de. "Solicitud de Habeas Corpus para la Orangután Sandra. Comentario a propósito de la Sentencia de la Cámara Federal de Casación Penal de la Ciudad Autónoma de Buenos Aires, 18 de diciembre de 2014." http://www.derechoanimal.info/images/pdf/GFB-Habeas-Corpus-Sandra.pdf. Web. 28 June 2016.

Balcombe, Jonathan. "Fishes Have Feelings, Too." *New York Times*. 14 May 2016. Web. 14 May 2016.

Baranda, Consolación. "Ciencia y humanismo: la *obra de agricultura general* de Gabriel Alonso de Herrera (1513)." *Criticón* 46 (1989): 95–108. Print.

Barbero Richart, Manuel. *Los códices etnográficos: El "Códice Florentino."* Alcalá de Henares: Universidad de Alcalá de Henares. Servicio de Publicaciones, 1997. Print.

Barrera-Osorio, Antonio. *Experiencing Nature: The Spanish American Empire and the Early Scientific Revolution*. Austin: U of Texas P, 2006. Print.

Bekoff, Marc. "Cognitive Ethology: The Comparative Study of Animal Minds." *A Companion to Cognitive Science*. Eds. William Bechtel and George Graham. Malden, MA.: Blackwell, 1998. 371–9. Print.

Beusterien, John. *Canines in Cervantes and Velázquez: An Animal Studies Reading of Early Modern Spain*. Farnham, UK: Ashgate, 2013. Print.

Braun, Lucien. *Conrad Gessner*. Genève: Editions Slatkine, 1990. Print.

Broom, Donald, et al. "Pigs Learn What a Mirror Image Represents and Use It to Obtain Information." *Animal Cognition* 78.5 (2009): 1037–41. Print.

Brumec, Yesica. "Sandra, la 'persona no humana' que espera hacer historia en Argentina." *La voz* 24 December 2014. Web.

Bulliet, Richard W. *Hunters, Herders, and Hamburgers: The Past and Future of Human-Animal Relationships*. New York: Columbia UP, 2005. Print.

Calvo, Fernando. *Libro de albeytería, en el qual se trata del cavallo y mulo, y jumento, y de sus miembros y calidades y de todas sus enfermedades, con las causas, y señales, y remedios de cada una dellas*. Salamanca: Juan Fernández, 1587. Print.

Cantor, Maurício, Lauren G. Shoemaker, Reniel B. Cabral, César O. Flores, Melinda Varga, and Hal Whitehead. "Multilevel animal societies can emerge from cultural transmission." *Nature Communications* 6, Article number: 8091 (2015) doi:10.1038/ncomms9091. Web.

Capen, Stephen. "*The Futurist Radio Hour*: An Interview with Paul Auster." *Conversations with Paul Auster*. Ed. James M. Hutchisson. Jackson, MS: UP of Mississippi, 2013. 100–5. Print.

Cardenas, Anthony. "Horses and Asses: Don Quixote and Company." *RLA* 2 (1990): 372–7. Print.

Casas, Bartolomé de las. *Historia de las indias*. Vol. 2. Ed. André Saint-Lu. Caracas, Venezuela: Biblioteca Ayacucho, 1986. Print.

Cervantes, Miguel de. *The Adventures of Don Quixote*. Trans. John Michael Cohen. Hammondsworth, UK: Penguin Books, 1956. Print.

– "The Colloquy of the Dogs." *Exemplary Novellas*. Ed. and trans. Michael Harney. Indianapolis: Hackett Publishing Company, Inc, 2016. 447–512. Print.

– "The Deceitful Marriage." *Exemplary Novellas*. Ed. and trans. Michael Harney. Indianapolis: Hackett Publishing Company, Inc., 2016. 431–46. Print.

– *Don Quixote*. Translated by Edith Grossman. New York: Harper Collins Publishers Inc., 2003. Print.

– "El coloquio de los perros." *Novelas Ejemplares*. Ed. Harry Sieber. Madrid: Cátedra, 1980. 297–359. Print.

– *El ingenioso hidalgo don Quijote de La Mancha*. Ed. Luis Murillo. 2 vols. Madrid: Castalia, 1978. Print.

– *Los trabajos de Persiles y Sigismunda*. Ed. Juan Bautista-Avalle Arce. Madrid: Castalia, 1985. Print.

– *The Trials of Persiles and Sigismunda*. Translated by Celia Richmond Weller and Clark A. Colahan. Berkeley: U of California P, 1989. Print.

Chalmers, David J. *The Conscious Mind: In Search of a Fundamental Theory*. New York: Oxford UP, 1996. Print.

– *How Smart Are Dogs?* Dir. Julia Cort. Nova ScienceNOW. *NOVA-Official Website/PBS*. 9 February 2011. Web. 16 October 2016.

– "Materialism and the Metaphysics of Modality." *Philosophy and Phenomenological Research* 59.2 (1999): 475–96. Print.

Covarrubias Orozco, Sebastián de. *Tesoro de la lengua castellana o española*. Madrid: Luís Sánchez, 1611. Print.

Crane, Susan. *Animal Encounters: Contacts and Concepts in Medieval Britain*. Philadelphia: U of Pennsylvania P, 2013. Print.

Crowley, Stephen J., and Colin Allen. "Animal Behavior." In *The Oxford Handbook of Philosophy of Biology*. Edited by Michael Ruse. New York: Oxford UP, 2008. 327–48. Print.

Cruz, Juana Inés de la. "Poema 92: Arguye de inconsecuentes el gusto y la censura de los hombres que en las mujeres acusan lo que causan." *Renaissance and Baroque Poetry of Spain*. Ed. and trans. Elias Rivers. Long Grove, IL: Waveland Press, Inc., 1966. 322–4. Print.

Darwin, Charles. *The Descent of Man, and Selection in Relation to Sex*. 2 vols. London: John Murray, 1871. Web.

Daston, Lorraine. "Intelligences: Angelic, Animal, Human." *Thinking with Animals: New Perspectives on Anthropomorphism*. Ed. Lorraine Daston and Gregg Mitman. New York, NY: Columbia UP, 2005. 37–58. Print.

De Waal, Frans. "What I Learned from Tickling Apes." *New York Times*. 10 April 2011. Web.

DeYoung, Randy, and Karl Miller. "White-tailed Deer Behavior." *Biology and Management of White-tailed Deer*. Ed. David G. Hewitt. Boca Raton, FL: CRC Press, 2011. 311–54. Print.

Dennett, Daniel. *The Intentional Stance*. Cambridge, MA.: MIT Press, 1987. Print.

Deyermond, Alan D. *Historia de la literatura española 1: La edad media*. Barcelona: Editorial Ariel, 2008. Print.

Dostoyevsky, Fyodor. *Crime and Punishment: The Coulson Translation, Backgrounds and Sources, Essays in Criticism*. Trans. Jessie Coulson. New York: Norton, 1989. Print.

Dunston, Emma J., et al. "Exploring African Lion (*Panthera leo*) Behavioural Phenotypes: Individual Differences and Correlations between Sociality, Boldness and Behaviour." *Journal of Ethology* 34.3 (2016): 277–90. Print.

Eco, Umberto, et al. "On Animal Language in the Medieval Classification of Signs." *On the Medieval Theory of Signs*. Ed. Umberto Eco and Costantino Marmo. Amsterdam: John Benjamins Publishing Company, 1989. 3–41. Print.

Egerton, Frank N. "A History of the Ecological Sciences, Part 11: Emergence of Vertebrate Zoology during the 1500s." *Bulletin of the Ecological Society of America* 84.4 (2003): 206–12. Print.

El Saffar, Ruth. *Cervantes,* El casamiento engañoso, *and* El coloquio de los perros. London: Grant and Cutler: Tamesis, 1976. Print.

Erdöhegyi, Ágnes, et al. "Dog-Logic: Inferential Reasoning in a Two-Way Choice Task and Its Restricted Use." *Animal Behaviour* 74.4: 725–37. Print.

Esopete Ystoriado. 1488. Edited by Victoria Burrus and Harriet Goldberg. Madison, WI: Hispanic Seminary of Medieval Studies, 1990. Print.

Favreau, Robert. "Le thème iconographique du lion dans les inscriptions médiévales." *Comptes rendus des séances de l'Académie des Inscriptions et Belles-Lettres* 135.3 (1991): 613–36. Print.

Feist, James D. "Behavior of Feral Horses in the Pryor Mountain Wild Horse Range." Diss. University of Michigan, 1971. Print.

Fernández de Oviedo y Valdés, Gonzalo. *Historia general y natural de las Indias*. Vol. 2. Ed. Juan Pérez de Tudela y Bueso. Madrid: Atlas, 1959. Print.

– *Sumario de la natural historia de las Indias*. Ed. Manuel Ballesteros. Madrid: Historia 16, 1986. Print.

Fernández, Enrique. *Anxieties of Interiority and Dissection in Early Modern Spain*. Toronto: U of Toronto P, 2015. Print.

Few, Martha, and Zeb Tortorici, eds. *Centering Animals in Latin American History*. Durham, NC: Duke UP, 2013. Print.

– "Introduction: Writing Animal Histories." *Centering Animals in Latin American History*. Ed. Few, Martha and Zeb Tortorici. Durham, NC: Duke UP, 2013. 1–28. Print.

Floridi, Luciano. "Scepticism and Animal Rationality: The Fortune of Chrysippus' Dog in the History of Western Thought." *Archiv für Geschichte der Philosophie* 79.1:27–57. Print.

Foley, Michael P. *Why Do Catholics Eat Fish on Friday?: The Catholic Origin to Just About Everything*. New York: Palgrave Macmillan, 2005. Print.

Forcione, Alban K. *Cervantes and the Mystery of Lawlessness: A Study of* El casamiento engañoso y El coloquio de los perros. Princeton, NJ: Princeton UP, 1984. Print.

Freund, Daisy. "How Animal Welfare Leads to Better Meat: A Lesson from Spain." *Atlantic* 25 August 2011. Web. 1 September 2016.

Fudge, Erica. *Brutal Reasoning: Animals, Rationality, and Humanity in Early Modern England*. Ithaca, NY: Cornell UP, 2006. Print.

Fugazza, Claudia, et al. "Do as I … Did! Long-Term Memory of Imitative Actions in Dogs (*Canis Familiaris*)." *Animal Cognition* 19.2 (2016): 263–9. Print.

Gallup, Gordon G. "Self-Awareness and the Emergence of Mind in Primates." *American Journal of Primatology* 2.3 (1982): 237–48. Print.

Gasta, Chad. "'Señora, donde hay música no puede haber cosa mala': Music, Poetry, and Orality in Don Quijote." *American Association of Teachers of Spanish and Portuguese* 93.3 (2010): 357–67. Print.

Geist, Valerius. *Deer of the World: Their Evolution, Behaviour, and Ecology.* Shrewsbury, UK: Swan Hill Press, 1999. Print.

"General History of the Things of New Spain by Fray Bernardino de sahagún: The Florentine Codex." *World Digital Library*. U.S. Library of Congress. 3 February 2016. Web. 16 November 2016.

Gerbi, Antonello. *Nature in the New World: From Christopher Columbus to Gonzalo Fernández de Oviedo*. Trans. Jeremy Moyle. Pittsburgh: U of Pittsburgh P, 1985. Print.

Gessner, Konrad. *Historiae Animalium*. Zurich: Froschauer, 1551. Print. Facs. ed.

– *The history of four-footed beasts and serpents and insects*. Translated and adapted by Edward Topsell (1607, 1658). Intro. Willy Ley. Republication of 1658 edition. 3 vols. NY: Da Capo Press, 1967. Print.

Gieling, Elise Titia, et al. "Assessing Learning and Memory in Pigs." *Animal Cognition* 14.2 (2011): 151–73. Print.

Gómez-Centurión Jiménez, Carlos. *Alhajas para soberanos: los animales reales en el siglo XVIII: de las leoneras a las mascotas de cámara*. Valladolid: Junta de Castilla y León, Consejería de Cultura y Turismo, 2011. Print.

González Echevarría, Roberto. *Celestina's Brood: Continuities of the Baroque in Spanish and Latin American Literatures*. Durham, NC: Duke UP, 1993. Print.

– "El prisionero del sexo. El amor y la ley en Cervantes." *Temas* 32 (2003): 15–45. Print.

– "The Life and Adventures of Cipión: Cervantes and the Picaresque." *Diacritics* 10.3 (1980): 15–26. Print.

González, Julio, et al. "Reading *Cinnamon* activates Olfactory Brain Regions." *NeuroImage* 32.2 (2006): 906–12. Print.

Grady, Joseph Edward. "Foundations of Meaning: Primary Metaphors and Primary Scenes." Dissertation, University of California, 1997. Print.

Greer, Margaret. "Diana, Venus and Borrowed Dogs: On Hunting in *Don Quixote*." *Cervantes y su mundo*. Ed. Robert A. Lauer and Kurt Reichenberger. Vol. 3. Kassel: Reichenberger, 2005. 201–22. Print.

Griffin, Donald R. "Progress toward a Cognitive Ethology." *Cognitive Ethology: The Minds of Other Animals. Essays in Honor of Donald R. Griffin*. Ed. Carolyn A. Ristau. Hillsdale, NJ: L. Erlbaum Associates, 1991. 3–17. Print.

Guerrini, Anita. *The Courtiers' Anatomists: Animals and Humans in Louis XIV's Paris*. Chicago: U of Chicago P, 2015. Print.

Held, Suzanne, Michael Mendl, Claire Devereux, and Richard W. Byrne. "Behaviour of Domestic Pigs in a Visual Perspective Taking Task." *Behaviour* 138.11 (2001) 1337–54. doi: 10.1163/156853901317367627. Web.

Henzen, Wilhelm, et al., eds. *Inscriptiones urbis Romae latinae. Pars quinta, Inscriptiones falsas urbi Romae attributas comprehendens*. Berlin: Apud Georgium Reimerum, 1885. Print.

Herrera, Gabriel Alonso de. *Agricultura general de Gabriel Alonso de Herrera. Corregida según el testo original de la primera edición publicada en 1513 por el mismo autor*. 4 vols. Madrid: Imprenta Real, 1818. Print.

Herz, Rachel. *The Scent of Desire: Discovering Our Enigmatic Sense of Smell*. New York: William Morrow, 2007. Print.

Heyes, Cecilia M. "Theory of Mind in Nonhuman Primates." *Behavioral and Brain Sciences* 21.1 (1998): 101–48. Print.

Horowitz, Alexandra. *Inside of a Dog: What Dogs See, Smell, and Know*. New York: Scribner, 2009. Print.

Huet, Marie-Hélène. *Monstrous Imagination*. Cambridge, MA: Harvard UP, 1993. Print.

Hutson, Matthew. *The 7 Laws of Magical Thinking: How Irrational Beliefs Keep Us Happy, Healthy, and Sane*. New York: Hudson Street Press, 2012. Print.

Ibarretxe-Antuñano, Iraide. "Metaphorical Mappings in the Sense of Smell." *Metaphor in Cognitive Linguistics: Selected Papers from the Fifth International Cognitive Linguistics Conference, Amsterdam, July 1997*. Ed. Raymund W. Gibbs, Jr, and Gerard J. Steen. Amsterdam: John Benjamins, 1999. Print.

Irigoyen García, Javier. *The Spanish Arcadia: Sheep Herding, Pastoral Discourse, and Ethnicity in Early Modern Spain*. Toronto: Toronto UP, 2014. Print.

Isidore of Seville, Saint. *The Etymologies of Isidore of Seville*. Trans. Stephen A. Barney et al. Cambridge; New York: Cambridge UP, 2006. Print.

Jaen, Isabel, and Julien Simon, eds. *Cognitive Approaches to Early Modern Spanish Literature*. New York and Oxford: Oxford UP, 2016. Print.

Jiménez, Juan Ramón. *Platero y yo*. Ed. 18a. Madrid: Cátedra, 1998. Print.

Kaminski, Juliane, and Marie Nitzschner. "Do Dogs Get the Point? A Review of Dog-Human Communication Ability." *Learning and Motivation* 44.4 (2013): 294–302. Print.

Keiper, Ronald. *The Assateague Ponies*. Centreville, MD: Tidewater Publishers, 1985. Print.

Kiley-Worthington, Marthe. "Nonhuman Mind-Reading Ability: Commentary on Hamad on *Other Minds*." *Animal Sentience: An Interdisciplinary Journal on Animal Feeling* 2016.070 (2016). *Animal Studies Repository*. The Humane

Society of the United States and Institute for Science and Policy. N.d. 28 August 2016. Web.

Kinkade, Richard P., and John E. Keller. "Myth and Reality in the Miracle of *Cantiga 29.*" *La corónica* 28.1 (1999): 35–73. Print.

Kreilkamp, Ivan. "Petted Things: *Wuthering Heights* and the Animal." *Yale Journal of Criticism* 18.1 (2005): 87–110. Print.

Kusukawa, Sachico. "The Sources of Gessner's Pictures for the *Historia Animalium.*" *Annals of Science* 67.3 (2010): 303–28. Print.

Lakoff, George, and Mark Johnson. *Metaphors We Live By*. Chicago: U Chicago P, 1980.

– *Philosophy in the Flesh: The Embodied Mind and Its Challenge to Western Thought*. New York: Basic Books, 1999. Print.

Latini, Brunetto. *The Medieval Castilian Bestiary: From Brunetto Latini's Tesoro. Study and Edition*. Study and Edition by Spurgeon Baldwin. Exeter, Devon: University of Exeter, 1982. Print.

Leblanc, Michel-Antoine. *The Mind of the Horse: An Introduction to Equine Cognition*. Cambridge, MA: Harvard UP, 2013. Print.

Lemasson, A., et al. "Horse (*Equus Caballus*) Whinnies: A Source of Social Information." *Animal Cognition* 12.5 (2009): 693–704. Print.

Lent, Peter C. "Mother-Infant Relationships in Ungulates." *The Behaviour of Ungulates and Its Relationship to Management*. Ed. Valerius Geist and Fritz R. Walther. Vol. 1. IUCN Publications New Series. Morges, Switzerland: International Union for Conservation of Nature and Natural Resources, 1974. 14–55. Print.

Liberatori, Elena. "Asociacion de Funcionarios y Abogados por los Derechos de los Animales y Otros contra GCBA sobre amparo." Ciudad de Buenos Aires, 21 de octubre de 2015. EXPTE. A2174–2015/0. http://www.ijudicial.gob.ar/2015/la-ciudad-debera-garantizar-un-habitat-adecuado-para-la-orangutana-sandra/. Web.

Lovejoy, Arthur O. *The Great Chain of Being: A Study in the History of an Idea*. Cambridge, MA: Harvard UP, 1936. Print.

López Medel, Tomás. *De los tres elementos: tratado sobre la naturaleza y el hombre del nuevo mundo*. Ed. Berta Ares Queija. Madrid: Alianza Editorial, 1990. Print.

Mancing, Howard. "Rocinante." *The Cervantes Encyclopedia*. Vol. 2. Westport, CT: Greenwood Press, 2004. 618. Print.

– "Sancho Panza's Theory of Mind." *Theory of Mind and Literature*. Ed. Paula Leverage et al. West Lafayette, IN: Purdue UP, 2011. 123–32. Print.

Manuel, Juan. *El conde Lucanor*. Madrid: Castalia, 1984. Print.

Marino, Lori, and Christina M. Colvin. "Thinking Pigs: A Comparative Review of Cognition, Emotion, and Personality in *Sus Domesticus.*"

International Journal of Comparative Psychology 28.1 (2015): np. *eScholarship*. N.d. Web. 16 October 2016.

Marshall, Justin, and Kentaro Arikawa. "Unconventional Colour Vision." *Current Biology* 24.24 (2014): R1150–R54. Print.

Martin, Adrienne L. "Zoopoética quijotesca: Cervantes y los estudios de animales." *eHumanista/Cervantes* 1 (2012): 448–64. Web. 28 August 2016.

Martyr Anglerius, Petrus. *De orbe novo, the Eight Decades of Peter Martyr d'anghiera*. Trans. Francis Augustus MacNutt. 2 vols. New York: G.P. Putnam's Sons, 1912. Print.

Martínez de Espinar, Alonso. *Arte de ballestería y montería, escrita con método, para excusar la fatiga que ocasiona la ignorancia*. [1644]. Ed. Eduardo Trigo de Yarto. Madrid: Ediciones Velázquez, 1976. Print.

Martínez-Bonati, Félix. "Towards a Formal Ontology of Fictional Worlds." *Philosophy and Literature* 7.2 (1983): 182–95. Print.

Masson, Jeffrey Moussaieff. *The Pig Who Sang to the Moon: The Emotional World of Farm Animals*. New York: Ballantine Books, 2003. Print.

Matute, Ana María. "Fausto." *El tiempo*. Barcelona: Mateu, 1963. 159–79. Print.

Maupassant, Guy de. *The Works of Maupassant. Mont Oriol Part I, Part II, and Other Stories*. Trans. Albert M.C. McMaster, A.E. Henderson, and Mme. Quesada. New York: Classic Publishing Co., 1911. Print.

Melville, Elinor G.K. *A Plague of Sheep: Environmental Consequences of the Conquest of Mexico*. Cambridge Cambridge UP, 1994. Print.

Menéndez Pidal, Gonzalo. *La España del siglo XIII: leída en imágenes*. Madrid: Real Academia de la Historia, 1986. Print.

Montaigne, Michel de. "Apology for Raimond de Sebonde" (2.12, pp. 137–373) in *Essays*. Trans. Charles Cotton. Ed. William Carew Hazlitt. 3 Vols. London: Reeves and Turner, 1877. Hathi-Trust/Web.

Morales Muñiz, Dolores Carmen. "Leones y águilas. Política y sociedad medieval a través de los símbolos faunísticos." *Animales simbólicos en la historia: desde la protohistoria hasta el final de la edad media*. Ed. María Rosario García Huerta and Francisco Ruiz Gómez. Madrid: Editorial Síntesis, 2012. 207–30. Print.

Morgado García, Arturo. "La visión del mundo animal en la España del siglo XVII: el bestiario de Covarrubias." *Cuadernos de Historia Moderna* 36 (2011): 67–88. Print.

– "Una visión cultural de los animales." *Los animales en la historia y en la cultura*. Ed. Arturo Morgado García Moreno and José Joaquín Rodríguez. Cádiz: Servicio de Publicaciones de la Universidad de Cádiz, 2011. 13–41. Print.

Myers, Kathleen. *Fernández de Oviedo's Chronicle of America: A New History for a New World*. Austin: U of Texas P, 2007. Print.

Nadeau, Carolyn. *Food Matters: Alonso Quijano's Diet and the Discourse of Food in Early Modern Spain*. Toronto: U of Toronto P, 2016. Print.

Nagel, Thomas. "What Is It Like to Be a Bat?" *Philosophical Review* 83.4 (1974): 435–50. Print.

Nordenfalk, Carl. "The Five Senses in Late Medieval and Renaissance Art." *Journal of the Warburg and Courtauld Institutes* 48 (1985): 1–22. Print.

Norton, Marcy. "Animal (Spain)." *Lexikon of the Hispanic Baroque: Transatlantic Exchange and Transformation*. Ed. Evonne Levy and Kenneth Mills. Austin: U of Texas P, 2013. 17–19. Print.

– "Animal (Spanish America)." *Lexikon of the Hispanic Baroque: Transatlantic Exchange and Transformation*. Ed. Evonne Levy and Kenneth Mills. Austin: U of Texas P, 2013. 21–3. Print.

– "The Chicken or the *Iegue*: Human-Animal Relationships and the Columbian Exchange." *American Historical Review* 120.1 (2015): 28–60. Print.

O'Connor, Doreen M. "*She* Is the Cat's Mother: (Dis)Engaging Women in *Don Quixote*." *RLA* 2 (1990): 499–504. Print.

O'Keefe, J., and L. Nadel. *The Hippocampus as a Cognitive Map*. Oxford: Oxford UP, 1978. Print.

Ödberg, F.O. "Some Aspects of the Acoustic Expression in Horses." *Ethologie und Ökologie bei der Haustierhaltung*. Ed. K. Zeeb. Darmstadt: Kuratorium.für Technik und Bauwesen in der Landwirtschaft, 1974. 89–105. Print.

Olkowicz, Seweryn, Suzana Herculano-Houzel, et al. "Birds have primate-like numbers of neurons in the forebrain." *Proceedings of the National Academy of Sciences (PNAS)*. 13 June 2016, doi: 10.1073/pnas.1517131113. Web.

Ordóñez Villa, Montserrat. "Rocinante y el asno, personajes cervantinos." *Razón y fábula* 8 (1968): 57–75. Print.

Pagden, Anthony. *European Encounters with the New World: From Renaissance to Romanticism*. New Haven, CT: Yale UP, 1993. Print.

Palesca, Claude, and Dolores Pesce. "Guido of Arrezo." *Grove Music Online*. Oxford UP. 11 February 2013. Web. 16 November 2016.

Paul, Anne Murphy. "Your Brain on Fiction." *New York Times* 17 March 2012. Web. 17 March 2012.

Pavel, Thomas. *Fictional Worlds*. Cambridge, MA: Harvard UP, 1986. Print.

Pepperberg, Irene M. *Alex & Me: How a Scientist and a Parrot Discovered a Hidden World of Animal Intelligence – and Formed a Deep Bond in the Process*. New York: Collins, 2008. Print.

Pereira, Gómez. *Antoniana Margarita: reproducción facsimilar de la ddición de 1749*. Ed. and trans. José Luis Barreiro Barreiro et al. Santiago de Compostela: Universidad de Santiago de Compostela, 2000. Print.

Pérez, Luis. *Del can y del caballo*. Valladolid: Adrián Ghermart, 1568. Print. Facs. ed.

Pierce, Jessica. "Emotional Pain in Animals: An Invisible World of Hurt. Recognizing the Psychological Effects of Animal Abuse." *Psychology Today* (2012). 28 August 2016. Web.

Pinon, Laurent. "Conrad Gessner and the Historical Depth of Renaissance Natural History." *Historia: Empiricism and Erudition in Early Modern Europe*. Ed. Gianna Pomata and Nancy G. Siraisi. Cambridge, MA: MIT Press, 2005. 241–67. Print.

Pliny, the Elder. *Natural History*. Vol. 3. Trans. Harris Rackham. Loeb Classical Library. 2nd ed. 1983, reprinted 1997. Cambridge, MA: Harvard UP, 1997. Print.

Poggioli, Renato. *The Oaten Flute: Essays on Pastoral Poetry and the Pastoral Ideal*. Cambridge, MA: Harvard UP, 1975. Print.

Pollos Herrera, Justino. "Algunos vocablos y locuciones albeiterescas o chalanescas en las obras de Miguel Cervantes." *ACer* 19 (1981): 185–96. Print.

– "Rocinante y El rucio en el *Quijote* de Avellaneda." In *Cervantes: Su obra y su mundo*. Ed. Manuel Criado de Val. Madrid : EDI-6, 1981. 837–48. Print.

Porter, Jess, et al. "Mechanisms of Scent-Tracking in Humans." *Nature Neuroscience* 10.1 (2006): 27–9. Print.

Povinelli, Daniel J. "Panmorphism." *Anthropomorphism, Anecdotes, and Animals*. Ed. Robert W. Mitchell et al. Albany: State University of New York, 1997. 92–103. Print.

Powers, Mary "The Uniqueness of Rocinante." *RLA* 2 (1990): 520–3. Print.

Proops, Leanne, et al. "Cross-Modal Individual Recognition in Domestic Horses (*Equus caballus*)." *Proceedings of the National Academy of Sciences of the U.S.A.* 106.3 (2009): 947–51. Print.

Ramírez, Mariana A., and Alfred Rodríguez. "Whistling in the Dark: Chapters 19 and 20 of Part I of *Don Quijote*." *Cervantes: Bulletin of the Cervantes Society of America* 16.2 (1996): 107–13. Print.

Real Academia Española. *Diccionario de autoridades*. 3 vols. Madrid: Gredos, 1963. Print. Facs. ed. of *Diccionario de la lengua castellana*. Madrid: F. del Hierro, 1726–39.

Ritvo, Harriet. *The Animal Estate: The English and Other Creatures in the Victorian Age*. Cambridge, MA: Harvard UP, 1987. Print.

Rodríguez Freyle, Juan. *El carnero*. Caracas: Biblioteca Ayacucho, 1979. Print.

Ruiz Gómez, Francisco. "El hombre y las animalias. Discurso simbólico de la razón." *Animales simbólicos en la historia: desde la protohistoria hasta el final de la edad media*. Ed. María Rosario García Huerta and Francisco Ruiz Gómez. Madrid: Editorial Síntesis, 2012. 253–75. Print.

Ruiz, Juan (Arcipreste de Hita). *Libro de buen amor*. Madrid: Castalia, 1988. Print.

Ryan, Marie-Laure. *Possible Worlds, Artificial Intelligence, and Narrative Theory*. Bloomington: Indiana UP, 1991. Print.

Sahagún, Bernardino de. *Códice florentino de Fray Bernardino de Sahagún. Reproducción facsimilar del ejemplar que conserva la Biblioteca Medicea Laurenziana.* 3 vols. Florence: Talleres Casa Editorial Giunti Barberá, 1979. Print.

– *Historia general de las cosas de Nueva España.* Vols. 1 and 3. Ed. Angel María Garibay K. México: Editorial Porrúa, S.A., 1956. Print.

Salazar y Acha, Jaime. *La casa del rey de Castilla y León en la Edad Media.* Madrid: Centro de Estudios Políticos y Constitucionales, 2000. Print.

Schaller, George. *The Serengeti Lion: A Study of Predator-Prey Relations.* Chicago: Chicago UP, 1972. Print.

Scham, Michael. *Lector Ludens: The Representation of Games and Play in Cervantes.* Toronto: U of Toronto P, 2014. Print.

Serpell, James. *In the Company of Animals: A Study of Human-Animal Relationships.* Cambridge: Cambridge UP, 1996. Print.

Seyfarth, Robert M., and Dorothy L. Cheney. "The Structure of Social Knowledge in Monkeys." *Animal Social Complexity: Intelligence, Culture, and Individualized Societies.* Ed. Frans B.M. De Waal and Peter L. Tyack. Cambridge, MA: Harvard UP, 2003. 207–29. Print.

Shepherd, Gordon. *Neurogastronomy: How the Brain Creates Flavor and Why It Matters.* New York: Columbia UP, 2012. Print.

Simerka, Barbara. *Knowing Subjects: Cognitive Cultural Studies and Early Modern Spanish Literature.* West Lafayette, IN: Purdue UP, 2013. Print.

Sobejano, Gonzalo. "El 'Coloquio de los perros' en la picaresca y otros apuntes." *Hispanic Review* 43.1 (1975): 25–41. Print.

Spolsky, Ellen. "Cognitive Literary Historicism: A Response to Adler and Gross." *Poetics Today* 24.2 (Summer 2003): 161–83. Print.

Stankowich, Theodore, and Richard G. Coss. "Effects of Risk Assessment, Predator Behavior, and Habitat on Escape Behavior in Columbian Black-Tailed Deer." *Behavioral Ecology* 18.2 (2007): 358–67. Print.

Steinbeck, John. *Travels with Charley: In Search of America.* 50th anniversary ed. New York: Penguin Books, 2012. Print.

Still Alice. Directed by Richard Glatzer and Wash Westmoreland. 2014. Sony Pictures Classics, 2014. Film.

Stubbs, George. *La cacería del Grovesnor.* 1762. Private collection. Print.

Sweetser, Eve. *From Etymology to Pragmatics.* Cambridge: Cambridge UP, 1990. Print.

Taube, J.S., et al. "Head Direction Cells Recorded from the Postsubiculum in Freely Moving Rats." *Journal of Neuroscience* 10 (1990): 420–47. Print.

ten Donkelaar, Hendrik Jan, et al. "The Limbic System." *Clinical Neuroanatomy: Brain Circuitry and Its Disorders.* Ed. Hendrik Jan ten Donkelaar. Heidelberg: Springer, 2011. 633–710. Print.

Toynbee, Jocelyn Mary Catherine. *Animals in Roman Life and Art*. Ithaca, NY: Cornell UP, 1973. Print.

Turner, Mark. *The Literary Mind*. New York; Oxford: Oxford UP, 1998. Print.

Tyler, Stephanie J. "The Behaviour and Social Organization of the New Forest Ponies." *Animal Behaviour Monographs* 5.2 (1972): 87–196. Print.

Urbina, Eduardo. "Cervantes y *el Quijote* en la narrativa de Paul Auster." *Proceedings of the 2. Congresso Brasileiro de Hispanistas, 2002, São Paulo (SP) [online]*. São Paulo: Associação Brasileira de Hispanistas, 2002. *SciELO Proceedings*. N.d. Web. 14 October 2016.

Valle Ojeda Calvo, María del. "Una forma de ocio cortesana y popular en el teatro del siglo de oro: la corrida de toros." *Materia crítica: formas de ocio y de consumo en la cultura áurea*. Ed. Enrique García Santo Tomás. Madrid: Iberoamericana-Vervuert, 2009. 77–101. Print.

Vannoni, Elisabetta, et al. "Acoustic Signaling in Cervids: A Methodological Approach for Measuring Vocal Communication in Fallow Deer." *Cognition, Brain, Behavior* 9.3 (2005): 551–65. Print.

Varner, Gary E. *Personhood, Ethics, and Animal Cognition: Situating Animals in Hare's Two-Level Utilitarianism*. New York: Oxford UP, 2012. Print.

Vauclair, Jacques. "Categorization and Conceptual Behavior in Nonhuman Primates." *The Cognitive Animal: Empirical and Theoretical Perspectives on Animal Cognition*. Ed. Marc Bekoff et al. Cambridge, MA: MIT Press, 2002. 239–45. Print.

Vives, Juan Luis. "La Razón." *Tratado del Alma*. 1538. Trans. José Ontañón. Ediciones de la Lectura, 1916. 85–96. Print.

Voisenet, Jacques. "El simbolismo animal según los clérigos de la edad media: entre el dualismo maniqueo y la polivalencia." Trans. Mercedes Pachón Reyna. *Animales simbólicos en la historia: desde la protohistoria hasta el final de la edad media*. Ed. María Rosario García Huerta and Francisco Ruiz Gómez. Madrid: Editorial Síntesis, 2012. 187–205. Print.

Wagschal, Steven. "The Smellscape of Don Quixote: A Cognitive Approach." *Cervantes: Bulletin of the Cervantes Society of America* 32.1 (2012): 125–62. Print.

Wolski, T.R., et al. "The Role of the Senses in Mare-Foal Recognition." *Applied Animal Ethology* 6.2 (1980): 121–38. Print.

Woollett, Anne T., and Ariane van Suchtelen. *Rubens & Brueghel: A Working Friendship*. Los Angeles: J. Paul Getty Museum, 2006. Print.

Worden, William. "The First Illustrator of Don Quixote: Miguel de Cervantes." *Ekphrasis in the Age of Cervantes*. Ed. Frederick de Armas. Lewisburg, PA: Bucknell UP, 2005. 144–55. Print.

Zunshine, Lisa, ed. *Introduction to Cognitive Cultural Studies*. Baltimore: Johns Hopkins UP, 2010. Print.

Index

TORONTO IBERIC

1 Anthony J. Cascardi, *Cervantes, Literature, and the Discourse of Politics*
2 Jessica A. Boon, *The Mystical Science of the Soul: Medieval Cognition in Bernardino de Laredo's Recollection Method*
3 Susan Byrne, *Law and History in Cervantes' Don Quixote*
4 Mary E. Barnard and Frederick A. de Armas (eds), *Objects of Culture in the Literature of Imperial Spain*
5 Nil Santiáñez, *Topographies of Fascism: Habitus, Space, and Writing in Twentieth-Century Spain*
6 Nelson Orringer, *Lorca in Tune with Falla: Literary and Musical Interludes*
7 Ana M. Gómez-Bravo, *Textual Agency: Writing Culture and Social Networks in Fifteenth-Century Spain*
8 Javier Irigoyen-García, *The Spanish Arcadia: Sheep Herding, Pastoral Discourse, and Ethnicity in Early Modern Spain*
9 Stephanie Sieburth, *Survival Songs: Conchita Piquer's* Coplas *and Franco's Regime of Terror*

10 Christine Arkinstall, *Spanish Female Writers and the Freethinking Press, 1879–1926*
11 Margaret Boyle, *Unruly Women: Performance, Penitence, and Punishment in Early Modern Spain*
12 Evelina Gužauskytė, *Christopher Columbus's Naming in the* diarios *of the Four Voyages (1492–1504): A Discourse of Negotiation*
13 Mary E. Barnard, *Garcilaso de la Vega and the Material Culture of Renaissance Europe*
14 William Viestenz, *By the Grace of God: Francoist Spain and the Sacred Roots of Political Imagination*
15 Michael Scham, Lector Ludens*: The Representation of Games and Play in Cervantes*
16 Stephen Rupp, *Heroic Forms: Cervantes and the Literature of War*
17 Enrique Fernandez, *Anxieties of Interiority and Dissection in Early Modern Spain*
18 Susan Byrne, *Ficino in Spain*
19 Patricia M. Keller, *Ghostly Landscapes: Film, Photography, and the Aesthetics of Haunting in Contemporary Spanish Culture*
20 Carolyn A. Nadeau, *Food Matters: Alonso Quijano's Diet and the Discourse of Food in Early Modern Spain*
21 Cristian Berco, *From Body to Community: Venereal Disease and Society in Baroque Spain*
22 Elizabeth R. Wright, *The Epic of Juan Latino: Dilemmas of Race and Religion in Renaissance Spain*
23 Ryan D. Giles, *Inscribed Power: Amulets and Magic in Early Spanish Literature*
24 Jorge Pérez, *Confessional Cinema: Religion, Film, and Modernity in Spain's Development Years (1960–1975)*
25 Joan Ramon Resina, *Josep Pla: Seeing the World in the Form of Articles*
26 Javier Irigoyen-García, *"Moors Dressed as Moors": Clothing, Social Distinction, and Ethnicity in Early Modern Iberia*
27 Jean Dangler, *Edging towards Iberia*
28 Ryan D. Giles and Steven Wagschal (eds): *Beyond Sight: Engaging the Senses in Iberian Literatures and Cultures, 1200–1750*
29 Silvia Bermúdez, *Rocking the Boat: Migration and Race in Contemporary Spanish Music*
30 Hilaire Kallendorf, *Ambiguous Antidotes: Virtue as Vaccine for Vice in Early Modern Spain*
31 Leslie Harkema, *Spanish Modernism and the Poetics of Youth: From Miguel de Unamuno to* La Joven Literatura

32 Benjamin Fraser, *Cognitive Disability Aesthetics: Visual Culture, Disability Representations, and the (In)Visibility of Cognitive Difference*
33 Robert Patrick Newcomb, *Iberianism and Crisis: Spain and Portugal at the Turn of the Twentieth Century*
34 Sara J. Brenneis, *Spaniards in Mauthausen: Representations of a Nazi Concentration Camp, 1940–2015*
35 Silvia Bermúdez and Roberta Johnson (eds), *A New History of Iberian Feminisms*
36 Steven Wagschal, *Minding Animals in the Old and New Worlds: A Cognitive Historical Analysis*

www.ingramcontent.com/pod-product-compliance
Lightning Source LLC
LaVergne TN
LVHW041114090826
844660LV00062B/939/J

* 9 7 8 1 4 8 7 5 0 3 3 2 1 *